Maryland and Delaware Canoe Trails

By Edward Gertler
A Paddler's Guide to Rivers of the Old Line and First States
Fifth Edition
Seneca Press
2002

Printed on Recycled Paper

Preface

This fifth edition of *Maryland and Delaware Canoe Trails* comes exactly 22 years after the first edition rolled off the press. It comes none too soon. There have been so many changes. The population of Maryland and its neighboring states has ballooned. Housing tracts have replaced fields and woods; dual highways have replaced country lanes; and there are more boaters and fishermen enjoying (and competing for) our streams. There have been positive changes too, such as more parks and preserves, and improved water quality in once polluted streams. The sport has continued to change too. There is a vastly improved selection of boats, equipment, and materials, and an increased availability of good instruction. So old barriers are falling. Rapids and falls once portaged are now being run. Serious whitewater is no longer the domain of decked boats only. And the rise of sea kayaking has made paddling Maryland's and Delaware's tidewaters a pleasure rather than an ordeal. Also, the adventure population, those who paddle, ski, hike, etc., are aging and their tastes are changing. And, last but not least, I have probably changed a little too.

I got into guidebook writing to answer a question so frequently asked of me: "Where's a good place to go canoeing around here?" That is not such an easy question to answer, particularly since boaters' tastes vary so widely. So I have taken the approach of presenting, as completely as possible, the entire selection of fresh-flowing streams and many of the most scenic tidewater routes. With such a selection, any paddler should be able to find some waters to suit his or her tastes. Then armed with this guidebook, plus a few excellent guides to the neighboring states, the eager paddler should never again claim ignorance as a reason for staying home.

The scope of this book is admittedly arbitrary and reflects my boating tastes or simply what I have so far explored. Although identified as a Maryland and Delaware guidebook, I saw no reason to exclude tiny District of Columbia or to snip off many streams' headwaters just because they are over the state line. On the other hand, I had to curb this logic for the Susquehanna and Delaware rivers or this book would be called *Maryland, Delaware, Pennsylvania, New Jersey, and New York Canoe Trails,* and you would get a hernia if you tried to lift it. As the paddler of a solo canoe, I prefer small, sheltered waters, be they tiny torrents, swamps, or tidal estuaries. Also, being lazy, I like current and hate wind. So, comprehensive as this book may be, I know I omitted some beautiful stretches of open shoreline and remote Chesapeake Bay island circuits that sea kayakers would just gobble up. My apologies, and I will continue to do better with each future edition (particularly after I get a better boat).

Finally, I point with pride, and in a few instances embarrassment, that I have paddled or portaged every bit of every waterway described in this book. Be assured that if I recommend carrying a dam or falls, it is because I carried (or wished that I had). And if I say that you will see no houses in a certain gorge, it is because I saw no houses when I was there. And so on. Of course, rivers are dynamic and ever-changing: trees fall, houses are built, dams wash out, and fences are strung. I am sure that there will be differences in the streams as I saw them and as future paddlers will see them. So complement this guide with lots of good judgement on the river; scout when there is a question; and carry when there is any doubt. May this book be the catalyst for many safe and enjoyable trips.

Ed Gertler

Acknowledgements

I have found that it is much easier soloing a canoe through whitewater than soloing the production of a book. So I shall now sing about a few unsung heroes. First of all, thanks go to Roger Corbett, who was the logistical mastermind behind the initial edition. Roger helped me plot and plan, offered advice, gave guidance, and generally shared the fruit of years of experience gained in assembling his own guidebooks. In one way or another, he also helped in subsequent editions too. Roger also guided me to Don Rau of Word Design, who was responsible for converting a few thin, black diskettes into the readable print and format that follows. Those diskettes contained good text thanks to Elizabeth Pennisi, a professional journalist, who donated a pair of perfectly good eyes to edit and proof. Finally, thanks go to cartographer Megan Kealy who has coached me on technique and, more recently, patiently weaned me from pen and ink to mouse and keyboard in order to do all those maps.

I wish to acknowledge the numerous paddlers who have helped me explore these streams. But most notably, praise goes to Pete and Barb Brown and Tom and Paulette Irwin. These poor souls have suffered through countless mismeasured mileages, mistimed and mislocated take-outs, misread gradients, misinterpreted weather forecasts, and other such abuse, all in the name of exploring one more new river. And when the going got too tough, they still would be kind enough to run my shuttles. And besides being good paddling companions, the Browns are fine photographers, Barb having contributed the all too representative back cover photo. Since much of my exploring was done alone, I shall take this opportunity to thank the scores of motoring strangers who were kind enough and brave enough to stop, pick up, and shuttle the funny, bearded, neoprene-clad hitchhiker with purple paddle in hand. And thanks to the people living by the put-ins who watched my equipment, while I was shuttling.

I want to thank the officials. The personnel of the U.S. Fish and Wildlife Service, Blackwater and Prime Hook National Wildlife Refuges were ever so helpful to my exploration of their waterways. Thanks goes to Bob Davison and Jim Rymer of the Maryland State Highways Administration for their help in providing up to date map information. Thanks to the staff of Patuxent River Park in helping me with some last minute exploration of their domain. I am grateful for the help of numerous staff at the state offices of the U.S. Geological Survey. Lastly, praise goes to the personnel of the Delaware Department of Transportation whose promptness in filling map orders was amazing.

Finally, bibliographic credit goes to the amazing American Guide Series books for Maryland, Delaware, and Pennsylvania, that were produced during the 1930's by the Writers' Program of the Works Progress Administration. Further credit goes to the more recently published *Maryland, A New Guide to the Old Line State* by Papenfuse, Collins, Stiverson and Carr. These references have proven to be a bountiful source of interesting historical and cultural background information. Finally, *Delaware's Outstanding Natural Areas And Their Preservation,* by Lorraine Fleming, provided a mind-boggling, in-depth inventory of Delaware's natural assets, making it easier for me to set my priorities.

Contents

Chapter 1   *Introduction* 1

Chapter 2   **The Youghiogheny River Basin** 15

Youghiogheny River, Bear Creek, Casselman River, North Branch Casselman River

Chapter 3   **The Potomac River Basin** 29

Potomac River, North Branch Potomac River, Savage River, Georges Creek, Wills Creek, Brush Creek, Little Wills Creek, Jennings Run, Evitts Creek, Town Creek, Flintstone Creek, Fifteenmile Creek, Sideling Hill Creek, Tonoloway Creek, Little Tonoloway Creek, Licking Creek, Big Cove Creek, Conococheague Creek, Back Creek, West Branch Conococheague Creek, Antietam Creek, West and East Branches of Antietam Creek, Catoctin Creek, Monocacy River, Marsh Creek, Rock Creek (Pa.), Toms Creek, Middle Creek, Big Pipe Creek, Little Pipe Creek, Linganore Creek, Bennett Creek, Seneca Creek, Little Seneca Creek, Rock Creek, Anacostia River, Northwest Branch, Mattawoman Creek, Nanjemoy Creek, Zekiah Swamp Run and Wicomico River

Chapter 4   **West Chesapeake Bay Drainage** 147

St. Mary's Coast, Patuxent River, Little Patuxent River, Middle Patuxent River, Western Branch Patuxent River, Calvert Coast and Parker Creek, West River and Rhode River, Severn River, Patapsco River, South Branch Patapsco River, Gwynns Falls, Jones Falls, Herring Run, Gunpowder Falls, Little Falls, Western Run, Little Gunpowder Falls, Winters Run

Chapter 5   **The Susquehanna River Basin** 189

Susquehanna River, Conowingo Creek, Octoraro Creek, Deer Creek

Chapter 6 Rivers of the Eastern Shore 201

Northeast River Tributaries, Big Elk Creek, Great Bohemia Creek, Chester River, Wye River, Choptank River, Tuckahoe Creek, Kings Creek and Miles Creek, Taylors Island Passages, Honga River, Worlds End Creek and Farm Creek, Blackwater River and Little Blackwater River, Transquaking River, Chicamacomico River, Island Creek and Pokata Creek, Nanticoke River, Broad Creek, Hitch Pond Branch and James Branch, Marshyhope Creek, Barren Creek, Rewastico Creek and Quantico Creek, Wicomico Creek, Monie Creek, Manokin River and Kings Creek, Janes Island and Cedar Island, Pocomoke River, Nassawango Creek, Dividing Creek, Pitts Creek, Marumsco Creek

Chapter 7 The Christina River Basin 265

Christina River, White Clay Creek, Red Clay Creek, Brandywine Creek

Chapter 8 Delaware Bay Drainage 279

Appoquinimink River and Blackbird Creek, Smyrna River and Leipsic River, St. Jones River and Murderkill River, Mispillion River, Cedar Creek and Slaughter Creek, Broadkill River and Old Mill Creek, Prime Hook Creek

Chapter 9 Atlantic Ocean Drainage 297

Assateague Island Canoe Trail

Chapter 10 Storm Drains and Flash Floods 301

Index 303

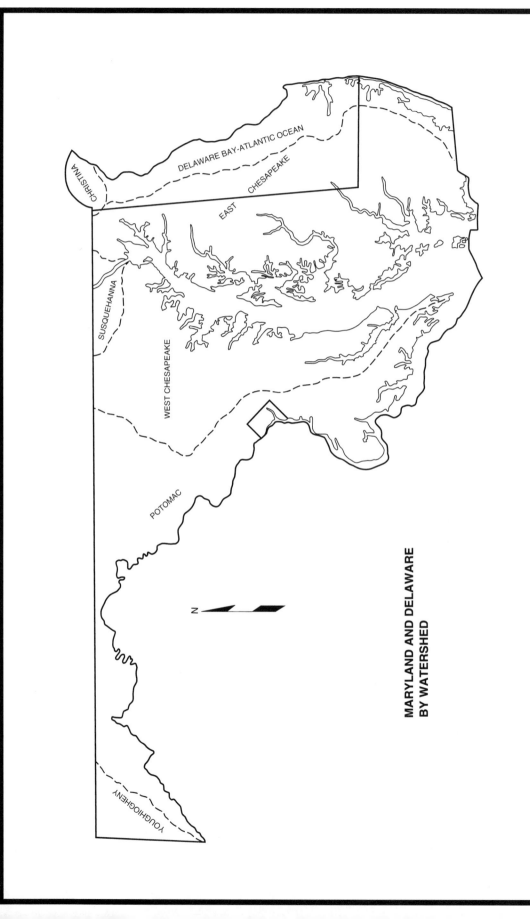

MARYLAND AND DELAWARE
BY WATERSHED

DELAWARE BAY-ATLANTIC OCEAN

CHRISTINA

EAST CHESAPEAKE

SUSQUEHANNA

WEST CHESAPEAKE

POTOMAC

YOUGHIOGHENY

N

Chapter 1
Introduction

My idea of a good canoeing guidebook is that it should tell you where to go and what you need to know both before you leave and when you get there. It should present an inventory and description of boatable waterways. It should provide all the hard data necessary to plan a trip; yet it should be pleasant and interesting to read, so as to provide some good armchair canoeing on a frozen winter's evening. In addition, I believe that good maps are necessary to tie together all the strange names and to explain the shuttle far better than words can. Such a package, hopefully, will answer the question of where to go canoeing, whether the inquirer is a thrill-seeking expert or the most casual or timid beginner.

Recognizing that a lot of beginners and novices might be using this book, there was a temptation to dedicate much of this chapter to how to canoe. While I have included a few basic tips, I have refrained from adding any more because the wealth of literature and club, Red Cross, and commercial boating instruction available in this area can do a much better job. I urge you to use these resources. Those few basic tips that I did include, here and scattered throughout the text, are those that will help you to better use this guide and understand the information that it provides. These include articles on hazards, reading water, judging tides, navigating roads, etc. I have also taken the liberty to preach about conservation, etiquette, and ways that you can help improve the sport. I beg that you take the time to read and consider the content of those few paragraphs. The pressures on our water resources grow every year. Only care and energy from you, the user, can assure a rosy future for our pastime. Enough said for now.

So let's get down to the important stuff.

How To Use This Book

I have organized this book by major watersheds, starting in the west. Each chapter progresses from the headwaters to the mouth. When the branches have branches, they have been ordered in the same manner. In addition, to orient you I have included a watershed map with each chapter's introduction. If you are searching for streams in a specific area, this arrangement will be convenient. If you are alphabetically oriented, check the alphabetical index at the end of the book. This index is also annotated to identify advanced whitewater sections, to help serious whitewater paddlers get to the meat of these states.

Each river report starts with a (usually) brief **Introduction.** This section may locate the stream, identify its outstanding qualities or deficiencies, or present some historical or contemporary color.

Next the **Section** is identified. I have selected sections most often because there was some unifying characteristic to that stretch, either aesthetic, the nature of the whitewater, or duration of its boatable season. Sometimes the section is just what comprises a good day's run. And on many small streams, it is simply the whole stream.

Each section begins with a table of vital statistics: gradient, difficulty, distance, time, width, scenery, and map.

Gradient describes how steeply the stream drops. It is expressed as feet per mile and comes from dividing the total drop of the segment by its length. Runnable gradients range from zero on lakes and tidewater to as much as 200 feet per mile on little torrents like Conowingo Creek. If the gradient is sufficiently unevenly distributed, I have also included the gradient of the steepest stretch, for example 1.5 miles @ 50fpm.

The gradient is a general indication of the likelihood of rapids. The higher the gradient, the more rapids or riffles you are likely to encounter. The difficulty is likely to increase with gradient too. High water levels or uneven distribution of drop, however, can produce difficult whitewater with relatively low gradients. For example, look at the pool and drop nature of the 27-fpm lower Yough in Pennsylvania or the 8-fpm Potomac between Great Falls and tidewater. Conversely, an evenly distributed steep gradient on a small stream can result in surprisingly easy whitewater, as on 80-fpm Big Cove Creek in Fulton County, Pennsylvania.

Difficulty is based on the international whitewater rating scale that runs from 1 to 6 and a smooth water scale that goes from A to C. I have expanded the whitewater numbers to include + and – to improve its precision. I have expressed difficulty as a range (example 1 to 3+) because few rivers stay the same difficulty for very far. If a stream includes a markedly different stretch or one bad rapid, I have set that difficulty off with a comma (example 1,4–). The inventors of the rating scale intended it to be quite descriptive and objectively applied. It can be interpreted as follows:

    A. **Smooth Water.** This is a condensation of the A to C scale which describes if there is current and how much. Since current velocity varies according to both flow and cross-sectional area of the stream, it is meaningless to describe typical current velocity. If a stream is flat, that is all that matters.

    1. **Easy.** Short, straightforward riffles usually formed by gravel or sand bars, low ledges, or constrictions of the river. Waves are less than one foot high, and little maneuvering is required. Routes are easy to determine, and all riffles are followed by adequate rescue opportunity.

    2. **Medium Difficulty.** Rapids are more frequent, composed of waves less than two feet high and in regular patterns with easy eddies. There are more rocks and obstructions, but maneuvering is still easy and rescue spots are still plentiful.

    3. **Difficult.** Rapids are long and require extensive maneuvering. Both ledges and waves are up to three feet high, and waves are often irregular. The course is not always easily recognizable. Rescue opportunities are spaced farther apart.

    4. **Very Difficult.** Long, pushy, extended sets of rapids with high, irregular waves. Boulders and ledges block the course and, along with powerful crosscurrents, require abrupt and intricate turns. The course is often difficult to recognize and scouting is often necessary. Rescue is difficult.

    5. **Exceedingly Difficult.** Long, heavy rapids with high, irregular waves and powerful crosscurrents, or steep, complex, boulder-clogged rapids with poor visibility. Big drops and powerful hydraulics are unavoidable, and the ability to catch small, fast eddies is essential for control. Rescue is very difficult and scouting is often unavoidable.

    6. **Utmost Difficulty.** All the difficulties stated in Class 5 carried to the extreme. Running such water involves an unusual risk of life.

The objective classification system, unfortunately, can be influenced by subjective assessments, including such variables as experience of the rater, size of his or her ego, effect of adverse weather, and the number of wipe-outs, swims, and rolls associated with a particular trip. There has been a trend in recent years, as paddle skills and equipment improve, to downgrade river ratings. The North Branch Potomac between Kitzmiller and Bloomington, for example, was regarded as an expert's-only run in the 50's and early 60's. So since they considered it at the limits of their ability, paddlers rated it Class 5. Now, some people begin their whitewater paddling on that section. Of course, the river has not changed any. But we certainly have a different perspective of what is, for example, "pushy," "powerful," or "unavoidable." What is particularly important to recognize is that Class 6 does not hold a monopoly on risk of life. If you are improperly prepared, almost any grade of whitewater can hurt you. In fact, most whitewater casualties that have happened in recent years to competent whitewater paddlers have occurred on only Class 3 and 4 water.

To standardize my ratings in this book, I have intended them to describe the given stream at a level of about six inches of runnable water. If you encounter higher or lower water, be prepared for a different difficulty. Since there is no standardization of ratings between various guidebooks, do not count on my application of the rating scale to necessarily match with that of other authors. I tried to take the middle of the road, but the best way for you to compare ratings is to start with a stream rated well within your ability and then take it from there. Finally, please note that this is a whitewater rating system only and thus only addresses conditions encountered on an ideal unobstructed stream. In reality, many of these states' small streams are complicated by fallen trees, fences, and other strainers that greatly increase the difficulty and risk involved in paddling these streams. To this, add factors of water temperature, air temperature, and your physical condition to determine if you can handle a given class of difficulty.

Distance is expressed in statute miles and is rounded off to the nearest tenth of a mile. The number describes the distance from one end of the stream segment to the other, even if there is no convenient access to one of those points. This is all pretty straightforward until one must describe big rivers, such as the Potomac or Susquehanna, or estuaries. For big rivers, the distances are measured from point to point along the centerline of the stream. For wide estuaries with irregular shorelines, the distance follows the route of a paddler travelling about a hundred yards off shore, but who shortcuts across sharp embayments.

Sometimes distance does not tell the whole story. For example, a battle through a mile of the strainer-choked Zekiah Swamp Run will consume about as much time and effort as 10 miles on the upper Potomac at highwater. And battling a mile of head winds on the Choptank is far different from a mile of sprightly Fifteenmile Creek. So you must allow for this with time.

Time is also included, expressed in hours and rounded off to the nearest half hour. This represents paddling and portaging time only. Be sure to allocate extra time for lunch, scouting, and rescue. Add additional time for large groups and if you are in poor physical condition.

Width is expressed in feet, unless otherwise noted.

Scenery is self explanatory. I can sometimes be hard to please, especially since I explore many streams in the cold months when there is no foliage to hide the trash, summer homes, industry, etc.

Maps listed are those applicable to that section. The numbers correspond to those on the lower right hand corner of the map.

Next **Hazards** are listed. This inclusion is usually redundant, but better safe than sorry. You will note that I have often indicated which dams and falls are runnable. Unless otherwise stated, if I have declared a drop runnable, it is because I have tried it successfully. As a rule, I discourage beginners and novices from following my lead, because the consequences to the unprepared can be as serious as death in a keeper hydraulic. On the other hand, experienced paddlers who understand these risks might as well enjoy as much drop as the stream has to offer. But do so at your own risk.

Water Conditions describe the best time of year and under what hydrological and meteorological conditions one can expect to find adequate water in the stream. Since I detest driving long miles and endless hours, while wasting gallons of precious gasoline, to find an empty river, the time spans recommended for catching a stream are slightly conservative. The creeks may retain water longer than indicated, but do not count on it.

Most freshwater streams in this book are small and convey a rapid runoff. Some general rules describe when you should most likely find water in them. First, best flow conditions occur between November 1 and April 15. One reason is that this is the time that large frontal storms, which drop large amounts of rain over a wide area, roll through these states. Summer showers, in contrast, can be incredibly heavy, but they often only dump on a few square miles. Another cold weather advantage is that vegetation, which in summer consumes a tremendous amount of moisture, is dormant. Second, in the highlands of western Maryland, with its climate equivalent to a northern state, snow often accumulates for a few months and then, over one or two weeks in spring, melts, assuring wonderful and consistent, raised water levels. Finally, for tidewater streams, all of the above does not matter. There is always water there.

As mentioned earlier, the volume of flow can determine the difficulty, not to mention the floatability, of a stream. To determine how much water there is, we use a **Gauge**. A gauge is a point of reference that relates the stream height at a given point to the volume of water flowing down the stream. Sometimes it is as simple as a joint on a bridge pier, how high an indicator rock protrudes, or the depth of a representative riffle. Better yet, many streams have numbered staff gauges, sometimes just hash marks painted on a bridge abutment, sometimes enamel-coated, metal staffs marked into precise increments.

The best of these gauges are United States Geological Survey (USGS) streamflow gauging stations. You can usually identify a USGS gauge as a tall, rectangular concrete tower, often located near a bridge. Some others consist of a vertical corrugated pipe with a green, wooden or metal box on top. These stations have flow-measuring and recording instruments inside and often have a readable staff outside. The gauge scale is usually set so that the stations will never report a negative level. Hence, zero canoeing level on a stream may read, for example, 2.0 feet on the USGS gauge.

Unquestionably, the best way to quantify water conditions is in flow, which we express in units of cubic feet per second (cfs). Flow is best because the amount of water needed to get down a river rarely changes. In contrast, stream bed scouring, sediment and gravel deposition, or even water weed growth can dramatically change the relationship between depth at the gauge and the amount of flow. So, if flow information is available, favor it over height, especially as this guidebook edition ages.

There are a variety of ways to read the gauges. You cannot beat an on-site inspection for reliability, and that is your only choice for the more primitive gauges and more obscure USGS gauges. For scores of gauges, however, you can obtain information in advance by phone and by computer. By far, the best source is the internet in general, and specifically the USGS's site at <http://water.usgs.gov.real-time.html>. You can find similar information and more (such as rainfall amounts) on the National Weather Service's site at <http://iwin.nws.noaa.gov>. Other sites, such as that of American White-water, <http://www.awa.org/awa/online/gauges.html>, and many local paddling clubs have links to the USGS site. The USGS site, which is updated every few hours, usually gives both flow and height. Click on a specific gauge, and you can study a hydrograph to determine how quickly the stream is rising or falling.

If you do not have internet access, there are good but less comprehensive phone sources. The most common practice is to call the National Weather Service River Forecast offices. For this book, the most useful of these is the Washington, D.C. Forecast Center, reached at 703-260-0305. They give Potomac and Monongahela basins readings. For the Susquehanna Basin, call the State College Forecast Center at 814-234-9861. For Monongahela Basin readings only, call the Pittsburgh Forecast Center at 412-262-5290. All of these gauge readings are also available from a commercial Dial 900 service called Waterline. Call 1-800-945-3376 for information.

One final word about UGSG gauges. The Weather Service and USGS perform a tremendous service to the paddling community by making these readings available to us. Washington River Forecast Office, for example, maintains a multiple-line recording, changed twice a day, just for recreational users. In these budget-trimming times, we cannot take these services for granted. So if you use these phone numbers, please take the time to write the Director of the National Weather Service, 8060 13th Street, Silver Spring, Maryland 20910 or the Director of the USGS, 807 National Center, Reston, VA 20192, and let him or her know how much you appreciate the service. It helps at budget time.

Other gauges include painted or wooden staff gauges, put on bridge piers and abutments for further flood monitoring. Pennsylvania is particularly well-endowed with these. On some popular streams, canoeists have painted simple gauges, usually marked at foot or half-foot increments, usually on bridge piers and abutments. This system, developed and refined in this area by the late Randy

Carter, a renown and widely travelled whitewater canoeist and guidebook author, usually establishes the zero mark to represent the minimum possible level of navigation. However, you must realize that paddlers possess varying ideas of what constitutes "too low," depending on such variables as the gauge painter's boating prowess, boat materials and construction, and degree of aversion to boat repair and maintenance. So the boater who runs a river by an unfamiliar canoe gauge that reads zero may be a real gambler. As for my definition of zero, it is the level at which you unavoidably start scraping in more than a few shallows, unless I have specified otherwise.

For each river I have tried to include a gauge that you can inspect on site and, if possible, a call-in or online gauge. Where there is a call-in or online gauge on a nearby stream, I have included readings that must be only regarded as rough correlations.

Understand that gauges have their limits of usefulness. Unless otherwise stated, the recommended gauge level reflects the stretch adjacent to the gauge. Since high water moves like a big wave, especially on small, flashy streams, an adequate level at the gauge may be already too low 10 miles upstream. So it helps to know if the stream is rising or falling. You may, for example, call Washington on Friday and find that Kitzmiller is reading 5.0 feet. But when you arrive on Saturday, it has already dropped to 4.2 feet. So it is often wise to start calling gauges two days before you go paddling, to detect a trend. Also, when using the roughly correlated gauges mentioned before, remember that the correlation holds best if there is snow melt or a uniform rainfall. So do not count on these gauges in showery summer months.

If you are paddling tidewater, then wind and tides assume the importance that levels have on non-tidal streams. The Weather Service's Washington Center, at 703-260-0505, provides a lower Chesapeake Bay weather forecast that includes wind and tide information. For more precise wind information, a private service called Iwindsurf.com provides almost continuously updated wind information for stations throughout the tidewater region. Call 1-800-765-GALE for information or visit its website at www.iwindsurf.com. Also, the National Weather Service provides wind information on its webstite <http://www.nws.noaa.gov/er>. Look for Philadelphia, Sterling, and Wakefield districts. For tide information, try <http:/www.tidesonline.com>.

Maps accompany each river description, most importantly to answer shuttle and access questions. Except for the usually exaggerated river widths, the maps are spatially accurate. To help you break the stream into a trip of suitable length, I have included as many river mileages as possible. These are the little numbers hugging the rivers, and they denote the distances between the little arrowheads. It was not practical to include mileages on some tidal waters, however, because the irregular shorelines of these waters offer seemingly infinite choices of itineraries. These arrowheads do not necessarily denote access points. Sometimes I have simply placed them at landmarks, such as high bridges and mouths of major tributaries, just so you can mark your progress on your trip. In general, though, you can assume that most bridges afford some degree of public access and that those dead-ending roads that I have included will also get you to a public, or friendly private, access point. I have also occasionally included roads that dead end at the water, but are not open to the public. These have been included should you need an emergency access point. On tidewater and some of the bigger rivers, the states or counties have provided special public access for boaters in the form of ramps or parking areas. These are often singled out, where space permits, as "Access." As for gauges, I have included most gauges that you must inspect on site and some call-in gauges.

Stalking The Elusive Shuttle Road

Once that you have selected a river to run and confirmed that it probably has some water in it, you still have to find your way there and shuttle your vehicles. An ordinary gas station road map should accomplish the former and the accompanying maps in this guidebook should take care of the latter. I have found, however, that even the best directions and maps can be rendered useless if you cannot distinguish the names of the roads.

Shuttling the various rivers described in this volume may involve navigation of roads in as many as five states. In doing so, you will find your most valuable and essential landmark is the common road sign. While interstate, federal, and state primary roads are almost always easily identified, figuring out the secondary roads can be confusing because of the varying and sometimes subtle labeling techniques.

The system in Maryland is simple. Secondary roads are named, not numbered, and names are found on ordinary street signs mounted on high metal or wood poles at intersections. In some rural areas, such as Allegany County, look for street names on mailboxes.

Delaware numbers its secondary roads on tiny white signs attached to the posts of stop signs at the intersections. The signs identify the road that you are on and the road that it is intersecting, each marked by appropriate arrows. The roads are also often, but not always, labeled on yellow warning signs that announce upcoming intersections. Northern Delaware, in addition, names its roads, and these are displayed on regular street signs.

Pennsylvania is a bit confusing because of its inconsistency. Pennsylvania now identifies its state-maintained secondary roads, called State Routes (SR), by four-digit numbers. They are posted on small white signs, about 12 inches by 18 inches, set on street corners at eye level. Some localities, in addition, give regular names to these roads, and post them on street signs. Township-maintained secondary roads are usually identified by a three-digit number prefixed by the letter T (T354 for example). They are usually posted on street signs, if they are posted at all. Some townships also assign and post regular names for these roads, and others post both (T354, Maple Road for example). On my maps, I have tried to identify all roads by at least their number, even if there are currently no signs identifying them. I have done so in hope that the county or township will some day come along and post these roads. In addition, I have tried to include the regular name, as posted (and spelled) on the street signs. On the maps, if a road bears both a name and a number, I have put the number in parentheses.

West Virginia labels roads with names on common street signs or pairs of numbers on small green and white signs.

Virginia makes navigating easy, identifying roads with three-digit numbers (which all tend to look alike). They are conspicuously displayed on small white signs and, in addition, these signs tell you if the road dead ends, and if so, how far.

Needless to say, vandalism, exotic driving habits, and target practice take their toll on these friendly monuments, thus rendering this dissertation useless at times. So an investment in a good topographic map might also be well worth your while.

River Manners

In spite of all the posted lands in these states, most streams suffer no access problems. But with the increased popularity of river running, this situation could change, if we do not abide by some basic principles of river etiquette. The following suggestions address most of the sort of actions that have made us unwelcome. Please remember these so that you never spoil the fun for others who follow.

1. When possible, always ask permission to cross, park on, or camp on private land. Most people are glad to share a corner of their land if you just grant them this formality of respect.
2. Find a secluded spot for changing your clothes. Public nudity is incredibly offensive to many people, both in backwoods and "enlightened" urban areas, especially when you bare yourself right in front of their house, family, etc.
3. Do not block roads or driveways, even just to slow down for a brief chat. If you cannot find a decent shoulder, keep moving until you do. Otherwise, not only do you create a safety hazard, but you might get a ticket. Too many times paddlers have been known to park in and block driveways, without permission. Besides being a serious breach of etiquette, you could be responsible for blocking a fire truck or ambulance from its destination. How would you feel then?

4. If you are floating down a creek and a landowner tells you to "git," then git. Arguing or obscenely gesturing will get you nowhere, will only exacerbate his grudge against paddlers, and besides, you were headed in that direction anyhow. A humble demeanor or apology can often shame a hothead into a more mellow stance.

5. Do not damage those horrible barbed wire, electric, and other fences. They are there to keep the farmer's livestock in during the 99% of the year when the creek on which you are floating is only ankle deep. They are not there to intentionally hurt you.

6. Litter leaves hard feelings, so do not litter, even if the stream is already trashy.

7. Be discreet about where you start fires, ask permission where possible, use other people's fire rings at popular campsites, leave as little evidence of your fire as possible, and of course, thoroughly douse your fire when you are done.

8. Be nice to fishermen, even if a few are not nice to you. Give them a wide berth, do not run over their lines, keep the noise down when passing by, and avoid the popular fishing streams during the first week of trout season. Remember, they enjoy the river as much as you do. And if that does not sway you, remember that there are far more fishermen than canoeists, they are better organized, they have more economic clout, and have more friends in the state legislatures.

No Paddler Is An Island

The growing popularity of paddling has resulted in the appearance of paddling communities and clubs in about every sizable town. Is there such a group in your neighborhood? A membership in a canoe club will be the best buy for your boating dollar that you will ever find. Besides affording you the chance to meet other people of similar interests, many clubs conduct excellent educational programs. Here is a chance to quickly acquire techniques that might take you years to learn on your own, and it is free. Clubs serve as a marketplace to buy and sell the highly specialized equipment that newspaper ads could never serve. This is the place to keep up with the latest techniques, materials, and other consumer information. If a new safety hazard appears on a nearby stream, this will be your first opportunity to learn about it, other than the hard way. If an access problem arises, this is where you learn about it first. Essentially a club is your contact with the world of paddling, and no matter if you go boating once a year or every week, or if you are a rugged loner or a group person, you will get the most out of the sport if you keep in touch.

Clubs have another important function. They give you the strength of numbers needed to get your way in this world. It has been clubs that have succeeded in getting special recreational water releases from reservoirs on the Savage River and North Branch Potomac River. Club input and cooperation has helped guide management decisions on publicly owned rivers such as the lower Yough in Ohiopyle, Pennsylvania or the Potomac River near Washington. Clubs have helped local rescue squads to improve their river rescue capability. Clubs have spearheaded river conservation movements and stopped destructive dam projects. Essentially, clubs are your river lobby. They are your paddlers' union. Your support of a club, if only by adding your name to its roster, increases its clout to protect your favorite streams and your right to enjoy them with a minimum of interference.

The following are some clubs that serve the area described in this guidebook. Since most club contacts change from year to year, an inquiry at the nearest outdoors specialty shop should produce an address for those clubs that do not possess a perennial address.

> Baltimore: Greater Baltimore Canoe Club (P.O. Box 1841, Ellicott City, MD 21041)
> Chester County, PA: Buck Ridge Ski Club (P.O. Box 179, Bala Cynwyd, PA 19004)
> Frederick: Monocacy Canoe Club (P.O. Box 1083, Frederick, MD 21701)
> Hagerstown: Mason Dixon Canoe Cruisers
> Harrisburg, PA: Canoe Club of Greater Harrisburg
> Lancaster, PA: Lancaster Canoe Club

Philadelphia, PA: Philadephia Canoe Club (4900 Ridge Ave., Philadelphia, PA 19128)
        Appalachian Mountain Club, Delaware Valley Chapter
Pittsburgh, PA: Pittsburgh AYH (6300 5th Ave., Pittsburgh, PA 15232)
        Three River Paddling Club
Virginia: Coastal Canoeists (P.O. Box 566, Richmond, VA 23204)
Washington, D.C.: Blue Ridge Voyageurs
        Canoe Cruisers Association (P.O. Box 3236, Merrifield, VA 22116)
West Virginia: West Virginia Wildwater Association (P.O. Box 8413, S. Charleston, WV
    25303)
Wilmington, DE: Wilmington Trail Club (P.O. Box 1184, Wilmington, DE 19899)
York, PA: Conewago Canoe Club

The Importance Of An Education

Believe it or not, the hapless fellows in the movie "Deliverance" (the suburbanites, not the perverts) are real and common phenomena of our nation's rivers. For it seems that a dumb myth persists in this land—a myth in which many individuals believe that the ability to masterfully handle a canoe is instinctive. Unfortunately, too many of these people who have ventured forth to demonstrate their born-to-canoe theory have become the clients of the local rescue squad, mortician, etc. If you are a raw novice contemplating using this book, you will enjoy it much more if you first accumulate a little education. Now if you go to the local library or book store and obtain a "how to canoe" book, you are on the right track. But you will find it much more effective, efficient, and enjoyable to be taught by a real, live paddler.

It is very easy to learn to paddle, especially if you live in or near the area covered by this guidebook. First of all, you can call your local Red Cross chapter, which usually conducts a schedule of basic canoeing classes each summer. These courses teach you details of the canoe and equipment, basic flat-water handling skills, and rescue. Next, contact any of the local clubs listed earlier. Most of these conduct basic flatwater and whitewater paddling classes and offer trips to join where you can practice your newly acquired skills in the presence of more experienced individuals. Note that even if you do not aspire beyond smooth water paddling, the knowledge of boat handling and understanding currents gained from a basic whitewater course will be of great value to you elsewhere. Finally, if you have lots of money to spare, there are a fine selection of private paddling schools located around Washington, D.C., Ohiopyle/Confluence, Pennsylvania, and up and down the Appalachians, where you can receive more intense, advanced, and personal instruction. These schools also have the advantage of providing your equipment and other logistical needs. So as you can see, the opportunities to become a master of your craft are there. Please use them.

Save The River

It is unfortunate, but if something can go wrong with a river, it will. This is especially true in a densely populated region like Maryland and Delaware. For this reason, it is important that we paddlers take the initiative as watchdogs of our favorite streams. But this responsibility is made easier thanks to the existence of a few dedicated organizations, four of which I particularly urge you to support.

1. **American Rivers.** We river lovers are fortunate to actually have an official lobbying organization representing us in the big seat of power, Washington, D.C. They go by the name American Rivers. They are a small and dedicated band who fight for the preservation of free-flowing streams and fight against needlessly destructive projects such as certain dams, river channelization, etc. They are our David fighting our numerous river-eating Goliaths. Please support them (and help yourself) by

joining. Individual memberships are $20 per year, sent to American Rivers, 1025 Vermont Ave. NW, Washington, D.C. 20005. Keep a friend in high places.

2. **American Whitewater Affiliation.** This is a national paddling organization oriented towards whitewater enthusiasts. They have channeled a lot of their energy into defending river access and preventing hydroelectric projects from destroying prime whitewater streams. In our region, they have been instrumental in protecting the Savage and Youghiogheny rivers. Membership is $25 per year, sent to P.O. Box 85, Phoenicia, NY 12464.

3. **The Potomac Conservancy.** This organization was originally formed to protect the sight line along the Potomac below Great Falls, which has been threatened by some really grotesque, unchecked development. It is growing to become an advocacy group for the entire Potomac, our premier river. Do join or send contributions to P.O. Box 9121, Arlington, VA 22219.

4. **The Nature Conservancy.** These people fill a similar function as the Natural Lands Trust, but their emphasis is on preserving ecologically important areas. We paddlers have benefitted from this pursuit because they have protected almost all of Nassawango Creek and parts of Kings Creek (Talbot), the Choptank River, and North Branch Potomac. To join or contribute to their Maryland-Delaware Chapter, write The Nature Conservancy, 2 Wisconsin Avenue, Suite 410, Chevy Chase, Md 20815.

Further River Reading

Good river running does not end at the state line. So here is a list of the fine guidebooks that cover the surrounding neighborhoods.

> *Garden State Canoeing* by Edward Gertler (Seneca Press, 530 Ashford Rd., Silver Spring, MD 20910)
>
> *Keystone Canoeing* by Edward Gertler (Seneca Press, 530 Ashford Rd., Silver Spring, MD 20910)
>
> *Virginia Whitewater* by H. Roger Corbett (Seneca Press, 512 Monet Drive, Rockville, MD 20850)
>
> *Wildwater West Virginia,* by Paul Davidson, Ward Eister, Dirk Davidson, and Charlie Walbridge (Menasha Ridge Press, P.O. Box 59257, Birmingham, AL 35259)
>
> *Canoeing Guide to Western Pennsylvania and Northern West Virginia* by American Youth Hostels, Pittsburgh Council (AYH, Inc. 6300 Fifth Ave., Pittsburgh, PA 15232)

Supplementary Maps

While the maps in this book can fulfill most of your needs on land, for the water you may want something extra. This is particularly true for paddling tidewater, with its confusing wetland channels and complex shorelines. Of course the best maps are USGS 7½-minute quadrangles, but they are expensive and not always readily available. National Ocean Service nautical charts (or commercial versions of them) are also excellent, but they do not double as road maps. Here are some suggestions for substitutes.

For tidal tributaries of the Western Shore in Maryland, navigating is relatively easy. You mainly need a detailed map to determine the length of your itinerary. County maps by the Maryland State Highway Administration (SHA) are adequate. They come in scales of an inch to a mile and inch to 1.5 miles. The Maryland Geological Survey publishes excellent county topographic maps at a scale of one inch to the mile (though cultural features may not always be current, and the maps are folded in a hideous manner). SHA's grid maps, which are drawn to the same scale as USGS quadrangles (one inch to 2,000 feet) but cover twice the area are good deals. Equally good buys are the ubiquitous Alexandria Drafting Company (ADC) county street map books, also to the scale of USGS maps.

For the Virginia side of the Potomac, the Virginia Department of Transportation county general highway maps are cheap but, at a scale of one inch equals two miles, barely adequate. ADC books cover Fairfax, Prince William, and Stafford counties. For the northern Neck, if you photocopy and enlarge a section from the superb DeLorme state road atlas, you have got yourself a good map.

For the Eastern Shore, confusing marshy byways can challenge the best navigator. So USGS quadrangles, SHA grid maps, or ADC map books are a must for most. ADC does not cover Somerset County. Maryland Geological Survey county maps are adequate for good navigators.

For Delaware, the state Department of Transportation's county general highway maps are adequate (scale: one inch to 1.5 miles). ADC covers New Castle and Kent counties.

To obtain these maps:

USGS: 7½-minute quadrangles are $4.00 per map plus $3.50 shipping. Send order to USGS, Bureau of Information Services, Box 25286, Denver, CO 80225 or call 703-648-6892. Local outdoor stores are also a potential source, though their stocks usually favor mountainous destinations.

Maryland SHA: Both full size, black and white county general highway maps (one inch to one mile) and color (one inch to 1.5 miles) are $2.00 per map and grid maps are $2.50. Send order to SHA, Map Distribution, 2323 West Joppa Rd., Brooklandville, MD 21022 or call 410-321-3518.

Maryland Geological Survey: County topographic maps are $5.00 plus $1.00 for shipping. Send order to Maryland Geological Survey, 2300 St. Paul St., Baltimore, MD 21218 or call 410-554-5505.

ADC: Most county street map books are $11.95. You can find them at most convenience stores, supermarkets, bookstores, drug stores, and ADC, 6440 General Green Way, Alexandria, VA 22312 or call 1-800-ADC-MAPS.

Virginia DOT: County general highway maps are $.25 each. Send order to Virginia Department of Transportation, Administrative Services, 1401 Broad Street, Richmond, VA 23219 or call 804-786-2838.

Delaware DOT: County general highway maps are $2.00 each. Send order to Delaware Department of Transportation, Contract Administration, P.O. Box 778, Dover, DE 19903 or call 302-739-4348.

DeLorme: Atlases for Virginia, and Maryland and Delaware are $16.95 each. You can find them in most bookstores or order from DeLorme Mapping Company, P.O. Box 298, Freeport, ME 04032 or call 1-800-227-1656, Ext. 6200.

Geography And Geology

Rivers do not just happen, but rather are a product of the environment through which they flow. If the paddler has a general understanding of this environment, particularly the geology and geography of the area, then he can more easily find the streams best suited to his tastes.

Although Maryland and Delaware combined encompass only a modest area, their unusual wedge-shaped configuration manages to pack a wonderfully varied collection of topography into those meager boundaries. Geologists neatly divide the states into three "provinces"—the Appalachian, Piedmont, and Coastal Plain. Furthermore, the Appalachian Province is subdivided into the Allegheny Plateau, Valley and Ridge, and Blue Ridge districts.

Starting in the far west, the Allegheny Plateau extends from beyond the West Virginia line to Dans Mountain, which is just west of Cumberland. This is a rolling upland punctuated by a series of long, gently rising ridges which are underlain by fairly flat alternating layers of sandstone, coal, shale, and limestone. Streams in this region tend toward the extreme, either meandering peacefully about high, fairly open valleys or plunging violently through deep, V-shaped canyons. Often the transition between the extremes occurs quite abruptly. This area also holds title to Maryland's most rotten weather. The high ridges are buffeted by the cold winter storm systems that roll out of the northwest and, in the process, scrape out copious quantities of moisture. It is common to lose 10 to 15 degrees F and go from sunshine to snowfall in the 10-mile drive from Cumberland to Frostburg.

Next comes the Valley and Ridge District, which extends from Cumberland east to Hagerstown. A drive down U.S. Rte. 40 between these two towns will no doubt convince you that this is a very descriptive name. As a general rule, the valleys evolve from narrow, rugged, and semi-wild on the west to wide, fairly flat, and well cultivated in the east. The streams in this region wind about like drunk snakes, but within the confines of very straight valleys. Occasionally these streams will cut through a ridge to get to another valley, and it is here that one can best expect to find whitewater in this district. Finally, huge deposits of limestone underlying this area make it a caver's delight.

The Blue Ridge District is a narrow strip occupied by South Mountain, Catoctin Mountain, and the valley in between. There is only one stream, Catoctin Creek, that flows entirely within this region whose scenery in Maryland, while pretty, does not look much different from the Valley and Ridge District to the west. Geologists will blanch at this callous assessment.

Next, extending from the Blue Ridge east to an imaginary line connecting Washington, Baltimore, and Wilmington is the Piedmont Plateau. This is a very rolling land dominated by beautiful, old farms on the west, sprawling cities on the east, and transition in between. The streams of this region flow in every direction, sometimes straight, sometimes crooked, but almost always flat. On the eastern edge of this region, however, where the Piedmont meets the coastal plain, all eastward flowing rivers drop over a band of old, hard rock referred to as the Fall Line. The nature of the Fall Line can vary from stretches of gentle riffles to the violent cataracts of the Great Falls of the Potomac.

All lands to the east of the Fall Line fall in the coastal plain. The plain on Maryland's Western Shore (of the Chesapeake Bay) is rolling and sometimes even rugged while, in contrast most of the lands east of the Chesapeake Bay are as flat as a pancake. One thing is for sure, the streams of the coastal plain are invariably peaceful. Most of the stream mileage here was flooded out by the ocean thousands of years ago, creating hundreds of miles of tidal estuaries. The most spectacular example of this is the Chesapeake Bay, which fills the former lower Susquehanna River Valley. This watery area is heaven on earth for sailboaters, power boaters, sea kayakers, waterfowl watchers, fishermen, seafood lovers, etc. It can be good for canoeists too, if they are selective about weather and tides. The remaining rivers of this area are swamp runs, which are free-flowing, fairly swift, tiny, and wild, but often very obstructed by the lush vegetation that surrounds them.

Help Set The Author Straight

Writing a canoeing guidebook is frustrating. I just know that right at this moment, as I write this page, somewhere in Maryland a flash flood is moving some rock in a stream bed to somewhere different than where I said it was. And some farmer is stringing barbed wire across, some tree is falling across, and some beaver is damming up some stream that I called "unobstructed." The State Highway Administration is probably changing a route number, and some bored delinquents are probably shooting holes in the street sign that marks the crucial turn on one of the shuttles. And shifting gravel probably has caused some gauge to now read two feet off what I said it should.

It is hard to nail a moving target. So help me out. Do not be shy. If you find any mistakes or changes, I welcome your comments. Just write Seneca Press, 530 Ashford Road, Silver Spring, MD 20910 and help build a better guidebook. Sure as you will hit another rock, there will be another edition out some day.

Glossary

In order to reach as many people as possible, I have tried to limit the amount of canoe jargon in my descriptions. The newcomer may, nevertheless, still be baffled by a few commonly used river terms. So I have included this brief glossary.

Advanced: Paddler who is competent at maneuvering his or her boat, reading the water, and staying out of trouble in Class 4 or greater whitewater.

Beginner: A person who knows little or nothing concerning basic strokes, canoe handling, and how a river works. Seldom gets out paddling more than once or twice a year.

Braiding: Situation where a stream channel splits, and then the split splits, and then the split split splits, ad nauseum, to form a pattern resembling a braided rope. Such areas can often spell trouble because narrow and shifting channels are prone to strainers.

Camps: A local term, especially common north of Maryland, for vacation homes and cabins. These often also take the form of old school buses, tarpaper shacks, and trailers. A string of these along an otherwise pretty river is called a river slum.

Hole (a.k.a. hydraulic, keeper, stopper, souse hole): A depression in the water caused by water flowing over a rock or ledge to displace the water at the bottom of the drop. This results in a recirculating surface current that can slow down or trap boats that enter it.

Intermediate: Paddler who understands the principles of boat handling and the river, and can roughly move his or her boat to where desired on up to Class 3 water.

Left (or Right): One side as distinguished from the other, when one is facing downstream.

Low-water Bridge: A low concrete slab or culvert bridge designed to function only at low water levels, and to accept inundation without damage at high water. A poor man's special, but a paddler's headache.

Novice: Paddler who has learned the basic canoe strokes, simple fast water maneuvers, such as eddy turns and ferrying, and understands the nature of currents, eddies, holes, etc., but has not become proficient at using all that knowledge.

Playing: Activity where skilled whitewater paddlers practice precise boat maneuvers by using the current. This includes surfing, hole sitting, and catching eddies for fun. If this still makes little sense, a brief whitewater canoeing lesson would be worth a thousand words.

Shuttle: Complex car positioning exchange undertaken by groups of paddlers to make sure that when they reach the take-out, they have a way to get back to the put-in.

Strainer: Any obstacle across the current that allows water to flow through while trapping any floating scum or debris, including boats and boaters. Very dangerous. In this book I have usually used this term to denote fallen trees, logjams, and brush. I have usually separately detailed the man-made strainers.

Weir: A little dam, but often just as dangerous as a big dam, because of its hole.

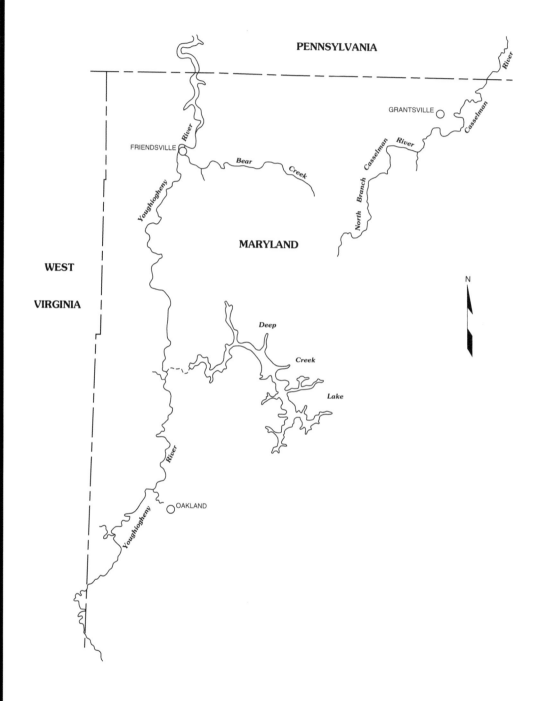

Youghiogheny River Tributaries

Chapter 2
The Youghiogheny River Basin

The Youghiogheny and its tributaries drain 1,748 square miles of rugged plateau country in West Virginia, Maryland, and Pennsylvania. Roughly 400 square miles of that area is in Maryland. This is the only basin in the state that drains to the westward-flowing Ohio River system. Maryland's portion of the Youghiogheny watershed is a thinly populated territory possessing no cities or even large towns. Light agriculture, logging, coal mining, and tourism are the major activities of this region. Most of the basin's waterways, navigable or otherwise, are deeply incised into the landscape, rushing at the bottom of steep-walled, rhododendron-clothed gorges. This is a wild and lonely corner of the state and the rivers truly reflect this character.

The following streams are described in this chapter:

Youghiogheny River

Bear Creek

Casselman River

    North Branch Casselman River

Youghiogheny River

Youghiogheny River

INTRODUCTION: A lot of nice things can be said about the Maryland section of the Youghiogheny (called the "Yough" by most people). But to 99% of the paddling community it is known for only one thing. It is the big whitewater challenge. Probably no section of a river in the East is so famous and sought after to test one's technical boating ability as is this river from Sang Run to Friendsville.

The Yough, unfortunately, has also been a troubled river. The trouble all started when the State of Maryland designated the segment from Millers Run to Friendsville as a Wild and Scenic River, a status which regulates land use in the canyon in order to preserve the natural qualities of the river corridor. Local landowners, a traditionally independent lot, did not receive this restrictive legislation well, especially since the State did not even offer to buy their land or at least buy scenic easements. So some of those people who lived in that stretch from Hoyes Run to Sang Run chose to express their distaste for the government's action by posting their land and denying access to the river to all outsiders. This included fishermen, hunters, and hikers, as well as boaters. There was a period during which boaters attempting to put in at Sang Run were harrassed, threatened, and even had their vehicles vandalized. This situation, fortunately, has cooled off considerably. If you stick to the public boaters access a few hundred yards above the Sang Run bridge, you should have no problems.

Protection of the river corridor remains unsettled. There have been incidents of illegal logging in the canyon. The County or State have periodically tried to weaken the protective laws or restrict boater access. Back in the 1980s, the Natural Lands Trust attempted to buy land or scenic easements in the corridor, ultimately to turn it all over to the State. But that never worked out. The State, has done little since then to show that it is interested in seriously protecting the Yough. Most recently, the State has been tampering with the dam releases to promote a cold water fishery in the river. This could affect the availability of boatable water and reduce the predictability of the release schedule.

Now, overcrowding is becoming an issue between Sang Run and Friendsville. The rise in commercial rafting coupled with an unprecedented boom in private boating has caused some congestion during dry spells when everybody must squeeze onto a two-hour water release from a power plant. Once again the State will no doubt be drawn into the issue. The outcome of its efforts we can only nervously anticipate.

Section 1. U.S. Rte. 50 to Millers Run						
Gradient	Difficulty	Distance	Time	Width	Scenery	Map
4	A to 1,2	16.1	5.0	10-40	Good	1

TRIP DESCRIPTION: This section makes it possible for a status-conscious novice to go out and spend a lovely, safe day on the river and then go home and brag to all his friends about how he ran the Upper Yough. From Rte. 50 to Crellin, the Yough is a tiny brook that twists and turns through a woodland or pastoral setting in a fairly remote upland valley. The water is mostly flat and swift. But one fairly long, boulder-studded rapid (Class 2) just above Crellin, where Dilly Road follows the river, might challenge the novice. A town park, just above the confluence with Snowy Creek, provides a convenient take-out at Crellin. Below Crellin the Yough begins passage through an attractive wooded gorge that more or less brackets the river all the way to its mouth at McKeesport, Pennsylvania. With Snowy Creek and then the Little Yough joining, the stream grows noticeably larger. But it continues mostly smooth with only an occasional riffle. For too many years the Little Yough has also conveyed Oakland's raw sewage. Completion of a sewage treatment plant in 1988 has ended that problem.

The end of this section, Millers Run, is a wretched access point and can be difficult to locate. But it is the last chance to get out before the river changes personality. So to get there, go south on the Oakland-Sang Run Road 0.3 miles from the intersection with Mt. Nebo Road. There, at the bottom of the hill, you should find a tiny brook. That is Millers Run, up whose bed you can walk to get from the river. If that does not appeal to you, double back northbound for about 0.15 miles, uphill, until you see a vetch-covered meadow that provides a clear and dry, but steep, path to the river.

HAZARDS: Between Rte. 50 and Crellin, there are the debris-choked remains of a low-water bridge (above Sunnyside Road) and always the possibilty of some deadfalls.

WATER CONDITIONS: Runnable during spring within a few days of hard rain or during a thaw.

GAUGE: There is a USGS gauge (on USGS website), with an outside staff, about an eighth of a mile above Md. Rte. 39 on river left (reached by dirt road on left bank). A flow (level) of 360 cfs (3.0 feet) is about minimum for starting at Rte. 50. For rough winter and spring correlations, the USGS gauge at Kitzmiller, on the North Branch Potomac (on USGS website or call Washington), should be reading over 630 cfs (3.9 feet).

Section 2. Millers Run to Sang Run Road						
Gradient	Difficulty	Distance	Time	Width	Scenery	Map
36*	1 to 5-	10.5	4.0	30-50	Excellent	1
*3.5 @ 90fpm						

TRIP DESCRIPTION: This section is commonly referred to as the Top Yough and is for top paddlers only. One starts with a relaxing 3.5-mile paddle down fairly placid waters through quiet woods before the bottom drops out of the river. Here, abruptly, the Yough plunges over a few complex ledges with sticky holes followed by a relatively easy slalom through the boulders and over tiers of shallow ledges for one mile down to Swallow Falls Road. Swallow Falls is about a hundred yards downstream, where you can land on the left brink and then carry both the falls and a vicious eight-foot ledge just downstream. For about the next two miles the river is characterized by long, steeply dropping, boulder-clogged rapids. You can scout most rapids from the eddy, except for a nasty one about a mile below Swallow Falls where all the water funnels steeply down a complex route on the left. Undercut rocks and jammed debris make this a rapid of consequence. Scout first. The river calms down as it approaches the Hoyes Run Power Plant, just below which a short walk up a private road on the right leads to a public fisherman's access area. The final three miles to Sang Run allow you to cool down on riffles and easy rapids through a more open valley. Finally, do not get so engrossed with the whitewater that you miss viewing the beautiful falls just a few yards up Muddy Creek from its confluence with the Yough. This is just downstream of Swallow Falls, on the left.

HAZARDS: Swallow Falls, which is about a hundred yards down easy rapids from the Swallow Falls Road bridge. Just downstream is a jagged eight-foot ledge with a deceptively powerful hole at the bottom.

WATER CONDITIONS: Winter or spring within a few days of hard rain or during thaw.

GAUGE: Staff gauge on downstream side of the right pier of Sang Run Road bridge is useable only when the power plant at Hoyes Run is not generating. This usually means weekends and early mornings on weekdays. At such times, 1.7 feet is about minimum and 3.0 feet is about the upper limit

Youghiogheny River
Bear Creek

for most paddlers. During winter and spring, 440 cfs (3.5 feet) at the USGS Kitzmiller gauge, on the North Branch Potomac (call Washington), roughly correlates to adequate water on the Top Yough. A better choice is the USGS gauge near Rte. 39 (on USGS website or inspect on site). Look for at least 255 cfs (2.8 feet).

Section 3. Sang Run Road to Friendsville (Md. Rte. 42)						
Gradient	Difficulty	Distance	Time	Width	Scenery	Map
52*	2 to 5	9.4	4.0	30-50	Excellent	2
*3 @ 100fpm +						

TRIP DESCRIPTION: This section is referred to as the Upper Yough and has the whitewater that made this river famous. Specifically, what makes it so special are four miles of unrelenting boulder piles, ledges, blocked views, cryptic passages, menacing undercuts, and technical difficulties. At lower levels the typical rapid is tight, has poor visibility, requires quick and precise maneuvering, and has an eddy or small pool at the bottom. At higher levels the passages open up but are still complex, visibility is still poor, and waves and holes become big and vicious. Strength, a good brace, and a roll are essential, and rescue opportunities are few and far between. The seriousness of this section is reflected in there being only a two-foot difference between being too low and too high to run.

One has over two miles of riffles and flat water on which to warm up before confronting Gap Falls, a sloping five-foot ledge that is run near the left. From here it is all downhill through too many rapids to describe in detail. Just remember, everything is runnable. It is entirely possible to eddy hop down this river, doing all of your scouting from your boat. If you are going to need to get out and scout, then start as early as possible for it is going to be a very long day. A better option though for most first timers is to run with someone who knows the way down. If you do not know any such person, wander into Friendsville, a base for commercial rafting and a hangout for private boaters. You should be able to find someone there who will take you under their wing. In fact, for a reasonable fee, some of the companies, such as Precision Rafting, and independent guides now offer some professional quality guide service for newcomers.

The rough stuff ends at Kendall, now just a name on the map but once a busy logging camp. Remaining is a soothing two-and-three-quarter-mile coast over continuous easy rapids and then riffles, all of which would be considered prime whitewater on most other streams.

You probably will not notice it on your first run, but this is a very beautiful tour. People's recollections from their first trip generally tend to omit trees, boulders, sky, and other normally obvious scenery. But there are cliffs, graceful hemlocks, falls on side streams, rhododendron gardens, and beautifully sculpted boulders. It is a true wilderness river.

The currently most popular take-out point in Friendsville is on the left bank below the Main Street bridge. Since this and most other Friendsville access points are within sight of houses and people, please use discretion when changing clothes, etc. Though it adds another mile to the trip, the least offensive place to finish is at the town park off the Friendsville-Addison Road. Please do not alienate the one group of Yough residents who are still friendly to boaters.

HAZARDS: The entire four miles from Gap Falls to Kendall may be hazardous to your health. Besides offering the normal bumps and abrasions inherent to such a rocky stream, the boulders on this river are very round and undercut. So it is not a good place to swim. On the other hand, it is not necessarily a safe river to get out of either. During the summer you must watch out for rattlesnakes which find the numerous boulders a splendid place to sun themselves (one more reason not to scout from shore). If disaster should strike, remember that a foot trail on an old logging railroad grade follows the right bank from roughly a mile below Gap Falls to Friendsville.

WATER CONDITIONS: Found up during winter and spring within a few days of hard rain or during a thaw. But why freeze? During a normal summer you can usually run the Upper Yough on most weekdays, when the power company releases water from their hydroelectric station at Hoyes Run. Water is usually released in the late morning and early afternoon, the water arriving at Sang Run around noon to 1:00 P.M. On the other hand, in dry summers this release (which locals refer to as "the tide") may only last for two hours and occur only one or two days per week. Additionally, there are usually scheduled first Saturday of the month releases during summer, but beware, these resulting crowds are staggering. A power company public information recording (call 814-533-8911) provides that week's release schedule. Summer rains also occasionally boost the river to runnable levels on weekends.

GAUGE: The staff gauge on the Sang Run Road bridge should read 1.7 feet for a minimal level, and consider 3.0 feet as maximum, although it has been successfully run in excess of 3.5 feet by a few. On weekends or any other time the power plant is not running, you can use the USGS gauge at Friendsville (on USGS website or call Pittsburgh or Washington). Friendsville at 580 cfs (3.15 feet) corresponds to roughly 1.95 feet at Sang Run (normal release level when natural river flow is low).

Section 4. Friendsville (Md. Rte. 42) to U.S. Rte. 40 (Jockey Hollow Boat Ramp)						
Gradient	**Difficulty**	**Distance**	**Time**	**Width**	**Scenery**	**Map**
27*	A to 2-	10.1	3.5	50-1,600	Good	2
*gradient down to reservoir						

TRIP DESCRIPTION: The last section of Maryland's Yough belongs again to the novice. There is about one mile of free-flowing river over mild gravel bar and rock garden rapids to the backwater of Yough Reservoir. The reservoir is relatively narrow and fringed by high slopes that are just about free of any development. It is really a pleasant place to paddle if you go early in the season when it is full and early in the morning when it is calm and unpopulated. If you do not go at such times, you can look forward to slogging through disgusting mudflats to get in and out and to being buzzed by power boat jockeys while fighting aggravating headwinds. Take out at the public launching ramp (Jockey Hollow) off U.S. Rte. 40 about a half mile west of the bridge over the reservoir. If water is too low to start at Friendsville, go two and a half miles north from the center of town on the Friendsville-Addison Road to Selbysport, where a short, steep road descends on the left down to the lake.

HAZARDS: Being run over by a water skier on Yough Lake.

WATER CONDITIONS: The free-flowing section usually has enough water during spring and early summer, except after a long dry spell. It is also passable on summer weekdays, late in the afternoon, from dam releases. The lake is best in late spring or early summer when the drawdown is minimal.

GAUGE: None. Judge riffles at the Rte. 42 bridge.

Deep Creek Lake

If this guidebook were being published in 1900, this description would be of Deep Creek, not Deep Creek Lake. It would describe two sections. Section 1 probably would have been a winding, novice run through an upland valley. Section 2 would have been a thundering descent into the Yough gorge — the domain of steep creek experts in plastic boats (had polyethylene been invented then). But the reality is that a dam went in about 1925, flooding that big valley and diverting the water around the steep section through a tube to an electric generating station.

What we have today is a big lake with heavily developed shores and waters infested with motorboats and personal water craft. If that does not bother you, this is certainly a roomy place to paddle. With the lake's many arms, you can explore, find shelter from the wind, and near the heads of those arms, maybe even find a bit of relative solitude. In summer, the waters get warm enough for comfortable swimming.

The best point for access is from Deep Creek Lake State Park.

Bear Creek

INTRODUCTION: Bear Creek is an attractive little trout stream that gushes into the Yough at Friendsville. It is difficult to catch at canoeable levels, so should you happen upon favorable water and have enough daylight for a descent, do not pass up this gem.

Section 1. U.S. Rte. 219 to Friendsville (Friendsville-Addison Rd.)						
Gradient	Difficulty	Distance	Time	Width	Scenery	Map
81	2 to 4	7.3	2.0	15-25	Good	2

TRIP DESCRIPTION: Put in just downstream of the high Rte. 219 bridge where Bear Creek Road crosses the creek. The first three miles are suitable for the intermediate paddler, as the waters rush over gravel bars and small boulder patches through a gorge-like valley. You can count on confronting some fallen trees and other woody hazards, usually in fast spots.

About three miles above Friendsville the stream draws close to the road and the gradient begins to grow and grow. This is where the advanced paddlers take over with many starting at the pipeline crossing and steel bridge located two miles above Accident Friendsville Road. After a boulder introduction, the creek begins to flush over sandstone ledges up to five or six feet high. Some of these have technical, sloping configurations that require expert boat handling ability. It is a worthy tributary to the mighty Upper Yough.

HAZARDS: Strainers and the whitewater.

WATER CONDITIONS: Canoeable in spring, only within a day of hard rain or during a rapid thaw.

GAUGE: There is a USGS gauge (on USGS website) in Friendsville a few hundred yards below Accident Friendsville Road. A flow of 240 cfs (2.8 feet) is a relatively low but good first-time level for the entire run. If there is enough water to get down the rapid above the Addison Friendsville Road, there is enough water elsewhere.

Mine Over Matter

The plateau off which the Yough drops is underlaid by vast deposits of coal. Most of it is the semi-bituminous variety, which is a high-grade product preferred for use by the steel industry. The coal exists in several layers, called seams, the largest and most worked being the 14-foot-thick Pittsburgh Seam. Deep-lying seams of coal are extracted by a complex system of shafts, tunnels, vents, and conveyors appropriately called deep mines. There are only a few of these in Maryland. The bulk of the coal is extracted from seams close to the surface of the land by simply scraping off the soils and rock above and then just scooping up the coal. This practice is appropriately called surface, or strip, mining.

Coal was discovered in Maryland as far back as 1782, near Georges Creek. But mining did not really pick up until the railroad arrived about 70 years later. Since then, the coal industry has operated on cycles of boom or bust. The petroleum shortages of the 1970's brought the most recent comeback, and new mines have sprouted up everywhere.

Traditionally the boater could always tell if there was mining in the area by dead rivers, orange rocks, and water that tasted like a rusty nail. The acid river would also do a number on concrete bridge piers and the paint on nearby houses. Strip mines meant scarred and denuded hillsides, and deep mines meant smoldering tailings piles. And any paved roads would soon be ground to potholes and rubble under the wheels of the heavily loaded coal trucks. So the paddler could only be thankful that there was not coal under more of the State.

Today mining has become less of a trauma on the landscape. Maryland's tough environmental rules on surface mining now regulate the methods of mining, require control of sediments and acidic drainage, and require complete reclamation of the site when the mining is completed. One deep mine in Garrett County is now cleaning its wastewater so well that it is raising trout in its final treatment pond. Some major polluting abandoned mines now have treatment systems on their discharges. Other past damage has been mitigated when new mines open on top of old, unreclaimed mines, because the new mine assumes complete responsibility for reclamation of the site. A fringe benefit of the 1970s boom was that the price of coal made it economical to go back and sift the coal from the old tailings (gob) piles, resulting in the disappearance from the landscape of many of these eyesores. Nevertheless, much controversy continues as to whether coal mining can really be kept compatible with a good environment. One thing is for certain, the paddler will be the first to know.

─── Casselman River ───

INTRODUCTION: The Casselman River is the Youghiogheny's largest tributary, born at the confluence of the North and South branches and joining the Yough about 10 river miles north of the Mason-Dixon Line at Confluence, Pennsylvania. As it cuts down into the Yough gorge it creates miles of good scenery and novice to intermediate whitewater. But the initial miles in Maryland are relatively tame and make a fine run for novices, when the weather is warm enough. The stream flows through a Mennonite and Amish enclave, the influence of which surfaces, among other places, in some of the valley's attractive barn architecture and in the fine eateries around Grantsville (some closed on Sundays).

Section 1. Md. Rte. 495 to Salisbury, Pa. (Pa. Rte. 669)						
Gradient	Difficulty	Distance	Time	Width	Scenery	Map
15	1 to 2–	11.9	3.5	15-35	Good	3

TRIP DESCRIPTION: The put-in at Md. Rte. 495 is on the North Branch a few yards above the confluence with the South Branch. Initially the Casselman is flat, deep, and narrow, winding through a pretty, pastoral valley close by Rte. 495. After about a mile and a half, it leaves the road and cuts into a wooded gorge, all the while rushing over almost continuous riffles formed by cobbles and small boulders. When it leaves the gorge it passes, in quick succession, under I-68, Rte. 40, and the big, graceful stone arch of the old Casselman Bridge.

Built in 1816 to carry the National Road across the river, the Casselman Bridge was, at that time, the largest of its kind in the country. Building such an innovative project apparently did not inspire the bridge's contractor to confidence. For legend has it that he was so worried that the bridge would not stand that the night before the formal grand opening, he had his workmen remove the supporting framework just to make sure of its integrity and avoid a lot of embarrassment.

Below Rte. 40, riffles and easy rapids continue to be frequent, though the gradient decreases with each mile. By the time the Casselman reaches Salisbury, it is mostly flat. Views from the river are of woods, pasture, and some big, lovely farm houses and barns. Finally, thanks to successful acid mine drainage abatement programs, this once polluted stream is now again a productive trout habitat.

HAZARDS: None.

WATER CONDITIONS: Canoeable in spring within a few days of hard rain or during a thaw.

GAUGE: There is a USGS gauge (on USGS website or inspect on site) about a half mile downstream of Rte. 40, at River Road bridge. This gauge should read at least 160 cfs (1.8 feet). For just eyeballing it, the riffles at the put-in should all be passable. Roughly, the USGS gauge at Markleton, many miles downstream (call Pittsburgh or see USGS website), should read over 950 cfs (3.0 feet). Also, for an even rougher winter and spring correlation, Kitzmiller gauge, on the North Branch Potomac (call Washington), should read at least 690 cfs (4.0 feet).

Fun And Games Off The River

Most paddlers head to the Youghiogheny Basin to get away from it all, finding paddling and just enjoying the great outdoors sufficient recreation. But even out here in the sticks there are occasional interesting diversions in the form of happenings, events, and festivals to occupy a piece of your time. Take Friendsville, for example, that quiet little town at the confluence of Bear Creek and the Yough. On the third Saturday of every July the air fills with the sweet sounds of the Annual Fiddler's Contest featuring the finest and some not-so-fine regional artists. Just across the West Virginia Line from Garrett County is Preston County, a cold and rugged plateau land that has at least found success in growing buckwheat. The county is so proud of this that every September they celebrate a weekend-long Buckwheat Festival at Kingwood, the county seat. Fanciers of buckwheat cakes will go hog wild at this extravaganza. And then when spring arrives, and the rivers begin to rise, so does the sap, especially in the sugar maples. Sugar maples are common trees in these cold, high elevations and tapping them for their sweet sap is vigorously pursued. Meyersdale, Pennsylvania, a small town on the Casselman River, just north of Salisbury, celebrates with an annual Maple Sugar Festival. It would sure be nice if we could only coordinate this with the Buckwheat Festival.

North Branch Casselman River

INTRODUCTION: The North Branch of the Casselman River drains the high plateau valley between Negro and Meadow mountains in Garrett County. This is the heart of Maryland's icebox, so it is best to shoot for this gem during spring thaw. In spite of the presence of some strip mining in the area, it affords a very pretty run through a most isolated corner of the state.

Section 1. Dung Hill Road to Md. Rte. 495						
Gradient	Difficulty	Distance	Time	Width	Scenery	Map
44	1 to 3	5.7	1.5	10-25	Very Good	3

TRIP DESCRIPTION: The fun starts immediately, as one can shoot the metal culvert tubes under Dung Hill Road (only in Garrett County can the high beak baggers ascend such prizes as The Dung Hill, Pee Wee Hill, Roman Nose Mountain, Snaggy Mountain, Monkey Lodge Hill, or Contrary Knob). Initially the clear stream is smooth, but it flows very swiftly, rushing through escape-

Casselman River
North Branch Casselman River

25

proof alder thickets at the base of a pastoral valley. In spots these alders arch completely across the creek and, though passable, should be approached with utmost caution. The North Branch then enters a gorge, dashing down easy rapids formed by boulders and small ledges. Things calm down above Durst Road, but below there the stream enters another gorge, filled with long rock gardens and a few exciting boulder patches. Both gorges are lush with hemlock and rhododendron. The gentle finish at Rte. 495 hints little of the fun upstream.

HAZARDS: Overhanging alders and fallen trees, aggravated by narrow, island-formed channels.

WATER CONDITIONS: Canoeable in spring within two days of hard rain or after a rapid thaw. Since this stream drains bogs and swamps, it holds its water better than most streams this small.

GAUGE: There are joints in the concrete piers of the Md. Rte. 495 bridge. On the downstream side, the fourth joint below the top represents a minimal but enjoyable level. This roughly corresponds to 500 cfs (2.6 feet) on the USGS gauge near Grantsville (see USGS website or inspect on site). If the Casselman looks runnable from bank to bank at the rapid just below U.S. Rte. 40, go up and check out the North Branch.

Upper Potomac River Tributaries

PENNSYLVANIA

GETTYSBURG

Rock Creek

Marsh Creek

Middle Creek

Toms Cr

Big Pipe Creek

Little Pipe Creek

River

Linganore Creek

FREDERICK

MARYLAND

Monocacy

Bennett Creek

Little Seneca Creek

Great Seneca Creek

Potomac

ROCKVILLE

Northwest Branch

Rock Creek

River

D.C.

Anacostia River

VIRGINIA

N

Mattawoman Creek

WALDORF

Zekiah Swamp Run

LA PLATA

Nanjemoy Creek

Potomac

River

Lower Potomac River Tributaries

Chapter 3
The Potomac River Basin

The Potomac is the longest and most diverse river system in Maryland. The basin encompasses almost 15,000 square miles of Maryland, Pennsylvania, West Virginia, and the District of Columbia. It reaches from the cold, high plateau of the Alleghenys to the broad waters of the Chesapeake Bay and tidewater. The Potomac and its tributaries flow through wild mountain gorges, open farm country, and lush swamps; past heavy industry; and through the nation's capital. Its waters vary from fresh to brackish and clean to foul. Its temperament ranges from the raging cataracts of Great Falls or rushing mountain torrents like the Savage to the peaceful meanderings of the Antietam or marshes of Allens Fresh. You can fish for trout in its mountain headwaters, fish for bass in its broad main stem, and go crabbing in its tidal reaches. You can spend a day just playing the rapids in the Mather Gorge or spend two weeks floating and camping the long, lazy Potomac, Monocacy, or Conococheague. You can be buzzed by swallows beneath the C&O Canal aqueduct that spans Seneca Creek or be buzzed by jet airliners while paddling under the approach path to National Airport. The variety of experiences are infinite, and you can always count on some good boating to be enjoyed somewhere in the basin.

The following streams are described in this chapter:

Potomac River
    Potomac River (Tidal)
    North Branch Potomac River
        Savage River
        Georges Creek
        Wills Creek
            Brush Creek
            Little Wills Creek
            Jennings Run
        Evitts Creek
    Town Creek
        Flintstone Creek
    Fifteenmile Creek
    Sideling Hill Creek
    Tonoloway Creek
        Little Tonoloway Creek
    Licking Creek
        Big Cove Creek
    Conococheague Creek
        Back Creek
        West Branch Conococheague Creek

Antietam Creek
        West and East Branches Antietam Creek
Catoctin Creek
Monocacy River
    Marsh Creek
    Rock Creek
    Toms Creek
        Middle Creek
    Big Pipe Creek
        Little Pipe Creek
    Linganore Creek
    Bennett Creek
Seneca Creek
    Little Seneca Creek
Rock Creek
Anacostia River
    Northwest Branch
Mattawoman Creek
Nanjemoy Creek
Zekiah Swamp Run and Wicomico River

North Branch Potomac River
Potomac River

Potomac River

INTRODUCTION: If any river in Maryland can be called "Old Reliable," it is unquestionably the Potomac. When the Potomac on those very rare occasions gets too low to float, then it is time to give up on rivers and go to the bay or the ocean. When it gets too frozen to paddle, then it is time to give up on paddling and go skiing. Reliable flow means reliable whitewater. When most other streams in the state are a jumble of wet rocks, the rapids at Harpers Ferry and on the lower Potomac remain interesting. But most of the Potomac is usually docile and, as such, always provides plenty of opportunity for novice paddling and leisurely canoe-camping. Much of the left bank of the river is protected by the C&O Canal National Historical Park, thus alleviating to a large extent the problem of trespass inherent with camping on most streams. The Park provides reliable camping with its 32 hiker-biker campsites between Oldtown and Washington. Finally, if you are poaching, smuggling, running from the law, or have any other reason to be concerned with the location of political boundaries, you can rely on the Potomac to never float you out of Maryland, as the whole river, right up to the right bank, belongs to "The Old Line State."

Section 1. Oldtown, Md., to Paw Paw, W.Va. (Md. Rte. 51, W. Va. Rte. 9)						
Gradient	**Difficulty**	**Distance**	**Time**	**Width**	**Scenery**	**Map**
4	A to 1	10.9	3.5	100-500	Good	4

TRIP DESCRIPTION: One can start a Potomac cruise right at the junction of the North and South branches. But putting in 2.1 miles upstream at the low-water toll bridge over the North Branch at Oldtown, Maryland, is much more convenient.

As you float past the confluence of the two branches, you may notice that the left bank is pretty sorry looking. This is the legacy of the great storm of November, 1985, which dumped rain on the South Branch's headwaters at an intensity that would be expected only once in 500 years. The resulting floodwaters surged out of the South Branch, collided with that left bank, and scoured away the lush bottomland forest. You are seeing just the scars.

This section of the Potomac follows a relatively straight, eastward course as it cuts through the lovely, low hills and ridges of Allegany and Hampshire counties. Except for a short reach near Town Creek, where noise from Rte. 51 can be heard from the river, one enjoys the impression of remoteness. These miles run mostly flat, broken by a few riffles formed by tiers of low ledges. The water, unfortunately, often still suffers some slight odor and discoloration from upstream pollution on the North Branch. If this presents a problem on a hot summer day, the wilting paddler in search of a swimming hole can find excellent refuge by paddling a few yards up such clear and clean side streams as Town Creek (left) or the Little Cacapon (right).

The take-out is reached by a dirt road branching off W. Va. Rte. 9 at Paw Paw, just east of the bridge over the Potomac. Or you can continue around the bend another mile to a National Park Service access area (Tunnel Access), off of Md. Rte. 51 just west of the railroad overpass, a half mile west of Paw Paw. This spot affords more parking space.

HAZARDS: None.

WATER CONDITIONS: Canoeable most of summer, except after a prolonged drought.

Potomac River

5

GAUGE: USGS gauges on the main stem at Paw Paw and at Hancock and on the North Branch at Cumberland (call Washington or see USGS website for all three), should report at least 440 (3.5), 610 (2.8), and 330 (2.4) cfs (feet) respectively.

Section 2. Paw Paw, W.Va., to Little Orleans, Md.						
Gradient	Difficulty	Distance	Time	Width	Scenery	Map
3	A to 1	21.7	7.0	200-400	Very Good	5

TRIP DESCRIPTION: If John Smith (the first European known to have seen the Potomac) had first set eyes upon the Potomac from the top of Sideling Hill, he probably would have named it the "Snake River." For about 25 miles, from Paw Paw to Sideling Hill Creek, the river coils down a serpentine path as it cuts what is almost a canyon through the foothills between Town Hill and Sideling Hill. The valley is thinly inhabited and, except for the presence of a well-travelled railroad line, it presents a fairly wild riverscape that has long been very popular with canoe campers. Although this section can easily be covered in a day at most levels, the favorite procedure is to make it an overnighter, with a camp stop at the Sorrel Ridge Canal Campsite. Even if you do not camp here, it is worth a stop to hike up the towpath to explore the old C&O Canal Tunnel. The current through "The Paw Paw Bends" is usually strong and, though most of the way is flat, there are still lots of riffles formed by low ledges. The water is clean and usually fairly clear, and the fishing is usually rewarding. Take out at the launching ramp at the mouth of Fifteenmile Creek.

HAZARDS: None.

WATER CONDITIONS: Runnable all year, except after an unusually bad drought.

GAUGE: USGS gauges at Paw Paw and Hancock (call Washington or see USGS website) should respectively report at least 340 (3.3) and 460 (2.6) cfs (feet).

Section 3. Little Orleans, Md., to Hancock, Md.						
Gradient	Difficulty	Distance	Time	Width	Scenery	Map
2	A to 1	16.6	5.0	300-600	Good	5

TRIP DESCRIPTION: This section makes an ideal canoe-camping extension to the Paw Paw Bends cruise. To Great Cacapon, W.Va. the atmosphere is mostly wild (except when the trains roar by) and the scenery is dominated by beautiful Sideling Hill and Cacapon Mountain. One can enter or leave the Potomac at Great Cacapon by way of a state access area on the Cacapon, about 50 yards above its mouth.

Below Great Cacapon the mountain views continue to be pretty, but the riversides are marred by miles of often shoddy summer homes and shacks. The river glides swiftly throughout this section over a rocky bottom with occasional riffles formed by tiny ledges. Watch out for one strong, straightforward riffle through the ruins of the old C&O Canal Dam No. 6, above Great Cacapon. A launching ramp at the mouth of Little Tonoloway Creek in Hancock allows an easy exit.

HAZARDS: None.

WATER CONDITIONS: Runnable anytime.

Potomac River

Section 4. Hancock, Md., to Williamsport, Md.						
Gradient	Difficulty	Distance	Time	Width	Scenery	Map
2	A to 1–	28.2	9.0	400-700	Good	6

TRIP DESCRIPTION: This section can be divided into two comfortable runs of 14 miles each by gaining access at the McCoys Ferry launching ramp. To McCoys Ferry the Potomac is flat, yet maintains a strong current, even at low water. The bottom remains rocky. The trouble with this section is that I-70 runs so close to the river that it sounds as if one is paddling down the median strip. But the scenery of wooded hills and bluffs is attractive and, with a good pair of earplugs, this can provide pleasant cruising.

Seven miles of deadwater, backed up by C&O Canal Feeder Dam No. 5, begin at McCoys Ferry. The dam entails a rough carry on the left side. Below the dam, micro-ledges and old rubble weirs built to support fish traps create a few riffles. Some beautiful, towering, white limestone cliffs on the right make these last few miles the best part of the trip. Take out at the town park in Williamsport, just below the junction of Conococheague Creek (approached via West Salisbury Street).

The campground at historic Fort Frederick State Park provides another popular intermediate access point. If you use this spot, please park your car at the visitor center, not at a campsite, as the latter deprives some potential camper of the use of that site.

HAZARDS: Dam No. 5. Carry on the left.

WATER CONDITIONS: Runnable anytime.

GAUGE: USGS gauge at Hancock (call Washington or see USGS website) can read down to 400 cfs (2.5 feet), maybe even lower.

Section 5. Williamsport, Md., to Dam No. 4						
Gradient	Difficulty	Distance	Time	Width	Scenery	Map
2	A	15.6	5.0	400-700	Poor	7

TRIP DESCRIPTION: The trip starts off with a short portage on the right around a four-foot dam at Potomac Edison's power plant. At extremely high levels (like over 11.0 feet at Hancock) the dam washes out, but at any normal levels approach with the utmost caution, and carry. The river flows two and a half miles before the 13 miles of deadwater behind Dam No. 4 begins. This might be tolerable if the river were scenic. But, instead, the banks on most of this stretch are lined by a most distasteful display of summer dwellings. These include mobile homes, old school buses, trailers, shacks, and anything else that someone thought of to keep the rain off their heads, all often crammed together like a long parking lot. In warm weather count on competing with motorboats and water skiers for the right-of-way. Dam No. 4 is easily carried on the left. But a better idea is to put in here and skip this section.

HAZARDS: A four-foot dam at the power station at Williamsport (carry on right) and Dam No. 4, (carry on the left).

WATER CONDITIONS: Canoeable all year.

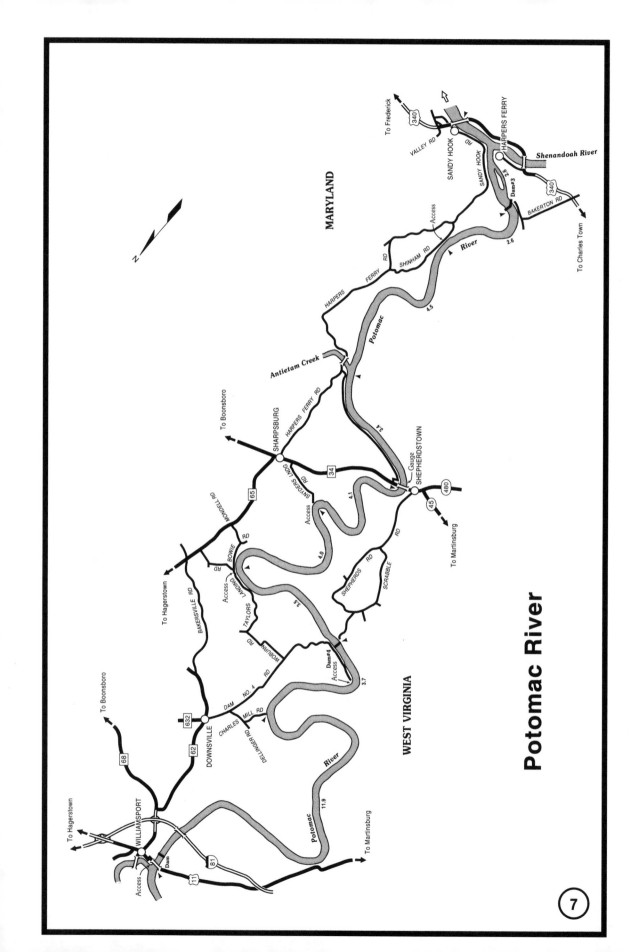

GAUGE: USGS gauge at Hancock (call Washington or see USGS website). Late summer flows drop below 790 cfs (3.0 feet). While nothing is too low, be sure to handle high levels (over 3,300 cfs or 5.0 feet) with care when approaching Dam No. 4.

Section 6. Dam No. 4 to Harpers Ferry, W.Va. (Dam No. 3)						
Gradient	Difficulty	Distance	Time	Width	Scenery	Map
2	A to 1	22.1	7.0	300-900	Good	7

TRIP DESCRIPTION: This is an attractive section without too much second home development and, on those stretches where it does exist, the dwellings are better spaced and of a more tasteful design than those upstream. The first five miles below the dam include many easy riffles best enjoyed at low water levels (under 790 cfs or 3.0 feet at Hancock), which expose old fishtrap weirs and low ledges. One particularly interesting spot, called The Horsebacks, is found a few miles below Dam No. 4. Here the river weaves through a staircase of tiny ledges that run parallel to the direction of the river. The rest of the way to Shepherdstown is flat. The 11.6 miles from Dam No. 4 to Shepherdstown is a nice day's trip. It is possible to take out at the gauging station on the right about 500 yards below the Rte. 34 bridge.

Below Shepherdstown wooded bluffs and the approaching Blue Ridge dominate the scenery. There are some small, ledgy riffles down to Antietam Creek and a few isolated ledges farther downstream, but the rest of the way is flat. One can take out at Dargan Bend (Shinhan Landing) launching ramp on the Maryland side about eight miles below Shepherdstown, or on the West Virginia side about 2,000 feet above Dam No. 3. You can reach the latter point by turning north off U.S. Rte. 340 onto Bakerton Road (Secondary Rte. 27) at the four-way intersection 1.5 miles west of the bridge over the Shenandoah River. Follow this road 1.5 miles to a railroad underpass and turn right immediately beyond.

HAZARDS: None.

WATER CONDITIONS: Always enough water.

GAUGE: None is necessary. Typical late summer low flows are around 1,200 cfs (2.0 feet) at the USGS gauge at Shepherdstown (call Washington or see USGS website).

Section 7. Harpers Ferry (Dam No. 3) to Point of Rocks, Md. (U.S. Rte. 15)						
Gradient	Difficulty	Distance	Time	Width	Scenery	Map
4	1 to 2+	13.5	4.0	1,000-2,000	Very Good	8

TRIP DESCRIPTION: For these 13 miles the Potomac cuts through the ancient Blue Ridge and its foothills and, in the process, forms the first whitewater since its headwaters. Start by carrying Dam No. 3 on the Maryland side or, if the level is medium or lower (under 3,300 cfs or 5.0 feet at Hancock, 4,900 cfs or 3.7 feet at Shepherdstown), by lifting over the left end of the dam itself. The dam has some tempting, runnable looking breaches, but they all bristle with old iron reinforcing rods. At moderate levels, the following mile and a half, known as The Needles, is an intricate, ledgy staircase that has long been a favorite novice whitewater run. Rocky as this section may be, only the most extreme droughts render it unnavigable. On the other hand, if the river is high, novices should skip this section altogether, as bank to bank the broad river rolls along powerfully and is spotted with

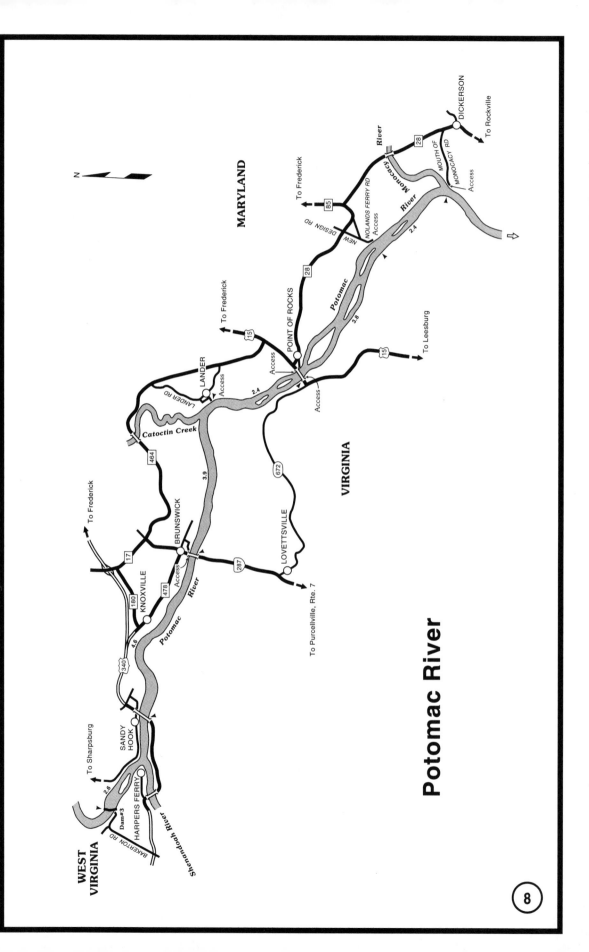

Potomac River

8

waves and souse holes that are always much larger than they look from the bank. A swim here in high water would be a long one, and in cold weather this could be potentially fatal.

If you have never been to Harpers Ferry before, be sure to stop and spend some time there. Besides being picturesque and historical, this town benefits from the National Park Service's practice of not only restoring old shops, homes, and businesses, but also of peopling them with interpreters, dressed in the garb of the times (and occupation). They will answer your questions, spin interesting yarns, and offer you at least an approximate feeling of what it was like to be in Harpers Ferry 140 years ago.

The Shenandoah River joins at Harpers Ferry and at summer levels often doubles the flow of the Potomac. About a half mile below the confluence, the river tumbles over a series of jagged ledges, the rocky spine of the Blue Ridge. The river always carries enough water to run these ledges along the Maryland side. The ledges form two distinct drops, the second and by far the bounciest of which is named Whitehorse Rapids. At medium to high levels, boaters wishing to avoid heavy water can opt for a variety of more technical routes through the ledges to the right.

Below Whitehorse and U.S. Rte. 340, the river glides through a beautiful maze of rocks and islets to another gap, this time through South Mountain (left) and Short Hill (right, now Virginia). Once again the Potomac tumbles over a staircase of ledges to form two short, easy rapids. The remainder of the run is smooth, but swift, past wooded bluffs, more rocks and islands, and finally through a gap in Catoctin Mountain. Take out at the launching ramp beneath the Maryland end of the U.S. Rte. 15 bridge.

Other popular access points to this section of river are above U.S. Rte. 340 at the wayside picnic area in Virginia (mile 2.5) and Lock 30 under Md. Rte. 17 bridge, Brunswick, Md. (mile 7.0). Traditionally, boaters have also used the tourist parking area about a hundred yards up the Shenandoah in Harpers Ferry. But as of this writing, the park has prohibited boater access at this spot. Hopefully this ill-conceived policy will soon change. But check first. Paddlers be warned that automobile break-ins are becoming a growing problem along this popular section of river. Choose your parking spot carefully.

HAZARDS: Carry Dam No. 3 at start.

WATER CONDITIONS: This is always runnable below the Shenandoah, with The Needles sometimes becoming marginal during late summer low flow.

GAUGE: USGS gauges at Hancock, Shepherdstown, and Harpers Ferry (call Washington or see USGS website) should respectively read at least 610 cfs (2.8 feet), 910 cfs (1.8 feet), and 2.8 feet for The Needles. Levels over five feet on Hancock and Harpers Ferry gauges or Millville gauge (on Shenandoah) mean relatively high water conditions. Novices should avoid such levels if the water is cold.

Section 8. Point of Rocks, Md. (U.S. Rte. 15), to Violets Lock						
Gradient	Difficulty	Distance	Time	Width	Scenery	Map
1	A	26.1	8.5	1,000-2,200	Good	8,9

TRIP DESCRIPTION: The Potomac leaves the mountains for good now and settles down to a leisurely coast across the Piedmont. The river through here is wide, fairly straight and, while flat, still possesses a good current. There are some wooded bluffs here and there, but the usual scenery is a uniform line of trees on each bank—silver maples, sycamores, willows, and box elders as far as you can see. There are also some unusually long islands which, along with the absence of railroads (below Monocacy) and highways, make this a prime section for camping. These islands do well at screening from sight some pockets of riverside development that foul the Virginia side. Also on the Virginia side,

Potomac River

some office buildings and apartments that loom beyond the streamside buffer are now visible from mid-river, especially in winter. The most significant civilized intrusion is the power plant below the mouth of the Monocacy.

This plant, while not the most beautiful sight in the world, has produced two synthetic whitewater gems. The huge volume of cooling water discharged down a short canal to the river creates a very playable chain of standing waves at low levels (under 2,850 cfs or 3.0 feet on the USGS gauge at Little Falls). Higher levels diminish the drop and the phenomenon is inundated. The only catch to this wonder is that under optimal late summer low flow conditions the water is also very hot, hence creating one of the rare situations where a soaking wet paddler could keel over from heat stroke. A more recent development is an artificial whitewater course developed in the concrete-lined channel just upstream. This is entirely on private property and available to authorized training athletes only. But you should take a peek through the fence at this fascinating flush.

Access to the power plant discharge is best gained at Mouth of Monocacy Boaters' Access, a mile and a half upstream, or at the Dickerson Warmwater Access, a mile downstream. Some good access points to the rest of this section include Nolands Ferry Access (mile 3.8), Whites Ferry (mile 12.6), Edwards Ferry (mile 17.4), Algonkian Park (mile 23.5), and Seneca Creek (mile 25.8).

HAZARDS: None.

WATER CONDITIONS: Canoeable all year.

GAUGE: None necessary. USGS gauge at Point of Rocks (call Washington or see USGS website) gets down to around 1,420 cfs (0.8 feet) in late summer low flows.

Section 9. Violets Lock to Great Falls						
Gradient	Difficulty	Distance	Time	Width	Scenery	Map
4	A to 2–	7.3	2.5	1,300-3,000	Very Good	9

TRIP DESCRIPTION: The Potomac now gently begins its 180-foot descent over the Fall Line to tidewater. A special feature of this section is that it is paralleled by the usually rewatered C&O Canal, thus relieving the paddler of the burden of setting up a car shuttle, as is necessary on most other streams.

The section starts with the river rushing over the rubbly ruins of the C&O Canal Dam No. 2 and then for the next mile through a maze of islands, rocks, and easy riffles. The Potomac is a wide river through here. If you prefer something more closed in, especially if the river is high and powerful, ferry over from Violets Lock to the Virginia side where you will find a small channel splitting off perpendicularly from the river just above Dam No. 2. This channel is the washed out remains of the old Patowmack Canal, part of a pre-C&O Canal navigational venture of George Washington's to bypass the Fall Line rapids. Spiced with numerous rubbly or ledgy riffles, this passage has long delighted novice whitewater boaters. Many say it reminds them of a bayou with gradient. A popular practice is just to run these riffles, then ferry over to the Maryland side for a short carry up to the C&O Canal, and finally ascend the canal, a loop of a little over two miles.

Below here the river is split in half by three-and a half-mile-long Watkins Island and further subdivided by dozens of other islands. Except for a pair of riffles at a pipeline crossing, the river drifts lazily all the way to Great Falls. Paddlers taking the extreme left side of the river will find a low weir at the Potomac River Water Filtration Plant. It can be scrapey at low levels.

This section ends just above Great Falls. Take out at Maryland's Great Falls Park, on the left. Make sure you know where the Washington Aqueduct water supply dam is, and take out well above. To wash over this dam would be nasty, but your troubles would just be beginning, as Great Falls develops just downstream. STAY AWAY.

Potomac River

HAZARDS: Possible trees on the Patowmack Canal, and Great Falls Dam at the trip's end. Do not mistake this little dam for the falls, which are just downstream.

WATER CONDITIONS: Always runnable, though novices should avoid this section at high levels (over 22,000 cfs or 5.0 feet at Little Falls) because of the danger of being drawn into the falls downstream. At low levels (under 2,850 cfs or 3.0 feet at Little Falls) Dam No. 2 will be scrapey.

GAUGE: USGS gauge at Little Falls (call Washington or see USGS website).

Section 10. Great Falls						
Gradient	Difficulty	Distance	Time	Width	Scenery	Map
200	5 to 6	0.4	1.0	200-2,000	Excellent	10

TRIP DESCRIPTION: While Great Falls is just pretty scenery for most of us, for a growing number of advanced boaters, it is a runnable rapid. Perhaps equally amazing is that the National Park Service, which is usually very skittish about such activities, has kept an open mind and cooperated with the paddling community to permit this activity. We are indeed fortunate to have this choice, and even if this is not every paddler's cup of tea, simply having the opportunity to watch others meet the challenge is most rewarding.

Great Falls is actually a series of falls, ranging from steep rapids to sheer drops of over 20 feet. There are also man-made drops on a channel along the Maryland side that were part of a failed attempt as a fish ladder. You can view the falls from observation decks on both sides of the river. People have navigated dozens of different routes, including the fish ladder passage. The water level often dictates their choice. Most runs are done at low water, but that threshold is edging ever upward.

If you wish to paddle the falls, please play by the rules. You must register in advance with the Maryland Department of Natural Resources. Registration forms are distributed by the American Whitewater Affiliation (address: 1430 Fenwick Lane, Silver Spring, MD 20910, or call 301-589-9453). Runs should be before 9:00 am or after 6:00 pm, preferably on weekdays, so as minimize the attractive nuisance potential. You may only approach the falls from downstream, carrying up over the rocks and cliffs — a questionable requirement probably to winnow out less dedicated sorts. An unwritten rule is to talk first with experienced falls runners, join them, and abide by their warnings and advice. Please do not be the fool whose death or dramatic rescue episode causes the suspension of this privilege.

HAZARDS: Deceptive power of even low water levels, pinning spots, and inherent orthopedic danger of jumping big drops.

WATER CONDITIONS: Most runs are done at levels of under 6,000 cfs or 3.5 feet, levels which are most commonly found between mid-June and November.

GAUGE: USGS gauge at Little Falls (call Washington or see USGS website).

Section 11. Great Falls to Washington, D.C. (Chain Bridge)						
Gradient	Difficulty	Distance	Time	Width	Scenery	Map
8	A to 3–, 4	10.4	3.5	60-1,500	Excellent	10

TRIP DESCRIPTION: This final section is the Potomac's finest. It has the best whitewater, the most dramatic scenery and, at least in the Mather Gorge below Great Falls, a wilderness character normally unthinkable in the heart of a major metropolitan area.

Normal healthy people wishing to remain normal and healthy will want to portage Great Falls. This is easily accomplished by carrying down the C&O Canal towpath 800 yards to the second lock (Lock 17) below the old Great Falls Tavern and following a well-trod path that branches off to the right. This path winds about a hundred feet to a sand beach on a lagoon cut off from the main river by Rocky Island. This puts you at the bottom of a wild, rockbound gorge that extends for over a mile downstream.

If the level is under 8,500 cfs (3.8 feet), paddle off to your right and carry or drag over the slippery, slimy rocks to the main channel. Relaunch at a passage that local paddlers refer to as the S-Turn. At low and moderate levels it is possible to paddle and portage from here upstream to within sight of the falls. At a variety of levels, the two rapids on this upstream stretch (Fish Ladder and Observation Deck rapids) offer great surfing. Going downstream is a turbulent flush through a short and narrow reach of rock gorge ending with a wavy but uncomplicated ride through Rocky Island Rapid.

When the river is above 8,500 cfs (3.8 feet), water flows into the sand beach lagoon and it now becomes an arm of the river. At such levels it is now possible to paddle straight downstream from the put-in or off to the extreme left, plunging over some small but twisting drops. These routes are recommended for paddlers uncomfortable with heavy whitewater. The alternative route is the main channel, through the S-Turn, which becomes extremely turbulent at levels over 10,400 cfs (4.0 feet). At such levels, Rocky Island Rapid develops into a long chain of big, breaking waves and becomes the premier playing spot on the lower Potomac.

Below Rocky Island the river widens and after a short pool rushes over a short bouncy drop called Wet Bottom Chute. From here to the end of the Mather Gorge the river is flat, in a sometimes turbulent sort of way. The mellowness of this portion of the river affords a welcome opportunity to soak in the beauty of the gorge's jagged 80-foot cliffs. You will no doubt be sharing this reach with hoards of rock climbers who enjoy these cliffs from an even closer perspective.

The gorge ends with a wide, easy rapid on the left hand bend above the confluence with Difficult Run. These rapids provide an ideal and, in warm weather, safe training area for neophytes. The tributary, Difficult Run, is worth a short hike up a good trail to admire its rocky, plunging course and perhaps contemplate as a destination the next time it rains.

The next few miles of the Potomac comes as a large, lazy river with a few good drops and riffles thrown in for spice. This is an island-studded stretch decorated by wooded bluffs and occasional little rock cliffs or outcrops. About a quarter mile below Difficult Run is the most popular access to the lower Potomac. It is a trail down from the parking area by MacArthur Boulevard, across the road from Old Angler's Inn Restaurant.

A half mile downstream the river splits around Offut Island, recognized by its bold, rocky upstream face. Take the left side for the most exciting ride, except at low water when it almost dries up. A half mile farther downstream the river splits around two large islands. The most interesting passage is down the right channel over Yellow Falls, a three-foot double ledge. The other two channels drop more gradually and dry up in low water. Another mile through a long rock garden brings you to Stubblefield Falls, a short, easy, bouncy rapid.

From here on down to Brookmont is mostly smooth water that glides through rock gardens and dozens of small islands. These islands and the adjacent bottomlands, especially on the southern exposed Maryland side, are a wildflower lover's paradise during April and May. You will recognize Brookmont by a monolithic concrete pumping station on the left bank of the river.

The pumping station marks the location of Brookmont Dam. This insignificant-looking, two-foot weir has gained as bloody a reputation as Attilla the Hun. For years the reversal from this little drop would annually trap and drown at least one, sometimes several, unsuspecting boaters. In 1986 the Corps of Engineers finally modified the dam's left half (between Snake Island and the Maryland bank) to destroy the reversal. While the danger appears to have been greatly reduced, many paddlers still choose to get out well above and carry down the C&O towpath to the pool below or land at the head of Snake Island and carry. As additional incentive for this option, keep in mind that you can be fined for running the dam. As for the river to the right of Snake Island, very little water flows over there at low water. At higher levels also avoid this side as its sharp and considerably higher drop, its reversal, and its rocky outflow create a nasty trap. Just below Brookmont Dam is a curving rubble dam, C&O Canal Dam No. 1, which you can run just to the left of Snake Island.

If you are uncomfortable in big, powerful, and turbulent water, then end your trip at Brookmont (at Lock 6). The river soon changes radically as it funnels down to a final narrow, rocky plunge to tidewater. Immediately below the dams, the river filters through some rock gardens, narrows, and then rushes through some bouncy but uncomplicated chutes as it rushes on toward Chain Bridge. Within sight of the bridge, where the river and downstream visibility appear blocked, get out and scout. This is Little Falls. It is a steep, heavy rapid split down the middle by a pair of jagged, rocky islands. Depending on the level, you can run either side with each choice having its special problem. At very low levels (less than 1,850 cfs or 2.8 feet) the Maryland channel is rocky but safe, while the most popular and exciting route is the diagonal left to right descent between the islands. But before you attempt this diagonal route, beware of the deceptively dangerous pinning potential on the head of the rocky island.

Up to 10,400 cfs (4.0 feet) the Maryland side is dependable and relatively conservative, but to get there you must fight what can be an awesome current to avoid being swept against the head of the lower island. From 10,400 cfs (4.0 feet) to roughly 37,000 cfs (6.0 feet) the paddler can take the more straightforward Virginia side, but in doing so must avoid being snared by a vicious hole on the right side of the head of the second island.

Finally at levels over 37,000 cfs (6.0 feet), the island becomes buried and Little Falls is simplified into a long, heaving mass of giant waves, boils, and whirlpools extending past Chain Bridge. The major hazard now is the center pier of Chain Bridge which forms a powerful recirculating eddy that might hold you and your boat for the rest of your short life.

Access to this section is good. In addition, you can do much of this section as a circuit paddle, using the rewatered sections of the C&O Canal. Popular access points include the observation platform at the Virginia Great Falls Park, the parking lots opposite Anglers Inn on MacArthur Blvd., Carderock Recreation Area (lower end), Lock 8 (79th St., Cabin John), Sycamore Island, and Lock 6 at Brookmont. For just running Little Falls, most people start at Lock 6 and paddle up the canal or its parallel feeder canal and enter the river just above Dam No. 1. It is most convenient to take out at the pumping station at the foot of the rapids (low concrete structure on the left) and follow a straight concrete roadway back to the canal and then paddle and portage back to your car. Or you can continue another mile downstream on tidewater to Fletchers Cove where you can drive your vehicle almost to the riverbank.

HAZARDS: High water. Surging, high-speed current combined with vertical rock banks make escape for the swimming paddler extremely difficult in the narrow Mather Gorge or at Little Falls. On the wide stretches, the shear distance from shore breeds the potential for a marathon swim. Either situation could be lethal when the water is cold.

Brookmont Dam. This structure has earned a reputation as a "drowning machine" over the years. Recent modifications of its left half have done much to diminish the danger. But it is still too soon to give it a clean bill of health, so portage at all but low levels.

Little Falls. The power of the big river being constricted through this narrow, rocky channel allows only a narrow margin of error. If there is any question about this section, hike in first and scout. If you still have doubts, then skip it.

WATER CONDITIONS: There is always enough water for paddling. The problems arise when there is too much, a situation most likely to occur in winter or early spring.

GAUGE: There is a USGS gauge at the Brookmont Pumping Station (identified as Little Falls, call Washington or see USGS website). For the river above Brookmont, levels of 6,000 cfs (3.5 feet) to 16,000 cfs (4.5 feet) bring out the best bounce in most rapids. For the Little Falls section, levels of under 4,000 cfs (3.2 feet) are best for the relatively inexperienced or those troubled by big water. Above 16,000 cfs (4.5 feet), only expert boaters with strong rolls should venture down this last mile of whitewater.

Potomac River

CLARA BARTON PKWY

120

CANAL

Fletchers Boathouse

GEORGE WASHINGTON MEMORIAL PKWY

RD

SPOUT RUN PKWY

66

WHITEHURST FWY

K ST

Thompson Boat Center

Rock Creek

ROCK CR PK

T. R. Is.

B

C

D

27   Access

Pentagon

1

395

GEORGE WASHINGTON MEM. PKWY

Washington National Airport

Four Mile Run

Washington Marina

WASHINGTON ST

ALEXANDRIA

Hunting Creek

95

495

FRANKLIN ST

1

95

495

N

ARLINGTON

VIRGINIA

A - CHAIN BRIDGE
B - KEY BRIDGE
C - THEODORE ROOSEVELT BRIDGE
D - ARLINGTON MEMORIAL BRIDGE
E - WOODROW WILSON BRIDGE
F - S. ROYAL ST
G - JONES POINT DR

WASHINGTON

DISTRICT OF COLUMBIA

Washington Mon.

1

395

Tidal Basin

OHIO DR

OHIO DR

Washington Channel

Potomac

River

Hains Pt.

Anacostia

River

S. CAPITOL ST

S. CAPITOL ST

SUITLAND PKWY

Access

295

Blue Plains

Oxon Cove

95

495

F

G

Access

E

Jones Pt.

1

11

State Of The River Address

For a river that has been subjected to almost 350 years of civilization, the Potomac has held up quite respectably. Partly it remained this way because enough residents cared to protect it from pollution and dams. Will you pick up the torch when the next threat arises?

The Potomac in recent decades has suffered a widespread reputation as an open sewer. This has been unfortunate and unfair, as most of the river flows quite clean with normally clear waters supporting healthy populations of bass and other cleanwater species; providing a safe boating and swimming environment; and providing a safe drinking water supply for numerous towns along the river. On the other hand, the section passing through Washington, D.C. — the portion most visible to the nation and the media — has suffered horribly in past years from discharges of raw or partially treated sewage, combined sewer overflows, and street runoff. From hence came its notorious reputation. Since the early 1970's, however, the federal and local governments have built new and upgraded old sewage treatment plants, separated some of the combined sewers, and stopped raw sewage discharges. By 1978 conditions had so improved that the Interstate Commission on the Potomac River Basin, a basin watchdog agency, pronounced the river through Washington to be clean enough for swimming.

The Potomac has remained remarkably free of dams for such a major river. There are only two Corps of Engineers-built dams in the basin, Savage River and Jennings Randolph, and there are a few large municipal and industrial water supply impoundments. The Corps long ago drafted plans for a huge system of reservoirs across the basin, including one that would drown the Potomac from just above Great Falls back up into Frederick County, a reservoir at Sixes Bridge on the Monocacy, and one on Town Creek. Most of these proposals have been fought and defeated, with Jennings Randolph Dam so far the only survivor. An even more encouraging development for us friends of the river has been the construction, by the Corps, of a pumping station on tidewater just below Little Falls. This is the structure that we paddlers see as a concrete observation deck on the river left above Chain Bridge. For you see, most of those Corps dams were justified as necessary to meet future water supply demands of the Washington Metropolitan Area. But planners pointed out that there was already a huge reservoir of fresh water lodged in the estuary between Little Falls and the beginning of brackish water at Fort Washington, And with the elimination of so much of Washington's pollution, we could now tap this as an emergency drinking water source. So why build dams when for a fraction of the cost and with minimal environmental damage we could, if the Potomac's flow ever drops below our demands, just pump up this existing water supply? For once, good sense prevailed.

Potomac River (Tidewater)

INTRODUCTION: When the Potomac turns tidal, it transforms into an entirely different waterway. In its remaining 90 miles, it changes from fresh to salty. It widens from 150 feet at the foot of Little Falls to seven miles above Point Lookout. Traffic on tidewater is dominated by motorboats, including commercial shipping and even an occasional warship. And, of course, this reach never lacks for water.

One of the nicest features of the tidal Potomac and its tributaries is the benign nature of its tides. They are almost inconsequential. The currents are usually gentle enough for the average paddler to overcome easily. The range is typically only a few feet. So mistiming a tide will slow you somewhat, but not stop you, and might only deny you access to the shallow upper reaches of tributaries.

Because of the size and shape of the Potomac estuary, it is appropriate to modify the format of the trip descriptions. I have divided this reach into five sections. The first, that which flows through the District of Columbia, is relatively narrow and therefore, as with most streams in this book, is

Potomac River
Mattawoman Creek

MARYLAND

VIRGINIA

ALEXANDRIA

To Waldorf

12

described from the vantage of one paddling straight down the center of the river. But below the District, because the river is so wide, most paddlers would probably favor a shore. So I have described the river from that perspective, not only following each shore, but also probing up most tidal tributaries. Distance and time are not projected because they depend on how closely you follow the shoreline and how many tributaries you probe. The widths given below are those of the Potomac proper.

Section 1. Chain Bridge to I-95						
Gradient	**Difficulty**	**Distance**	**Time**	**Width**	**Scenery**	**Map**
0	A	11.7	5.5	150-3,700	Good	11

TRIP DESCRIPTION: A few decades ago, this section of river was branded a national shame. Raw or partially treated sewage from Washington and its suburbs rendered its waters a stinking, gray health hazard. Today those same waters are often clear and support luxuriant beds of aquatic grasses, schools of game fish, and flocks of waterfowl. Except after a rain, when street runoff and some remaining combined sewers foul things up, contact with the river is perfectly safe. Sadly, for many, the Potomac has yet to shed its poor public image.

You cannot put in from the high, shoulderless approaches to Chain Bridge. Instead, launch into the C&O Canal from a small parking area along the Clara Barton Parkway about a tenth of a mile above Chain Bridge and paddle upstream about 200 yards. Here a 200-yard portage down a wide, smooth path will deliver you to the pumping station at the foot of Little Falls. Beginners should avoid the pumping station put-in if Little Falls USGS gauge reads over 6,000 cfs (3.5 feet), as medium water levels bring swift and treacherous currents while higher levels create huge standing waves to Chain Bridge and even below. Another option is to put in at Fletchers Boathouse and paddle as much of the mile upstream as you can.

From Little Falls to Key Bridge, the Potomac passes through a mostly natural setting. On the Virginia side, high wooded bluffs rise right from the water's edge. The busy George Washington Parkway runs along its crest, mostly out of view, though not out of hearing. On the District side, equally high ground rises behind a narrow strip of wooded bottom lands. A single level of the C&O Canal runs parallel and offers a convenient way to return to the start. The river channel is as narrow as 150 feet at the foot of Little Falls and as much as 70 feet deep near Fletchers Boathouse.

Key Bridge marks the beginning of the big city. On the right looms the high-rise glass and glitter of Rosslyn. On the left, Georgetown's renovated waterfront presents an equally dazzling facade, which contrasts with the hilltop medieval spires of Georgetown University or the turn-of-the-century, riverside boathouses by Key Bridge. Shortly below is that palace-like mirage called the Kennedy Center. In between is one last natural refuge, Theodore Roosevelt Island, a former plantation and now a jungle-like patch fortunately penetrated by a good trail system. Perhaps the most interesting time to be paddling around the foot of Theodore Roosevelt Island is about 9:00 pm on July 4th where and when you will find one of the best spots in the city for viewing the fireworks over the Washington Monument.

By law, Washington has a unique, low-rise, horizontal skyline that intentionally accentuates the city's famous landmarks. From the river you will easily spot the Capitol's dome, Washington Monument, the Lincoln and Jefferson memorials, and National Cathedral.

From Georgetown to National Airport, both banks are park land. A two-mile-long strip on the left is East Potomac Park, originally created as a disposal area for muck dredged from the river. At its north edge is the cherry-tree-fringed Tidal Basin, whose two outlets are regulated by tide gates. Short carries will get you in and out, but be prepared for five-foot-high seawalls at the east end. The east side of East Potomac Park is bordered by Washington Channel, an interesting route past seafood markets, restaurants, marinas, and the stately campus of Fort Lesley J. McNair. The tip of the park is called Hains Point, where you will find The Awakening, a bizarre likeness of a slumbering giant rising out of the earth.

Potomac River
Nanjemoy Creek

VA RTE. 608 - BROOKE RD
VA RTE. 610 - NEABSCO RD
VA RTE. 629 - ANDREW CHAPEL RD
VA RTE. 630 - COURTHOUSE RD
VA RTE. 633 - POSSUM POINT RD

N

MARYLAND

VIRGINIA

To Waldorf

LA PLATA

BEL ALTON

301

PORT TOBACCO

CHAPEL POINT RD

Access, Chapel Pt. St. Pk.

POPES CREEK RD

EDGE HILL RD

POPES CREEK

Access

Port Tobacco River

6

Mary Dr

CEDAR POINT NECK RD

BRENTLAND RD

Cmpgd.

BLOSSOM POINT RD

Burgess Creek

DURHAM CHURCH RD

Hillitop Fork

Nanjemoy Creek

301

218

To Richmond

206

218

206

Chotank Creek

River

225

425

Mattawoman Creek

Access

IRONSIDES RISON RD

General Smallwood State Park

FRIENDSHIP LANDING RD

425

Access

6

224

Maryland Point

Thorne Gut

224

Chicamuxen Creek

To Washington

Neabsco Creek

610

Leesylvania State Park

Powells Creek

Accesses

633

Quantico Creek

FULLER RD

Access

Access

QUANTICO

RUSSELL RD

Access

Chopawamsic Creek

1

DUMFRIES

TRIANGLE

Mallows Bay

Potomac

Aquia Creek

Aqua-Po Park

608

Accokeek Creek

Potomac Creek

629

BROOKE

630

STAFFORD

1

696

FAIRVIEW BEACH

218

BUTLER RD

212

BUS 17

FREDERICKSBURG

13

This is a noisy reach because across the river is busy Washington National Airport. Airplane lovers will delight in the almost continuous procession of planes coming and going. At the airport's north end you can probe the lagoon of Roaches Run Waterfowl Sanctuary. But be sure that you are strong enough a paddler to overcome the tidal surge through the connecting culvert. The alternate connecting route, a portage across the busy George Washington Parkway, is a game of Russian roulette. At the south end of the airport you can probe up the mouth of Fourmile Run. But you will find only channelized urban ugliness.

Continuing down to the Wilson Bridge, on the Virginia side, on past the Washington Sailing Marina and some wooded park land, you come to Alexandria. Its interesting waterfront includes old ships, restaurants, pricey condos, rotting docks, and a power plant. If you follow the District side, the former Bolling Air Force Base offers only a high riprapped bank for a view. It is followed by the huge Blue Plains Sewage Treatment Plant, a major reason why the river's waters are now so clean. Come here during cold weather, and you will find yourself amid scores of bass boats, as the warm effluent makes this a fish resort. Just below is Oxon Cove, whose wooded shores would make it an attractive retreat were it not for the rafts of floating trash (my favorite was the floating red easy chair) washed down from the streets of the Oxon Run watershed. Swampy shores mark the remainder of this trip.

Access on this reach is pretty good, though uneven. From top to bottom, best spots on the Virginia side are at the causeway to Theodore Roosevelt Island, the Columbia Island Marina, Lady Bird Johnson Park (just across the George Washington Parkway from the marina), the public ramp at north end of National Airport at Roaches Run, the public ramp at the Washington Sailing Marina, and beneath the Woodrow Wilson Bridge at Jones Point Park (approached from S. Royal Street). Best spots on the District side are Fletchers Boathouse, Thompson Boat Center, and the parking area at Hains Point.

HAZARDS: Motorboats (particularly bass boats) and a small volume of commercial shipping.

WATER CONDITIONS: Tidal, so there is always enough water. Beginners should avoid the river above Fletchers Boathouse when the water is high.

GAUGE: Little Falls USGS gauge (call Washington or see USGS website).

Section 2. Maryland Side: I-95 to U.S. Rte. 301						
Gradient	Difficulty	Distance	Time	Width	Scenery	Map
0	A	Variable	Variable	0.5 - 3.5 Miles	Fair to Very Good	12,13

TRIP DESCRIPTION: Both sides of the Potomac from Washington to Rte. 301 are a pleasant surprise in that they are graced with numerous and often lengthy segments of undeveloped shoreline. Bird life abounds, most notably in the form of bald eagles and great blue herons. The fishing is good, as is the water quality. The scenery is both beautiful, varied, and stimulating.

There are two negative features on this section. First, shameful deposits of flotsam, mainly washed from the streets of the metropolitan area, litter the shoreline. Fortunately, its concentration gradually decreases with the miles downstream.

Second, hydrilla can be a problem in the first 30 miles. This attractive submerged (barely) water plant was at one time feared as the vegetable that would devour the Potomac—sort of an aquatic kudzu. But its spread has been limited and has instead proved an asset for the river in that it provides food and cover for fish and fowl, absorbs nutrients, and filters sediment and motorboats from the water. Nevertheless, you may find yourself cursing the weed as it is nearly impossible to paddle through and mats of it often clog the near-shore waters and some tributaries. Since it dies off during winter, that season and spring are the best times to avoid its grasp.

There is no access at the Maryland end of the Wilson Bridge, so the next best choice is Jones Point Park on the Virginia side. Heading south, you first encounter a broad, scenic cove fringed by high, wooded shores. How long its wild state continues is uncertain, as there have long been elaborate plans here to construct an complex of hotels, marinas, etc. So enjoy it while it lasts. At the south end rise the 100-foot heights of Rosier Bluff, atop which are the ruins of Fort Foote, one of a ring of earthen batteries built during the Civil War to defend Washington. Look for some rotting pilings and a small brick building, from which you can follow a trail to the top (this is a potential access point if you are not cardiovascularly challenged). An interpretive trail winds through the ruins of the fort and past two huge cannon. For the next mile the waterfront is developed, until Broad Creek.

Enough of Broad Creek remains natural to merit a detour. You can ascend about a mile to where shallows and marsh seem to block further progress. But if you probe around, you will find a narrow channel in the center that leads up into the marsh and even into the swampy woods before deadfalls become an obstacle.

After about two miles of moderately developed shoreline comes Fort Washington. The present structure was completed in 1824, replacing an earlier fort that the British destroyed during their invasion of Washington in 1814. Stop here at least long enough to climb the bluff and ramparts for a stunning view of the river bend. If you do not mind the 100-yard carry between the lower parking lot and the lighthouse, this park is a potential access point. The fort marks the mouth of Piscataway Creek.

Piscataway makes a pretty side trip. The high, wooded north shore is generally attractive, but marred by a big marina and few fancy houses. The south shore is mostly wild, except for one spot at its upper end where a big sewage treatment plant hides behind a neo-colonial facade. At the head of the wide water, narrow channels hug both the north and south shores, leading up into marsh and swamp. The channels join and, even at low tide, you can ascend up to Rte. 210. There is deep-water access to Piscataway via Farmington Landing (free), located at the foot of Wharf Road, or via Fort Washington Marina (pay).

For the next six miles, much of the Potomac shoreline is wild, ranging from eroded banks to swamp. The quality of this setting is no accident. Years ago, citizens concerned about preserving the view from Mount Vernon formed a land trust (The Accokeek Foundation) that, through easements and public purchase, have staved off objectionable development. Hidden on the cut banks about a mile and a half below the mouth of Piscataway (look for a small fishing pier) is the National Colonial Farm. This is a living history museum that depicts a small colonial tobacco farm. It is well worth the modest admission fee to visit. Access to this reach is at the public landing at the end of Md. Route 227, Marshall Hall, and at the fishing pier of the National Colonial Farm.

One final point of interest about this reach is that it is where the boundary between fresh and brackish water occurs. While you will not immediately be able to taste the difference, subtle visual hints such as landings with work boats and piles of crab pots suggest a changing river.

The wildness is briefly broken by the little settlement of Fenwick. But just below is one the prettiest spots on the Maryland side — Pomonkey Creek. Depending on how thick the hydrilla is, you can follow its winding course about a mile and a half through marsh backed by high, wooded slopes. There is yet little development here.

Two miles of wooded bluff alternating with swamp characterize the Potomac below Pomonkey, though impending development threatens this. Potomac Heights follows, where houses perch a la Malibu upon eroded bluffs. After Potomac Heights comes the Naval Surface Warfare Center at Indian Head. Though the bluffs continue through much of the reservation, scrubby vegetation, junk, and drab military structures make for mediocre scenery. The river view changes here also, for with Occoquan Bay across the way, you are exposed to nearly four miles of beautiful open water. If the wind is out of the northwest, however, this can be a liability.

The broad estuary of Mattawoman Creek (described separately) enters next. The public ramp on this creek, at General Smallwood State Park, is the first public access point since Marshall Hall and the

Zekiah Swamp Run
Wicomico River
Potomac River

To Waldorf

LA PLATA

6

To Waldorf

488

BEL ALTON

BEL ALTON NEWTOWN RD

Swamp   Run

6.5

To Leonardtown

5

Zekiah

5.9

6

POPES CREEK RD

301

PENNS HILL RD

OLIVERS SHOP RD

231

POPES CREEK

To Newmarket, Rte. 5

EDGE HILL RD

NEWBURG

Newport Swamp Run

5.1

234

Potomac

257

Access

COFFEE HILL RD

4.9

River

Chaptico Creek

CHAPTICO

WILSON RD   ISSUE

Access

CHAPTICO WHARF RD

Southern Park

ROCK POINT RD

Wicomico

3.6

238

254

COBB ISLAND   Access

Access   BUSHWOOD RD

CLEMENTS

239

242

234

To Waldorf

520

470

5

River

RIVER SPRINGS RD

AVENUE

McIntosh Run

242

HATCHET THICKET RD

Access

GOLDEN THOMPSON RD

St.   Clements   Bay

245

LEONARDTOWN

COLTONS POINT   Museum

Access

St. Clements Island St. Pk.

Breton Bay

Access

ABELLS WHARF RD

5

BRETON BEACH RD

244

To St. Mary's City

Potomac River

To Waldorf   To Hollywood

5   245

LEONARDTOWN

Access

Breton   *Bay*

Access

ABELLS WHARF RD

BRETON BEACH RD

5

244

Potomac

249

CALLAWAY

GREAT MILLS

FLAT IRON RD

Eastern Branch

5

249

PINEY POINT

Piney Pt. Light

Access

St. George Creek

ST. GEORGE ISLAND

St. Mary's   *River*

ST. MARY'S CITY

St.   *Inigoes*   *Creek*

ST. INIGOES

To Lexington Park

235

BEACHVILLE RD

St.

FOX HARBOR RD

Access

WYNNE RD   RIDGE

N

River

5

Pt. Lookout State Park

Access

Pt. Lookout

15

last until Friendship Landing on Nanjemoy Creek. If you are not bothered by open water crossings, it may be best to approach much of this isolated reach from such Virginia accesses as Quantico, Aqua-Po Beach Park, or Fairview Beach.

The river now follows a great bend, the southern tip of which is called Maryland Point. The 17 miles from Mattawoman to Maryland Point is a wonderful trip. Development is spotty. In between are long stretches of either swampy shores or wooded or eroded bluffs. Be sure to leave time for side trips up tributaries. The largest, Chicamuxen Creek, which is just below the mouth of Mattawoman, funnels into a narrow, marsh-bound passage with little development. The real gems though are farther downstream — particularly Mallows Creek and Thorne Gut — whose marshy routes cut back into the riverside bluffs. It is easy to miss their mouths, so look for marshy breaks in the otherwise wooded shorelines. Sand bars at the mouths of some such creeks, bar entrance at low tides.

The most interesting feature of this reach is the ship graveyard at Mallows Bay. After World War I, over 200 surplus merchant ships were brought to these shallow waters for salvage or disposal. What remain today are rows of timbers and spikes barely protruding from the water. The best way to appreciate this spot is to climb the bluff at the north end of the bay, from which angle the ships' outlines become obvious.

From Maryland Point to the mouth of Nanjemoy Creek, the shoreline is mostly developed. Its best quality is the view downstream and across the river. Nanjemoy Creek is described separately.

From Nanjemoy Creek to Port Tobacco River, the Potomac's shore is mostly undeveloped, lying within a military reservation. So look, but do not land, as live ordnance may be a problem. Mostly you see 20-foot eroded mud banks with many toppled trees. At a few points the banks dip to marsh. One such spot, about a mile or two below Nanjemoy, has a narrow passage that leads to a beautiful little pond.

Port Tobacco River offers a scenic side trip past high ground with well-spaced development. Only at its upper end does it get too civilized. Perhaps the best place to appreciate Port Tobacco River is from high above, from the yard of St. Ignatius Church near Chapel Point. The church is beautiful too. Though the present structure dates only back to 1798, it represents the oldest continuously active parish in the country. As for Port Tobacco, it is long gone, a victim of terminal siltation. There is public access to Port Tobacco River at Chapel Point State Park, private access via Goose Bay Marina and Campground, and de facto access to the upper end at the foot of Mary Drive.

The Potomac shoreline from Port Tobacco River to Rte. 301 is mostly undeveloped. This is a beautiful reach punctuated by some high clay cliffs. Part way down is Popes Creek—a cluster of popular seafood restaurants. Native Americans apparently found this spot ideal for similar purposes, as they left a shell pile covering 30 acres as much as 15 feet deep (both the native Americans and the shells are long gone). You can take out on this side of Rte. 301 via privately-owned Aqua-Land, or cross the river to the public ramp at the Virginia end of the bridge.

HAZARDS: Watch for metal bars in waters of Mallows Bay.

WATER CONDITIONS: Tidal.

GAUGE: None.

Section 3. Maryland Side: U.S. Rte. 301 to Point Lookout						
Gradient	Difficulty	Distance	Time	Width	Scenery	Map
0	A	Variable	Variable	1.8 - 7 Miles	Fair to Good	14,15

TRIP DESCRIPTION: The serrated shoreline of the lower estuary offers hundreds of miles of exploring. Unfortunately, too many miles of these shores have been devoured by development. So you will have to be content with scattered little prizes, such as a sandy beach, a marshy creek head, or a fossil-studded cliff.

From Rte. 301 to the Wicomico River, the shoreline is pretty continuously developed. First there is a big power plant, then houses, houses, and more houses. One pleasant wild reach remains intact below Swan Point. You can get in and out of the river at Southern Park (follow the path from the western end of the ball field); up the Wicomico at the end of Rock Point Road; at a tiny park at the end of Rte. 254, Cobb Island Road; and at the south end of the Rte. 254 bridge to Cobb Island.

The Wicomico River (not to be confused with the one on the Eastern Shore) is described separately. From the Wicomico to Colton Point, the shoreline ranges from moderately to densely developed. In contrast are the wild masses of St. Catherine and St. Clements islands. The former is private while the latter, which was the site of Maryland's first settler's landfall, is public and invites exploration. For some background on this spot, visit the St. Clements Island Museum in Colton. For access, the ends of Whites Neck Road (Md. Rte. 520) and River Springs Road, at the mouth of Whites Neck Creek, are public landings. You can also slip in at the county park and museum at Colton, or pay to launch at St. Patrick's Creek Campground and Marina about a mile up St. Patricks Creek.

Rounding Colton Point you behold St. Clements Bay, a pleasing body of water that with high tide you can follow up to Rte. 234. Except for around St. Clements Shores, development is well spaced, and on the lower east shore, even sparse. An attractive marsh caps the upper end of the bay. To reach the highway, follow the channel at the center of the marsh, not the more likely-looking bay to the west. About halfway up the marsh is an s-bend with a fork. Against your instincts, go right. This will curve around and lead you into swamp and then dry woods. You may have to lift over a strainer to reach the road.

The mouth of St. Clements Bay leads into Breton Bay. With mostly high and dry banks, Breton Bay curves up through a flat and then rolling landscape. Development is widespread, but tastefully spaced. Above Leonardtown, the course winds into a beautiful marsh, and then swamp. With a high tide, you can make it up what is now called McIntosh Run to Rte. 234. Perhaps the nicest face of Breton Bay is an undeveloped reach near its west mouth. If you search carefully, you can find a tiny channel that leads into wild Fresh Pond. Also gracing the lower bay on the west is St. Francis Xaviers Church and an adjacent parish house, which have stood there since 1640. There is public access to Breton Bay at Abells Wharf and in Leonardtown at the foot of Rte. 236, Washington Street.

From Breton Bay to Piney Point, the shoreline alternates between densely developed beach communities and natural reaches. There is also the big oil terminal at Piney Point. The waters off the undeveloped reaches are usually shallow, which may perhaps lessen their desirability for development. There are several little side streams which remain fairly unspoiled, also thanks to their shallowness. With a high tide they invite exploration. A county park protects the beautiful little Piney Point Lighthouse, which has stood there since 1836. The only public access to this section is a park at the bridge to St. George Island and at the lighthouse.

The St. Mary's River joins just beyond St. George Island. The most scenic way to get there is by the inside passage, St. George Creek. From end to end, wild, piney shores, marsh, and a few farm structures grace the view of its far side.

The St. Mary's is a handsome river. Almost up to St. Mary's City, much of its west side remains wild, lined by cut banks and little beaches. Well-spaced houses and farms follow the upper river. You can make it up the St. Mary's almost to Great Mills. With a high tide, you can reach Rte. 5 via the Eastern Branch.

On the east side of the river is St. Mary's City, which is mostly composed of the attractive campus of St. Mary's College. Be sure to check out the convincing replica of the *Dove*, which is moored at the foot of the hill. The *Dove* was one of two ships that brought the first English settlers to what was to become Maryland. Just downstream of the school is an interesting clay cliff loaded with fossil shells. Shores are more built up below town, and if you probe up St. Inigoes Creek, it is absolute suburbia up there. With high tide, you can make it up to Rte. 5 either via St. Inigoes Creek or its tributary, Church Creek. A military base lines the shore below St. Inigoes, but below there are farms and lonely beaches. The only public access to the St. Mary's is at the college, where Rte. 5 touches the river. You can unload on the posted shoulder and then park in numerous lots on campus.

The remainder of the Potomac again alternates between developed and deserted shores. Perhaps the nicest spot is about a mile of lonely beach in Point Lookout State Park. The beach occupies the equivalent of a barrier island, behind which the lagoons of Lake Conoy and Pt. Lookout Creek make worthy side trips. There are public access areas just inside Smith Creek, (at the end of Beachville Road) and at the State Park (pay). You can also get in/out at the picnic area near the point and around the point at the fishing pier.

HAZARDS: The wider river means more exposure, hence worst winds and waves.

WATER CONDITIONS: Tidal.

GAUGE: None.

Section 4. Virginia Side: I-95 to U.S. Rte. 301						
Gradient	Difficulty	Distance	Time	Width	Scenery	Map
0	A	Variable	Variable	0.5 - 3.5 Miles	Fair to Very Good	12, 13

TRIP DESCRIPTION: Though crowded by an even greater, festering, oozing blob of suburbia, the Virginia side of the river offers a trove of pleasant getaways close to the big city. The scenery is varied. Access is relatively good. And less than 20 miles from the White House, there is some of the best bald eagle watching in the region.

You can launch right underneath the Woodrow Wilson Bridge at the foot of Jones Point Road, which places you on the very southern tip of the District of Columbia. Rounding the point, which is graced by an old lighthouse, you enter a bay, much of which is mud flats at low tide. This is Hunting Creek. If you can find the shallow channel (near the north side), you can follow it under the George Washington Parkway bridge and about a mile beyond. Though a bland passage and noisy (the Beltway runs parallel), it and its vegetated buffer provide a good refuge for waterfowl and waterfowl loving paddlers. Proceeding down river — just past Belle Haven Marina — there begins a two-mile strip of wetlands, the marshy upper part of which is called Dyke Marsh. You can paddle by it, or examine it closely by probing a series of twisting channels called "guts." And if that is not enough, a bike trail provides a view from high ground and boardwalks. Paddlers seeking only a marsh trip can launch at the Belle Haven Marina ramp (pay) or from the nearby picnic area (free).

After Dyke Marsh is an enclave of fancy homes followed by national park land that extends almost to Mount Vernon. This narrow strip, dominated by the noisy parkway and crowded bike path, offers some access to the river, the best of which is Riverside Park, at the mouth of Little Hunting Creek. At its mid-point, the park's boundaries bulge to accommodate the bluff once occupied by Fort Hunt, a 19th-century battery that complemented Fort Washington to protect Washington, D.C. from invaders who never came.

Just before Mount Vernon is Little Hunting Creek. You can poke up Little Hunting Creek over two miles at high tide and up its North Branch for about a half mile. For a built-up creek, Little Hunting is attractive, as its neighbors have generally set their houses back from the water and landscaped their yards well. Farther upstream, marsh and wooded shores create a fairly wild illusion. Copious quantities of trash flushed from the headwaters are its most serious blemish.

The Mount Vernon estate preserves over a mile of shoreline. You can see Mr. Washington's famous mansion only briefly from the river. So land and go visit it. Below there, much more contemporary fancy homes line the shore for about two miles, well up into the horn-shaped mouth of Dogue Creek. With a high tide, you can ascend Dogue Creek to a little beyond Rte. 235 and its old stone grist mill. The last short reach of Dogue remains in a natural state. The grist mill is a good point of access to Dogue, as is the park at the Mount Vernon Road bridge, just inside Walker gate of Fort Belvoir. The west shore of Dogue Creek is mostly natural, wooded, and high, as is the next mile of the Potomac. We can thank the U.S. Army for protecting the view. Ironically, Fort Belvoir is the home base of the U.S. Army Corps of Engineers, long viewed by some as a metaphor for environmental destruction.

The next bulge to the right is Gunston Cove, which splits into two arms — Accotink Bay and Pohick Bay. Protected by Fort Belvoir, a regional park, and Gunston Hall Plantation, this is a delight- ful piece of water. Its shores are mostly high, wooded, and wild, with much of the Belvoir section set aside as a wildlife refuge (further irony). Accotink Bay is a particularly great place to observe wading birds because it is so shallow that, at low tide, any bird with legs becomes a wading bird. And you will be a beached whale if you do not pay attention to where you are going. While most of Accotink is silted in, even at low tide it is possible to probe up into its beautiful marshes and swamp almost a mile and a half by an elusive channel whose mouth is about a hundred yards off the west shore. With a little wading, you can even make it up to Poe Road. Pohick Bay is navigable for almost two miles at low tide and probably almost up to Old Colchester Road at high tide. Deep water access to these bays is good. You can reach the mouth of Accotink Bay (at a place called Tompkins Basin) in Fort Belvoir via Warren Road (free) or the mouth of Pohick Bay via the boat launch area (pay) at Pohick Bay Regional Park. To enter Ft. Belvoir, you must go to Tully Gate, where you can get a visitor's pass. For more information, call 703-806-3104.

Heading back into the Potomac and making the sharp turn around Hallowing Point, you pass a few miles of fairly heavy development and then return into a superb natural setting. It is this way because much of Mason Neck, which is the land between Gunston Cove, the Potomac, and Occo- quan Bay, has been preserved within a national wildlife refuge and state park. The neck's Potomac side starts with a beautiful marsh penetrated by a maze of guts, at least three of which are passable even at low tide. In contrast, the remaining two miles to Occoquan Bay are lined by wooded bluffs and dirt cliffs. Near-shore waters tend to be shallow along here.

Continuing around Mason Neck from the Potomac, you enter Occoquan (native American for "hooked inlet") Bay. The waters continue shallow and are lined by bluffs and dirt cliffs, but they are now broken by short swampy enclaves. In spite of a robust population of motorboats, the combina- tion of Occoquan Bay, Belmont Bay, and Occoquan River makes a fine paddling destination. The average paddler could spend a weekend circumnavigating these waters and their tidal tributaries.

At the head of Belmont Bay lies possibly the prettiest destination on the tidal Potomac, Kanes Creek. This narrow route extends back about a mile into the hilly woodlands of the state park. Marshy coves, holly groves, soaring eagles, and an air of isolation are just a few of the qualities that will charm you. A canoe launch by the visitors center along Belmont Bay, a half mile south of Kanes Creek, makes for easy access.

Past Kanes Creek, the north side of Belmont Bay continues to be mostly undeveloped, but as you enter the narrowing waters of the Occoquan River, houses and then marinas appear. On up beneath the busy spans of the railroad, Rte. 1, and I-95 bridges, a steep mostly wild north side contrasts with marinas, industry, and townscape on the hilly south side. Shortly above the town of Occoquan, a mostly dewatered bed of jagged fall line rock marks the head of navigation. You can get into the river around here in the town of Occoquan at the municipal parking lot beneath the Rte. 123 bridge (beware, this touristy village can become gridlock on nice weekends); at the foot of Old Colchester Road (Rte. 825), which is a public landing, but with no parking; and at the boat ramp (pay) at Occo- quan Regional Park.

The west side of the bays is generally pleasing. Except for the houses at Featherstone Shores and the fence bordering a small military installation, most of the shore appears wild. Part lies within the bounds of two small national wildlife refuges. Particularly nice is a two-mile strip of wetlands south of Featherstone Shores. You can penetrate the swampy upper half at three points and then follow the narrow, winding channel of parallel flowing Farm Creek. At low tide the ruins of an old bridge may force a short carry. Below Farm Creek, swamp turns to marsh, and a railroad trestle marks the mouth of Neabsco Creek.

Once you pass the clot of houses and marinas at its mouth, Neabsco Creek provides a scenic side-trip. Framed by hilly, wooded shores, this is a shallow bay with the deepest water on its south side. At its upper end are spatterdock-filled shallows followed by marsh. The deepest water now shifts to the north side where you can explore crooked channels far into the marsh, almost up to the power line crossing below Rte. 1.

The name Neabsco comes from native American for "at point of rock." At the south entrance to Neabsco is Freestone Point, an imposing bluff and 100-yard reach of sandstone cliffs and boulder-strewn shoreline. Hard rock is indeed an unusual sight in the coastal plain. Freestone Point and the following mile of Potomac shoreline is protected by Leesylvania State Park. Leesylvania was once the estate of Henry "Lighthorse Harry" Lee, Revolutionary War hero and father of General Robert E. Lee. The park offers numerous access choices, including a canoe launch at its southern end. The southern end marks the mouth of Powells Creek.

Powells Creek is a beautiful estuary whose natural surroundings are violated only by a power line crossing at its upper end. Do not take this condition for granted as the land immediately to the south was under serious consideration as the site for a giant theme park called Legoland in the early '90s. As on Neabsco, the deepest water is toward the south side. You can probe only a short way into the marshy and swampy head before the channel completely disperses.

From Powells Creek to Quantico Creek, there are some high, wooded banks and bluffs. But these qualities are offset by some houses, the railroad, an oil terminal, and the giant power plant at Possum Point.

Quantico (native American for "by the long stream") Creek makes an only mediocre side trip. There is a lot of development along its north shore. In contrast, the high south shore, which is within the Marine Corps base, remains mostly wild, wooded, and even graced with some more exposed rock. At the upper end, a channel follows the north side up into the marsh, which unfortunately brushes up against the commercial and industrial backside of Dumfries. With a high tide and a lift over a beaver dam, you can make it all the way up to the eastbound lane of Rte. 1 in Dumfries. Especially as you stand on the beaver dam, it is truly difficult to imagine that in colonial times, before siltation smothered these waters, seagoing ships could also ascend to this town. There is access to the deep end of Quantico Creek via a Virginia Power Company access located 2.2 miles down Possum Point Road from Rte. 1 and via a ramp on the marine base just below the railroad trestle. This ramp is approached from the town of Quantico, via Sherwood Drive and the Naval Medical Clinic (look for ramp signs).

The marine base lines the Potomac shoreline with buildings, a marina, and an airfield. Lonely Chopawamsic Island is the only token parcel of nature remaining. But a trip up Chopawamsic Creek more than compensates.

Chopawamsic (native American for "by the separation of outlet") Creek is a lovely estuary whose wild shores are protected as a natural area/wildlife refuge. The waterbirds seem to have figured this out. The deep water favors the south side as, unfortunately, so does the hydrilla. The channel into the marsh, on the other hand, is on the north. If you are really into wetlands, by lifting over beaver dams you can probe even farther into the upper marsh before the water totally disperses. You can enter Chopawamsic near its mouth via a ramp reached by driving to the war museum, turning right (upstream), and following the paved, then gravel road through a park. You can sometimes get in at the foot of the airfield. Also, you can reach the upper estuary via a canoe launch and wildlife viewing area 1.4 miles down Russell Road from Rte. 1.

Potomac River

MARYLAND

VIRGINIA

COLES POINT

Access 679

HAGUE

To Callao

612

612 Beales Mill

626 Dam Run

202

621 Creek

Lower Machodoc Creek

Nomini Bay

Nomini

Currioman Bay

Access

To Kilmarnock

622

643

645

609

Access

MONTROSS

Potomac River

214

R.E. Lee Birthplace

3

347

Access

Westmoreland St. Pk.

204

Popes Creek

COLONIAL BEACH

Access

Washington Birthplace Nat. Mon.

3

Access

OAK GROVE

Monroe Bay

205

Creek

Access

Mattox

205

To Fredericksburg

631

Potomac River

To La Plata, Waldorf

Roster Creek

Creek

Access

301

DAHLGREN

206

218

Williams Creek

Upper Machodoc

To Richmond

N

16

The several miles from Chopawamsic Creek to Aquia Creek provide a pleasant passage. Much of the wooded shoreline remains wild. Gone are the big bluffs, but except for one marshy mile, the banks are all solid, sometimes eroded, and in the first two miles, decorated by more of those sandstone outcrops. The near-shore waters are generally shallow and often clogged by rafts of hydrilla. There are also the overgrown remains of several abandoned or wrecked ships.

In spite of development (patchy on north side, more heavily on south), Aquia (native American for "seagull") Creek is a pleasing destination. It cuts back into hilly terrain, though its banks are relatively low with many marsh-fringed coves. Particularly nice is a side trip up unspoiled Boars Creek, a north shore tributary entering a half mile east of the railroad bridge. Aquia eventually necks down into an initially attractive marsh-bound passage that leads to marinas and into the heart of a huge residential and waterside development. The head of tidewater falls about a half mile short of Rte. 1. After a hard rain, you could begin a one-way trip starting at the highway. The only deepwater access to Aquia is at Aqua-Po County Park. There is an entrance fee that is reasonable for residents and a rip-off for others.

The short reach from Aquia Creek to Potomac Creek is mostly developed, except for a high, eroded bluff. Examine this closely as it is just a trove of fossils.

Potomac Creek is definitely worth a visit. Except for the first mile, to Accokeek Creek, the north side is completely wild. Can you spare some time for Accokeek? Once past a patch of houses, this twisting tributary takes you on a pleasant trip up into a broad, isolated marsh. Potomac Creek also leads to marshy head and then a little way farther into a swamp before strainers and diverging channels block the way. Returning along the south shore, there is scattered development that increases toward the mouth. At the mouth, another fossil-filled bluff demands close examination.

From Potomac Creek to Fairview Beach, except for one ostentatious structure, the shoreline remains undeveloped. Private access at Fairview is possible at the marina at the lower end of town. Developed shores continue below Fairview to the boundary of Caledon Natural Area.

Caledon is a gem — 2,600 acres of wild land with trails through old hardwood forest and, of course, a lovely shoreline. The waterfront varies between high banks, grassy flats, and swamp.

From Caledon to Mathias Point, the river bends northward and the natural landscape continues. About two miles below Caledon, Chotank Creek provides a beautiful side trip up a lonely marsh. Below Chotank, clay cliffs and wooded bluffs, eventually topped by houses, line the river.

At Mathias Point, the river turns south again and development again lines the banks. At a swampy point about a mile above the Rte. 301 bridge, a sandbar juts downstream for hundreds of yards, diverting you far towards midstream, an inconvenience on a windy day. A public ramp on the north side of the bridge provides an easy exit.

HAZARDS: Personal watercraft and bass boats.

WATER CONDITIONS: Tidal.

GAUGE: None.

Section 5. Virginia Side: Rte. 301 to Smith Point						
Gradient	Difficulty	Distance	Time	Width	Scenery	Map
0	A	Variable	Variable	1.8 - 7 Miles	Fair to Very Good	16, 17

TRIP DESCRIPTION: Like the Maryland side, much of Virginia's lower Potomac shore and tributaries have succumbed to intensive shoreline development. But the river's vastness, some wild tributaries, and historic landmarks are good reason to continue down into this region, called the Northern Neck, and on towards the Chesapeake.

Potomac River

From the Rte. 301 bridge to the mouth of Upper Machodoc Creek (pronounced Ma-Show'-Doc), the waterfront belongs to the U.S. Naval Surface Weapons Center. This means a mix of wild shores and ugly military structures.

Turning up Upper Machodoc, you encounter more mysterious military structures, then marinas and the town of Dahlgren. The town also crowds Williams Creek, which you can ascend to Rte. 206, a de facto access point, or even to Rte. 301. While the west side of Williams Creek is largely natural, houses dot the west side of Machodoc up to Rte. 218. Across the broad waters, the east side of the creek is all navy property and is mostly undeveloped (except for a million no trespassing signs). By far, the best paddling is above Rte. 218, where the marsh-fringed creek wriggles for about three miles into a remote, hilly setting.

The three miles from Machodoc to Rosier Creek evolve from riprapped banks in the naval reservation to high undisturbed banks and bluffs in the stretch below. If you turn up Rosier Creek, you will find development at first, but a return to nature in the marshy upper end. Ahead is Potomac Beach and Colonial Beach, over four miles of bulkheads, public beach, and development — a stretch worth skipping. On the back side of Colonial Beach is Monroe Bay, a completely developed waterway. There is a public ramp on its north side, just inside its mouth. A mile down the Potomac, Mattox Creek joins.

You will miss little by skipping the heavily developed portion of Mattox Creek below Rte. 205, so put in at the bridge and paddle upstream. This is a beautiful route that you can follow for about two and a half miles through marsh and woods. Tidewater ends at a beaver dam, which you should ascend, and then poke about its serene pond. There is also a pretty side trip up a tributary that joins from the east just above Rte. 205.

From Mattox Creek to Popes Creek, the near-shore waters are shallow. But hug the waterfront anyway, as it is composed of high clay banks or low cliffs, deposits which shed lots of sharks' teeth onto the sands at their base. There is public access at the picnic area at the mouth of Bridges Creek. From Bridges Creek down to Popes Creek and on up the west side of that tributary is federal land — the George Washington Birthplace National Monument.

Popes Creek is a worthy detour. This quiet backwater leads you past farms, colonial structures, and on up into a pretty marsh ending at an ancient, earthen milldam. Much of the creek is shallow at low tide. Also, because of the funneling effect of its narrow mouth, be prepared for a stiff tidal current at the entrance and continuing through a confusing tangle of channels that divide the marsh just upstream. One can launch into the creek from the picnic area a half mile above the mouth and avoid these difficulties.

Below Popes Creek, waterfront development is heavy to the edge of Westmoreland State Park, which has a public ramp (modest park entrance fee). Just below the ramp and beach begins a bold line of high, multihued clay cliffs and wooded bluffs. These deposits also shed sharks' teeth. A few miles down river is a break in the cliffs, in which is nestled an old mill, part of the Stratford Hall Plantation, the birthplace of Robert E. Lee. This is a potential access point (park entrance fee) and an excuse to do some more terrestrial touring. After another mile, houses begin to crown the riverside bluffs until the Potomac bulges into Virginia as Curriomen and Nomini bays.

Curriomen and Nomini bays are separated by a long string of grass- or shrub- covered, sandy islands. You can make a good circuit tour by putting in at Curriomen Landing, a public landing at the foot of Rte. 622, and following the Potomac side of the islands and mainland side of Curriomen Bay. The islands, which are privately owned, are also rich in teeth, probably transported from the cliffs upstream. High, eroded, and mostly undeveloped banks line the landward side of shallow Curriomen Bay.

At the head of Nomini Bay is Nomini Creek. Though much of its shoreline is developed, this is still an attractive waterway. The farther upstream you go, the thinner the development is and the higher the surrounding land. By far the best paddling is above Rte. 621, where the view is of high, wooded hillsides and thin marshy fringes. About a mile and a half above this bridge the creek forks. Nomini is to your right and can carry you another half mile into marsh and spatterdock. The left choice is Beales Mill Run, which leads you up through marsh, then swamp to an old, earthen milldam above Rte. 612. Carry over the dam. The pond is empty, but you can pole and paddle up another half mile of narrow channel through the grassy bed of the pond in a wilderness-like setting.

Below the mouth of Nomini Creek, you follow the east side of Nomini Bay. The shore is initially undeveloped with a pretty beach, but shallow water keeps you far away. Soon after, houses appear and line the shore to Cabin Point, the mouth of Lower Machodoc Creek.

Most of the shoreline of Lower Machodoc Creek and its tributaries is developed. You can find a few small, undisturbed parcels here and there, mostly at the marshy heads of the creeks. There is public access to the creek in Coles Point, behind the store and marina at Branson Cove.

From Lower Machodoc Creek to Bonum Creek, most of the Potomac waterfront is developed. So are the little side creeks, though more moderately. Bonum Creek is marked by a jetty and has a public landing at the foot of Rte. 763. It offers some attractive but moderately developed scenery.

The first third of the way from Bonum Creek to the Yeocomico River is scenic, with 10-foot cutbanks backed by fields or woods. After that, houses line the waterfront.

The Yeocomico (native American for "four houses") is an attractive waterway, in spite of extensive development. Its many arms offer miles of paddling opportunity, while the relatively high surrounding terrain provides good shelter on breezy days. Most of its arms are wild on their upper reaches. Particularly good destinations are upper Lodge Creek, which leads up through marsh then swamp almost to Rte. 360, and upper Mill Creek, a narrow passage through marsh and past holly- and laurel-covered hills, ending at Courtney Pond. The best choice, however, is Hampton Hall Branch of the West Yeocomico River. Above Rte. 202, it is completely wild, lined by wooded and laurel-bound 30-foot bluffs. With a high tide, you can follow it up to the dam of Gardy Millpond. Carry over the dam onto one of the prettiest spots on the lower Potomac. The pond's two prongs are flanked by steep hills choked in mountain laurel. Come and paddle here in late May when it all blooms.

Access to the Yeocomico system is good. There are public landings on Lodge Creek at Lodge Landing, foot of Rte. 712; on Gardy Millpond; and on the West Yeocomico at Mundy Point Landing, foot of Rte. 620 (subtle dirt road to your left that looks like a private drive). You can launch into Hampton Hall Branch at Rte. 202; into Mill Creek at Rte. 620, Courtney Millpond; into Kinsale Branch at the north end of the bridge in Kinsale; and into the Shannon Branch of the Northwest Yeocomico at Rte. 610. Finally, you can pay to use many of the Yeocomico's numerous private marinas.

It is a short hop down the Potomac from the Yeocomico to the next major tributary, the Coan River. This reach is initially developed, but the second half yields a beautiful sand beach backed by low fields, woods, marshes, and ponds.

The Coan is another river that maintains its beauty in the face of development. Rounding the point at Lewisetta, most of the arms to the west, such as The Glebe are built up (though The Glebe's north bank remains wild). Much of the Coan is only lightly developed. The surroundings are high and wooded. Particularly nice is its Mill Creek tributary. With a high tide, you can follow the Coan up to Rte. 360, but finding the last bit of the route can be confusing. Heading up through marsh, bear left. Then, about 150 yards before the highway, an unlikely looking channel emerges from a swampy clump of trees to your right. That is the passage to the highway. There are two deep-water public accesses to the upper Coan, Forest Landing at the foot of Rte. 612, and Rowes landing, at the foot of Rte. 601. There is also private access at the marina at Lewisetta.

Most of the remainder of the Potomac is built up. You can find some relief by probing the side streams. Hull Creek, whose narrow mouth generates a stiff tidal current, is the biggest and best example. The river, however, has a dignified end as the mouth at Smith Point is within the bounds of a nature preserve.

These final miles can be a temperamental reach to navigate. With a fetch that reaches to the Bay Bridge, this is an exposed shore with rough waters. The shallowness of the waters generates some nasty surf, so beware.

The only public access to this reach is the landing at Vir-Mar Beach (foot of Rte. 643). If you are going to Smith Point, enter the Little Wicomico River and take out at the Sunnybank Ferry.

HAZARDS: An unfavorable wind can build up big waves on this exposed shoreline.

WATER CONDITIONS: Tidal.

GAUGE: None.

North Branch Potomac River

INTRODUCTION: The North Branch of the Potomac, as a matter of historical tradition, is considered the headwaters of the Potomac. This proves to be an embarrassing origin for our "national river." The North Branch has suffered decades of abuse, pollution, and devastation, the scars of which are hard to ignore. In contrast with the agricultural valley and wild gorges of the South Branch, the North Branch has been a valley dedicated to industry. Its bottomlands have been the sites for factories producing plate glass, tires, synthetic fibers, and paper; its canyons have provided passage for railroads to cross the high Allegheny ridges; and its surrounding hills have yielded the coal to generate electricity for Eastern cities and to fire iron and steel furnaces from Pittsburgh to Japan. The price of this development has been half a river poisoned to death by acid mine drainage, hillsides scarred by mining and pollution, and a valley filled with stinking air.

Why go there then? Because the times are changing rapidly. Many of the old factories are closed now, and those that remain have taken great strides to reduce their pollution. The coal mining industry can no longer rape and run, and there are even efforts to repair some of the old mining destruction. Trout now thrive in formerly dead waters. So the blighted areas are shrinking, and in between are miles of beautiful and natural riverscape and acres of land that have healed over from past abuses. Besides, some of the best whitewater in the Potomac Basin is up here (although it tastes like a rusty nail).

Section 1. Henry, W.Va., to Gormania, W.Va. (U.S. Rte. 50)						
Gradient	Difficulty	Distance	Time	Width	Scenery	Map
38	1 to 3	8.4	2.5	15-30	Good to Fair	18

TRIP DESCRIPTION: The North Branch officially starts at Fairfax Stone, an ancient boundary stone marking the western limit of Lord Fairfax's enormous domain. The stone is located just beyond the southwest tip of Garrett County, inside West Virginia (Virginia in Fairfax's day). Only six miles downstream, the North Branch gathers enough water, at times, to float a canoe. The put-in is about seven miles southwest of Gormania on W. Va. Rte. 90, where the highway permanently leaves the river at Island Creek Coal Mine. Initially the stream meanders swiftly between alder-bound banks and rushes over easy rock garden rapids through less than spectacular scenery. But the North Branch soon springs to life, tumbling continuously over a bed of small boulders and ledges of all sizes. When it is bank full, however, all the technical complexity washes out into a roaring flume that is short on eddies but overstocked with big waves and nasty diagonal holes—a run rivaling the Savage River for excitement and pushiness. The most interesting spot is located a short distance above Wilson where the river plunges over a sloping seven-foot ledge that is run to the right of center at low levels and left of center at high water. The stream returns to a sluggish state below Bayard and stays that way to Gormania. Take out on the left bank below Rte. 50.

North Branch Potomac River

18

HAZARDS: Possible strainers.

WATER CONDITIONS: Canoeable winter and spring during rapid snow melt or within two days of hard rain.

GAUGE: USGS gauge at Kitzmiller (call Washington or see USGS website) should report at least 1,720 cfs (5.2 feet).

Section 2. Gormania, W.Va. (U.S. Rte. 50), to Kitzmiller, Md.						
Gradient	Difficulty	Distance	Time	Width	Scenery	Map
47	3 to 4+	14.9	5.0	30-70	Good	18

TRIP DESCRIPTION: If you are the kind of paddler who loves to bloat yourself on mile after mile of continuous wild whitewater, then you should have been here before they built the Jennings Randolph Dam. From Steyer to Bloomington, Md., there were 30 almost unbroken miles of the splashy stuff, or you could have put in on the Stony River at Virginia Power's dam, near Mount Storm, W.Va., and made that a 38-mile trip. It was not out of the question, furthermore, to complete either one of these runs in a day and, in the process, on the Stony River option, to drop a phenomenal distance of 2,140 feet from start to finish. Luckily the dam left intact the best of the North Branch's whitewater, this section from Gormania to Kitzmiller. And rest assured that this section should be sufficient to satisfy all but the most demanding whitewater enthusiasts.

The first two miles to Steyer, an alternate put-in, contain nothing more difficult than easy gravel bar rapids. The scenery is hilly but unspectacular, and the water is tan from acid mine drainage. Below Steyer, the stream begins dropping over more ledges and forming more hydraulics than you ever dreamed could exist. As you play these beautifully-formed holes to exhaustion, think of all the poor slobs lining up on a hot summer's day at the famous Swimmers Hole on the lower Yough for just a few paltry seconds of play time. Things get even more interesting at the junction with the Stony River, as the North Branch becomes noticeably more powerful and pushy.

About a half mile below Stony starts a series of three big, memorable ledges. The first is a sloping, complex affair entered on the left and finished on the right. At the second, you aim for the middle and shut your eyes. The third ledge is a sloping, jagged, complex drop that you can run on the right.

Now begins mile after mile of nonstop small ledges, boulder patches, giant cobble bars, and a lot of maneuvering to get through it all. If you travel this at high water (over 2,820 cfs (6.0 feet)), look forward to moving at high velocity, bouncing down some big waves, and having to avoid some terminal holes. Aside from the water quality, some lingering damage from the 1985 flood, and the railroad (which is certainly comforting as a rescue feature), the scenery is beautiful, consisting of cliffs, hemlocks, rhododendron thickets, and big, forested canyon walls.

At Shallmar, two miles above Kitzmiller, the natural beauty is diminished by stripmine scars and a dredged and levee-bound river channel. This channel becomes tediously shallow at lower levels. Take out at either end of the MD. Rte. 38 bridge in Kitzmiller.

HAZARDS: Give extra attention to the three ledges described above and an inconveniently placed old bridge pier a few miles downstream on the left.

WATER CONDITIONS: Runnable winter and spring during snow melt and within two to four days after a hard rain.

GAUGE: A USGS gauge at Kitzmiller, located about two blocks below Rte. 38 on the left (call Washington, see USGS website, or inspect on site), should read at least 970 cfs (4.4 feet). The level is optimal for both open and decked boats at 1,520 cfs (5.0 feet), and 2,820 cfs (6.0 feet) indicates a big and ferocious river waiting for you upstream.

North Branch Potomac River

⑲

	Section 3. Kitzmiller, Md., to Jennings Randolph Dam					
Gradient	Difficulty	Distance	Time	Width	Scenery	Map
36	A to 3	8.5	3.5	40-2,200	Good	19

TRIP DESCRIPTION: The next 17 miles of almost continuous intermediate grade whitewater has now been cut in half by the Jennings Randolph Dam. Few whitewater paddlers will care to bother with the first half of the section from Kitzmiller to the dam as only three miles of free-flowing river and particularly good scenery remain. Because there is no access to the head of the reservoir, at least five and a half miles of deadwater paddling to either the dam, Howell Boat Launch Area, or the new Maryland launch area (at end of Mt. Zion Road) is unavoidable. But on the bright side, many of the scars from the massive railroad relocation and old strip mining have been revegetated, making the lake, with each year, an increasingly attractive place to paddle (providing that you do so when the pool is high and the mud flats are covered). Also, improving water quality has made the lake a reasonable fishing hole.

Next comes the dam. Even the thought of portaging this nearly 300-foot-high barrage would exhaust most paddlers. But for those inclined towards tackling such challenges, a road up and down the right edge of the dam makes this grim goal semireasonable. Since the Corps considers portaging on the dam trespassing, however, you might as well find other forms of aerobic exercise.

HAZARDS: Hernia and fines from attempting dam portage.

WATER CONDITIONS: Winter and spring within a week of hard rain or during snow melt.

GAUGE: USGS gauge at Kitzmiller (call Washington, see USGS website, or inspect on site) should read at least 580 cfs (3.8 feet) to run down to the lake.

Section 4. Barnum, W.Va., to Bloomington, Md.						
Gradient	Difficulty	Distance	Time	Width	Scenery	Map
33	1 to 3	6.6	2.0	40-70	Good	19

TRIP DESCRIPTION: As of this writing, the option of starting your cruise at the dam is not very encouraging, as the Corps of Engineers does not allow private vehicles onto the road down to the tailrace area. Hopefully this will soon change. Until then, these restrictions leave the only vehicle access via a narrow road into Barnum, putting you in about a mile and a half below the dam.

This has become a most popular run because of a series a scheduled water releases from the dam and because of the quality of the whitewater and scenery. The passage from Barnum to Bloomington is pretty, snaking through a wooded canyon whose walls are healing well from the trauma of the railroad relocation and past mining abuse. Rapids here, as on the section above the lake, are often long, dropping over huge bars of cobbles and small boulders, with a few low ledges thrown in for variety. One set of ledges about halfway between Barnum and Bloomington (on the right side near the end of a series of long islands) has long been the nemesis of less experienced paddlers. Here lurks one particularly deep and nasty hole known to surprise the unexpecting, inexperienced paddler. So be on the lookout.

The put-in at Barnum is a developed boaters' access, with good parking and changing house/toilets. During the scheduled releases, there is a modest entry fee that supports the Mineral County Parks Department, which was instrumental in developing the site and helping paddlers secure these releases.

Take out at Bloomington at a public access on the left, just upstream of the stone-arch railroad bridge. There is little parking space there, so park in the lot up the hill in Bloomington at the school. An alternate take-out is right at the confluence with the Savage River, or at the old bridge just upstream. The parking situation is tenuous, with many people using the old bridge approach (Westvaco's) or the parking lot of the two-story red brick building across the road (private). Please take care to avoid provoking the, so far, very tolerant landowners by avoiding public nudity, not blocking any entrances, and not smoking near those vertical metal pipes along the Savage River side of the parking lot (they are gasoline tank vents).

HAZARDS: None.

WATER CONDITIONS: In spring, once the reservoir is full, what flows in flows out, so that the river is runnable within a week of hard rain. The Corps strives to juggle the reservoir outflow to best address downstream water quality management, flood control, and the Washington Metropolitan Area's emergency water supply needs. In doing so, it usually releases a low, constant flow that is at best only a bare minimum for paddlers. As part of their water quality program, however, the Corps occasionally releases a combined surge from Jennings Randolph Dam (850-900 cfs) and from Savage River Dam (200-250 cfs) for 24 to 48 hours, from late July through October, to flush accumulated sediments from the river bed. These are definitely volumes that will delight any boater. Currently, the Corps only announces these releases a week beforehand. At that time the news is announced on the

Washington River Forecast recording and the Corps' hotline, and is disseminated through the grapevine to interested canoe clubs. As of this writing, a coalition of commercial outfitters and the private paddling organizations has been working to secure special recreational releases that can be announced months ahead of time. Presently, there are usually four two-day recreational releases of about 900 cfs scheduled every other weekend during April and and then two days on both Labor Day and Columbus Day weekends.

GAUGE: Call Corps (Baltimore) hotline at 410-962-7687 or consult their website at http://www.nab-wc.usace.army.mil/wc/index.html to find the discharge out of the dam or see Barnum gauge reading on USGS website. Consider a flow of 380 cfs the minimum flow for most people's tastes, though 250 cfs will still get you down the river. Any scheduled releases will be announced on the Washington River Forecast, USGS website, and Corps recordings and website.

Section 5. Bloomington, Md., to Keyser, W.Va.						
Gradient	Difficulty	Distance	Time	Width	Scenery	Map
22	1 to 2	7.5	2.5	60-100	Good to Fair	20

TRIP DESCRIPTION: If you have a head cold or acute hayfever, you may be specially qualified to run this stretch of river. For you will be the only member of your party not repulsed by the stench that fills this valley, a byproduct of the paper mill at Luke.

The trip starts with a 0.7-mile paddle down a gentle rapid, followed by a short pool to a small, unrunnable dam at the Westvaco paper mill. A short, steep, and slippery lift up through a break in the vegetation on the weed-choked right bank, followed by a short, easy walk gets you around the barrier. You then float past the paper mill, which if not beautiful, is certainly interesting and immense. Easy boulder-patch rapids and gravel bars carry one past the mill and through the tri-towns of Luke, Westernport, and Piedmont. Westernport was so named as it was the upper limit of navigation on the Potomac. If you have trouble with the rocks and holes on this section, just think about trying to work a loaded coal barge down it.

Below Westernport the river cuts a deep, attractive gorge through Dans Mountain. The rapids are often fairly long, dropping over a few ledges and patches of small boulders and cobbles. The gradient levels off approaching Keyser and the scenery becomes junky again. There is an easy take-out beneath the long U.S. Rte. 220 bridge, on the right. To find it, get off of Rte. 220 onto W.Va. Rte. 46, east. Go about three blocks to Main Street and turn left. Follow this to the end, and turn left onto Potomac Drive and follow to the bridge.

HAZARDS: Carry the dam at the paper mill on the right or, at low levels, lift over the crest on the right. If the water is high, watch out for a powerful, surprise hole, on the left, at the bottom of a long rapid about a mile below the huge Westvaco warehouse, which is a few miles below Westernport.

WATER CONDITIONS: Runnable winter and spring during snow melt and within a week of hard rain. Also, special releases from Savage and Jennings Randolph dams provide delightful levels.

GAUGE: USGS gauge at Luke (call Washington or see USGS website) should report at least 395 cfs (2.5 feet). If you are using dam releases, you can call Corps (Baltimore), or sometimes you can get a reading on the Washington River Forecast recording. The combined outflow from Jennings Randolph and Savage dams should be at least 400 cfs. If you use special dam releases, particularly the relatively short race releases, be sure not to start too early or you may actually outrun the water.

Section 6. Keyser, W.Va., to Allegany Fairgrounds						
Gradient	Difficulty	Distance	Time	Width	Scenery	Map
8	1	21.5	7.0	60-100	Good to Very Good	20

TRIP DESCRIPTION: If the water, air, and litter ever get cleaned up, this will become one of the most popular novice trips in Maryland. The river winds back and forth through a seemingly isolated valley, away from highways, and even the ever present railroad is usually set back from sight. The mountainsides are periodically lined by the biggest, most ornate, and most beautiful shale and sandstone cliffs in the Potomac Basin. The current through here is usually strong while the whitewater never amounts to more than straightforward gravel bar type riffles. The only exciting point is a runnable five-foot rubble dam behind the new prison (luckily set back from the river).

This is a long section that many people will prefer to shorten. Unfortunately, points of access are few, far between, and usually involve long walks or steep climbs. If you leave or enter at Pinto, you face a steep climb or descent at the Rte. 956 bridge. For the fairgrounds access, turn off Rte. 220 onto Moss Avenue, cross the railroad tracks, and turn right. Follow the paved road around the south edge of the grounds and then strike off across a meadow on a dirt track. Those with conventional vehicles will want to walk the last hundred yards. Be sure you can recognize this spot from the river.

HAZARDS: A five-foot dam of jagged rubble behind the prison can be a trouble spot for beginners. More experienced boaters should have no trouble running a growing breach in the center.

WATER CONDITIONS: You will find the nicest canoeing conditions in winter and spring, except after a long dry spell, and during special releases from Jennings Randolph or Savage dams. If you do not mind a little scraping, you can float this through most normal summers.

GAUGE: USGS gauge at Pinto (call Washington or see USGS website) should report at least 300 cfs (1.5 feet).

Section 7. Allegany Fairgrounds to Wiley Ford, W.Va. (W.Va. Rte. 28)						
Gradient	Difficulty	Distance	Time	Width	Scenery	Map
4	A to 1	6.8	2.5	80-100	Good to Poor	20

TRIP DESCRIPTION: The paddler who bypasses this section will not have missed much. After a pretty start past the last of the great shale cliffs, the scenery slowly succumbs to the visual blight of the Cumberland area. Houses, factories, railroads, and trash become more frequent. Pools get longer and the riffles shorter until, upon entering Cumberland, the current dies in a long pool that leads into a leveed flood channel. The pool ends at a 15-foot dam located directly under the Rte. 28 bridge between Cumberland and Ridgeley. Carry on the right. Below the dam and the concrete confluence of Wills Creek, the dredged out river flows straight and often tediously shallow. A more natural riverscape finally resumes approaching Wiley Ford.

The take-out at Wiley Ford is steep and the parking is poor. A better idea is to take out 1.3 miles downstream, near the Cumberland Sewage Treatment Plant. To get there, turn off Virginia Avenue, in South Cumberland, onto Offutt Street and follow to the end, which is at a town park. You can park there, a hundred yards from the river, or, even better, continue just past the treatment plant where a dirt road on its downstream perimeter will bring you almost to the river bank.

HAZARDS: Beware of the unrunnable 15-foot dam in Cumberland, beneath the Rte. 28 bridge.

WATER CONDITIONS: Best in winter and spring, but passable in all but the driest summers.

GAUGE: USGS gauges at Pinto and Cumberland (call Washington or see USGS website) should report at least 260 cfs (1.4 feet) and 330 cfs (2.4 feet) respectively.

Section 8. Wiley Ford, W.Va., to South Branch Potomac River						
Gradient	Difficulty	Distance	Time	Width	Scenery	Map
4	A to 1	20.2	6.5	80-100	Good	4

TRIP DESCRIPTION: Below Wiley Ford, the impact of Cumberland dwindles as the river now flows by high, wooded banks and bluffs and through some small mountain gaps in a thinly populated area. A few big junk piles are its worst flaw. The water retains some of that papermill odor, but it is tolerable. Most of the water is now flat with the only excitement being at a three-foot rubble dam, runnable on the right, about eight miles below the start.

The confluence with the South Branch is two miles beyond the low-water toll bridge at Oldtown. To reach the confluence, cross the toll bridge into West Virginia, pass under the railroad, and turn left 200 yards beyond onto Arnold Stickley Road. Follow a mile and a half until it hits the South Branch, just above the mouth. Most people will simply choose to finish at Oldtown.

HAZARDS: Three-foot dam at the former Pittsburgh Plate Glass plant, run on right, and the low-water bridge at Oldtown can be a problem at high water.

WATER CONDITIONS: Passable in all but the driest late summers.

GAUGE: Cumberland USGS gauge (call Washington or see USGS website) should read at least 330 cfs (2.4 feet).

Savage River

INTRODUCTION: The Savage is probably Maryland's most famous whitewater river, even more widely known than the Upper Yough. Much of this fame comes from being this country's premier racing stream. The combination of five miles of continuous, powerful, and complex rapids backed by assured, controlled water releases from a reservoir has made this the site of national championships races in slalom and wildwater, the 1972 Olympic Trials, international races, and the 1989 World Whitewater Championships. And since these releases usually occur when most other small streams are low, they have proven to be a boon to cruisers. Finally, the Savage deserves credit as an educational aid, for the one minute on and next minute off character of its controlled flow provides an ideal opportunity for the paddler to study just what stream bottom structure makes whitewater so wild.

Section 1. Avilton Lonaconing Road to Merrill						
Gradient	Difficulty	Distance	Time	Width	Scenery	Map
68	2 to 3,6	6.5	2.0	10-25	Excellent	21

TRIP DESCRIPTION: With only a minuscule mountain watershed, the upper, upper Savage is rarely boatable. Such a shame. For this is as beautiful a whitewater run as you will find in Maryland—a passage resembling a scaled-down version of West Virginia's Laurel Fork of the Cheat. From the time you leave the few camps at the put-in until you reach the camps at Blue Lick Run (just above Merrill) you will be in the wilderness. The creek wriggles down a tight little gorge at the foot of Four-mile Ridge in complete isolation. Rock cliffs and formations are everywhere, their rugged profiles dappled with lichens, draped with ferns, and often engraved by striations that geologists call cross-bedding. Groves of hemlock impart a green friendliness to the gray winter forest that usually coincides with high water on this stream.

With this section's steep gradient the rapids are almost continuous, with just enough pause to allow you to savor the scenery. Rapids are formed by cobble bars, lots of ledges (some up to three feet high), and some boulders. There are many sharp turns and pile-ups into undercut rocks. So if the lower Yough's Dimples Rock Rapid troubles you, then you are in for some excitement here. About four miles into the run, on a straightaway, is a steep rapid clogged by jagged, severely undercut boulders. Most will choose to carry the first two drops (on right), especially if they see how much water is flowing under the boulders. This being a tiny stream, trees are an occasional problem, always in fast spots. Finally, watch out for a strand of barbed wire by the camps above the take-out.

HAZARDS: Carry the dangerous rapid described above. Expect a few fallen trees and that barbed wire below Blue Lick Run.

WATER CONDITIONS: Canoeable winter and spring within a day of hard rain or during rapid snow melt.

GAUGE: Just enough water to cleanly run the ledgy rapid immediately above the put-in bridge is just enough to do a bumpy run down the creek. For calling ahead, the USGS gauge near Barton (actually it is located about two and a half miles above Big Run, see USGS website) should be over 260 cfs (2.3 feet). For a rough correlation, look for sharp rises in gauges on Wills Creek, Georges Creek, and Casselman River.

Section 2. Merrill (Westernport Road) to Savage River Dam						
Gradient	Difficulty	Distance	Time	Width	Scenery	Map
48*	A to 2	8.8	2.5	10-30	Fair to	21
*until lake					Very Good	

TRIP DESCRIPTION: This is the unsavage part of the Savage River. From the bridge at Merrill to Big Run Campground, it offers about six miles of often intimate, hemlock and rhododendron-fringed cruising down a narrow, thinly inhabited valley. But although the valley's permanent population is small, there are many houses, usually scattered clusters of summer camps, that periodically blemish the riverside view. The water can be fairly clear and the rapids are numerous and easy, dropping over a bed of cobbles and small ledges. At full pool the reservoir begins just above Big Run. It is short and narrow with steep, undeveloped shores. So if the lake is full, with no ugly mud flats to mar the scene, it is a beautiful place to paddle. For those boaters, however, who are allergic to flatwater, Big Run Campground is an easy egress point.

HAZARDS: Fallen trees and overhanging rhododendron in fast spots.

WATER CONDITIONS: Up in winter or spring within two days of hard rain or during a rapid snow melt.

GAUGE: The put-in rapids are a good spot at which to judge the flow. The USGS gauge near Barton (see USGS website) should read over 175 cfs (2.0 feet). Do not bother checking the USGS gauge on Section 3. Manipulation of flow by the dam renders it unreliable.

Section 3. Savage River Dam to mouth						
Gradient	Difficulty	Distance	Time	Width	Scenery	Map
75	3 to 4	4.7	1.5	20-30	Good	21

TRIP DESCRIPTION: To reach the uppermost put-in, follow a narrow dirt road that branches off the Savage River Road at the left end of the new concrete bridge below the dam. If the road is not gated, you can drive to the end of a grassy field and carry about a hundred feet to a small pool at the end of the emergency spillway channel.

Now begins the big flush. The next pool is one exciting mile downstream, behind the five-foot-high Piedmont Dam. One has the choice of running the dam via a narrow breach located several feet off the left bank (good but exciting) or via a curving, rock-studded channel through the deteriorated and undercut right abutment (not recommended). Use discretion on running this dam if the river above 1,000 cfs.

About a half mile below Piedmont Dam is a narrow concentration of heavy and turbulent white-water known as the Triple Drop, the final drop of which has a strong hole best run on the right. Just below is the toughest problem on the river, Memorial Rock Rapid, recognized by a large, pointed boulder sticking out of the water about 10 feet off the left bank. Run just to the right of this rock to avoid a big, submerged rock and mean hole, or sneak on the extreme left at high levels.

Below Memorial Rock the really big pressure is off, and many conservative paddlers choose to start at the church just downstream of Memorial Rock. The river continues just as exciting and pushy, and you should take this stretch just as seriously as above. The best take-out is on the North Branch Potomac on the left a few yards below the mouth.

HAZARDS: Piedmont Dam, which is run as described above or easily carried on the left. Fallen trees are also an occasional problem.

WATER CONDITIONS: Caught only for brief periods following hard rain or big snow melt, in winter and spring. Infrequently scheduled race releases offer occasional treats. Finally, sometimes the flush releases for the North Branch include 200 to 300 cfs from the Savage River Dam.

GAUGE: USGS gauge (call Washington or see USGS website) above first bridge should read at least 210 cfs (1.7 feet) for a bare minimum level for the most hardcore plastic boaters. Race releases over the years have varied from 900 cfs (3.1 feet) to 1,400 cfs (3.7 feet), all fine levels. It is also easy to assess the level from the road. Daily discharge from Savage River Dam is also available from Corps of Engineers (Baltimore) at 410-962-7687 and from their website.

What's That I Smell?

Anyone who paddles the Savage or North Branch Potomac cannot help but be aware of the presence of Westvaco's paper mill at Luke. Ugly as it may be, it is a fascinating mass of technology that is worth a pause to study. The plant is one of the world's largest producers of fine paper, fine paper being the high quality, smooth, glossy paper used in magazines, picture books, etc.

To understand the mill one must understand papermaking, which briefly is as follows. First, the raw material for this paper is largely hardwood, which is stored in the woodyard on the right bank just below the new Rte. 46 bridge. Before use, the logs must be debarked. Nothing is wasted as the bark is shipped next door as raw material to supply a charcoal plant. The wood is then chipped, and the chips are "digested" under heat and pressure in a caustic brew. Digestion dissolves the lignin, a natural glue that binds the wood fibers together. The fibers are also physically agitated to break them apart, literally beating them to a pulp, a disgusting-looking slurry of cellulose fibers. The fibers (now called pulp) are removed, rinsed, and bleached and are now ready for paper making, which entails spraying the pulp evenly upon a large, moving, cloth conveyor belt called a "felt." As the felt moves along, a finish that may contain clays, pigments, or starch is also sprayed on. Excess water (called "whitewater" in the industrial jargon) drains through the felt, and blasts of hot air complete the drying process. The result, voila, paper.

How much of this affects you the paddler? First, the plant uses the huge volume of over 60 million gallons a day of water from the North Branch, which at low flows can amount to almost half the flow in the river. Before Jennings Randolph dam came on line, to conserve water when the river was low, the plant would pump its uncontaminated cooling water (about half the water used here) back to the head of the plant where the water is sprayed into the air to cool it and hence into the river where it can reenter the plant's intake. The strange metal pipes you see bristling along the left bank upstream of the mill are for this recycling system. The wastewater from digestion, called "black liquor," used to go into the river, but now is totally processed for reuse in the towering building next to Rte. 135 and at the rotary kiln across the river. All other contaminated wastewater flows to a treatment plant downstream. The plant removes most harmful pollutants, but unfortunately the stink and some discoloration remains. Speaking of stink, most of the frightening looking white clouds billowing from the mill are just steam. With all of the drying, cooking, and cooling, over six million gallons of water daily go up the stacks as steam. This, unfortunately, also still smells. The high stack was built so to disperse these and other gases, or else this would be one foggy and smoggy valley. The dead mountainside across the river was Westvaco's doing, a result of past abuse. But, with air quality improved, vegetation is now rapidly reclaiming these slopes.

Georges Creek

INTRODUCTION: Georges Creek has long been the shame of Maryland, but it is not as bad as it once was. It flows through a valley whose mountainsides are still scarred and tortured by decades of mining abuse. The narrow bottomlands along the stream remain crowded with roads, railroad tracks, and a chain of decaying towns; while old cars, washing machines, torn plastic, and all the other debris of civilization are strewn about the stream's bed and banks. The water, on the other hand, has improved. Much of the sewage, which used to flow untreated from every building, now flows down a sewer to a new treatment plant. Although acid continues to seep from abandoned mines, reclamation has eliminated some old sources. So there are fewer reasons now for paddlers to overlook this elusive but excellent piece of whitewater.

Section 1. Midland (Md. Rte. 36) to mouth						
Gradient	Difficulty	Distance	Time	Width	Scenery	Map
69	3 to 4	10.5	2.5	15-30	Poor	13

TRIP DESCRIPTION: Georges Creek drains a six-mile-wide trough between Dans and Big Savage mountains. It is fed by numerous brooks that steadily swell its flow in wet weather. So you can select a put-in by driving upstream until you consider it too small or shallow for floating with the prevailing water level. Suggested put-ins are at the Rte. 36 bridge halfway between Midland and Lonaconing or behind a ball field about three quarters of a mile upstream.

In general, Georges Creek is a pushy run as it tumbles continuously over gravel bars, rock gardens, and small ledges. In addition, there is man-made excitement such as cables, low bridges, retaining walls, debris, bridge piers, and one nasty five-foot weir in Barton. Carry the latter. The volume grows noticeably with each mile and, by the time it reaches Barton, Georges Creek can be a powerful torrent. Things then get increasingly interesting as the river begins dropping through boulder patches and over sets of sloping, often complex, five- or six-foot ledges.

The last good take-out on Georges Creek is at the American Legion Hall in Westernport, on the right bank about 100 yards upstream of Md. Rte. 135. Otherwise continue down the North Branch about a third of a mile to the town park just upstream of the big wastewater treatment plant in Westernport.

HAZARDS: A five-foot concrete dam just below the lower bridge in Barton (behind the church) has a nasty hole. Carry, though that is nasty too. Logs, low bridges, and debris coupled with high stream velocity and poor eddies can be dangerous.

WATER CONDITIONS: Most likely caught up in winter and spring after a heavy rain. Steep and sometimes denuded slopes and a small watershed means a quick and intense runoff.

Wills Creek
Little Wills Creek
Brush Creek
Jennings Run

To Bedford

MADLEY

6.8

Little Wills Creek

Brush Creek

2022

PACKSADDLE RD (T407)

Falls

2.0

PINE VALLEY RD

2019

2020

1.2

1.1

CARTER HILL RD (T754)

Wills

Falls

Creek

FAIRHOPE

2019

5.7

3004

HYNDMAN

3.2

GLENCOE

3.4

TOOLAND RD (T755)

PHILSON RD (T377)

To Rte 160

2015

2.4

To Rte 60, Pleasant Union

96

Creek

3001

Wills

PALO ALTO

5.5

PENNSYLVANIA

N

ELLERSLIE

36

Schellsburg Rd/ Forest Grove Rd

MARYLAND

1.8

Park

CORRIGAN-VILLE

36

Jennings

3.4

Run

Creek

2.3

Wills

40

To Hancock

Gauge

CUMBERLAND

2.3

68

RIDGELEY

North Branch Potomac River

22

GAUGE: There is a USGS gauge on Md. Rte. 36 a half mile south of its bridge over Georges Creek just outside of Westernport at Franklin (call Washington, see USGS website, or inspect on site). As a minimum, it must read about 275 cfs (4.5 feet). Otherwise, judge conditions from the road.

Wills Creek

INTRODUCTION: Most paddlers do not even know Wills Creek exists, even though, if they are from Washington or Baltimore, they pass over it every time they travel to the Yough, Cheat or Savage. This is too bad, for given a good rain this watershed offers the advanced paddler one full weekend of exciting and challenging whitewater boating in a setting ranging from the scenic to the strange. Besides the variety of the main stem, there are also three paddleable tributaries: Brush Creek, Little Wills Creek, and Jennings Run. Together they comprise the best and closest whitewater package accessible to the Baltimore-Washington area.

During July of 1984 one of those once-in-a-lifetime storms zeroed in on the basin of Wills Creek, dumping five inches of rain in two hours on already rain-soaked ground. The storm generated a flood that devastated the towns of Fairhope and Hyndman, the river road, and the railroad. But the towns, the railroad, road, and stream have been rebuilt, with busy bulldozers pushing up riprapped banks, channelizing the bed, and relocating boulders. It is a mess from the boater's point of view. But take comfort in that time heals all wounds. Experience on other flood-devastated streams has demonstrated that vegetation will reclaim the banks, and future high water will move the boulders and gravel back to exactly where the river pleases. Future paddlers will never suspect what Wills Creek looked like back in 1984.

Section 1. Glencoe (SR2015) to Fairhope (SR2019)						
Gradient	**Difficulty**	**Distance**	**Time**	**Width**	**Scenery**	**Map**
61	2+ to 3+	4.3	1.5	15-30	Very Good	22

TRIP DESCRIPTION: Upper Wills Creek provides a zesty rush down continuous, bouncy little rapids, punctuated by sets of exciting ledges with individual drops of up to three feet. Although this run is mostly of intermediate difficulty and is considerably easier than Section 2, you should be overqualified to attempt it, as you will need to avoid two dangerously situated waterfalls; one which could destroy your boat and one which could destroy your health.

You can start at the highway bridge in Glencoe, or better yet, start 2.5 fun-filled miles upstream. To reach this upper access point from Fairhope, take the first right in the center of Glencoe and then, a tenth of a mile beyond, turn left. Follow this rough dirt road 2.5 miles upstream to where you will find a house, a road to the right, a small creek, and then a trail on the left that leads a hundred yards down to the water.

To Glencoe the tiny stream rushes over gravel bars and a few ledges in a mostly uncomplicated manner, which is fine since alder-and brush-choked banks make escape or rescue difficult. When you reach Glencoe, begin counting railroad bridges. For directly beneath the fifth bridge is the first falls. If you lose count, this bridge has a tunnel at its downstream end, labelled Falls Cut Tunnel. The falls has a six-foot vertical drop that goes splat onto a rock. Scout this and carry left, or if the level permits and you want to live dangerously, eddy out on the right brink and lift over the slippery and sloping rocks to the pool below. A half mile below the confluence with Brush Creek is the Railroad Cut Falls. This is a man-made cataract, blasted out of rock by the railroad to bypass a hairpin loop of the creek and thus eliminate the need for two bridges. Paddle down as far as your good sense or nerves allow you, and carry on the left.

HAZARDS: There are trees above Glencoe and the two falls below. Before setting up the shuttle, the paddler should hike up the railroad grade from Fairhope to establish some landmarks (most notably a black cliff on the river right and a concrete retaining wall on the left) so as not to miss that last very important eddy.

WATER CONDITIONS: Canoeable in the winter and spring during snow melt or within two days of hard rain.

GAUGE: None. Roughly, the USGS gauge at Eckhart Junction (call Washington, see USGS website, or inspect on site) should be over 1,375 cfs (4.8 feet).

Section 2. Fairhope (SR2019) to Hyndman (Pa. Rte. 96)						
Gradient	Difficulty	Distance	Time	Width	Scenery	Map
73	2+ to 4+	5.5	1.5	20-35	Fair	22

TRIP DESCRIPTION: These are five miles of probably the most enjoyable and challenging whitewater in the Potomac Basin. The first few miles, which cut through Big Savage Mountain, are a memorable tumble over a mostly bouldery bed. At low levels it is an often tedious and incredibly rocky natural slalom suitable for both open and decked boats. At medium levels it becomes powerful and pushy, with complexity that includes not only dodging boulders, but also powerful holes. At higher levels the rocks are all covered, eddies gone, and there is just one long rapid of big waves and huge holes.

The initiation rites commence about 150 yards below the Fairhope put-in. There is a sloping, four-foot diagonal ledge with a powerful stopper which, if entered in the middle, will grab you and violently thrust you to the right before maybe releasing you. This can be traumatic to right-sided canoeists. The timid should sneak on either side. About a mile downstream is a short, boulder-choked rapid called Yo Yo (a preflood name given for the tenacity of one hole) that you can see from the shuttle road where it dips fairly near to the river. With menacingly undercut boulders and jammed debris, your only route choice here is to sneak down the extreme right (if it is free of debris). After the second bridge the stream widens and conditions begin to gradually mellow. At low levels this wide stretch becomes impassable before that above, especially since the bulldozers have changed the stream bed.

Set in a deep canyon, this was once a pretty run. But for the time being, the flood damage has messed all that up. So you might as well keep your eyes on the rapids.

HAZARDS: If your skills are insufficient, the whitewater will be a hazard.

WATER CONDITIONS: Canoeable in winter and spring during snow melt and within three days of hard rain.

GAUGE: The USGS gauge at the intersection of U.S. Rte. 40 and Md. Rte. 36, Eckhart Junction (call Washington, see USGS website, or inspect on site), should be at least 700 cfs (3.9 feet). Roughly, the USGS gauge at Kitzmiller, on the North Branch Potomac (call Washington or see USGS website), should be 1,050 cfs (4.5 feet) and the USGS gauge at Markleton, on the Casselman River (call Pittsburgh or see USGS website), should be over 950 cfs (3.0 feet).

Section 3. Hyndman (Pa. Rte. 96) to Eckhart Junction						
Gradient	Difficulty	Distance	Time	Width	Scenery	Map
21	A to 2+	13.0	4.0	30-50	Fair to Poor	22

TRIP DESCRIPTION: Wills Creek has now broken out of the Allegheny Plateau and settles into a more gentle pace through a trough nestled between the Allegheny Front and Wills Mountain. The run is initially busy, dropping over cobble bars in a bouncy and uncomplicated manner. One particularly steep rapid, about a mile below the start, can throw up waves that are big enough to swamp an open canoe. But the rapids gradually shorten, and the pools grow longer, with one particularly long, straight, and dead pool below Ellerslie.

The scenery through here is disappointing. While the valley is pretty, the view of it from the water is poor, obscured by high banks and dense vegetation. The last two miles are also scarred by large-scale quarrying on the side of Wills Mountain.

HAZARDS: Low bridge about a mile below Corriganville might be impassable at high water.

WATER CONDITIONS: Canoeable in winter and spring during snow melt and within a week of hard rain.

GAUGE: Minimum is roughly a little less than that for Section 2, whatever that is. USGS gauge at Eckhart Junction (call Washington, see USGS website, or or inspect on site) should be 640 cfs (3.8 feet). Roughly, USGS gauge at Kitzmiller, on North Branch Potomac (call Washington or see USGS website), should be 1,050 cfs (4.5 feet).

Section 4. Eckhart Junction to mouth						
Gradient	Difficulty	Distance	Time	Width	Scenery	Map
20	2 or 6	2.3	.25	40-60	Unusual	22

TRIP DESCRIPTION: Did you ever stand on a city street during a rain, watching a piece of flotsam float down the gutter, and wonder what it would be like if that flotsam was your boat and the gutter was a river? Here is your big chance. The last 1.4 miles of Wills Creek through Cumberland is now, courtesy of the magical hand of the Corps of Engineers, a giant trapezoidal concrete storm drain, i.e. a real live paved river.

You make your entry via The Narrows, a massive gap cut by Wills Creek through Wills Mountain. Here massive white cliffs, among the most spectacular in the Potomac Basin, rise above the rocky, but surprisingly easy, stream. Although the creek shares the gap with U.S. Rte. 40 and a busy railroad line, it is beautiful. Then comes the U.S. Rte. 40 bridge and "The Channel."

Once into "The Channel" the paddler is committed. It is indeed a strange sensation to travel down a high velocity river of uniform width, uniform depth, and with no eddies, or nothing even to grab onto. Even if one could stop, the sloping concrete walls are capped by vertical concrete walls which are capped with chain-link fences, meaning no escape. The gradient, luckily, is expended over gentle inclined planes which usually have incredibly uniform, channel-wide surfing waves at the bottom. One exception is a hydraulic beneath the first railroad bridge through which you can punch with a good running start or sneak on the extreme left. Take out directly across the North Branch where one can drive a car up to the back side of the levee.

HAZARDS: The whole channel is a hazard if you flip. While this is an easy, uncomplicated run (providing that you do not broach on a bridge pier), a swimmer or inverted boater would be severely beaten and abraded. Since there is no way out until the end, this would be a long swim where you would capture the true essence of what keelhauling is all about.

WATER CONDITIONS: Winter or spring during any wet spell or after locally intense showers.

GAUGE: Same as Section 3.

Brush Creek

INTRODUCTION: Brush Creek drains an isolated piece of plateau northwest of Fairhope, Pennsylvania. This seldom run torrent makes an ideal introduction to a Wills Creek run when the water is up and, if the water is really high, makes a reasonable alternative to an overly pushy Fairhope to Hyndman flush.

Section 1. Pack Saddle Covered Bridge (T407) to mouth						
Gradient	**Difficulty**	**Distance**	**Time**	**Width**	**Scenery**	**Map**
75	2 to 4–	3.2	1.0	20-30	Excellent	22

TRIP DESCRIPTION: Brush Creek is a beautiful, mini-wilderness passage that enters Wills Creek just above the Railroad Cut Falls at Fairhope. It flows through a wild, wooded gorge that is decorated by falls, rock cliffs, hemlock, and rhododendron, and is only civilized by one road bridge and a cluster of rustic log structures. Rapids formed by boulders, gravel, and ledges are almost continuous, separated only by short pools. There is an unrunnable 10-foot falls beneath the covered bridge at the put-in, and, about a mile downstream, there is a steep tier of ledges that form a chute dropping about 10 feet. Take out above Railroad Cut Falls on Wills Creek, about a half mile below the confluence with Wills Creek.

If water is extra high, the purist can add on about three miles to this run by starting at SR2017, a half mile northwest of Johnsburg. Although the scenery is fine, an alder jungle and numerous dangerously placed fallen trees will make this an expedition.

HAZARDS: Steep ledge rapid about a mile below the start. If you decide to carry, look for an old logging railroad grade on the left.

WATER CONDITIONS: Canoeable winter and spring during snow melt and within two days of hard rain.

GAUGE: None on creek, but you can judge conditions at the put-in. USGS gauge at Eckhart Junction, on Wills Creek (call Washington or see USGS website), should probably be close to 1,470 cfs (4.9 feet).

Little Wills Creek

INTRODUCTION: Little Wills Creek flows down a narrow valley between the Allegheny Front and Wills Mountain to enter Wills Creek just below Hyndman. It draws most of its flow off of the well-watered Allegheny Plateau, and you can generally look forward to finding it canoeable if upper Wills Creek has water. Pa. Rte. 96 accompanies this run and is never more than a half mile away.

Section 1. Madley (Pa. Rte. 96) to mouth						
Gradient	Difficulty	Distance	Time	Width	Scenery	Map
39	1 to 2+	6.8	2.0	15-25	Good	22

TRIP DESCRIPTION: Fans of small, shallow, and busy streams will delight in Little Wills Creek. It provides a descent down almost continuous easy rapids that are formed by gravel bars and rock gardens. Swift flatwater provides periodic pauses. The proximity of the highway has resulted in some trash and other eyesores, but most of the time the view is only of farmland and mountainsides.

Put in on Wolf Camp Run, at the village of Madley. The take-out at the junction with Wills Creek is poor. So continue on down Wills Creek for a half mile to a road bridge accessible from Hyndman.

HAZARDS: Fallen trees where the stream occasionally braids (not visible from the highway).

WATER CONDITIONS: Canoeable in winter and spring during snow melt and within two days of hard rain.

GAUGE: If Wolf Camp Run looks passable at the Rte. 96 bridge, then there is plenty of water on Little Wills. Roughly, the USGS gauge at Eckhart Junction (call Washington or see USGS website) should read over 1,375 cfs (4.8 feet). Even more roughly, the USGS gauge at Saxton, on the Raystown Branch (call State College or see USGS website), will be running about 3.5 feet.

Jennings Run

INTRODUCTION: Jennings Run drops off the Allegheny Front to join Wills Creek at Corriganville, two miles above The Narrows. This is a great target for bored whitewater paddlers looking for cheap thrills and chills when their regular favorites are too high to attempt.

Section 1. Barrelville (Md. Rte. 36) to mouth						
Gradient	Difficulty	Distance	Time	Width	Scenery	Map
75	4	3.4	1.0	15-20	Poor	22

TRIP DESCRIPTION: Jennings Run is 3.4 miles of nonstop terror. It has only one rapid, also 3.4 miles long, formed by ledges, boulders, gravel, tree trunks, and one demolished bridge. Eddies are rare and you can bet that they will not be where the fallen trees are. The water is muddy, and the bank scenery, if you notice it, consists largely of views of the highway and nearby houses. Bland fare. On the other hand, the nearness of Rte. 36 can be comforting as it greatly facilitates rescue and escape. The best take-out for this run is a few yards up Wills Creek from the confluence, at a town park.

HAZARDS: The ruins of a concrete bridge about halfway down the creek requires a tricky cross current maneuver that could result in a serious broach if not executed properly. Also expect some fallen trees in bad spots.

WATER CONDITIONS: Canoeable during winter or spring, only immediately after a heavy rain.

GAUGE: None. Judge condition from the highway.

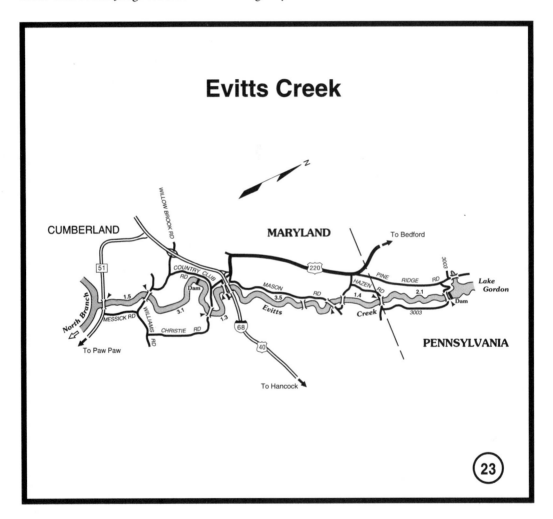

Evitts Creek

INTRODUCTION: Evitts Creek occupies the narrow trough between Wills Mountain and Evitts Mountain northeast of Cumberland, Maryland. With its limited watershed and two water supply reservoirs that intercept a substantial piece of its flow, this is a good stream to take advantage of when everything else is in flood. Do not be discouraged by its proximity to an urban area for this lively run is still quite attractive.

Section 1. Lake Gordon Dam to Md. Rte. 51

Gradient	Difficulty	Distance	Time	Width	Scenery	Map
21*	1 to 2+	12.9	4.0	15-40	Good	23

*reaches 100 fpm in Pa.

TRIP DESCRIPTION: To reach the put-in, drive north on U.S. Rte. 220 3.5 miles past the exit from U.S. Rte. 40 to where Pine Ridge Road (no sign) continues straight ahead at the fork, while Rte. 220 bends to the left. Follow Pine Ridge Road about two miles, turn right onto Dam Road and follow this to the bridge over Evitts Creek. This is immediately below Lake Gordon Dam. Between Dam Road and Hazen Road (Maryland State Line), the creek rushes busily and with a surprising amount of pushiness over rapids formed by gravel and small ledges and over a sharp two-foot ford best run to right of center. The route passes through wooded ravines and past shale cliffs and little meadows. To U.S. Rte. 40/I-68 the gradient gradually decreases, but the stream flows over a continuous series of riffles and easy rapids over a rocky and gravelly bottom, complicated now and then by a barbed wire fence or downed tree. The scenery here is more open with more roads and houses.

Below Rte. 40 the creek slows to fast flat water with occasional riffles. There are more houses and civilization now, but it continues to wind against enough wooded hillsides and cliffs and through enough open fields to maintain attractiveness. It also passes by a small amusement park and through a golf course. The latter has a three-foot dam that is run down exciting but easy chutes in the center or on the right. Take out just above Md. Rte. 51 on the left. The creek joins the North Branch Potomac about a quarter mile downstream after passing under the railroad yards (through a most impressive tunnel) and the C&O Canal aqueduct.

HAZARDS: Watch for fallen trees and barbed wire above Rte. 40 and the weir described above. Also, below the community college, there may be a strainer caused by a collapsed swinging bridge.

WATER CONDITIONS: First of all, you need some period of sustained wet weather to fill Lake Koon and Lake Gordon. After those conditions are granted, Evitts is runnable within two days of a hard rain.

GAUGE: None. Rapid at foot of Lake Gordon should be passable to do upper creek.

——— Town Creek ———

INTRODUCTION: Town Creek flows out of the heart of Bedford County, Pennsylvania to wind across the center of Allegany County and enter the Potomac below Oldtown, Maryland. This is rugged mountain country where numerous level-topped ridges fringe valleys filled with steeply rolling hills. These hills are all sit upon limestone so that, besides some very scenic canoeing, this neighborhood offers a lot of interesting caving for the explorer who seeks to see the land from every angle.

Section 1. Chaneysville, Pa., to U.S. Rte. 40

Gradient	Difficulty	Distance	Time	Width	Scenery	Map
15	1 to 2–	15.1	5.0	10-30	Very Good	24

Town Creek
Flintstone Creek

PENNSYLVANIA

MARYLAND

Match Line

CHANEYSVILLE

Sweet Root Creek

Elk Lick Creek

Wilson Run

ABEY RD (2002)

326

4.7

Match Line

4.7

T323

2.5

T305

T306

Town Creek

7.9

326

Flintstone Creek

To Cumberland

DOLLY RD

40

BLACK VALLEY RD

CHANEYSVILLE RD

68

FLINTSTONE

To Hancock

N

4.0

TOWN

OLD WILLIAMS RD

CREEK

3.6

MERTEN AVE

RD

1.5

PUMPKIN CENTER

JACOBS RD

OLIVER BELTZ RD

2.8

BEAR HILL RD

WAGNER RD

Town Creek

6.9

CREEK RD

MANIFORD RD

GREEN RIDGE RD

PACK HORSE RD

LOWER TOWN

2.9

2.8

To Cumberland

51

OLDTOWN

1.3

Potomac River

24

TRIP DESCRIPTION: Town Creek is formed by the confluence of Sweet Root Creek, Elklick Creek, and Wilson Run. Put in a half mile southeast of Chaneysville, on Elklick Creek (watch out for fences), or a half mile south of town where Pa. Rte. 326 swings close to Town Creek (be sure to get permission from landowners first).

Town Creek meanders through a sparsely inhabited valley. The stream bumps up against countless little shale cliffs while winding through woodlands and by attractive farms. Near Hewitt it carries you beneath one lovely, white covered bridge. The fairly clear water rushes over numerous short, easy riffles, formed by gravel and some broken ledges. The only complications are three low-water bridges and maybe a fallen tree or new fence. Finish your cruise at the old Rte. 40 bridge, just downstream of the main highway.

HAZARDS: Low-water bridges, trees, or fences.

WATER CONDITIONS: Canoeable in winter or spring within three days of hard rain.

GAUGE: USGS gauge (see USGS website) below Pack Horse Road, near Oldtown, should read over 300 cfs (3.9 feet). Roughly, USGS gauge at Saxton, on Raystown Branch (call State College or see USGS website), should be over 1,560 cfs (3.2 feet).

Section 2. U.S. Rte. 40/I-68 to mouth						
Gradient	Difficulty	Distance	Time	Width	Scenery	Map
9	A to 1	25.8	8.0	20-35	Good	24

TRIP DESCRIPTION: This section is not quite as lively nor is it as pretty as the upper section, but it is a little easier to catch at a runnable level. Woodlands and small farms dominate the valley scenery, and there are some pretty cliffs here and there. The impression is that you are far from any place important or busy. The main flaw here is the frequent presence of summer homes, though they are generally well-spaced, unlike the congested slums found along the Potomac. The water is likely to be fairly clear. Though a generally tranquil stream, Town usually has a strong current and lots of riffles.

You can easily break this long section into shorter trips via several bridges and fords. Most of the necessary access and shuttle roads are slow, narrow, and crooked. Allow enough time for this. If you choose to float Town all the way to its mouth, you will be rewarded by the old C&O Canal aqueduct and a nice set of rocky riffles through the site of an old mill dam. To reach the mouth, drive about a half mile east on Rte. 51 from its bridge over the creek to the first dirt road on your right. This leads to a old railroad grade, which you can then follow to the creek.

HAZARDS: None.

WATER CONDITIONS: Canoeable winter and spring within four days of hard rain.

GAUGE: Same as Section 1. If the first riffle below the confluence with Flintstone Creek is deep enough to float, all but perhaps a few of the widest riffles will be passable.

Another Point Of View

Nothing so rounds out a river tour as a good bird's eye view of that river. The more aggressive and prosperous paddler can go out and charter an airplane. But for the more frugal and down-to-earth majority, knowing where to drive or hike for a good view should suffice. Here are a few recommended scenic overlooks in the Potomac Basin.

North Branch Potomac at Luke: It is possible to gain a panoramic if not scenic view of this industrial valley from old W.Va. Rte. 46. Cross the North Branch from Westernport into Piedmont, West

Virginia and find some local who can give you directions to the old alignment of Rte. 46, as there are no longer any signs. This precariously perched road may be closed (it should have been condemned years ago), but it is well worth hiking up.

Wills Creek Narrows: It is possible to drive up, from the Cumberland side, to Lovers Leap on the northeast rim of this spectacular gap.

Potomac River above Paw Paw: Land at the mouth of the second tiny creek on the right, about a mile below where the Little Cacapon River joins the Potomac. Climb onto the railroad grade and from there follow a primitive path that ascends the knife-edge ridge that separates the creek ravine from the river. This affords grand views both upstream and down.

Potomac River below Paw Paw: Way back in the heart of Green Ridge State Forest, at the intersection of Merten Avenue and Stafford Road, is Banner Overlook. This affords an excellent distant view of the first loops of the Paw Paw Bends.

Potomac River near Doe Gully: About three crooked miles west of Little Orleans, on the Oldtown Road, look for a sign marking Carroll Road. Turn left here and follow Carroll Road a few hundred yards to an overlook onto a straightaway of one of the bigger of the Paw Paw Bends.

Potomac River at Prospect Peak: Ascend W.Va. Rte. 9 east out of Great Cacapon, West Virginia to a grand view of the river and Sideling Hill.

Potomac River at Harpers Ferry: A short climb to Jeffersons Rock in Harpers Ferry yields a view for which Thomas Jefferson thought worthy of a trip across the ocean. You can enjoy another fine view on the Maryland side of the Potomac, peering straight down on the town, by ascending a trail starting at the east end of the railroad tunnel. This will take you to the top of the big, black cliffs of Maryland Heights.

Potomac River in Mather Gorge: Foot trails run along both sides of this shallow gorge, offering a glut of fine scenery.

Town Creek: Drive north from Md. Rte. 51 on Green Ridge Road about 3.5 miles for good views of a big loop of Town Creek.

Flintstone Creek

INTRODUCTION: Flintstone Creek drains a tiny valley between Evitts Mountain and Tussey Mountain in Franklin County, Pennsylvania. Its exit from that valley, around Tussey Mountain and through Warrior Ridge into Town Creek, affords a short and exhilarating run for microstream enthusiasts.

Section 1. Flintstone Creek Road to mouth						
Gradient	Difficulty	Distance	Time	Width	Scenery	Map
46	1 to 3–	3.6	1.0	10-20	Fair	24

TRIP DESCRIPTION: This is a very tiny, busy run from start to finish, dropping over ledges, boulders, and gravel. There are ledges up to three feet high at the start, but they offer no problems. Fallen trees in fast spots are a hazard, so be alert. The scenery, unfortunately, is cluttered with houses, roads, and trash, but the river will usually manage to distract you. Take out on the east bank of Town Creek at the Old Rte. 40 bridge.

HAZARDS: Trees, logs, and, if you put in farther upstream, barbed wire fences.

WATER CONDITIONS: Canoeable winter and spring only within 24 hours of hard rain.

GAUGE: None, but you can easily assess the situation by driving up the riverside road from I-68/Rte. 40.USGS gauge (see USGS website) on Town Creek near Oldtown, should read over 1,220 cfs (6.5 feet).

Fifteenmile Creek

INTRODUCTION: Fifteenmile Creek drains the dry, shaley ridges of Buchanan State Forest in Pennsylvania and Green Ridge State Forest in Maryland. Consider it quite a prize to run, as it is really

Sideling Hill Creek

tiny and difficult to catch up. Its unorthodox direction of flow across the grain of Town Hill and the surrounding hills takes it through some rugged, uncivilized country and assures it a lively gradient.

Section 1. Scenic U.S. Rte. 40 to mouth						
Gradient	Difficulty	Distance	Time	Width	Scenery	Map
29	1 to 3–	10.4	3.5	10-40	Excellent	25

TRIP DESCRIPTION: Most of this run is through a beautiful, isolated, wooded gorge decorated by numerous shale cliffs and rock formations. Shady hemlock bends are common. This is a tiny and twisting stream where you are always close to the quickly changing scenery. And as a result, opportunities for surprising some wildlife are good here.

Fifteenmile Creek requires some skill to explore. There are lots of rapids and riffles formed by gravel bars and small broken ledges. At times the whitewater is pushy and almost continuous. In particular, you must be prepared for a few spots with hard right-angle turns where rapids pile up against cliffs (these spots drive home the value of leaning downstream like nothing else can). Also there are quite a few fallen trees to tangle with, especially where the stream splits around islands.

An easy put-in is found by following a dirt road (Fifteenmile Creek Road) north off Scenic Rte. 40, east of its bridge over the creek, to a bridge and ford. Also, starting along Fifteenmile Creek Road downstream of the forestry camp below U.S. Rte. 40 is easy. As for take-outs, you can use the low-water bridge at Little Orleans (which is usually not runnable), or better yet, proceed another half mile down to and under the C&O Canal aqueduct to a launching ramp at the confluence with the Potomac.

Unless you desire to reach some intermediate point, the best shuttle for Fifteenmile Creek is to take I-68/U.S. Rte. 40 (or Scenic Rte. 40) and Orleans Road. Back roads like Fifteenmile Creek Road or Mountain Road look shorter, but they are crooked, have only dirt or gravel surfaces, and in snowy weather they will be impassable. They are scenic, but not expedient.

HAZARDS: Trees everywhere and a low-water bridge at Little Orleans.

WATER CONDITIONS: Catch in winter and spring within two days of hard rain.

GAUGE: There is no gauge on the creek, but if the USGS gauges on Town and Sideling Hill creeks are respectively running over 600 cfs (4.9 feet) and 320 cfs (2.4 feet), it is likely Fifteenmile has enough water for a float. If riffle below Pratt Hollow (stream running down along Rte. 40 from the west) is passable, then the level is adequate.

Sideling Hill Creek

INTRODUCTION: All of the small Potomac River tributaries in the Appalachian ridge and valley region, from Evitts Creek to Licking Creek, are similar and pleasant canoe streams. But Sideling Hill Creek just puts all their finest qualities together and comes out with something better than all the rest. This crooked creek drains the eastern edge of Bedford County, Pennsylvania, and, after crossing a corner of Franklin County, enters Maryland to form the boundary between Washington and Allegany counties. Few creeks are as easy to locate. For travelers on U.S. Rte. 40/I-68, just look for the gaping, man-made notch that carries that highway through the summit of Sideling Hill. You can see it for miles. You will find the creek at the foot of the hill (west side).

Section 1. Purcell, Pa., (SR2011) to Old U.S. Rte. 40						
Gradient	Difficulty	Distance	Time	Width	Scenery	Map
16	A to 1	13.9	4.5	10-30	Very Good	26

TRIP DESCRIPTION: The put-in is at a secondary roadbridge (SR2011) over the West Branch, about a third of a mile above the confluence with the East Branch. If there appears to be enough water on either branch, then there is plenty on the rest of the creek. The following miles carry you past a few farms and a few summer cottages, but mostly through woods filled with hemlock and rhododendron. There are shale cliffs covered with ferns, moss, and lichen and, in mid-winter, with intricate ice decorations. The creek is graced by plenty of easy riffles separated by deep pools of hazy, green water. And if you enjoy all this, you will love Section 2.

HAZARDS: Possibility of fallen trees.

WATER CONDITIONS: Paddleable in winter and spring within two days of hard rain.

GAUGE: On Section 2, there is a USGS gauge at Ziegler Road (see USGS website). Minimum for Section 1 is about 285 cfs (2.3 feet). Also, if all of the riffle above the take-out looks passable, there will be enough water.

Section 2. Old U.S. Rte. 40 to mouth						
Gradient	Difficulty	Distance	Time	Width	Scenery	Map
16	1 to 2–	11.6	4.0	25-35	Excellent	26

TRIP DESCRIPTION: Lower Sideling Hill Creek is an almost wild river. The first half of this section passes through undisturbed woodlands largely within the bounds of a state wildlife management area. The stream twists and turns at the base of Sideling Hill, bouncing into beautiful cliffs and crumbly, shale slopes. It rushes over numerous rapids of gravel and broken ledges that can be quite tricky where they pile up against cliffs to form 90-degree turns. The gradient gradually moderates, and the woods yield to some farmland. But many of the farms are abandoned and going to seed. The creek makes a grand exit from its wilderness-like valley as it passes beneath the 110-foot arch of the old C&O Canal aqueduct and onto the broad Potomac where, a half mile downstream, opposite Lock 56 at Pearre, is an easy take-out.

HAZARDS: None.

WATER CONDITIONS: Canoeable winter and spring within four days of hard rain.

GAUGE: USGS gauge at Ziegler Road should read over 214 cfs (2.1 feet). Also you may find a painted canoeing gauge on at the old, stone bridge abutment at the put-in (these tend to come and go depending on the quality of the paint).

Valley And Ridge Close-up

Probably the most notable feature that you will observe while passing down Sideling Hill Creek and many other streams of the Valley and Ridge District, besides the strikingly beautiful rock formations, are the cliffs and slopes of crumbling shale. Shale is a sedimentary rock formed by consolidation of mud, mud that was deposited in a shallow sea millions of years ago. This is a soft rock that weathers by breaking away, piece by piece, as thin, smooth-faced, and sharp-edged fragments. Pick up a piece and you will find it easy to break. Piles of these fragments form the slopes that you keep seeing. As with sand, any rain that falls upon this coarse surface quickly percolates down into the debris and, in the process, leaches away many nutrients. As a result, a desert-like and barren environment is created that is only suitable for habitation by the heartiest of plant types. Notice that most of the trees that you see living (or dying) there are pine and eastern red cedar, both scrubby looking species adapted for hardship. A more interesting resident is the prickly pear cactus. Possessing pads that are only about four inches long, they blend easily into the shale background except for one glorious week, usually in mid or late June, when they show off their beautiful, rose-like, yellow blossoms. One other tenacious plant that you are likely to notice here, and also on the rocky cliffsides, is the columbine. This plant is most prominent in early May when it displays its intricate, red, drooping flowers that contrast so brilliantly with the grays and browns of the bare rock.

Tonoloway Creek

INTRODUCTION: Tonoloway Creek drains an area of rolling hills and low ridges east of Sideling Hill to join the Potomac River at Hancock. Most of its drainage and length is in Pennsylvania, its last few miles crossing Maryland at the state's narrowest point. The Tonoloway's valley is apple country, and many a hillside is decorated by the orderly patterns of orchards. Yet, little of this activity is apparent to the Tonoloway paddler, who sees and enjoys what seems to be the remotest of streams.

Section 1. Needmore, Pa., (U.S. Rte. 522) to mouth						
Gradient	**Difficulty**	**Distance**	**Time**	**Width**	**Scenery**	**Map**
10	A to 1	20.7	6.5	15-30	Good to Excellent	27

TRIP DESCRIPTION: Put in at U.S. Rte. 522 or one mile downstream at the tiny concrete bridge of T363, east of Needmore. The following miles to the confluence with Little Tonoloway Creek describe an incredibly serpentine course that advances you about one mile down the valley for every two miles paddled. While there are occasional farms and fields, most of the way is through woodlands, easily viewed over low banks. Almost every bend exposes pretty shale cliffs, and almost every northern exposure displays a cool green hemlock grove. Most of the surrounding hills are close by and steep, the combined effect being one of intimacy and remoteness. You speed through this setting on a strong current spiced with many easy riffles. Beginners can easily handle this trip. But, since the stream is so narrow, they must be ready to avoid an occasional fallen tree or other strainer.

Below the Little Tonoloway Creek confluence, Tonoloway is slightly larger and slower than above, while the surroundings are more settled and open. Nevertheless, it is still a pretty stretch to paddle. There are no really nice take-outs in Hancock, with the lesser of evils being to finish at the Timber Ridge Road bridge just below I-70.

HAZARDS: Watch for occasional deadfalls.

WATER CONDITIONS: Canoeable winter and spring within a day or two of hard rain. Below Little Tonoloway, it lasts a day longer.

To McConnellsburg

NEEDMORE

0.8

T363

522

6.5

Creek

LOCUST GROVE RD

T318

To Breezewood

Little

OLD 126

4.8

3007

Tonoloway

1.6

T335

(T332)
COVALT RD

655

Tonoloway

3006

1.0

T404

3.5

70

7.4

484

Creek

3011

MYERS RD

(T329)

WARFORDSBURG

1.9

1.6

2004

Dam

2005

484

Creek

2.3

928

PENNSYLVANIA

2005

N

3.2

40

68

PENNSYLVANIA AVE

TIMBER RIDGE RD #1

MARYLAND

To Cumberland

Tonoloway

522

70

40

HANCOCK

144

To Hagerstown

Potomac

River

Tonoloway Creek
Little Tonoloway Creek

27

GAUGE: If you can run the riffle at T363, then there is just enough water. USGS gauge upstream of Needmore (see USGS website) should report over 15 cfs (3.7 feet). For a rough correlation, the USGS gauge at Saxton, on the Raystown Branch (call State College or see USGS website), should be at least 1,560 cfs (3.2 feet) for the upper creek and 1,360 cfs (3.0 feet) for below Little Tonoloway.

——— Little Tonoloway Creek ———

INTRODUCTION: Considering that Interstate 70 follows over half of this course, it is amazing what a pleasant run Little Tonoloway is. It accomplishes this seemingly impossible feat by twisting behind little hills and cliffs, which not only block the view, but screen out the sound of the busy highway. Little Tonoloway does not have much of a watershed, so you must rush to catch it up, and that is where the interstate can be very useful.

Section 1. T318 to Deneen Gap						
Gradient	Difficulty	Distance	Time	Width	Scenery	Map
48	1 to 2	4.8	2.0	10-20	Very Good	27

TRIP DESCRIPTION: The put-in is at a township road branching off of Locust Grove Road, where the creek is almost small enough to leap across. This upper reach is reserved for those who feel comfortable on tiny strainer-strewn passages and who are quick enough to catch it with enough water. It is a gem that twists through a remote, wooded, gorge-like setting. There are many little shale cliffs and, should you be lucky enough to pass through in May, the surrounding forest is decorated by an uncommon, lavender variety of wild azalea. A good gradient over a cobble and ledge bed would provide a speedy passage were it not for the numerous deadfalls.

HAZARDS: Strainers.

WATER CONDITIONS: Canoeable winter and spring within a day of hard rain.

GAUGE: None. Roughly, USGS gauge on Tonoloway Creek near Needmore (see USGS website) should be over 100 cfs (4.4 feet).

Section 2. Deneen Gap to Johnsons Mill (SR2004)						
Gradient	Difficulty	Distance	Time	Width	Scenery	Map
21	1 to 2	9.6	3.5	10-25	Good	27

TRIP DESCRIPTION: To reach the put-in, get off I-70 (heading north) at Exit 32, turn right, then left, and park. The stream is about a hundred feet across the grassy field, down a steep bank. Little Tonoloway gets off to a lively start as it tumbles out of a gap in Sideling Hill and heads eastward, cutting across the geological grain of the land. Small ledges and gravel bars form almost continuous rapids, and there are many tricky spots caused by swift water sweeping under trees and roots on bends. The scenery alternates between rural and woodsy, while shale cliffs abound all the way. Around Warfordsburg, the pace slows, while the scenery degrades to prolonged views of the interstate highway and a large gravel quarry. There is a two-foot-high rock dam at the quarry, best run on the left. Below here

Licking Creek
Big Cove Creek

28

the good scenery returns, while the water is mostly slow. One gets a final splash, however, at a crumbling dam above Johnsons Mill. If not clogged with debris, there is a passable breach on the far left that drops into a juicy hole. The take-out is a tenth of a mile above the confluence with Tonoloway Creek.

HAZARDS: Trees and roots on bends on the upper creek. The broken dam above Johnsons Mill has a lot of potential for trouble.

WATER CONDITIONS: Canoeable winter and spring within a day of hard rain.

GAUGE: If the little ledges at the put-in are clearly passable, or if the rock dam at Mellott Quarry, near Warfordsburg, has a clean chute on the left, then the level is adequate. Roughly, USGS gauge on Tonoloway Creek near Needmore (see USGS website) should be over 20 cfs (3.8 Feet). For an even-rougher estimate, the USGS gauge at Saxton, on the Raystown Branch (call State College or see USGS website), should be over 2,450 cfs (4.0 feet).

Licking Creek

INTRODUCTION: Licking Creek starts on the west slope of Tuscarora Mountain, near Cowans Gap State Park, then twists and turns through eastern Fulton County and a corner of Franklin County, and finally enters Maryland to join the Potomac below Hancock. It cuts through a beautiful landscape of low parallel ridges, covered with orchards, forests, and pastures. Many of the roads in the area follow the ridgetops, which afford enough good views to make the shuttling for this stream as pleasant as the paddling.

Section 1. Knobsville (U.S. Rte. 522) to U.S. Rte. 30

Gradient	Difficulty	Distance	Time	Width	Scenery	Map
20	1 to 2–	7.8	3.0	10-20	Good to Very Good	28

TRIP DESCRIPTION: Only the real hardcore purist will want to put in at Rte. 522. Here the stream is no more than 10 feet wide, is shallow even at high water, and bristles with obstacles. After leaving Rte. 522, it immediately rushes through a long tunnel of arching alder bushes, best negotiated on your belly. You can avoid this masochism by starting three quarters of a mile downstream, at SR1007 bridge, leaving you with only fallen trees, barbed wire, foot bridges, and sharp turns for interest. Actually the reason for putting up with all this nonsense is that it is the only way to gain access to the full length of the beautiful, wooded gorge above Mellotts Mill. In here you will find the going easy, the riffles frequent, and the solitude almost complete.

HAZARDS: Multitude of strainers, both natural and man-made.

WATER CONDITIONS: Up only within 24 hours of hard rain, in winter and spring.

GAUGE: Judge riffles at Rte. 522. Roughly, USGS gauge on nearby Tonoloway Creek above Needmore (see USGS website) should be running over 40 cfs (4.0 feet). For an even rougher correlation, USGS gauge at Saxton, on the Raystown Branch (call State College or see USGS website), should read about 3,700 cfs (5.0 feet).

Section 2. U.S. Rte. 30 to Pa. Rte. 456						
Gradient	Difficulty	Distance	Time	Width	Scenery	Map
10	A to 1	34.5	10.0	20-30	Very Good	28

TRIP DESCRIPTION: The creek now settles into a course suitable for nonmasochistic novices in search of beauty and solitude. Like other rivers in these parts, Licking twists unbelievably, bumps up against a lot of pretty shale cliffs, flows mostly through woods, and passes an occasional farm. Below Andover, there are few roads or structures. The water is mostly flat, but there are enough riffles and strong current to make you feel that the stream is doing the work.

HAZARDS: Some fallen trees and fences in the first 10 miles. Watch for a low-water bridge several miles below Rte. 522.

WATER CONDITIONS: Canoeable winter and spring. Above Pa. Rte. 928, catch within three days of hard rain, and below, within a week of hard rain.

GAUGE: Roughly, look for at least 15 cfs (3.7 feet) at USGS gauge on Tonoloway Creek near Needmore. For a rougher correlation, the USGS gauge at Saxton should read at least 1,360 cfs (3.0 feet). If you are approaching from the south, use the concrete footing on the west pier of the U.S. Rte. 40 bridge as a gauge. The top upstream corner should be covered with about four inches of water to start at Rte. 30, and about one inch to start at Rte. 928.

Section 3. Pa. Rte. 456 to U.S. Rte. 40						
Gradient	Difficulty	Distance	Time	Width	Scenery	Map
5	A to 1	9.7	3.0	20-35	Good	28

TRIP DESCRIPTION: Rte. 456 marks the transition to a slower and less meandering stream flowing through an open, pastoral valley. The valley continues to be sparsely settled, and the surrounding scenery remains pretty. The take-out at U.S. Rte. 40 involves a steep climb up to a side road on the west (right) bank. If you have a high-clearance vehicle, follow that side road under I-70 and about 50 yards beyond cut back onto a parallel dirt lane that drops almost to the creek by the railroad bridge. You still must negotiate a slippery mud bank here. One other alternative is to shorten the trip one and three quarter miles and take out at the handy canoe access ramp at Camp Harding Park.

HAZARDS: Barbed wire fences are always a possibility.

WATER CONDITIONS: This is usually passable within a week or two of hard rain during winter or spring.

GAUGE: Use the concrete footing on the west pier of the Rte. 40 bridge. Three inches below the top of the upstream corner is a minimal but passable level. The riffle just above this bridge should look canoeable. As rough indicators using USGS gauges on nearby streams (see USGS website), look for at least 10 cfs (3.6 feet) at Needmore on Tonoloway Creek, 1,260 cfs (2.9 feet) at Saxton on Raystown Branch, 800 cfs (3.2 feet) at Fairview on Conococheague Creek, or 430 cfs (4.3 feet) at Shirleysburg on Aughwick Creek.

If You Are Not Afraid Of The Dark

Many paddlers have found caving (also called spelunking) to be an ideal complement to their sport. After all, look at how similar these two masochistic pastimes are. Both are enjoyed in a cold, wet, and often muddy environment. Both satisfy the urge to explore and to travel under one's own muscle and wit. Cavers, like decked boaters, often spend hours in cramped quarters and, like canoeists, use their knees a lot. Furthermore, the paddler's helmet can easily be converted to a lamp-bearing caver's helmet, and a wet suit can suffice for caver's coveralls, hence saving equipment costs.

Most of Washington and Allegany counties, and to a lesser extent Garrett and Frederick counties are underlaid with limestone, and this continues on north into Pennsylvania. Caves are formed when rainwater, which even without the adverse influence of man is slightly acidic, slowly dissolves away the limestone as it seeps into cracks and fissures in the rock. Similarly, some limestone drops out of solution to form deposits that become the lovely flowstone formations that decorate some caves. Driving through cave country one will often notice a telltale sign of caves — sinkholes — which are crater-like depressions in the landscape formed when the roofs of caves collapse. If you do not get the hint driving, the alert paddler cannot help but notice intriguing holes in the cliffs and rock outcrops along streams of this region. Crabtree Cave (now gated and for experienced cavers only) lies in the canyonside just above the Savage River Dam, River (Indian) Cave is prominent on a Potomac River cliff just below the mouth of Opequon Creek, and Revells Cave forms a fascinating, subterranean maze behind an outcrop along Licking Creek. These are just a few. If you are seriously interested in expanding your horizons below ground, two excellent guides have been published: *Caves of Maryland, 1971*, by the Maryland Geological Survey and *State of West Virginia Geological and Economic Survey, Volume XIXA, Caverns of West Virginia.*

Big Cove Creek

INTRODUCTION: Big Cove Creek, which is anything but big, starts up by McConnellsburg, Pennsylvania, and drains the eastern edge of Fulton County to feed Licking Creek. Like Licking Creek, it twists a lot and possesses copious quantities of peace, solitude, and beauty. Unlike Licking Creek, Big Cove can offer you the thrill of some real, live whitewater.

Section 1. T379, Rock Hill Road to mouth

Gradient	Difficulty	Distance	Time	Width	Scenery	Map
21*	1 to 3–	12.0	3.5	10-20	Very Good	28
*reaches 80 fpm						

TRIP DESCRIPTION: To reach the put-in, drive 2.3 miles north of Webster Mill on U.S. Rte. 522, and turn left onto a paved side road, making sure not to blink, so that you will not miss the creek. Big Cove Creek is extremely tiny at T379, flows across private property (open cow pastures), and access is across someone's front lawn. Accordingly, please ask permission to put in, and do not invade with a large party. For at least the first mile, count on finding lots of fences, some deadfalls, logjams, and herds of curious cattle on the banks, trotting downstream with you. The stream then leaves the cowpastures and burrows into a beautiful, wooded gorge. The gradient increases, and soon its waters are rushing over continuous gravel bars and some broken ledges. The pace does not abate until Big Cove Tannery, about five miles below the start.

Conococheague Creek
Back Creek

29

The novice might consider putting in at Big Cove Tannery, where Pa. Rte. 928 parallels the creek, as the water is much slower from here on. The passage past pasture and woods is similar to what one would see along Licking Creek. One can take out at a ford, just below the mouth, or continue about three miles down Licking Creek to Pa. Rte. 928.

HAZARDS: Watch for a deteriorating 18-inch wooden weir at Big Cove Tannery, visible from Rte. 928. It has a strong roller at high water, but can be run. Strainers are a menace throughout this creek.

WATER CONDITIONS: Canoeable winter and spring within a day of a downpour.

GAUGE: If everything that you cross over on the way looks really high, then this might be up. Roughly, USGS gauge on Tonoloway Creek (see USGS website) should read over 40 cfs (4.0 feet).

Conococheague Creek

INTRODUCTION: Conococheague is a native American phrase for "it is a long way." And indeed it is. Draining the prosperous Cumberland Valley of Franklin County, Pennsylvania, and Washington County, Maryland, Conococheague winds 71 canoeable miles from Caledonia State Park to its confluence with the Potomac at Williamsport. And if the mainstem proves insufficient to satiate you, it is fed by two navigable tributaries, the West Branch and Back Creek, also described in this guide.

The valley of the Conococheague, which is the northern extension of the Shenandoah Valley, is dedicated to agriculture. It is a sea of corn, cattle, and orchards, from South Mountain on the east to Tuscarora Mountain on the west. Since this is obviously civilized territory, you will probably best remember the Conococheague for its fine cultural features, such as well-built barns, farm houses of native limestone, covered and stone arch bridges, and the beautiful, old towns nearby, such as Mercersburg, Williamsport, and Greencastle. It is a setting to be savored, and, fortunately, most of this tour is gentle enough for most beginners to enjoy.

Section 1. Caledonia State Park (U.S. Rte. 30) to Chambersburg (U.S. Rte. 30)						
Gradient	Difficulty	Distance	Time	Width	Scenery	Map
22	1 to 2+	18.0	5.5	15-40	Fair to Good	29

TRIP DESCRIPTION: The main stem of Conococheague Creek starts on South Mountain, growing to canoeable size at the confluence with Carbaugh Run and Rocky Mountain Creek. Put in at the Rte. 30 bridge over Rocky Mountain Creek, or at the picnic area in Caledonia Park. The Conococheague drops steeply and continuously over gravel bars and rock gardens, and soon rushes off into a beautiful grove of giant hemlocks. Unfortunately, after a short, pleasant interlude in this shady corridor, the channel braids, putting you face to face with many of the fallen giants of this forest. The going gets easier below Caledonia, but fallen trees and split channels continue to cause occasional problems as far down as Scotland. Though the gradient moderates, the creek remains fast and riffly to Chambersburg. There are three dams on this section: a two-footer at Scotland, which may be run on the right; a seven-footer (Siloam Dam) four miles below Scotland, which should be carried on the left; and a seven-footer above Commerce Street in Chambersburg, carried on the right. Watch for a foot-high weir by Wilson College.

Although this segment passes through some thick woods and by some pretty rural areas, the scenery also includes too many mobile homes, gravel pits, logged over hillsides, and stretches of dredged creek bed. So, if whitewater is not your priority, start your tour below Chambersburg.

HAZARDS: Fallen trees, especially in Caledonia Park, and three dams.

WATER CONDITIONS: Canoeable winter and spring within a day of hard rain.

GAUGE: If the rapids at Rte. 30 look passable, then the level is fine. The USGS gauge at Fairview, Maryland (call Washington, see USGS website, or inspect on site), located a half mile upstream of Md. Rte. 494, on Wishard Road, should read about 1,300 cfs (4.0 feet) to start at Caledonia. With 800 cfs (3.2 feet) you can start as far up as Woodstock Road. For a rough guess, the USGS gauge at Hogestown, on Conodoguinet Creek (call State College or see USGS website), should be over 1,300 cfs (3.5 feet).

Section 2. Chambersburg (U.S. Rte. 30) to West Branch						
Gradient	Difficulty	Distance	Time	Width	Scenery	Map
6	A to 1–	26.8	8.5	30-60	Good to Very Good	29

Conococheague Creek (30)

TRIP DESCRIPTION: Below Chambersburg the Conococheague winds through a remarkably beautiful, predominately rural setting. Its banks are usually low, affording a panorama of what, from the boater's viewpoint, appears to be sparsely settled territory. Complementing this picturesque passage are three graceful stone arch bridges and an exceptionally long covered bridge.

These are peaceful miles, with the creek expending its small gradient over occasional riffles. Stay alert, however, for a few fences (electric fences are popular around here) and, below Chambersburg's sewage treatment plant, for a sharp-crested, three-foot weir that beginners and paddlers of delicate boats should carry. Twelve bridges allow you to break this section down into cruises of comfortable length.

HAZARDS: One weir and some fences.

WATER CONDITIONS: Canoeable winter and spring within three days of hard rain, above Back Creek, and for a week to two weeks after a hard rain below.

GAUGE: The USGS gauge at Fairview, Maryland (call Washington, see USGS website, or inspect on site) should read at least 400 cfs (2.4 feet) to put in at Chambersburg. For a rough guess, the USGS gauge at Hogestown, on Conodoguinet Creek (call State College or see USGS website), should read over 440 cfs (2.0 feet) to start at Chambersburg.

Section 3. West Branch to mouth						
Gradient	Difficulty	Distance	Time	Width	Scenery	Map
3	A to 1	27.0	9.0	60-100	Good	29,30

TRIP DESCRIPTION: With the addition of the West Branch, the Conococheague gets noticeably wider and slower. There are very few riffles and the gradient is expended in a mostly swift current. Unlike on many mild streams, most paddlers will probably want to avoid this section at minimal flows. At such times the relatively uniform configuration of the creek's bed would result in long stretches of tedious shallow water paddling. In fact, this would then be a good creek for canoe poling enthusiasts. Summer low water also brings an unusually dense growth of aquatic weeds to further slow your progress. The only excitement on this run would be if you choose to run the sloping five-foot dam at Kemps Mill, above Williamsport. You can run it down the center or carry it on the left.

The scenery along here alternates between wooded bluffs and views of farmland. These miles are well endowed with beautiful stone arch bridges, including the C&O Canal aqueduct at Williamsport. It can be a serene section. Be forewarned, however, that if the auto raceway across the river from Wilson is operating, bring some industrial strength ear plugs.

Start this section at either SR3005 over the main stem or SR3004 over the West Branch, just above their confluence. The finish has an easy take-out at the Williamsport Town Park (approached via West Salisbury Street), right at the confluence with the Potomac. The best intermediate access points can be found at Md. Rte. 494, mile 8.8; Broadfording Road, mile 11.4; and the lovely, old Wilson Bridge, mile 18.4 (just upstream of U.S. Rte. 40).

HAZARDS: Five-foot dam at Kemps Mill. Hearing impairment while passing auto raceway.

WATER CONDITIONS: Good levels usually exist during winter and spring within a week of hard rain. At least minimal levels usually prevail until mid summer in an average year.

GAUGE: The USGS gauge (call Washington, see USGS website, or inspect on site) located a half mile above Fairview Road (Md. Rte. 494) along Wishard Road, right bank, should read at least 230 cfs (1.9 feet) but 290 cfs (2.1 feet) is the minimum enjoyable level, considering the low water problems discussed above. Also you can judge conditions by observing the riffle above the abandoned stone arch bridge just upstream of the Cearfoss Pike bridge (approach from east bank). If the riffle is runnable, you will do just fine.

Back Creek

INTRODUCTION: Back Creek feeds into the Conococheague at the village of Williamson, Pennsylvania. It offers a mediocre run through uninspiring scenery, via mostly flat water. The best part of your day may be running the shuttle, which is much more scenic and no less an exciting way to enjoy this beautiful countryside.

Section 1. U.S. Rte. 30 to Williamson (SR3002)						
Gradient	**Difficulty**	**Distance**	**Time**	**Width**	**Scenery**	**Map**
3	A to 1	9.4	3.0	20-30	Fair	29

TRIP DESCRIPTION: After a dismal start as a channelized ditch running through a suburban housing development, Back Creek winds through fields and woods. Although the creek only murmurs through an occasional riffle, you must be alert for many electric fences and a four-foot milldam behind Williamson. Carry the dam on the right. Back Creek joins the Conococheague about a third of a mile below the town.

With high water, one can start above Rte. 30 at the Ruritan Park at SR4010, or even farther up at Keefer Road (T539), where the creek is called Rocky Spring Run. The route meanders through a delightful, pastoral setting with old farm structures and lots of contented cows. On the negative side, however, is a greater frequency of fences and increasing possibility that some farmer may find your presence disturbing.

HAZARDS: Watch for a dam at Williamson and fences elsewhere.

WATER CONDITIONS: Canoeable winter and spring within two days of hard rain.

GAUGE: Judge shallows at put-in. The USGS gauge at Fairview, on Conococheague Creek (call Washington, see USGS website, or inspect on site), should be over 810 cfs (3.2 feet). To start as far up as Keefer Road, look for over 2,000 cfs (5.0 feet).

West Branch Conococheague Creek

INTRODUCTION: The West Branch flows for almost the entire length of western Franklin County, Pennsylvania, before joining the main stem near Greencastle. In its early stages it is confined by high mountain ridges. But for the rest of the way, it is free to wander about a wide, rural valley where it grows to resemble the main Conococheague. All of this creek makes a suitable run for novices.

Section 1. Pennsylvania Turnpike to Fort Loudon (U.S. Rte. 30)						
Gradient	**Difficulty**	**Distance**	**Time**	**Width**	**Scenery**	**Map**
9	A to 1+	21.7	8.0	25-40	Good	31

West Branch Conococheague Creek

TRIP DESCRIPTION: To reach the put-in, drive north on Pa. Rte. 75, past the Pennsylvania Turnpike. A quarter mile past Fannett-Metal High School, turn right onto a secondary road (SR4006) and follow this to a concrete arch bridge over the tiny West Branch.

Most of this run down to Richmond Furnace is typical of rural Pennsylvanian brooks. The water is often flat, shallow, and fairly slow, while the scenery of fields, farms, and scrubby woods is pleasant. An old 12-foot dam backs a small lake at Fannettsburg, but there is an easy portage that begins about a hundred feet to the left of the spillway, follows the berm to the right, and ends at the foot of the spillway. The lake waters once powered a small hydroelectric plant, now crumbling away, that was unusual in that the generators were driven by a water wheel, rather than by a turbine.

Below Richmond Furnace the scenery turns woodsy, featuring pretty views of nearby mountains. The gradient and volume pick up, and pleasant riffles abound. So skip the upper reaches, start at Fannettsburg, and enjoy the final 16 miles of this section. Take out in Fort Loudon, at the town park by Mullen Street.

HAZARDS: Trees and fences, a dam at Fannettsburg, and, below Fannettsburg, four fords or low-water bridges, including an unusual double-decker low-water bridge.

WATER CONDITIONS: Canoeable winter and spring within two days of hard rain.

GAUGE: Riffle at put-in must be passable, as a bare minimum. Because the stream gathers many small tributaries, enough water at the start will grow to plenty by Richmond Furnace. The USGS gauge at Fairview, on the main stem (call Washington or see USGS website), should read at least 870 cfs (3.3 feet).

Section 2. Fort Loudon (U.S. Rte. 30) to mouth						
Gradient	Difficulty	Distance	Time	Width	Scenery	Map
7	A to 2–	21.4	7.0	30-60	Good	31

TRIP DESCRIPTION: At Fort Loudon, the West Branch leaves the mountains behind and spends its last miles winding about a wide valley. The scenery is predominately agricultural, with high banks partially obscuring visibility above Pa. Rte. 16, but with lower banks and improved visibility below Rte. 16. The stream hurries over plenty of riffles in its first few miles, but then slows to only fast flat water, occasional riffles, and easy rapids. You must carry a five-foot mill dam at Heisey Road (on left, across private property) and another five-footer a half mile below Licking Creek (also on left). Take out at SR3004, a quarter mile above the mouth. A recommended run is from Pa. Rte. 16, on the West Branch, to Cearfoss Pike, on the main stem, a total distance of 15 miles. Take-out access there, unfortunately, is now confined to a steep and long carry on the left, at the old bridge.

HAZARDS: Two small dams and possible fences.

WATER CONDITIONS: Canoeable winter and spring within a week of hard rain.

GAUGE: Judge riffles at Fort Loudon. Fairview USGS gauge (call Washington, see USGS website, or inspect on site) should be at least 500 cfs (2.6 feet). As a rough correlation, the USGS gauge at Hogestown, on the north-flowing Conodoguinet Creek (call State College or see USGS website), should be at least 520 cfs (2.2 feet).

Something Else To Think About

Because the scenery along these little creeks is so often closed in, it gives you, the paddler, a lot of time to contemplate trees. In doing so, you will find that a handful of species dominate the stream-bank scenery here and on most other streams from the Fall Line west to the Allegheny Front. The most prominent is the sycamore, which is recognized by its often impressive dimensions, its fuzzy brown seed balls, and its gray and pure white mottled bark that contrasts so brilliantly against a blue winter sky. Also, if one of your childhood pleasures was crunching through leaves in the late fall, then you should remember the big, brown, and curled sycamore leaf as the prize crunchable. Probably just as common as the sycamore is the silver maple, identified by its smooth, gray bark (not as smooth as beech) and thin-lobed leaves. The willow, especially black willow, displays long, thin branches bristling with long, thin leaves. The box elder has toothed, oval leaves in clusters of three, looking awfully similar to poison ivy. But this tree is most conspicuous after the leaves have fallen, exposing curtains of winged seeds that at a distance add a pastel hue, reminiscent of spring buds, to the stream-bank scenery. Finally, you may see the river birch, which you recognize by the curls of paperlike bark that peel from its trunk.

These trees live along the banks because they love water, lots of it. With the water table only a few feet below the surface, they require only a shallow root system to meet their needs. Shallow root systems, unfortunately, make poor anchors, and that is why water and wind topple so many of these giants across your favorite creeks. These species have little commercial value, so about the only other threats to their longevity are hungry beavers and the occasional foolish farmer who chops them down to gain a few more square feet of pasture.

Antietam Creek

INTRODUCTION: Antietam Creek drains the eastern edge of Maryland's Cumberland Valley, beneath the western slope of South Mountain. It is born at the confluence of the West and East branches, just north of the Mason-Dixon Line, and winds and twists for almost 41 miles to the Potomac River. It joins the Potomac just below Shepherdstown, West Virginia. This scenic country creek has long been a favorite for novice whitewater paddlers.

Section 1. Confluence E. and W. branches to Security, Md.						
Gradient	Difficulty	Distance	Time	Width	Scenery	Map
6	A to 1	12.3	3.5	30-50	Good	32

TRIP DESCRIPTION: The trip begins on the East Branch at Pa. Rte. 316, just a few feet above the point where the West Branch joins. This section of Antietam twists and turns through attractive farm country that is complemented by the normal array of big, decorated barns and sturdy, old farmhouses. The narrow stream is always fairly swift, and there are plenty of riffles. There is a scrapey three-and-a-half-foot weir to carry about two miles below Old Forge Road and a four-foot weir (with a nasty roller) located at the take-out, which is where Antietam Drive touches the creek at Security.

HAZARDS: Avoid the two weirs mentioned above, and watch for possible fences and fallen trees.

WATER CONDITIONS: Runnable winter and spring within a week of moderate rain.

Antietam Creek

32

GAUGE: There is no convenient gauge. The USGS gauge at Burnside Bridge (call Washington, see USGS website, or inspect on site) should read over 675 cfs (3.8 feet).

Section 2. Security to Funkstown (Oak Ridge Road)						
Gradient	Difficulty	Distance	Time	Width	Scenery	Map
4	A to 1	5.8	1.5	50-60	Poor	32

TRIP DESCRIPTION: Most paddlers will choose to bypass this section as much of it is relatively ugly. The attractive rural landscape of the upper section now yields to houses, unsightly commercial buildings, an old power plant, and an obnoxious quantity of stream bank trash. The water is mostly flat, part of it being the backwater of a three-foot weir at the former power plant (now a paper recycling plant) below Mt. Aetna Road. But you can finish with a splash by running a short, rocky rapid beneath the Oak Ridge Road bridge at Funkstown.

HAZARDS: Weir described above.

WATER CONDITIONS: Runnable most of normal winter and spring.

GAUGE: None.

Section 3. Funkstown (Oak Ridge Road) to Antietam (Harpers Ferry Road)						
Gradient	Difficulty	Distance	Time	Width	Scenery	Map
7	A to 2–	23.4	7.0	50-100	Good	32

TRIP DESCRIPTION: Except for some lingering odors from the local sewage treatment plant, Antietam Creek quickly recovers from its bad urban trip. Once past I-70, the scenery and atmosphere are again delightfully rural. In fact, on this section the human influence has enhanced its beauty and interest. Several graceful stone arch bridges, crumbling mills, and old farmhouses, also constructed from the plentiful native limestone, lend an Old-World charm to the journey. The mills have also served to spice up the run, as their crumbling or crumbled dams form some interesting and sometimes relatively heavy rapids at Poffenberger Road, Wagaman Road, Roxbury Road, Md. Rte. 34, and just above the take-out at the village of Antietam. Still intact is a six-foot dam at Devils Backbone Park (Md. Rte. 68), and this requires a carry. An old three-foot dam, about a mile downstream of Backbone Park, is in an advanced stage of obliteration and is easily negotiated. But its remaining chunks might create some rough water when the creek is high. In between all of this artificial whitewater are numerous riffles formed by low ledges and gravel. The lower portion of this section winds through Antietam Battlefield, Maryland's only major Civil War engagement.

Harpers Ferry Road, located a quarter mile above the mouth, is the most convenient take-out. But if you are a purist, you can continue to the mouth and then paddle up the Potomac a hundred yards to a well-worn, informal take-out below a C&O Canal campground.

HAZARDS: Dam at Devils Backbone Park.

WATER CONDITIONS: This is runnable through most of any normal winter and spring, except after a prolonged rainless period.

GAUGE: There is a USGS gauge by the old Burnside Bridge in the Antietam Battlefield (call Washington, see USGS website, or inspect on site). The phone/internet-reported levels should read at least 480 cfs (3.4 feet) feet to start at Funkstown, 220 cfs (2.8 feet) to start at Devils Backbone, and 165 cfs

(2.6 feet) to start near Keedysville. When using this gauge, keep in mind that, at least at lower levels, the reading reported on the internet or forecast recording is about a tenth of a foot lower than what you personally would read on the damaged outside staff.

Roots And Origins

The Antietam Valley and nearby Conococheague, Catoctin, and Monocacy valleys were settled in the mid 18th century by Pennsylvanians of German extraction (Pennsylvania Dutch). Most of these people had originally migrated from the fertile farmlands of the Palatinate section of Germany, and the rich farming tradition that they carried with them shows today in the neat, well-tended farms of southeast Pennsylvania and central Maryland. In the mid 18th century the proprietorship of Maryland, anxious to settle and stabilize its frontier and recognizing this group's skills and potential permanence, offered families 200 acres apiece of free land to lure them across the border. It worked, as told by geographical names like Funkstown, Myersville, Zullinger, Altenwald, and Poffenberger Road, which dot the countryside.

West and East Branches of Antietam Creek

INTRODUCTION: The West and East branches of Antietam Creek gather their waters from the farmlands and mountainsides surrounding Waynesboro, Pennsylvania. Considering how much interest, charm, and pleasure the main stem of Antietam offers, these branches seem to be improbable headwaters. One meanders its way through mediocrity, while the other is endowed with stretches fit for ex-Kamikaze pilots only. But to appease the curious, this is what you can expect to find just north of the Mason-Dixon Line.

Section 1. West Branch: Pa. Rte. 316 to mouth						
Gradient	Difficulty	Distance	Time	Width	Scenery	Map
16	A to 1	5.2	2.0	25-35	Fair	33

TRIP DESCRIPTION: The West Branch meanders about the open farmlands west of Waynesboro. The put-in is in a cow pasture, and that is the story much of the way. While the valley is attractive, eroded mud banks detract from and sometimes block the scenery. The water is fast, but gentle riffles make the only whitewater. Fences and trees repeatedly block the way and will plague the novice paddler, the kind of paddler for whom this run would otherwise be so suited. Take out at SR2006, just above the confluence with the East Branch.

HAZARDS: Trees and fences.

WATER CONDITIONS: Passable winter and spring within two days of rain.

GAUGE: None. For rough correlation, the USGS gauge (call Washington or see USGS website) at Burnside Bridge, on the Antietam, should read over 770 cfs (4.0 feet).

West Branch Antietam Creek
East Branch Antietam Creek

Old Forge Picnic Area

N

0.5

Antietam Creek

2.7

GLEN FORNEY

To Chambersburg

FISH & GAME RD
(2007)

2007

MENTZER GAP RD
(2007)

Creek

1.4

316

PRICES CHURCH RD

Dam

COUNTRY CLUB RD

Branch

997

To Greencastle

16

0.9

2.8

WAYNESBORO

OLD FORGE RD
(2007)

COLDSPRING RD
(T366)

Antietam

MARSH RD (2002)

(2012)

WAYNE
HEIGHTS

316

East

16

ROUZERVILLE

1.3

WELTY RD

West Branch

2.9

(T370)

PENNSYLVANIA

RD

997

0.9

LYONS

1.9

GOODS
DAM RD

IRON BRIDGE RD
(2006)

MARYLAND

33

60

To Hagerstown

Section 2. East Branch: Old Forge to Pa. Rte. 316						
Gradient	Difficulty	Distance	Time	Width	Scenery	Map
34	1 to 3+	9.9	3.0	20-40	Fair	33

TRIP DESCRIPTION: The East Branch starts out as a tiny terror dropping off the west slope of South Mountain at a gradient in excess of a hundred feet per mile. Put in at the Mont Alto Forest road bridge below Old Forge, or you can even start another three quarters of a mile upstream where the Appalachian Trail crosses the creek at the upstream end of the state forest picnic area. But only put in here if you have superb ability at stopping on a narrow, eddyless torrent or at abandoning ship in a flash, for fallen trees repeatedly block your way. The gradient gradually lessens, but trees and, later on, fences persist. The scenery, for which you will only have fleeting seconds to see while paddling, consists initially of pretty woodlands. But summer homes dot the valley downstream.

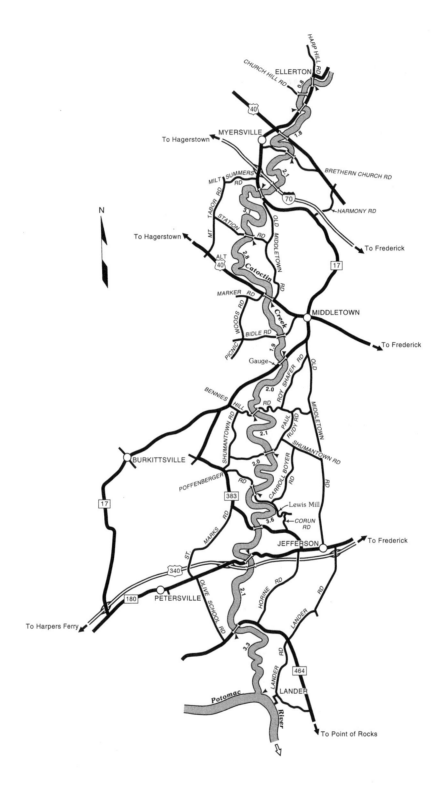

Catoctin Creek

By the time the East Branch reaches the Waynesboro Country Club (SR2007), the whitewater has mellowed substantially, but the creek remains mean. Passing through the golf course, the creek braids into several channels that would be canoeable if it were not for the frequent low foot bridges. At the lower end of the golf course the channels rejoin, and the stream then drops over a five-foot weir. Carry this on the right. Below the course, trees and fences continue to create an occasional annoyance.

The final four miles below Pa. Rte. 16 are usually free of trees and fences, and the segment is suitable for novices. The current is swift, and there are still plenty of riffles. The scenery assumes the typical rural landscape of the Antietam Valley.

HAZARDS: The upper creek is a high-speed obstacle course. The obstacles — trees and fences — appear as far down as Rte. 16. But with each mile downstream, negotiating them becomes more reasonable. Be prepared to carry foot bridges and a weir at the golf course.

WATER CONDITIONS: Canoeable winter and spring within a day of hard rain above Rte. 16 and within three days below.

GAUGE: None. For a rough correlation, the USGS gauge at at Burnside Bridge (call Washington or see USGS website), on the Antietam, should read at least 850 cfs (4.2 feet) for the far upper section and 720 cfs (3.9 feet) for the lower four miles.

Catoctin Creek

INTRODUCTION: Running down the western edge of Frederick County, Catoctin Creek drains the beautiful, rolling farmland of the Middletown Valley, between South and Catoctin mountains. It is a popular and delightful springtime novice run for those competent enough to handle sharp turns and occasional surprise strainers.

Section 1. Myersville (Brethern Church Road) to Middletown (Md. Rte. 17)						
Gradient	Difficulty	Distance	Time	Width	Scenery	Map
28	1	9.9	3.0	25-40	Good	34

TRIP DESCRIPTION: The recommended put-in is located just below U.S. Rte. 40. But it is possible for more experienced paddlers to start about four and a half miles upstream where Rte. 17 crosses the creek above Ellerton (at the intersection of Highland School Road) and enjoy a more challenging run over a steep and rocky bed complicated by fences, trees, and low-water bridges. This upper reach goes by the name of Middle Creek. The section below Brethern Church Road abounds with easy, gravel type riffles, but sharp bends and occasional fences or fallen trees can add a bit of challenge here. The surrounding countryside is mainly pastoral, but the noise from I-70 tends to disrupt the rural serenity that should fit with the scenery. So far, suburban encroachment on this valley is visible from the creek only near Myersville and Middletown.

HAZARDS: Trees and fences.

WATER CONDITIONS: Runnable winter and spring within two days of hard rain.

GAUGE: There is a USGS gauge downstream of the Rte. 17 bridge, south of Middletown. A reading of 2.5 feet is minimal.

Section 2. Middletown (Md. Rte. 17) to mouth						
Gradient	Difficulty	Distance	Time	Width	Scenery	Map
11	1	15.1	4.5	30-50	Good	34

TRIP DESCRIPTION: These miles of Catoctin Creek are deeply cut into the bottom of this rugged valley. The scenery is of pastoral and wooded hillsides; the whitewater is of numerous, easy riffles; and the fence/tree problems are only occasional. In addition to enjoying Catoctin's natural attractions, you may also find the old Lewis Mill of interest. Located along the creek, below Poffenberger Road, this attractive 180-year-old structure also features a complete solar heating system and a pottery studio and shop.

Many paddlers, preferring a convenient take-out and a shorter trip, finish the run at Md. Rte. 464, three miles above the Potomac. There is no road access to the mouth. So those preferring to go the whole way can take out at the state boaters' access at Lander, a half mile down the Potomac, or continue another two and a half miles to Point of Rocks (state landings at both ends of the U.S. Rte. 15 bridge). To reach the Lander take-out, cross the railroad tracks at the upstream end of town, turn left, follow the tracks for about 200 yards, and then follow the first road to the right.

HAZARDS: Possible trees or fences.

WATER CONDITIONS: Runnable winter and spring within three or four days of hard rain.

GAUGE: The USGS gauge at Rte. 17, south of Middletown, should read at least 2.3 feet.

Monocacy River

INTRODUCTION: The Monocacy is the second largest tributary to the Potomac in Maryland, draining almost a thousand square miles of prime agricultural land in Adams County, Pennsylvania, and Frederick, Carroll, and Montgomery counties in Maryland. Only the Shenandoah and the South and North branches of the Potomac, the first two being in Virginia and West Virginia, drain greater areas. The Monocacy's size makes it one of the more reliably floatable streams in the state. And that makes this stream a welcome commodity in this state of small creeks.

The river is officially born at the confluence of Marsh Creek and Rock Creek, right on the Mason-Dixon Line. In its passage to the Potomac, it collects several small tributaries that, if caught in wet weather, offer attractive and sometimes even exciting cruising. The scenery on this river is remarkably consistent, typified by a wooded bluff on one side, fields and farms on the other, and a million gawking cattle. The river is also consistent, typified by a generally strong current broken by an occasional approximation of a riffle. The scenery, unfortunately, suffers from too many over-the-bank trash dumps, the remains of which are usually strewn for miles downstream, and the water suffers from agricultural pollution, mostly a lot of mud and byproducts of gawking cattle. All in all though, it is a good retreat for a quiet day in the outdoors, relatively close to the population centers of the state.

Monocacy River
Toms Creek

35

**Monocacy River
Linganore Creek
Bennett Creek**

To Thurmont

To Baltimore

MT. PLEASANT

26

OLD ANNAPOLIS

2.4

McKAIG RD

GAS

HOUSE PIKE

75

15

3.5

4.5

HOUSE PIKE

Creek

2.3

LINGANORE RD

BOYERS

2.3

To Hagerstown

40

Dam

4.3

MILL RD

NEW LONDON RD

OLD

FREDERICK

Park

Lingnore

MARKET ST

GAS

PATRICK ST

To Hagerstown

70

SOUTH ST

144

NEW MARKET

340

15

REICHS

Park

70 40

To Baltimore

To Harpers Ferry

355

1.8

FORD RD

MONROVIA

REELS MILL RD

BALL

75

85

4.3

ARMBY CHURCH RD

BAKER VALLEY RD

270

80

N

BUCKEYSTOWN

Dam

80

URBANA

MICHAEL MILL RD

Park

FLINT HILL RD

MONOCACY BOTTOM RD

PARK MILLS RD

THURSTON RD

Creek

2.6

River

3.3

1.6

Dam

Bennett

4.3

DIXON RD

To Washington

OLAND RD

LILY

PONS RD

Gauge

THURSTON RD

CRISS FORD RD

MILLS RD

MT. EPHRAIM RD

Monocacy

2.5

85

Access

PARK RD

1.9

28

River

1.9

Potomac

Access

MOUTH OF MONOCACY RD

DICKERSON

Access

36

Section 1. Harney Road to mouth						
Gradient	Difficulty	Distance	Time	Width	Scenery	Map
3	A to 1	57.3	17.0	70-250	Fair to Good	35,36

TRIP DESCRIPTION: You can easily cover this river by dividing it into four moderately lengthed sections: Harney Road to Md. Rte. 77, a distance of 16 miles; Md. Rte. 77 to Devilbiss Bridge Road, 12 miles; Devilbiss Bridge Road to Pinecliff Park, 14 miles; and Pinecliff Park to the Potomac River, 16 miles. Or you can select your own length using any pair of at least 20 bridge crossings.

The stream from Harney to Rte. 77 is relatively narrow and, though mostly flat, is quite swift. A group can easily cover these miles in five hours of easy paddling at moderate water levels. About two miles below the start is Starners Dam, a three-foot weir that you should carry. There is a runnable two-foot weir about a quarter mile above the railroad bridge near Rocky Ridge. Except for some summer camps around Starners Dam, the scenery is typical Monocacyscape, wooded bluffs and pretty farms with occasional views of distant Catoctin Mountain.

Rte. 77, at which there is reasonable access at its southwest end, is conveniently located. For at Rte. 77, Double Pipe Creek joins and doubles the flow. The Monocacy responds by widening, slowing down, and by becoming even flatter than before, with the exception of one lively riffle at LeGore Bridge, an easy rapid through the remains of a low rubble weir near Buckeystown, and a series of rocky riffles above Park Mills bridge. From Rte. 77 to the Potomac the scenery changes little. In spite of encroaching suburbia, the view from the river remains remarkably uncluttered. The trip ends at the beautiful white arches of the old C&O Canal aqueduct. You reach this point from Rte. 28, east of the river, via Mouth of Monocacy Road.

HAZARDS: Carry the three-foot weir that is located about two miles below Harney Road.

WATER CONDITIONS: Runnable usually throughout any normal late fall, winter, spring, and early summer, up to mid-July. Summer shower activity often raises the river below Rte. 77 to passable levels even in late summer and fall.

GAUGE: For river above Rte. 77, use the USGS gauge at Rte. 140, near Bridgeport (see USGS website). Minimum is about 150 cfs (3.1 feet). A less reliable fall-back would be the USGS gauge near Frederick (call Washington or see USGS website). Minimum is likely to be about 750 cfs (2.9 feet). For the rest of the river, use the Frederick gauge. Minimum for the river between Rte. 77 and Rte. 26 is 350 cfs (2.1 feet) and for below Rte. 26 is 215 cfs (1.7 feet).

Head For the Hills

The western edge of the Monocacy Valley is dominated by the gentle bulk of Catoctin Mountain. Over 10,000 acres of this spur of the Blue Ridge, west of Thurmont, are protected and available for the public's enjoyment, as they lie within the bounds of Catoctin Mountain Park and Cunningham Falls State Park. The parks feature over 25 miles of hiking trails (which in winter make dandy cross-country skiing trails), nature trails and interpretive exhibits, campgrounds, swimming, lake and trout stream fishing, and points of interest such as Catoctin Furnace, Wolf Rock, and Cunningham Falls. It is a fine place to retreat to when your knees cannot take another hour in the canoe.

Marsh Creek
Rock Creek

To Chambersburg
SEVEN STARS

To Carlisle

To York

To Harrisburg

To Ortanna

30

34

30

116

GETTYSBURG

116

To Hanover

KNOXLYN RD

(3013)

BLACKHORSE

3.2

15

KNOXLYN-ORTANNA RD

TAVERN RD (T334)

116

CONFEDERATE AVE

BLACKSMITH SHOP RD

KNOBR RD (T325)

SCOTT RD (T331)

2.8

Gettysburg
National
Military
Park

HOSPITAL RD

3.5

97

To Westminster

(3005)

Dam

Creek

1.3

RD (T327)

SACHS RD (T417)

GOULDEN RD (T417)

Creek

WHITE CHURCH (T412)

PUMPING STATION RD

WATER WORKS

SCHRIVER RD (T328)

Marsh

1.6

BUS 15

SOLOMON RD

2.3

(T411)

CUNNINGHAM RD

(3006)

BARLOW-GREENMOUNT RD

RD

BULLFROG RD (3005)

(3008)

0.9

GREENMOUNT

BARLOW

To Two Taverns

BARLOW-TWO TAVERNS RD (2001)

ORPHANAGE RD (2010)

N

Dam

MARSH CREEK RD

2.6

BARLOW RD (2001)

3.0

134

YINGLING RD (T410)

FAIRPLAY

T404

RIDGE RD

15

NATURAL (T401)

DAM RD

(3002)

MASON-DIXON RD (3006)

1.4

(3002)

(T402) HORNER RD

MASON-DIXON RD

1.6

To Frederick

PENNSYLVANIA

2.0

River

MARYLAND

←BULLFROG RD

BOLLINGER SCHOOL RD

HARNEY RD

HARNEY

To Taneytown

37

Marsh Creek

INTRODUCTION: Marsh Creek drains the Blue Ridge foothills west of Gettysburg, Pennsylvania, pooling its waters with those of Rock Creek's, to form Maryland's Monocacy River. It flows through an attractive valley occupied by dairy farms and orchards—a picture of timeless tranquility. But this valley is best known for three days in July of 1863, when it was anything but tranquil. On those three days, the forces of the Civil War pitted 84,000 Union soldiers against 75,000 Confederate soldiers on the height of land between Marsh and Rock creeks. When the dust had cleared, over 50,000 casualties had earned the Battle of Gettysburg the distinction of being the bloodiest engagement of the Civil War. A trip on Marsh Creek gives you a perfect excuse to visit the nearby national military park and relive this important moment in our history.

Section 1. Seven Stars (U.S. Rte. 30) to Bus. Rte. 15						
Gradient	**Difficulty**	**Distance**	**Time**	**Width**	**Scenery**	**Map**
9	A to 1,2–	9.8	3.5	25-75	Very Good	37

TRIP DESCRIPTION: What a fine way to tour beautiful, rural Adams County, Pennsylvania. When not winding through deep woods, Marsh Creek glides past lovely, well-kept dairy farms, marked by herds of sleek cattle, sturdy old farm houses, and big, brightly painted barns decorated with hex signs. Because its banks are low, the paddler enjoys liberal views of all that is worth seeing.

Complicated only by a few downed trees early in the trip and one rocky rapid at the ruins of an old milldam, this section is suitable for novices. Generally smooth and straightforward riffles typify the run. One carry will be necessary to avoid a sharp, two-foot weir below the covered bridge downstream of SR3005.

HAZARDS: A weir at the Gettysburg Water Works and fallen trees.

WATER CONDITIONS: Canoeable winter and spring within two or three days of hard rain.

GAUGE: None on creek. Roughly, the USGS gauge near Bridgeport, on the Monocacy (see USGS website), should be over 300 cfs (3.6 feet). An even rougher indicator is the USGS gauge at Frederick (call Washington or see USGS website). It should be over 1,800 cfs (4.5 feet).

Section 2. Bus. Rte. 15 to Harney Road						
Gradient	**Difficulty**	**Distance**	**Time**	**Width**	**Scenery**	**Map**
12*	A to 3	6.0	2.0	50-100	Fair	37
*1 @ 40fpm						

TRIP DESCRIPTION: This section starts off with mostly flat water and another weir to carry (durable boats can clunk over), while flowing through fair scenery marred by summer homes. But after passing beneath U.S. Rte. 15, the creek cuts a short, wooded gorge through the hard diabase rock of Harpers Hill to create some interesting whitewater that climaxes with three exciting, complex, and boulder-choked rapids. Looking more like the Yough than Marsh Creek, this is by far the best piece of whitewater in the Monocacy Basin, short as it may be. The action concludes about a half mile below these rapids with a nasty plunge over a masonry-capped, four-foot ledge. You can run this via a tight slot to the right of center, or you can easily carry it. Below here Marsh Creek quickly reverts to its original tranquil pace and, except for easy rapid through a washed out dam below Rock Creek, stays that way to the Harney Road take-out, a half mile down the Monocacy.

HAZARDS: A thinly watered three-foot weir a half mile below Bus. Rte. 15, possible debris jams in rapids, and a sharp four-foot ledge below Harpers Hill Gorge.

WATER CONDITIONS: Same as Section 1.

GAUGE: Same as Section 1, except for below Natural Dam Road where minimum is about 150 cfs at Bridgeport..

Rock Creek

INTRODUCTION: Rock Creek is a generally mediocre stream that winds through mostly farmland, southeast of Gettysburg. Its waters are typically flat, and the scenery contains nothing particularly memorable. It is really not worth driving a long way for to paddle.

Section 1. Gettysburg (Pa. Rte. 97) to Harney Road						
Gradient	Difficulty	Distance	Time	Width	Scenery	Map
7	A to 1	10.4	3.5	20-50	Fair	37

TRIP DESCRIPTION: One can start on the southeast side of Gettysburg at Rte. 97, or if the water level is marginal, three and a half miles downstream at T411, below the welcome inflow of Littles Run. This first section, above T411, is drab and noisy, as it flows past a rock quarry and busy Rte. 15. Below here it is quieter. You occasionally see some pretty fern-fringed, shale outcrops and some attractive farm structures, but high mud banks tend to block any real views across the picturesque countryside. The only thing resembling whitewater on this trip is a curving rapid that dances through the ruins of an old dam above the take-out. The take-out is on the Monocacy, about a half mile below Marsh Creek. Best parking would be at the east approach of the Harney Road bridge.

HAZARDS: None normally. But fallen trees or a new fence are always a possibility.

WATER CONDITIONS: Canoeable in winter and spring within two days of hard rain.

GAUGE: None on creek. Roughly, USGS gauge near Bridgeport, on the Monocacy (see USGS website), should be over 300 cfs (3.6 feet). An even rougher indicator is the USGS gauge at Frederick (call Washington or see USGS website). It should be over 1,900 cfs (4.6 feet).

Toms Creek

INTRODUCTION: The waters of Toms Creek drain from the east slope of Catoctin Mountain near the Pennsylvania line west of Emmitsburg, Maryland. The creek offers the paddler a lot of easy whitewater while passing through a variety of attractive scenery which includes mountains, farms, and the campus of the National Emergency Training Center. It is a tiny and elusive stream that seldom carries canoe traffic.

Section 1. Carroll Valley (Pa. Rte. 16) to mouth						
Gradient	Difficulty	Distance	Time	Width	Scenery	Map
12	1 to 2–	10.7	4.0	14-40	Good	35

TRIP DESCRIPTION: The put-in is about a mile northwest of the state line. Here the stream is clear and shallow, rushing over a gravel bottom at the foot of Catoctin Mountain. Your clear passage through the riffles may be complicated by fallen trees or strands of barbed wire. Also, about a hundred yards upstream of Business Rte. 15, look out for a four-foot dam that you should carry. You have the option of running another four-foot dam (with a clunk), this one located on the Training Center campus. At moderate levels this second dam has a safe playing hydraulic at the bottom.

Below Emmitsburg the gradient slows, but there are still plenty of riffles and a swift current to carry you through a pleasant pastoral landscape. Sixes Road, the last possible take-out on Toms Creek, is narrow and offers poor parking. So one might consider continuing a mile and a half downstream to Sixes Bridge on the Monocacy where conditions are slightly better.

HAZARDS: Be alert for trees and fences on the upper creek and for two dams, described above, around Emmitsburg.

WATER CONDITIONS: Found up in winter and spring within a few days of hard rain.

GAUGE: There is a staff gauge at Annandale Road, river left, on the upstream face of an old, stone bridge abutment. It should be at least 1.6 feet. Roughly, the USGS gauge on the Monocacy at Bridgeport (see USGS website) should be over 300 cfs (3.6 feet) and, even more roughly, the USGS gauge at Frederick should be over 1,900 cfs (4.6 feet).

Middle Creek

INTRODUCTION: Middle Creek is born on the eastern slope of the Blue Ridge Mountains, and from there it flows through a lightly populated valley in Adams County, Pennsylvania, and Frederick County, Maryland, to join Toms Creek near Emmitsburg. Although both the creek and its watershed are tiny, its forested mountain headwater drainage seems to sustain floatable water levels long enough for the lucky paddler to exploit it. The finest quality of this stream is the presence of a delightful mile and a half of whitewater in a little gorge above Harney Road. It is well worth a visit when all the streams in the neighborhood are brimming.

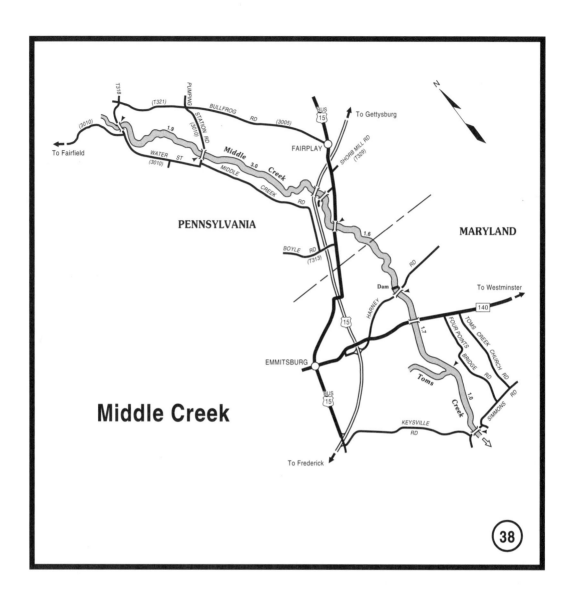

Middle Creek

38

Section 1. T318 to mouth						
Gradient	Difficulty	Distance	Time	Width	Scenery	Map
18*	A to 3–	8.2	2.5	15-25	Good	38
*1 @ 40fpm						

TRIP DESCRIPTION: The stream that you find at the put-in is not for the claustrophobic paddler, for it is only about 15 feet wide, and it squeezes even tighter downstream. Middle Creek starts off flowing over a bed that is peppered with fairly large, rounded boulders. But since the gradient is only modest, there is no great difficulty or danger here, just some interesting natural slaloming in a woodland setting. An occasional fallen tree and three stout cattle fences will require carries. The remaining miles to Business Rte. 15 wind in and out of fields and woods through what appears to be thinly settled countryside, which the paddler can easily view over the creek's low banks. The current through here is relatively sluggish, with only occasional riffles and easy rapids.

Below Business Rte. 15, Middle Creek begins an enjoyable descent, of low intermediate difficulty, over a rocky bed, through a gently sloped wooded gorge that cuts through the same mass of diabase rock that forms the exciting Harpers Hill Gorge on nearby Marsh Creek. The rapids are formed by small boulders and ledges. Although the rapids are neither as exciting nor as intense as those on Marsh Creek, the unusually sharp streambed rocks will keep you scrambling. The rapids end in the short pool of an eight-foot dam just upstream of Harney Road.

Harney Road marks a return to the mellow. Just below that bridge there is a sharp, two-foot weir that you can clunk over anywhere. After that the creek slows its pace, displaying at best some gentle riffles. Meanwhile, mud banks begin to rise and block out a large portion of the view of the pretty farm country beyond. There is no access to the mouth of Middle Creek, so continue another mile down Toms Creek to Keysville Road.

HAZARDS: Trees and fences will block the way on the upper stretches. Carry the old milldam above Harney Road on the left (easy). Be aware of the weir below Harney Road, especially when the water is very high.

WATER CONDITIONS: This is runnable within two days of hard rain, during winter or spring. Melting snow on Catoctin Mountain can sustain water even longer.

GAUGE: None. Judge conditions along the road near the put-in or at Harney Road, where the riffle below the dam should be clearly passable. Roughly, the USGS gauge on the Monocacy at Bridgeport (see USGS website) should be over 700 cfs (4.5 feet) and even more roughly, Frederick USGS gauge should be over 3,800 cfs (6.8 feet).

Big Pipe Creek

INTRODUCTION: Big Pipe Creek is the Monocacy's largest tributary. Together with its tributary, Little Pipe Creek, it drains much of the western half of Carroll County, flowing peacefully through a markedly rolling countryside of woodlands and well-kept dairy farms. In spite of its mild gradient, Pipe Creek, like other streams of the Piedmont, was once extensively exploited for its water power. Today five old mills still stand along the miles described below as reminders of the importance of even these two-bit cow pasture brooks to the development of this country.

Section 1. Mayberry Road to Detour (Md. Rte. 77)						
Gradient	Difficulty	Distance	Time	Width	Scenery	Map
9	A to 1	16.4	5.0	25-80	Good	39

TRIP DESCRIPTION: It is possible, right after a hard rain, to start at least as far up as Union Mills, Rte. 97, where Big Pipe is just a brook. These six miles reward you with some beautiful old mills (but no accompanying dams), including one at the put-in, and good scenery of fields, farms, and woods. The gradient is mild, and there are no difficult rapids. In fact, the water is mostly smooth. But fallen trees, barbed wire fences, beaver dams, and some wandering channels add some hardship to these miles. So the really inexperienced should start no higher than Mayberry Road.

Big Pipe Creek
Little Pipe Creek

To Thurmont

Monocacy River

Double Pipe Creek

77 1.6

DETOUR

B

3.6

C

3.1

A

Little

Gauge

194

To Emmitsburg

140

TANEYTOWN

To Frederick

194

Dam

KEYMAR

Big

2.2

CROUSE

MIDDLEBURG

2.0

MILL

RD

RD

RD

BROWN RD

Pipe

GOOD

SIMPSONS MILL RD

INTENT

JOHNSVILLE
RD

MIDDLEBURG

2.7

Pipe

HAPES MILL

RD

1.2

MILL

RD

TREVANION

SELLS

MILL

RD

HYSER

832

1.8

RD

Silver Run

Creek

4.3

RD

UNION BRIDGE

RD

OTTERDALE

Dam

2.0

1.3

1.8

140

BAYSHORES MILL

RD

UNGER

RD

RD

UNION BRIDGE

Creek

To New Market

Sams Creek

75

CLEAR

VIEW

RD

MAYBERRY

84

TYRONE

To Westminster

UNIONTOWN

A-NAYLORS MILL RD
B-SIXES BRIDGE RD
C-KEYSVILLE BRUCEVILLE RD

39

A bit more roomy and easier to catch Pipe Creek is born with the addition of Silver Run at May-berry Road. The initial few miles are still small, and a few trees and an occasional fence could impede your progress. But with the addition of Bear Branch and Meadow Branch, below Md. Rte. 832, the volume swells and the going gets easy. Just below Rte. 832 is a low-water bridge that at all but very high levels will demand a carry. There is a six-foot dam at Otterdale Mill. It has an easy carry on the right. This pretty, white mill still uses the waters of Pipe Creek for energy, not to grind grain anymore, but to directly power the compressors for a refrigeration unit. The closest thing to whitewater on Big Pipe are well-spaced gravel bar riffles, snag washovers, and an occasional, tiny rock weir.

This is a pretty creek. The scenery includes well-kept farms, overgrown fields, cool hemlock-cov-ered bluffs, and low sandstone and shale cliffs. They really know how to create lovely and lasting houses around these parts too, as evidenced, for example, by the proud old structure at Trevanion Road.

Little Pipe Creek joins just above the town of Detour, and the enlarged stream is now named Double Pipe Creek. Incidentally, Detour was once also called Double Pipe Creek, but the Western Maryland Railroad needed a shorter name to fit on their timetable. So for some unknown reason the name Detour was adopted. Detour is an easy and convenient place to take out. But if you are a purist, you can continue another mile and a half to Md. Rte. 77, just below the confluence with the Monocacy.

HAZARDS: Most people usually want to carry the low-water bridge by the park below Rte. 832 and the six-foot dam at Otterdale Mill.

WATER CONDITIONS: This is best caught up winter and spring within two days of hard rain. Unfortunately for we paddlers, water runs off faster in streams draining into the Monocacy from the agricultural lands to the east than from the forested slopes of Catoctin Mountain.

GAUGE: The USGS gauge at Bruceville, downstream left of the Md. Rte. 194 bridge, should read at least 1.7 feet (the outside staff only goes as high as 3.3 feet). For a rougher guess, the USGS gauge at Frederick, on the Monocacy (call Washington or see USGS website), should read approximately 1,450 cfs (4.0 feet) to negotiate the entire run.

Little Pipe Creek

INTRODUCTION: Little Pipe Creek starts on the west side of Westminster, Maryland, seat of beautiful, rural Carroll County. It gathers enough water to float a canoe by the time it reaches the town of Union Bridge and from there twists and turns along the Frederick County line to join Big Pipe Creek at Detour.

If we talked about streams as we do about some people, one would be tempted to call Little Pipe Creek a nerd. But if you look beyond the superficial perspective of the low-travelling paddler, it is not such a bland place. For example, the Little Pipe Creek Valley gives the impression of being just wall-to-wall farmland. But do not be fooled. Underlying this area are extensive mineral deposits, and there has been considerable activity about this region to extract this wealth. During colonial times copper was mined southeast of Johnsburg. And Maryland's only lead mine operated near Union Bridge around 1880. Today the most valuable mineral mined here is limestone. The huge Lehigh Portland Cement plant at Union Bridge consumes massive quantities of limestone pulled from its quarries along Sams Creek and farther up Little Pipe near New Windsor. Other quarries in the neighborhood mine the stone for use as aggregate for construction. Even the shale around here has worth as Lehigh Portland mines the material from a deposit southwest of here, near Woodsboro, where it roasts the rock to produce a special form of light-weight aggregate. So as you can see, for even the dullest of streams, there is often more to it than the rows of mud banks that meet the eye.

Section 1. Union Bridge (Md. Rte. 75) to Detour (Md. Rte. 77)						
Gradient	**Difficulty**	**Distance**	**Time**	**Width**	**Scenery**	**Map**
8	A to 1	9.6	3.0	20-40	Fair	39

TRIP DESCRIPTION: The suggested trip starts at Union Bridge, so named as the original bridge here over Pipe Creek united several Quaker settlements in the area. The start is hardly inspiring as the scenery, which includes houses, trash, and scrubby vegetation, is mostly drab, and the stream may be blocked by logjams or fences. Below Sams Creek, the volume increases enough to flush out most obstacles, and the scenery improves progressively with the appearance of pretty farms and small, red cliffs. Most of the water is flat. But a sharp, three-foot dam, located beneath the Conrail trestle above Rte. 194 requires a short but brushy carry. The take-out is just a short float down Double Pipe Creek.

HAZARDS: Trees, logjams, and fences come and go, mostly in the first few miles, and an unrunnable three-foot dam above Rte. 194 seems there to stay.

WATER CONDITIONS: Runnable winter and spring within two days of hard rain.

GAUGE: None. USGS gauge at Frederick, on the Monocacy (call Washington or see USGS website) should usually read at least 1,800 cfs (4.5 feet).

The Plague Of Fences

Certainly fences must be the most sinister trap found on the river. This bane of small stream enthusiasts is generally placed there by the farmers for the purpose of restraining their livestock. For while the cold, swollen torrent on which you are paddling may seem to be an effective enough barrier to these creatures, remember that in a few months, or even a few days, all that may remain are a few inches of easily fordable water. The most common variety of fences are barbed wire, electric, large-mesh woven wire, and board.

Barbed wire is the most frightening fence because of its potential to maim and its poor visibility until it is too late. Accordingly, one who travels a barbed wire infested stream while pushing darkness, paddling into the glare of the early morning or late afternoon sun, or paddling through a fog is really playing floating Russian roulette. Fortunately, there is often some slack in the stream-spanning strands of barbed wire. In such cases it is usually possible to avoid a carry by having one member of the party wade out (from downstream) and either lift or lower the strand for safe clearance of their companions.

You can recognize electric fences in that they are suspended from ceramic insulators. There is usually only a single strand of electrified wire. Contact with electric fences will not fry you, but it is certainly uncomfortable. These barriers work on the principle that after the average cattle bumps into a strand and is shocked by it, the beast will painstakingly avoid that strand ever after. This is so effective that after all of the cattle in a herd are "educated," it is seldom necessary to run the current through the wire. Only people, especially dumb paddlers, seem to never learn.

There is little to elaborate about woven fences. Just stay away from them as they are the ultimate in strainers. Also, remember that in their rusted state they can be difficult to see against a dark background.

Board fences consist of one or two stout cables from which are hung vertical wooden boards or sections of board fence. Locals often refer to these as cattle gates. When composed of sections, it is often possible to swing a section open enough to squeeze through a boat.

As vile as these contraptions are, please do not damage them as they are vital to the farmer-landowner. And if you really fear and detest fences, the best time to run a potentially fence infested stream is early spring after heavy ice has been broken out and flushed away by high water. Such an event will almost always rip out every lousy fence on the stream.

Linganore Creek

INTRODUCTION: Linganore Creek once offered a pleasant, uncomplicated cruise through the rolling farmlands of eastern Frederick County. Then, in the early '70s, private interests dammed the prettiest gorge on the creek to create a four-mile-long lake to be fringed by a housing development. You now get to run the leftovers.

Section 1. Md. Rte. 75 to mouth						
Gradient	Difficulty	Distance	Time	Width	Scenery	Map
11	A to 1	11.7	4.0	20-45	Fair	36

TRIP DESCRIPTION: This run starts out nicely enough, meandering through attractive woods and pastureland and past some pretty rock formations. The water is swift, muddy, and spotted with many easy riffles. This all ends below Gas House Pike with the backwater of Lake Linganore. The lake entails about four miles of deadwater paddling with scenery that is not particularly interesting unless you happen to be shopping for a homesite. The only reward for this lousy paddle, and a poor one at that, is to behold a relatively imaginative dam design. Back on a creek again, the scenery continues to be only fair as the route passes in and out of short, wooded gorges. The current remains swift. Linganore Road, about a quarter mile above the Monocacy, is your suggested take-out. For those who desire to float the whole way to the mouth, the next reasonable public access is one and a half miles down the Monocacy at Pinecliff Park.

HAZARDS: Carry Lake Linganore Dam on the left.

WATER CONDITIONS: Catch in winter and spring within a day of hard rain.

GAUGE: None. Very roughly, USGS gauge at Frederick, on the Monocacy (call Washington or see USGS website), should read at least 2,200 cfs (5.0 feet).

Bennett Creek

INTRODUCTION: Bennett Creek starts near Clarksburg, in western Montgomery County, flows into Frederick County, winds around the base of Sugarloaf Mountain, and empties into the Monocacy six miles above the mouth. It is a pleasant run through thinly populated, rolling, farm country that is probably doomed to become a part of suburbia. It is ideal for novices who are skilled enough to stop for trees, fences, and other strainers in a fast current.

Section 1. Md. Rte. 355 to mouth						
Gradient	Difficulty	Distance	Time	Width	Scenery	Map
11	A to 1	8.5	3.0	15-40	Good	36

Seneca Creek
Little Seneca Creek

TRIP DESCRIPTION: It is possible to drive right past this stream's put-in, as Bennett Creek is here only a 15-foot-wide brook meandering about a pastoral bottomland. Except for the persistent presence of a high voltage power line, this is a scenic cruise, passing mostly through farmlands above I-270 and mostly through woodlands below. The creek passes striking rock formations, well-preserved old houses, and the nearby bulk of lonely Sugarloaf Mountain. There are hundreds of little riffles over gravel bars and a few broken ledges. Fallen trees and logjams are common, but most have a passage around them. There is a low-water bridge about a mile below Little Bennett Creek that you must carry, and just below Park Mills Road bridge there is a four- and a half-foot dam. At least scout this. Take out at Lilypons Road bridge over the Monocacy, about a quarter mile below the confluence. You can save a steep carry by exiting just downstream, on the right, at the end of Criss Ford Road.

As you cruise down past the pretty hemlock-shaded slopes approaching Park Mills, try to picture yourself paddling through a major colonial industrial center. Almost 200 years ago a bustling, self-contained company town, structured around the manufacture of glass and peopled by over 300 immigrants (mostly German), was carved out of the wilderness near this spot. This was big-time industry by the standards of the time. Like many such ventures, it thrived for a while, then declined, and now birds, trees, and solitude give little hint of the area's former glory.

HAZARDS: You will encounter trees and logjams throughout, a low-water bridge below Little Bennett Creek, and a small dam below Park Mills. The dam is runnable in dead center, but it has a powerful reversal at the bottom that you had better consider most seriously before attempting.

WATER CONDITIONS: Canoeable winter and spring within two days of hard rain.

GAUGE: The USGS gauge on Mt. Ephraim Road, just upstream from Park Mills, should read at least 2.0 feet. To judge the level at the put-in, there should be at least six inches of water running over the little gravel riffle immediately below Rte. 355. Rough, remote indicators would be USGS gauges on Patuxent River near Unity (see USGS website) reading over 60 cfs (2.5 feet) and Seneca Creek at Dawsonville (call Washington or see USGS website) reading over 200 cfs (2.6 feet).

Seneca Creek

INTRODUCTION: Seneca Creek drains the heart of Montgomery County. Although the suburbs creep closer every year, it still affords a chance to paddle a small stream through fields and woods close to Washington, D.C. And with most of its miles now protected by Seneca Creek State Park, it looks as though we will continue to be able to enjoy this refuge for many years to come.

Section 1. Brink Road to Md. Rte. 28						
Gradient	Difficulty	Distance	Time	Width	Scenery	Map
10	A to 1	13.9	4.5	15-30	Fair to Good	40

TRIP DESCRIPTION: This section is officially called Great Seneca Creek, but it is really quite small. The stream winds about between often high mud banks through sometimes scrubby woods. Only a few power line crossings mar the sylvan solitude, while an occasional rock outcrop or hemlock-shaded bluff compensates for this. Above and below Clopper Road there is often some noise from some nearby shooting ranges. Though to my knowledge, no paddler has yet absorbed any stray bullets, at the range below Clopper Road the shooting is close enough that we have been showered by blasted shards of clay pigeons.

Seneca's mild gradient is expended over short gravel riffles, sand bars, and sunken logs. There are also a lot of deadfalls above the water and some huge logjams, many of which will block your way. But annual work trips conducted by the local canoe clubs have done much to reduce your carries. The best part of this section is located around Blackrock Mill Road, where the creek rushes through a pretty, wooded gorge, over some lively riffles, and past the old mill.

HAZARDS: Expect to carry fallen trees and logjams.

WATER CONDITIONS: Catch in winter and spring within a day of hard rain to start at Brink Road, and within a week of hard rain to start at Clopper Road. Expect this stream to become increasingly flashy as development covers more of the watershed.

GAUGE: The are USGS gauging stations on the right bank below Md. Rte. 28 bridge (see USGS website or call Washington) and on the left bank at Riffleford Road bridge (inspect on site). Respectively they should read at least 370 cfs (3.0 feet) and 4.5 feet to start as high as Brink Road and 170 cfs (2.5 feet) and 3.9 feet to start at Clopper Road.

Section 2. Md. Rte. 28 to mouth						
Gradient	Difficulty	Distance	Time	Width	Scenery	Map
7	A to 1	5.6	2.0	25-40	Fair to Good	40

TRIP DESCRIPTION: The stream, now joined by Little Seneca Creek, is a little larger, but still blocked occasionally by logs. It contains nothing more challenging than easy riffles, flowing over fine gravel and the crumbling ruins of an old weir. The view, when there is one, continues to be of fields and woods with a few pretty rock outcrops thrown in. The last half mile below River Road is a backwater of the Potomac. There is a public ramp at the old C&O Canal aqueduct, or you can avoid this section by exiting on the right, above River Road (private, ask permission), or left, about a hundred yards below the bridge.

HAZARDS: Strainers.

WATER CONDITIONS: Catch in winter or spring within a week of hard rain. Often passable into June.

GAUGE: USGS gauge at Rte. 28 should read at least 83 cfs (2.2 feet).

⎯ Little Seneca Creek ⎯

INTRODUCTION: Little Seneca Creek feeds its modest volume to Big Seneca Creek near Dawsonville. It offers two distinct paddling experiences—one for the pond paddler, the other for the creek boater. The former is the result of a 500-acre reservoir, named Little Seneca Lake, constructed to supplement the Washington Area's water supply in severe drought. Surrounded by Black Hill Regional Park, this is a quiet, safe and reliably watered refuge on the edge of the suburban tsunami. The latter is what remains of the natural creek, which is small and seldom runnable. And few paddlers would shed a tear if it were not for a patch of diabase, which is very hard rock. Little Seneca takes a rough ride as it flows across this patch, and its handful of resultant rapids has delighted most who have challenged its waters. This is a worthwhile outing if you live nearby.

Section 1. Little Seneca Lake						
Gradient	Difficulty	Distance	Time	Width	Scenery	Map
0	A	Variable	Variable	50-1,200	Fair to Good	40

TRIP DESCRIPTION: There is no recommended itinerary here. If you want to cut loose and closely follow the shoreline, you can do a circuit of about 13 miles. If you are looking for the most solitude and unspoiled scenery, head for the west arm or the upper east arm. Unfortunately, the park buffer does not screen the view of nearby neighborhoods to the east and south. The most desirable access is via formal launch sites, located on Clarksburg Road south of the bridge, on Black Hill Road, and near the Visitor Center. In season, you will share the lake with others (paddle craft and small sailboats), but fortunately no gasoline-powered motorboats.

Recreation here is regulated to the hilt. The most pertinent rule is that there is a launch fee. It is $4 for the daily permit (available at the launch sites) or $45 for a seasonal permit (available at Visitor Center). The lake is open during daylight hours only, from March 1 through December 15.

HAZARDS: None.

WATER CONDITIONS: Almost always full.

GAUGE: None.

Section 2. Hoyles Mill Road to mouth						
Gradient	Difficulty	Distance	Time	Width	Scenery	Map
19*	1 to 3–	3.6	1.5	15-25	Good	40
*0.5 @ 40fpm						

TRIP DESCRIPTION: The first interesting facet of this run is its put-in, which is a ford. Some paddlers have found amusement in driving their high-clearance vehicles right out into the torrent and unloading boats directly into the water, the ultimate in lazy person's launches. But be sure to check the depth before you try this stunt.

The muddy creek quickly reaches the diabase belt where it tumbles and twists through a series of boulder-clogged and fairly blind rapids. Below here the water quickly mellows to gravel-formed riffles, but look forward to a few fallen trees and maybe a fence to compound the difficulty. Take out a few yards down Seneca Creek at Md. Rte. 28.

Rounding out this run is pleasant scenery, mostly in the form of woods. Part of the surrounding land is park. Hopefully it will all be so someday, as the suburbs are rapidly closing in on the neighborhood.

HAZARDS: Trees and fences. The tight passages through the rapids also invite strainer problems.

WATER CONDITIONS: This is purely a flashy stream, so look for water only within 24 hours of a hard rain.

GAUGE: None on creek. But if the rains fell fairly evenly, the USGS gauge at Md. Rte. 28 (call Washington or see USGS website) should be at least 970 cfs (4.6 feet).

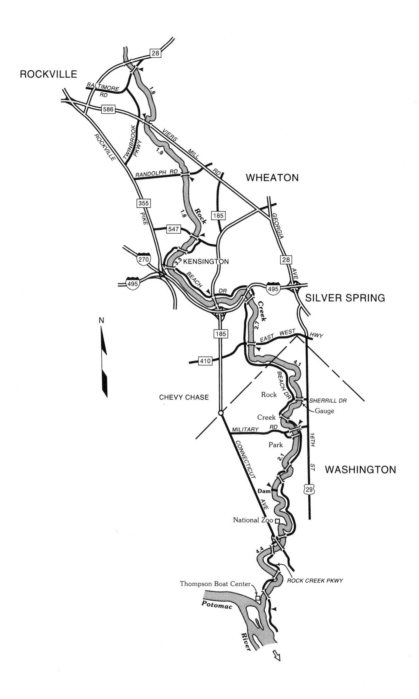

ROCKVILLE

WHEATON

KENSINGTON

SILVER SPRING

CHEVY CHASE

Rock
Creek
Park

WASHINGTON

SHERRILL DR
Gauge

National Zoo

Thompson Boat Center

ROCK CREEK PKWY

Potomac
River

N

Rock Creek

The Big Ditch

The longest nontidal waterway in the State of Maryland was at one time the 184.5-mile-long C&O Canal. This now mostly tree-filled ditch was conceived as a link between the early 19th-century port of Georgetown (part of what is now Washington, D.C.) and the vast, barely tapped market of the developing American midwest. As the name implies, the canal was to link the tidewater Chesapeake Bay, via Georgetown on the Potomac, to the Ohio River system. Construction started in 1828 and muddled along until 1850 and to Cumberland, Maryland. There financial difficulties spelled an end to further progress. Actually the canal was doomed from the start, for on the same day as its official groundbreaking ceremony, the B&O Railroad was also officially launched from Baltimore. The canal and the railroad engaged in a race for the west, a race that was easily won by the cheaper and technologically superior railroad. Nevertheless, the canal managed to survive until 1924 when one too many floods finally finished it off.

The engineering and construction of such a canal was no small feat in a day when earth moving was performed with only pick, shovel, wheelbarrow, and black powder. Just to get to Cumberland required constructing seven water supply dams across the Potomac, 74 lift locks, 11 stone aqueducts, and a 3,100-foot tunnel through a mountain (as a shortcut). Manning the project was a problem because the surrounding countryside was labor poor. So most workers had to be imported from overseas, especially Ireland. With all of these difficulties coupled with constantly tight money, it is a wonder that the glorious old ditch got as far as it did.

Today the canal and towpath are a recreational treasure. Twenty-two miles of the canal, from Georgetown to Violets Lock, and short sections near Oldtown and Big Pool are rewatered. Those desiring to paddle sections of the rewatered canal between Georgetown and Violets Lock can gain access at any of the points suggested for entering the parallel Potomac River. If you plan to do a continuous trip on this stretch, please note that at times certain segments may be dewatered. Almost always you can count on interruptions just below I-495 and a short gap below Great Falls. Also, an infestation of hydrilla has has pretty much rendered the watered reach from Carderock to Anglers Inn unfit for paddling, at least during summer. These rewatered segments offer not only beautiful calmwater canoeing, but also in a cold winter they convert to excellent outdoor ice skating rinks. The towpath is ideal for hiking, backpacking, and, upstream of Seneca, horseback riding. Are you tired of overcrowded, trailer-filled auto campgrounds? There are hiker-biker campsites about every five miles, outfitted with tables, latrines, and fireplaces, but inaccessible to cars. For an old weed-filled ditch, the C&O is not a bad place to visit.

Rock Creek

INTRODUCTION: Rock Creek slices down the middle of Montgomery County and Washington, D.C. to join the Potomac at Georgetown. Because it flows through a basin that has been almost completely urbanized, the creek has been reduced to functioning like a storm drain, with flows fluctuating in just a matter of hours between flash floods and trickles. Nevertheless, a spacious floodplain park in Montgomery County and, in Washington, one of the finest city parks in the nation, hide most of the surrounding sprawl from the paddler's sight. The creek is an ideal backyard refuge for those local paddlers who can get there in time. And even if you do get there too late to paddle, a system of horse and foot trails in D.C. and a bike trail in Maryland will allow you ample opportunity to at least follow Rock Creek along its banks.

Section 1. Rockville (Baltimore Road) to mouth						
Gradient	Difficulty	Distance	Time	Width	Scenery	Map
12*	1 to 3+	22.1	6.0	20-50	Good	41
*0.5 @ 80fpm						

TRIP DESCRIPTION: Most of the Montgomery County portion is characterized by fast flat water broken by easy gravel bar riffles. There are a lot of fallen or almost fallen trees, logjams, and snags in the upper part, but you can frequently paddle around or under them at medium levels. And at a few spots, oxbow channels offer fine bypasses around the tree-blocked main channel. A long, curving box culvert under the railroad tracks above Knowles Avenue offers a cheap thrill, flushing you through total darkness at high velocity. The entrance to at least one of the channels is usually obstructed.

The scenery behind the usually steep mud banks is mostly woods or open park land. Some highway noise, a few miles of Beltway, and festering clots of litter that collect against strainers are the only really obnoxious civilized intrusions. This section is at its best during summer when the dense foliage screens off much of the outside world, creating a steamy, jungle-like atmosphere.

As Rock Creek enters D.C., the surrounding slopes close in and form a lovely, shallow gorge that extends to the Potomac. At Military Road, the creek undergoes a total change in personality as the bottom suddenly drops out. This section plunges over the Fall Line at an initially violent rate of 80 feet per mile. There, sharp boulders fill the bed, current velocity increases, and the thick, muddy water reduces the visibility of underwater obstacles. The gradient eases off after a half mile and by Pierce Mill Dam, two miles below Military Road, the water is again mostly flat. Pierce Mill Dam is a picturesque, seven-foot-high structure with a churning, hungry-looking reversal at the bottom that makes a portage the best of decisions. Below here, Rock Creek is a smooth coast with only a few fords (scrapey), a low-water bridge, and pipe crossings to add excitement. A good bit of the right side below Pierce Mill is the National Zoo, where, if the wind is right, you may experience some unfamiliar sounds and smells. The exit into the Potomac is dramatic, with views of the Kennedy Center, Rosslyn, and the broad Potomac. Take out a few yards upstream at the docks of the Harry Thompson Boat Center (good parking just opposite Virginia Avenue).

Here is a final word of caution. The authorities frown on paddling the creek at rush hour because gawking motorists on nearby Beach Drive can easily be distracted into an accident which would quickly cause a mammoth traffic jam. This is a very real problem, so please stay away during rush hour.

With plentiful access, you can easily tailor a Rock Creek run to your tastes in distance or difficulty. You can squeeze in a few extra miles of scenic but logstrewn paddling by starting at Lake Needwood, Avery Road, or Southlawn Lane. East-West Highway is a good point at which to split the run described above. You can scout all of the D.C. section and part of Maryland from Beach Drive. But keep in mind that part of the D.C. portion of that road is closed to motor vehicles on weekends and other parts may be temporarily closed during rains because of flash flooding.

HAZARDS: Count on having to dodge or portage fallen trees, logjams, and, at high water, even floating picnic tables. Avoid Pierce Mill Dam (carried on right), about two miles below Military Road.

WATER CONDITIONS: Runnable within 24 hours of hard rain, but ideal water levels last for only a few hours after the rain stops.

GAUGE: There is a USGS gauge at Sherrill Drive (downstream left) with a staff on the right end of its weir. For the Fall Line section, about 2.5 feet is minimal and 5.0 feet is ideal. For the Fall Line, you alternatively can just scout t he first rapid or two below Military Road. For the rest of the creek, any riffle on a wide spot is an adequate indicator.

Anacostia River

Anacostia River

INTRODUCTION: The Anacostia is Washington's (and Maryland's) forgotten or, perhaps, ignored river. While the Potomac enjoys the title of "the nation's river," basks in the glow of Washington's monuments, and sparkles from a long and successful water pollution abatement program, the Anacostia remains the poor cousin. It flows through the rougher side of town and slinks in the shadow of power plants, freeways, and decaying neighborhoods. The quality of its relatively stagnant waters still leaves much to be desired. But do not write this off as a canoeing destination. For like the old brownstones of Capitol Hill, that have been restored from crumbling tenements to their former upscale glory, the Anacostia may be restored too. So if you live nearby, go decide for yourself.

Section 1. Alt. U.S. Rte. 1 to mouth						
Gradient	Difficulty	Distance	Time	Width	Scenery	Map
0	A	7.8	3.0	200-1,200	Fair	42

TRIP DESCRIPTION: Start at the public launching ramp, river left, just below Alt. Rte. 1 (Bladensburg Road). In colonial times, this point was the head of navigation for ocean-going ships. But years of siltation have left no evidence of this. Efforts to keep a channel by dredging have generated tons of muck that have been used to fill all the old marsh and bottomlands that once lined the Anacostia. So today the shape of the Anacostia is now mostly man-made. The riverside for the first mile is mostly undeveloped. Much of the parkland on the right side is reclaimed from an enormous, old municipal garbage dump. But this is not obvious, except for a few nostalgic-looking seagulls.

After passing beneath the busy Rte. 50 bridge, the river passes through a pleasing bit of swamp and marsh that at least looks fairly remote. There are backwaters here where you are likely to find abundant waterfowl. This area includes the beautiful Kenilworth Aquatic Gardens (worth a side trip). A little bit farther, on the right, is the graceful, rolling tract occupied by the National Arboretum (also worth a side trip). From this point on, stone or concrete seawalls gird the banks, and the surrounding lands are either open parks or other things. Other things include some power plants, RFK Stadium, marinas, and the Washington Navy Yard. The Navy Yard houses a war museum that maintains a sizable outdoor display of guns, torpedoes, and other armaments, partly visible from the river. Occasionally, visiting foreign warships dock here. At the mouth, completing the martial setting, is the pretty campus of the National War College.

There is no good access at the mouth. You could climb up the seawall near Hains Point to Ohio Drive. But a better idea is to paddle an extra mile, around Hains Point and its outlandish sculpture, up the Potomac to the launching ramp on the north side of National Airport at Roaches Run. For many of we aging children, watching the jets take off from National will be the high point of the cruise.

About the shuttle. You can drive almost all of it on freeways. But if you do not know your way around this area, you would be wise to attempt it first early in the morning of a Saturday, Sunday, or holiday. This is no place to ponder confusing turnoffs during rush hour. Finally, with only about two miles of walking, it is possible to do a one-car shuttle using the Metro between National Airport and Cheverly stations. How urban can you get?

HAZARDS: Avoid motorboats during summer.

WATER CONDITIONS: Canoeable anytime, except when frozen. Avoid within a day or two of hard rain, as the water quality will be foul.

GAUGE: None.

Northwest Branch

INTRODUCTION: The Northwest Branch is the aesthetically redeeming silver lining in the dismal cloud of the Anacostia Basin. This is a basin that provides countless textbook examples of the ill effects of totally urbanized watersheds, water pollution, erosion and sedimentation problems, surface mining abuse (sand and gravel), flash flooding, and suburban blight. Amazingly, however, this list does not include a relatively bad record of ravaging floods. For thanks to the wise foresight of the local bicounty planning agency, most of the floodplains were long ago purchased and converted to parkland. In one such park lies a narrow Fall Line gorge, and in this gorge runs the Northwest Branch, hidden for three and a half pleasant miles from the surrounding drab development. This and maybe even the section downstream is a worthwhile choice for the Washington or Baltimore area paddler who wakes up from an all night rain and wonders what to paddle.

Northwest Branch

43

Section 1. U.S. Rte. 29 to Hyattsville (38th Avenue)						
Gradient	Difficulty	Distance	Time	Width	Scenery	Map
25	1 to 3	8.1	2.5	25-50	Good to Poor	43

TRIP DESCRIPTION: Most paddlers will be interested in only cruising the first three and a half miles to Riggs Road (Adelphi Mill). The purist will want to put in right at the Rte. 29 bridge at the head of an enticing rapid. But before doing so, be sure to hike downstream (left bank) about 150 yards and decide if you care to risk a possible swim through the cataracts below. Either way, those without a death wish will want to portage around those drops, at least from the first bend, for a hundred yards via a well-worn trail high on the left bank, to a small grassy area below. The final four-foot ledge of this steep stretch has a narrow, clean slot on the right (if not clogged by logs), and at high levels you can run this dead center. Following the bouldery run-out below, the stream calms to just straightforward riffles and fast current through a lovely gorge with few views of houses and apartments that lie just beyond the rim. Directly under the high I-495 bridge rushes a narrow, twisting and, with more than a foot of canoeable water, pushy rapid. Poor visibility and chance of a surprise log make this one worth scouting. The stream slowly calms down again, but all the way to Riggs Road it maintains the ability to throw up some bouncy waves, rocky passages, and playable holes. A paved bicycle path and sewer right-of-way detract some from the wild atmosphere of the gorge, but nevertheless it is still pretty, especially in the summertime when the surrounding foliage is thick and steaming.

At Riggs Road the surrounding slopes diverge, and the stream enters the coastal plain. Now Northwest Branch winds about open parkland backed by houses, shopping centers, and apartments. The water now runs mostly smooth, but at a very high velocity. Paddlers must still be alert for trees, low bridges, and, most importantly, a sloping four-foot dam with a strong roller at the bottom. This dam is located just below Sligo Creek (right) within sight of two large gas storage tanks. Do not get swept into this trap. The take-out at 38th Avenue offers a final, bouncy, man-made rapid before the stream becomes channelized and levee-bound to tidewater at Bladensburg.

HAZARDS: First there is a series of large, vicious drops starting about a hundred yards below Rte. 29. Carry these on the left. Trees are an occasional problem all along. If water is really high you may have some bridge clearance problems. Finally, do not forget that four-foot dam with its deadly hydraulic, just below Sligo Creek.

WATER CONDITIONS: Runnable only within 24 hours of a hard rainfall. This is, unfortunately, a flash flooding type stream, and it gets more so each year as the watershed becomes increasingly developed.

GAUGE: There is a USGS gauge on the right end of the Queens Chapel Road bridge (Md. Rte. 500), but this tends to be meaningless when the height there reflects a crest that probably left the put-in two hours earlier. Accordingly, the only reliable way to judge the stream's fast-changing levels is to go to the put-in and, if water looks passable there, then exploit it immediately. If you start at Rte. 29, check out the rock garden at the foot of the cataract section. This represents the scrapiest spot that you will encounter.

The Rest Of The Watershed

As stated earlier, the Anacostia and its tributaries are not distinguished for their beauty. Oddly enough, the State of Maryland has passed a bill designating this a State Wild and Scenic River — a move that no doubt can only be attributed to some far out political chicanery that you or I will never understand. The Anacostia is fed by six major tributaries: Sligo Creek, Northwest Branch, Paint Branch, Little Paint Branch, Indian Creek, and Northeast Branch. Sligo has some excellent whitewater and flows through a pretty park. But it is difficult to catch up, and you may be harassed by park police when you try it. Paint Branch has an interesting and attractive fall line gorge, but most of it is off limits, flowing through the former Naval Surface Weapons Center (blocked by solid chain link fence and guarded by people with surface weapons). Little Paint Branch is little and ugly. Indian Creek has too many trees. And the Northeast Branch, while possessing one exciting, bouncy rapid at Riverdale Road, formed by the rubble dam at the head of the leveed flood channel, offers otherwise only the drabbest of excursions.

Mattawoman Creek

INTRODUCTION: Mattawoman Creek starts in Cedarville State Forest, forms part of the border of Prince George's and Charles counties, and then finally joins the Potomac at Indian Head. For most of its length it is small, winding, tangled, and choked—a classic coastal plain obstacle course. The paddler who makes it down that stretch will have done a real day's work. But there is also a tidal portion of the Mattawoman. And barring adverse winds, those miles require much less effort to paddle and offer one a setting that is pleasant and, in places, even a bit wild.

Section 1. Berry Road (Md. Rte. 228) to Md. Rte. 225						
Gradient	Difficulty	Distance	Time	Width	Scenery	Map
8	A to 1	10.6	10.0	10-20	Fair	12

TRIP DESCRIPTION: One can, and probably will, want to shorten this trip with access at Billingsley Road, Md. Rte. 227, or Bumpy Oak Road. There is no preferable section to attempt. They are all miserable, for fallen trees are evenly distributed with maddening frequency throughout the length. Understand that negotiating fallen trees is no safe endeavor. One risks breaking one's neck getting out on one of the many slippery, black, rotting ones and contracting terminal dermatitis after climbing or stepping onto one of the high and dry ones which often support lush growths of poison ivy (in winter recognized by hairy vines with pretty white clusters of berries). Those trees that are best portaged around have invariably fallen in dense patches of greenbriers, poison ivy, etc., through which you will almost invariably have to wade. Since this stream has some gradient, a misjudgment in water level could add dragging over gravel bars to your troubles. Finally, because the scenery includes power lines, some houses, and a wide, grassy right-of-way paralleling the left bank the whole way, the aesthetic compensation just does not justify the effort. If you want to paddle a swamp, try Zekiah or the Patuxent.

HAZARDS: Fallen trees, briers, poison ivy, and beaver dams.

WATER CONDITIONS: Passable in late fall, winter, and spring within a few days of rain.

GAUGE: There is a USGS gauge at Rte. 227 near Pomonkey (see USGS website or inspect on site). Look for at least 22 cfs (2.7 feet).

Section 2. Md. Rte. 225 to Smallwood State Park						
Gradient	Difficulty	Distance	Time	Width	Scenery	Map
0	A	6.1	3.0	20-3,000	Fair to Good	12

TRIP DESCRIPTION: A few more woody obstacles prevail in the first 150 yards below Rte. 225, at least at low tide. After that it is all clear sailing. And if you venture out on a windy day, take that statement literally. The first mile is by far the nicest—a mix of marsh and swampy shores partially protected by a state environmental preserve. The creek here remains relatively narrow with some potentially waterfowl-filled backwaters. Mattawoman then slowly widens and Indian Head and then the Naval Surface Warfare Center loom on the right, while the left shore remains mostly undeveloped. The naval plant manufactures rocket propellants and explosives, so do not plan on making any stops on that side of the creek. The launching ramp at General Smallwood State Park makes an easy take-out. The broad Potomac lies about a mile beyond. The bluffs on the left in this last mile support rich stands of mountain laurel. Bloom time is late May.

HAZARDS: There are some strainers at the start. Motorboats can be an annoyance on the tidal part. Finally, keep off the naval lands.

WATER CONDITIONS: Most of this is passable anytime, except when frozen or too windy. At low tide and low flow, there will probably be some dragging necessary in the first 150 yards.

GAUGE: None.

Nanjemoy Creek

INTRODUCTION: Nanjemoy Creek is a tidal tributary to the Potomac River in Charles County, Maryland, located only 40 miles south of Washington, D.C. Despite its proximity to the big city, it and its little tributaries—the Hill Top Fork, Burgess Creek, and Kings Creek—remain relatively undeveloped. This is a fine place for leisurely paddling, good bird watching, and for soaking up peace and quiet.

Section 1. Md. Rte. 6 to Friendship Landing						
Gradient	Difficulty	Distance	Time	Width	Scenery	Map
0	A	5.9	3.5	20-500	Very Good	13

TRIP DESCRIPTION: The suggested route for canoes is on the upper reaches of this creek, as it is far more intimate and far less exposed than the lake-like lower reaches. The put-in at Rte. 6 is at the absolute head of tidewater. The first few yards are narrow and shallow and may be complicated by a log or two. But then for the rest of the way it is all easy going. The banks are initially swampy, but that quickly gives way to broad marshes backed by graceful, wooded bluffs. A few houses and duck blinds are all the development that you will find until approaching Friendship Landing, and it is easy to imagine this as typical Chesapeake Bay country scenery that one might have enjoyed 300 years ago. Tempting camping opportunities abound here, but since this is all private land, please secure permission first. If you can ignore the ever-increasing bass boat traffic, you will have a fine trip. A public launching ramp at Friendship Landing provides easy egress.

HAZARDS: None.

WATER CONDITIONS: Tidal. Runnable year round, except when frozen.

GAUGE: None.

Gradient	Difficulty	Distance	Time	Width	Scenery	Map
0	A	Variable	Variable	250-6,000	Very Good	13

TRIP DESCRIPTION: The lower creek is a destination of contrasts. Its main body is wide and exposed, so that it is less often fit for canoeing (but fine for sea kayaking). On the other hand, it has three wonderful tributaries that are much more cozy. It suffers extensive shoreline development, but some equally long reaches remain wild too. Finally, it has limited access, but most of what you would care to see is within reach of Friendship Landing.

Striking eastward from Friendship Landing, the first bit of pleasant exploring is to be had by ascending Hill Top Fork. This is initially a wide, shallow estuary with a channel found on its east side. The creek rapidly narrows, though, and then twists for about a mile up through the marshes until you can advance no farther. The surrounding wooded bluffs are undeveloped, and the remote atmosphere is even more complete than back on Nanjemoy.

Continuing eastward, the north shore is largely marshy and wild, but there is eventually higher but flat ground upon which there are a few houses. The south shore is mostly dry, but development is light. After the creek turns hard right and widens, a major tributary enters on the left. This is Burgess Creek.

Burgess Creek is pretty. It twists through marshes for about three and a quarter miles, with only a few houses marring the isolation. At high tide, the head of navigation is where the marsh changes to swamp. Low tide will stop you about a half mile short of this point.

About a mile south of Burgess Creek is a gem of a side trip called Kings Creek. With high tide, you can ascend Kings for about a mile and a quarter. Its marshy path penetrates a totally wild setting. What a delight.

On the main body of the lower Nanjemoy, paddling is best on the east side. Except for a few military structures on the Blossom Point Proving Grounds, which borders about half of this section, the setting is undeveloped. This exposed shore suffers extensive bank erosion, as evidenced by the numerous trees that have tumbled from the resulting dirt cliffs. In contrast, the west shore is continuously developed, though the density decreases with each mile from the mouth.

There is no public access at or near the mouth. So if you venture that far, either double back to Friendship Landing, about five miles, or head down the Potomac to Goose Creek Marina (private, pay), about six miles.

HAZARDS: None.

WATER CONDITIONS: Tidal. Runnable year round, except when frozen.

GAUGE: None.

Zekiah Swamp Run and Wicomico River

INTRODUCTION: Zekiah Swamp cuts a north-south swath across Charles County from Cedarville State Forest to tidewater at the head of the Wicomico River. Draining the heart of this sodden woodland is Zekiah Swamp Run — a meandering, often braiding, sometimes rushing, and sometimes oozing ribbon of moisture. The swamp envelopes a sizable wilderness, less than an hour from the center of Washington, D.C., while the run is the best path for exploring it. And here is where the problem lies. For Zekiah Swamp Run is probably the most uncanoeable stream for its size in the state. If you are just a casual paddler, skip the description of Section 1. But if you feel that something worth seeing is worth fighting for, then read on.

If you do not feel like fighting, then maybe the Wicomico River is for you. The Wicomico is the estuary of Zekiah Swamp Run and Gilbert Swamp Run. To further confuse matters, the upper reaches suffer an identity crisis, the Zekiah arm being called Allens Fresh Run and the Gilbert arm being called Newport Swamp Run. Regardless of identity, these are broad, uncomplicated, often placid waters suitable for people who would rather relax.

Section 1. Md. Rte. 5 to Allens Fresh (Md. Rte. 234)						
Gradient	Difficulty	Distance	Time	Width	Scenery	Map
7	A to 1	12.4	15.0	3-30	Good	14

TRIP DESCRIPTION: Zekiah is the ultimate challenge to navigability. Like other troublesome small coastal plain streams, progress is repeatedly blocked by scores of fallen trees. But that is not all. The run periodically braids, not just into two or three channels, but dozens, all of which degenerate into trickles too small to float a boat. But that is not all. Cute, cuddly little beavers have dammed and flooded portions of the swamp, creating shallow ponds filled to the surface with dense growths of water weeds (even in winter). This forms a medium that is too thick to paddle through, but too thin to walk on or pole through. But that is not all. A lot of the dead, flooded, but still-standing trees in the beaver ponds have been cemented together by thick draperies of airborne vines that almost require the services of a machete to penetrate. Nevertheless, people (misfits) have occasionally beaten their canoes through this jungle and so can you. The described run is divided almost in half by Md. Rte. 6. Use this access. With progress sometimes measured inch by inch, even the most athletic should consider five to six miles of Zekiah a full day's work.

Having been forewarned of its faults, let us not overlook the charms of Zekiah. First and foremost, it is wild. The swamp is about a mile wide and surrounded by farms and more woodlands. Hence it is quiet down there. You will not see another soul, except maybe during hunting season. The water is clear and clean. There is no trash and litter and, except for an occasional deer stand, there is no development. The trees of the swamp are lovely, but particularly memorable are the dense groves of holly trees in the last few miles. Finally, the last few miles are an exception to the above mentioned hardships. Here the stream gushes its healthy volume down only a few channels, at least one of which is usually unobstructed. It even rushes over little riffles formed by bars of fine gravel. The last few hundred yards are tidal and, if you go there in early spring when the perch and shad are running, this stretch will be elbow to elbow with fishermen. Take out on the right at Rte. 234 bridge.

HAZARDS: During high water or, in the last few miles, even at normal levels, trees can be dangerous because of the strong current.

WATER CONDITIONS: Runnable late fall, winter, and spring except after a prolonged dry period.

GAUGE: There is a USGS gauge at Rte. 6 (see USGS website or inspect on site). Zero is unknown, but base winter flow is about 30 cfs (2.6 feet).

Section 2. Allens Fresh (Md. Rte. 234) to mouth						
Gradient	Difficulty	Distance	Time	Width	Scenery	Map
0	A	15.0	7.5	30 ft.-1.8 mi.	Good	14

TRIP DESCRIPTION: If you begin at Rte. 234, finding the put-in can be confusing. There are two bridges at Allens Fresh. Although the eastern span has the road sign saying Allens Fresh Run, you want the western span, which crosses the main channel and has a handy access on the upstream right side. Allens Fresh Run leads you via a relatively narrow path through expansive marshes backed by farms or wooded hills. It is a good setting for waterfowl watching. In the first quarter mile, however, also watch where you are going as, at low tide, the channel is narrow, shallow, and elusive.

When the river turns to the east, it becomes the Wicomico. If you desire more of the intimate marshy passages, look for a break on the left in about a mile. That is Newport Swamp Run which, at high tide, you can ascend to Rte. 234 (note that the sign at Rte. 234 bridge says Gilbert Swamp Run). Newport maintains a mostly narrow channel bordered by tall reeds, except in its uppermost reaches, where high ground closes in.

The left side of the river continues marshy for a few more miles to Budds Creek, which offers a short, pretty, side trip up into marsh. From Budds Creek to Chaptico Bay, the shore is solid, often marked by 10- to 20-foot eroded mud banks, largely wild except around the Wicomico Shores development.

Chaptico Bay and Run offer an attractive detour. The scenery varies, with a pastoral then wooded north side, developed south side, and marshy head. With a high tide, you can ascend to the edge of the town of Chaptico, about a quarter mile short of the Rte. 234 bridge.

The remainder of the Wicomico's left side is almost continuously developed. There are some beautiful side streams, however, such as Manahowie and Bramleigh creeks, that remain largely unspoiled.

The right side of the Wicomico is mostly high ground after Allens Fresh Run. Development is unevenly distributed and generally it is light, presenting a mostly wooded facade. Banks are often high and eroded, but there are plenty of nice places to land.

Deep water access to the Wicomico is pretty good. St. Mary's County provides evenly spaced public ramps at Wicomico Shores (near Budds Creek), Chaptico Wharf, and Bushwood Wharf. On the Charles County side, the foot of Rock Point Road (behind the old post office) is the only access.

HAZARDS: None.

WATER CONDITIONS: Tidal.

GAUGE: None.

Inside Swamps

Swamps and lowland floodplains are the closest that you will ever get in Maryland or Delaware to canoeing through a jungle. Since the rich botanical diversity of this environment is one of its finest features, the paddler should at least be able to recognize some of the more common tree types in this forest.

The most unusual tree found in the swamp is the bald cypress, and Maryland marks the northern limit of its range. Cypress has needles and cones like an evergreen, but sheds its leaves (needles) in the fall like a hardwood. The tree can grow to immense size and live to an incredible age. Even after it does die, its extremely rot resistant wood stays around for a long time. The most unusual feature of the cypress though are its knees. The knees are conical projections of the root system that rise from the water at the base of the tree to provide air for the roots. Most of the local cypress grows on the Eastern Shore. But the Western Shore has one small, beautiful stand, owned by The Nature Conservancy, found along Battle Creek in Calvert County. You cannot canoe through here, but a trail and boardwalk allow you to explore it by foot.

One of the most common swamp trees is the red maple. This usually modest-sized tree, with small, three-lobed leaves, distinguishes itself in autumn with a flaming display of red foliage. It stands out in the spring too when it is decked with tiny red flowers.

Another fall standout is black tupelo. This is another southern tree near its northern limit. You recognize this tree by its small oval leaves that turn scarlet in autumn and by its tiny blue-black fruit.

While Christmas comes but once a year, the coastal plain swamps are bountifully decked with holly year round. You will best appreciate the red fruit of the American holly after October, when they stand in such bold contrast to the gray and black of the winter swamp. Complementing the holly is an even brighter display of red berries born by the possumhaw, more a bush than a tree.

Another common tree, the sweet gum, is identified by its five-lobed, star-like leaves that also turn brilliant colors in fall and its burr-like seedpods. The pods, about an inch and a half in diameter, are also popular as Christmas decorations.

When patches of high ground appear in coastal plain swamps, beech trees also appear. Possessing paper smooth, gray bark and toothed, oval leaves and often reaching great size, these trees are best known as a destination for knife-wielding graffiti artists. These trees also bear small, chestnut-like burrs which yield two tetrahedral nuts per burr which in turn contain a most edible and delicious meat.

Finally there is poison ivy. True, this is not a tree. But it grows all over so many of them that it should be discussed here. Most people know poison ivy by its three shiny leaves. But since much swamp paddling may be done during the colder months, winter identification is important. At this time of year you can recognize poison ivy by its black, hairy vines and clusters of small, white berries. The author learned this lesson the hard way. It seems that upon first sighting the shrub he misidentified it as mistletoe and, it being a few weeks before Christmas, he decided to participate in tradition by picking a sprig, taking it back to his office, and hanging it over the doorway in hopes of coercing a kiss from the cute blond secretary down the hall. The days came and went, so did the secretary, and so did the mysterious rashes and chronic itching. After a few months he tossed the sprig away in disgust and without ever so much as a lousy peck on the cheek.

West Chesapeake Bay Tributaries

Chapter 4
West Chesapeake Drainage

The West Chesapeake Drainage encompasses all streams flowing into the Chesapeake Bay between the Potomac and Susquehanna rivers. Most of the streams described in this chapter start on the rolling, agricultural lands of the Piedmont. From there they tumble over the Fall Line to the coastal plain and, sooner or later, tidewater. The Fall Line descent, with its miles of whitewater, has proven a bonanza to the droves of whitewater paddlers that inhabit the nearby metropolitan areas. All these streams are small, with relatively short free-flowing portions. Then, upon reaching tidewater, they expand into broad and sometimes long estuaries. Also, above tidewater, most of the streams of this basin flow within the confines of wooded gorges. The exception is the Patuxent system, which possesses many miles that course through secluded swamplands. Either way, the rivers are usually remarkably hidden from their often urban and suburban surroundings and, hence, provide some fine paddling routes close to home. The estuaries, in contrast, have been extensively spoiled by shoreline residential development, industry, and bulkheading. For this reason, this chapters offers only the best selections for tidewater touring.

The following streams and shorelines are described in this chapter:

St. Mary's Coast
Patuxent River
    Little Patuxent River
       Middle Patuxent River
    Western Branch Patuxent River
Calvert Coast and Parker Creek
West and Rhode Rivers
Severn River
Patapsco River
    South Branch Patapsco River
    Gwynns Falls
    Jones Falls
Herring Run
Gunpowder Falls
    Little Falls
    Western Run
    Little Gunpowder Falls
Winters Run

Patuxent River Cattail Creek

To Damascus

MULLINIX RD

LONG COR RD

MILL RD

ANNAPOLIS ROCK RD

1.6

94

To Lisbon

108

ANNAPOLIS ROCK RD

JONES RD

JENNINGS CHAPEL RD

DAISY RD

Cattail Creek

UNION CHAPEL RD

To Cooksville

Patuxent

1.6

HIPSLEY MILL

River

3.3

650

To Laytonsville

HOWARD CHAPEL RD

3.2

97

Gauge

2.5

ROXBURY RD

RD

1.1

Gauge

0.9

Access

TRIADELPHIA

To Olney

3.3

Triadelphia

TRIADELPHIA

Access

GREENBRIDGE RD

RD

GREENBRIDGE RD

Access

Reservoir

0.7

650

Dam

BRIGHTON DAM RD

Gauge

HAVILAND MILL RD

RD

HIGHLAND RD

HOLLOW RD

To Clarksville

4.4

MINK

Patuxent

HIGHLAND

ASHTON

108

TUCKER LA

River

BROWN BRIDGE RD

216

EDNOR RD

1.6

Access

To Baltimore

650

MURPHY RD

SCAGGSVILLE

To Silver Spring

T. Howard

4.4

Access

Duckett

29

HARDING RD

To Baltimore

198

Reservoir

2.5

RIDING STABLE RD

Access

SUPPLEE LA

BROOKLYN BRIDGE RD

Dam

To Silver Spring

95

216

To Washington

LAUREL

N

44

St. Mary's Coast

INTRODUCTION: Here is a destination for paddlers seeking space. With a seemingly infinite Chesapeake on one side, low, lonely shores on the other, and little access in between, the reach between the mouths of the Potomac and Patuxent is a good escape.

Section 1. Solomons (Md. Rte. 4) to Pt. Lookout						
Gradient	Difficulty	Distance	Time	Width	Scenery	Map
0	A	28.4	14	5-10 miles	Good	48

TRIP DESCRIPTION: While this description follows from north to south, let the winds determine the direction of your trip, for this certainly is exposed water. Tides are weak, so do not worry about them, though a low tide could affect your success at probing up sidestreams.

At Solomons, one can put in either at the public boat ramp at Rte. 4, a mile to the south at the end of the Riverwalk, or across the river a half mile upstream of Rte. 4 along Patuxent Beach Road (across the street from the Boatel California). It is a poor start where the developed south shore yields to the drab, rip rapped fringe of the Naval Air Station. Though there are a few natural spots left within its bounds, usually about the only reward for passing by this stretch is the sight of some interesting aircraft. South of the base, the shore scenery alternates between wild and developed. Naval aircraft yield to bald eagles. In contrast to the Calvert Coast, there are no cliffs here, but many cut banks. There are beaches and a number of lagoons cut off from the Chesapeake by sand bars.

There is little public access to this stretch. The first possibility south of the naval base is Elms Beach County Park. It is open to vehicles April to November. At other times you will have to walk the half-mile road to the beach. The next possibility is Drury's Marina on the Northern Prong of St. Jerome Creek on Airedele Road, Ridge. For a $5 fee they provide a ramp, parking, and provisions. The last access is at Point Lookout State Park. You can get out at the picnic area near the point or about a mile north at the fishing pier.

HAZARDS: None.

WATER CONDITIONS: Tidal.

GAUGE: None.

Patuxent River

INTRODUCTION: The Patuxent is a river that has suffered at the hands of man in the name of progress. Most of its whitewater has been buried under two water supply reservoirs for suburban Washington. The reservoirs have intercepted most of its flow, allowing only a trickle to routinely flow past Laurel. When the river does flow, parts of it always run muddy from serious soil erosion problems in the basin, and until a few years ago, it smelled of sewage from too many poorly functioning sewage treatment plants. Much of it, nevertheless, has been maintained in a semi-wilderness character that makes for some attractive cruising right in the heart of the Washington-Baltimore megalopolis. Whether you are casting for bass in Duckett Reservoir, poking about the marshy fringe of Jug Bay, or

Patuxent River
Little Patuxent River
Middle Patuxent River

45

pulling a crab from a cove near Solomons, you will find it easy to forget the imperfections and appreciate the qualities of Maryland's second longest river.

Section 1. Mullinix Mill Road to Md. Rte. 97						
Gradient	Difficulty	Distance	Time	Width	Scenery	Map
18	A to 1	7.6	6.0	15-25	Good	44

TRIP DESCRIPTION: Mullinix Mill Road crosses the Patuxent only about five miles below its source, so do not expect to find a "river." The stream wanders through fairly mature woods, largely within the protection of Patuxent River State Park. The nearby terrain is initially hilly, even graced with some pretty rock formations, but the floodplain soon broadens. This is a typical Piedmont stream with lots of gravel-formed riffles with shallow sandy pools in between. It is also typical Piedmont in that it is plagued by deadfalls, though about halfway through the run, after the confluence with Cabin Branch, the coast is relatively clear. Nevertheless, be prepared for lots of extra exercise.

HAZARDS: Lots of strainers.

WATER CONDITIONS: Catch within a day of hard rain during late fall, winter, and spring.

GAUGE: There is a USGS gauge at Rte. 97 near Unity (see USGS website) with a staff attached to the right side of the bridge pier. Look for at least 210 cfs (3.5 feet) to start at Mullinix Mill Road and 175 cfs (3.3 feet) to start at Hipsley Mill Road.

Section 2. Cattail Creek: Union Chapel Road to mouth						
Gradient	Difficulty	Distance	Time	Width	Scenery	Map
19	A to 1	5.3	4.0	15-100	Good	44

TRIP DESCRIPTION: If you have time for extra paddling, there is about five miles of nice cruising on tiny, nearby Cattail Creek, which joins the Patuxent about a half mile below Rte. 97. Cattail is not within a state park, so its pleasant, crooked path takes you past farms and more houses. In addition to the usual gravel riffles, some interesting rapids are formed by patches of small boulders. A normal distribution of strainers will add to the sport. The final half mile of the creek is an attractive backwater of Triadelphia Reservoir. Take out at the W.S.S.C. access just below the confluence (see Section 4 for details).

HAZARDS: Lots of strainers, possibly including barbed wire.

WATER CONDITIONS: Catch within a day of hard rain during late fall, winter, and spring.

GAUGE: There is a staff gauge attached to the right abutment of the Rte. 97 bridge and one attached to the right abutment of the old bridge just upstream at Roxbury Mills. They should read respectively at least 1.9 feet and 2.6 feet.

Section 3. Brighton Dam Road to Md. Rte. 108						
Gradient	Difficulty	Distance	Time	Width	Scenery	Map
4	A to 1	4.4	1.5	15-30	Good	44

To Baltimore

450

450

BOWIE

3

To Washington

3.3

424

Gauge

50

To Annapolis

GOVERNOR BRIDGE RD

To Annapolis

DAVIDSONVILLE

214

4.5

LANDOVER RD

LOTTSFORD RD

ENTERPRISE RD

1.8

214

CENTRAL AVE

202

193

WATKINS PARK DR

2.1

WHITE HOUSE RD

LARGO RD

Western

BROWN STATION RD

5.4

202

725

UPPER MARLBORO

4

To Washington

OLD CRAIN HWY

WATER ST

CROOM STATION RD

To Waldorf

301

QUEEN ANNE BRIDGE RD

1.2

7.2

River

Patuxent

OLD CRAIN HWY

Access

To Rte. 2

408

Branch

3.2

3.3

N

Jackson Lndg. Park HQ

Jug Bay

1.7

382

CROOM AIRPORT RD

Selbys Lndg.

260

Mataponi Creek

4.1

CANDY HILL RD

FERRY LNDG RD

NOTTINGHAM

4

TANYARD RD

Hall Creek

CHANEYVILLE RD

5.3

2

To Annapolis

0.9

262

LOWER MARLBORO

MAGRUDERS FERRY RD

To Prince Frederick

Access

Patuxent River
Western Branch
Patuxent River

46

TRIP DESCRIPTION: This is a short and pretty beginners' run conveniently situated to Washington, Baltimore, Columbia, and Frederick. Reservoir-induced water starvation is the main reason that this stretch is not more popular. The little creek flows mostly back in the woods, running between usually high mud banks. Occasionally you will see some farms and houses. Frequently you will see beautiful rock outcrops, typically fringed by stands of hemlock. The water is very clean and mostly smooth, and the occasional riffles are short and insignificant. Several fallen trees should be your only difficulty on river. Off river, note that parking at all points other that the put-in is poor.

HAZARDS: Count on several trees or logjams.

WATER CONDITIONS: Most reliably up during a wet winter or spring when Triadelphia Reservoir is full and overflowing. In summer, usually only a trickle passes through the dam, but hydroelectric generation, mostly on weekdays and during business hours (peak electricity demand period) sometimes results in modest and floatable releases of water.

GAUGE: There is a UGSG gauge (inspect on site or see USGS website) by the picnic area below Brighton Dam. About 50 cfs (1.7 feet) is enough, though most would prefer about 100 cfs (2.0 feet) for the shallowest spots. A broad riffle near the lower end of the picnic area at the put-in is representative of the shallowest spots.

Section 4. Triadelphia and T. Howard Duckett Reservoirs						
Gradient	Difficulty	Distance	Time	Width	Scenery	Map
0	A	—	—	50-1,500	Good	44

TRIP DESCRIPTION: This section is composed of two water supply reservoirs that bracket Section 3. The lakes are attractive, especially early in the season when they are full and thus free of unsightly mud flats. Their usually hilly shores are almost all wooded, and there are also thick undergrowth groves of mountain laurel that burst into beautiful bloom in late May. Since only electric motorboats are allowed here, these are two lakes where you do not have to endure noise and fumes and worry about being run down.

The Washington Suburban Sanitary Commission owns these lakes. For you to boat on them, the Commission requires that you purchase a permit, costing 30 dollars for the season or three dollars for a day. You can secure this permit at the Commission offices at 14501 Sweitzer Lane, Laurel, at Sunshine Corner Store, at Spencerville Market, or at the reservoir office at Brighton Dam (convenient location, and open seven days a week, from 8:00 to 8:00). Boating is allowed from March 1 through December 15. The Commission allows direct access only at official launch areas (shown on map) although it would be permissible to paddle into either reservoir from above. The Commission has a long list of other "don'ts" also. If you do not have that list, the rule of thumb is that if whatever you are doing is fun, then you must be doing something wrong. Call (301) 774-9124 for additional information.

Finally, there is an isolated quarter-mile whitewater run hidden between Rte. 97 and the head of Triadelphia Reservoir. It is bouldery and one rapid approaches Class 3 at high water (rare). This is just too short to be worth most paddlers' trouble.

HAZARDS: None.

WATER CONDITIONS: Most of this is always canoeable, although the WSSC allows boating only from March 1 through December 15. If the lakes are low, the section of Duckett Reservoir from Rte. 108 to Browns Bridge will be free-flowing, exposing an old rubble weir and numerous gravelly or sandy riffles. Even at low flow, this stretch is mostly passable.

GAUGE: None.

Patuxent River

47

Gradient	Difficulty	Distance	Time	Width	Scenery	Map
7	A	16.7	10.0	30-40	Good	45

TRIP DESCRIPTION: Put in behind the municipal pool at the foot of 9th Street. If you have the skill and energy, it is possible to paddle, pole, or line upstream as far as I-95, a distance of about a mile. The path takes you over easy rapids, through the tail end of Rocky Gorge, and past some interesting mill ruins. Heading downstream, the initial passage through Laurel is softened by a narrow strip of park land. The stream then winds about dense, tangled woods, part of which have fallen across the stream. The trees and logjams in turn trap an incredible load of trash, including flood debris, milk jugs, plastic, tennis balls, and anything else you could imagine. Laurel's indiscriminate development of the river's floodplain has certainly aggravated this situation.

You can avoid most of this unpleasantness by putting in at Brock Bridge Road, located four and a half miles downstream and just above the Baltimore Washington Parkway. Just below here the stream enters the Patuxent Research Refuge and an amazing transformation occurs. The surrounding woods change to a healthy looking bottomland and swamp forest decorated here and there by big, graceful, silver, uncarved beech trees. The trash suddenly disappears, seemingly filtered out by upstream logjams. Unfortunately, navigation through here is a challenge, as the river periodically braids into numerous tiny channels, all liberally blocked by fallen trees. The channels reunite, the going is easy, then they split again, and so on and on and on. By the end of the long day you will feel as if you have fought your way down this river.

HAZARDS: Numerous fallen trees.

WATER CONDITIONS: Often carries runnable flows in wet years when reservoirs are full and hydroelectric plant is running. Runs high only when Duckett Reservoir is overflowing or after locally heavy rains fall downstream of the reservoir. Reservoir overflows are erratic. Obviously, if it is full and it rains hard, it overflows. But also, because the WSSC is under pressure to protect Laurel from the town's senseless, floodplain sprawl (the dam was never designed to function as a flood control structure), they often will release water from a full reservoir when there is a convincing forecast of rain.

GAUGE: There is a USGS gauge just below Rocky Gorge Dam (see USGS website). You need about 200 cfs (5.7 feet) to negotiate the riffles above 9th Street, but consider about 120 cfs (5.3 feet) a minimum for the rest of this section. You can do it even lower, but it will greatly increase the number of liftovers. Also you can judge the riffles near 9th Street.

Gradient	Difficulty	Distance	Time	Width	Scenery	Map
3	A	16.2	5.0	50-150	Good	46

TRIP DESCRIPTION: The Little Patuxent joins just above the put-in and adds enough flow and resultant width to now allow easy passage around most fallen trees. There is a strong current to Rte. 214, shortly below which tidewater begins. The river continues as on Section 5 to wind about a wide, forested floodplain and bump up against pretty, beech-covered hillsides. Below Rte. 214, the scenery degenerates with the appearance of several sand and gravel pits and renegade trash dumps.

HAZARDS: Snags and trees remain a problem above tidewater.

WATER CONDITIONS: Above Rte. 214, runnable most of year except after a prolonged dry spell. Below Rte. 214, it is always passable.

GAUGE: USGS gauge near Bowie (on USGS website) at U.S. Rte. 50 seldom gets lower than 120 cfs (4.1 feet), which is adequate for at least lightly loaded boats.

Section 7. Md. Rte. 4 to Magruders Ferry Road						
Gradient	Difficulty	Distance	Time	Width	Scenery	Map
0	A	15.3	6.5	200-2,500	Good	46

TRIP DESCRIPTION: This section of the Patuxent has pleased many paddlers who have found this to be the closest piece of fairly natural tidewater riverscape to Washington. This relatively wide, placid river describes great bends past marshes, wooded bluffs, and farms.

You can get some additional quality mileage out of this section by exploring some of the tributaries, in particular, Mataponi Creek and Hall Creek. These are wild, intimate gems. With a favorable tide you can ascend Mataponi for about a mile and a half and Hall for over two and a half miles. Mataponi is protected by Merkle Wildlife Management Area on one side and Patuxent River Park on the other. A trail and boardwalk system allows you to further explore this sanctuary on foot. Hall, whose broad freshwater marshes backed by unusually high, wooded hillsides will really charm you, apparently remains nice by luck.

Access to this section is fair. You can put in from Calvert County at the public dock at Lower Marlboro, in Anne Arundel County at Rte. 4, or in Prince George's County at Jackson Landing, Selbys Landing, or Magruders Ferry Road (Clyde Watson Boating Area). The latter three are in Patuxent River Park, which requires that you first obtain a permit for their use. Five dollars buys Montgomery and Prince George's County residents a day-use or annual permit (day use fee halved in off season). All others must shell out seven dollars for day use and ten dollars for annual. The park is open year round except for Christmas and New Year's days. For additional information, call the park at (301) 627-6074.

HAZARDS: None.

WATER CONDITIONS: Tidal. Always enough water on Patuxent, but tributaries can get pretty shallow at low tide.

GAUGE: None.

Section 8. Magruders Ferry Road to Solomons (Md. Rte. 4)						
Gradient	Difficulty	Distance	Time	Width	Scenery	Map
0	A	28.8	15.0	400 ft.-2 mi.	Good	47

TRIP DESCRIPTION: A different river now evolves. Vistas are long. With wide open and deeper water, there are sailboats and more motorboats. There is more development.

The lower Patuxent remains remarkably unspoiled considering its proximity to D.C. Much of this reach retains its rural flavor, with fields, colonial era houses, and tobacco barns easily visible upon the rolling landscape. Long stretches of shore remain undeveloped, with development being concentrated in pockets, such as around Solomons, Broomes Island, and Benedict. The most significant blemish is the giant power plant at Chalk Point, visible for several miles both upstream and down.

The waterfront is varied and interesting. Though generally high and dry, there are some good patches of wetlands such as those at the mouth of Battle Creek, at Broomes Island, and below Island Creek. On some stretches there are low cliffs of sand, multi-hued clay, and even rock. Particularly interesting are a deposit of gnarled, fossil-bearing rock at water level on the west side of the river near Hollywood Shores and Sotterly and on the east side below St. Leonards Creek.

The farther down river you paddle, the more you will share the water with non-paddle powered boats. Around Pt. Patience, the sharp spit that bends the river above Solomons, the river becomes absolutely congested, as this is a prime fishing venue. To wander between a bass boater and a good fishing hole is the rough equivalent of standing between a momma grizzly bear and her cubs.

The tributaries of this reach are often disappointing, for while the main river remains relatively undeveloped, these sheltered backwaters are lined with houses, bulkheads, piers, and boats. If you paddle to the heads of these, however, you may be rewarded. For example, about a mile of upper St. Leonards Creek and a half mile of upper Island Creek remain wonderfully wild with narrow channels threading through marshes backed by high, wooded hillsides. Holly and cedar add green on the grayest of winter days. The head of Battle Creek features the edge of its beautiful cypress swamp.

One tributary that will not disappoint you is Hunting Creek, located about four miles above Benedict. It has only a few houses on it, allowing plenty of seclusion in its marshy miles. The only direct access to this creek is from the south, at the end of Maurice Bowen Road. This is private property, so be sure to ask permission first.

If only the lower Patuxent were as isolated as its access points. There are far too few for such a long stretch of river. From the west, you can launch at Magruders Ferry Road (public, pay), shoulder of Rte. 231, shoulder of Trent Hall Road, Sandgates via private ramps at Cape St. Marys Marina and Seabreeze Restaurant (pay), beach at Greenwell State Park (free), Forest Landing (public, free), and foot of Clarks Landing Road. From the east, you have the pier at Kings Landing County Park (free), public ramp at Benedict (pay), private ramps at Len's Grocery and Lands End Marina in Broomes Island (pay), and public ramp at Rte. 4 in Solomons (pay).

HAZARDS: Motorboats.

WATER CONDITIONS: Tidal.

GAUGE: None.

Patuxent Postscript

A substantial portion of the upper Patuxent drainage is occupied by the new city of Columbia. A project of the Rouse Company, a progressive private developer, Columbia was started in the early 1960's with the goal of creating a complete city—a place touted by its architects as where one could work, live, and play, as an alternative to living in just another bedroom community. The project, unfortunately, did not work completely as planned, but must be at least credited as a good faith effort to manage the wanton suburban sprawl that has been devouring the countryside.

While Columbia attempts to cure our urban ills, there are facilities farther downstream devoted to solving our environmental problems. Patuxent Research Refuge conducts programs to protect and reestablish endangered species of wildlife, its most glamorous project being one to protect the whooping crane. Farther downstream at Calvert County's Jefferson Patterson Park, the Academy of Natural Sciences of Philadelphia Laboratory conducts water quality research while, at Solomons Island, near the Patuxent's mouth, the University of Maryland Chesapeake Bay Laboratory conducts estuarine research.

The coastal plain segment of the Patuxent flows through Maryland's tobacco belt. People have cultivated tobacco here from the first days of colonial settlement. Back then the economy revolved around the weed, and it was even an acceptable substitute for cash. The best means of transportation in those days was by boat, using the intricate network of tidal creeks. Most Maryland tobacco plantations clustered along tidewater for this reason. Many of the old plantation houses still stand, and though usually in private hands, many are opened for public inspection for a week or two each spring as part of various garden tours. Probably the most beautiful of these houses remaining along the Patuxent is Sotterly, a rambling structure located near the town of Hollywood. To serve those plantations that were landlocked, the colony authorized the construction of rolling roads. The roads received their name because tobacco was loaded into huge wooden casks, called hogsheads, and rolled (pulled by oxen, horses, etc.) over the roads to the nearest wharf. The name lives today, as in Rolling Road in Catonsville. Tobacco is no longer king in this state, but in southern Maryland it still occupies an important niche in the economy. And the large, gray curing barns, with their louvered walls, stand as monuments to its persistent, noxious presence.

Little Patuxent River

INTRODUCTION: The Little Patuxent starts on the Piedmont, north of Columbia, drops over the Fall Line near Savage, and finally meanders the remainder of its way across the Coastal Plain to meet the Patuxent at Rte. 3, north of Bowie. It is a diverse stream. It picks a pleasant path through an area that is increasingly urban, suburban, or industrial. It has some miles that will delight the white-water boaters, when they can catch its elusive high flows. And it has many miles of smooth water fit for the novice, that are easy to catch at canoeable levels. Conveniently close to a lot of paddlers, it is a prime refuge from our overcrowded world.

Section 1. Columbia (Entrance Road) to Savage (Foundry Street)						
Gradient	Difficulty	Distance	Time	Width	Scenery	Map
21*	1 to 2, 4	7.3	2.0	20-35	Fair to	45
*1.5 @ 56fpm					Good	

TRIP DESCRIPTION: Hurry. With much of its watershed now the streets, lawns, and roofs of Columbia, rain runs off fast, yielding only a brief period of canoeable water. You can start at the U.S. Rte. 29 bridge, but launching at Entrance Road lessens your chance of being hit by a speeding auto. The creek initially snakes through suburbs and some commercial areas. This is mostly a woodsy passage, though you will see some backyards and some office buildings. . The water is muddy and initially fast and flat, with simple riffles, but complicated by some strainers. After Guilford Road, rapids appear occasionally, and they become continuous below I-95. The surroundings through here are mostly wild, set in a deepening Fall Line gorge. Urban-tolerant wildlife, such as geese, ducks, beaver, and muskrat, are common here.

The last half mile, from where the Middle Patuxent joins, contains the whitewater climax of the trip. It is known as The Falls. Located just around the bend from the confluence, The Falls consists of a short, steep staircase of sharp ledges and drops a total of about 15 feet. Scout this. Although there is a feasible route down the left of center, the boater runs a serious risk of pinning vertically in the biggest ledge. A short carry on the left is recommended. A few hundred yards downstream, the swift river flows both by and under an old mill that has been renovated as a shopping mall and community center. Sometimes when debris jams at the upstream end of this structure, forming a dangerous strainer. So approach with caution. Take out at the ancient steel truss bridge (last of its kind) at Foundry Street.

HAZARDS: Trees and logjams on upper river. Scout The Falls and, if in doubt, carry.

WATER CONDITIONS: Runnable only within a day of hard rain. Best times are in winter and spring.

GAUGE: There is a USGS gauge located on the left bank downstream of Guilford Road. The outside staff should read at least 3.6 feet. For running The Falls, the USGS gauge at Savage (see USGS website) should be at least 250 cfs (4.6 feet).

Section 2. Savage (Foundry Street) to Md. Rte. 3						
Gradient	**Difficulty**	**Distance**	**Time**	**Width**	**Scenery**	**Map**
6	**A to 1**	**17.7**	**6.5**	**35-50**	**Fair**	**45**

TRIP DESCRIPTION: The trip starts off for the first three miles with many easy rapids and riffles over mostly gravel to Brock Bridge Road. Below Brock Bridge, the river is typically flat with a strong current. Low water exposes a few rocky riffles and many little riffles formed by bars of pea gravel. As small coastal plain streams go, the entire lower Little Patuxent has a low strainers-per-mile frequency. Also, most of those strainers exist on braided sections of its last several miles. The healthy flow of the stream has much to do with the low frequency. The inexperienced, however, will probably still consider the river an obstacle course. Bring along a saw and ease the path for others. There is a six-foot dam — recognized from above by a water treatment plant on the left — located just above Md. Rte. 198. Carry this, as there is an ugly, churning, and invariably lethal roller waiting for you at the bottom.

Most of the reach from the Baltimore-Washington Parkway to Piney Orchard Parkway/Patuxent Road flows through public lands — first the D.C. Childrens Center, then a corner of what remains of Ft. George G. Meade, and finally, the Patuxent Wildlife Research Center. The latter was formerly part of the army base and, though I have never seen any warnings to this effect, I recommend sticking to the water through here because of the remote possibility of old (possibly live) ordnance in the woods.

Most of the scenery along the lower Little Patuxent is woodlands, sometimes scrubby, but other times typified by beautiful patches of well-developed floodplain forest or beech-covered hillsides. This is a peaceful and seemingly remote area. Noise and junk at an auto raceway above Conway Road is the only significant blemish. As on the Patuxent, the water quality suffers at times from soil erosion. On the other hand, at winter base flows, this stream can be amazingly clear. So if someone ever puts a saw to a few fallen trees, this section could become a very popular run.

HAZARDS: Be sure to carry the six-foot dam at Fort Meade's water intake. There will be fallen trees throughout.

WATER CONDITIONS: Canoeable above Brock Bridge within three days of hard rain. Below there, it is up most of a normal late fall, winter, and spring.

GAUGE: There is a USGS gauge at Savage (on USGS website) on the median strip of U.S. Rte. 1, south bank, with a staff attached to a wooden post a few feet out from the bank. The top of the staff is about 5 feet (375 cfs). Minimum is 90 cfs (3.8 feet) to start at Savage and about 65 cfs (3.6 feet) to start below Brock Bridge Road. The staff gauge nailed to a piling on east abutment of Conway Road bridge should read at least 2.1 feet to start at Brock Bridge Road and 1.6 feet to start at Piney Orchard Parkway. Be forewarned, however, that this gauge has over the years been very changeable. You can also judge the condition of the first few miles at the put-in.

Middle Patuxent River

INTRODUCTION: The Middle Patuxent drains the middle of Howard County, entering the Little Patuxent at Savage, Maryland. It flows past the doorstep of the burgeoning new city of Columbia and then through a major industrial and transportation corridor. But hidden away in its gorge, the paddler would hardly know this. It is one of a half dozen Fall Line streams that, if given a good rain, can save the Washington or Baltimore area paddler a long drive to the mountains to find good scenery and whitewater.

Section 1. West Friendship (Md. Rte. 108) to Savage (Foundry Street)

Gradient	Difficulty	Distance	Time	Width	Scenery	Map
15*	A to 2-,4	18.9	3.5	25-35	Good	45
*1 @ 60fpm						

TRIP DESCRIPTION: It is truly difficult to imagine that the insignificant brook at Rte. 32 is a potential paddling route, but it is. For its first several miles, it twists down a broad wooded floodplain bordered by big, new, expensive houses. There is also a contrasting, exposed reach where the creek passes through the pretty fields of the University of Maryland Central Farm. Riffles are frequent but simple. Trees are also frequent, and limit this stretch's appeal to the hardy and experienced.

Below Homewood Road, much of the run is set in a shallow, wooded gorge whose only significant civilized intrusions are occasional road crossings, some sewer right-of-way scars, and one rock quarry (at I-95). At least half of this reach is now protected within a state environmental area and county parks. Progress continues to be slow because of fallen trees. Also steep mud banks and dense undergrowth beyond make these trees more troublesome than they are on most streams. Fortunately, a sizeable but unnamed tributary joins on the right about two miles below Rte. 108, and below that point downed trees seldom block the whole channel. The stream is also relatively sluggish with nothing more challenging than gentle gravel bar riffles, except for a stretch of interesting rock gardens above and a two-foot ledge below Cedar Lane.

A few miles below Rte. 29, the Middle Patuxent begins its descent of the Fall Line—a passage marked by numerous small rapids of rock gardens and little ledges. The Fall Line scenery is beautifully decorated with big rock outcrops that are often clothed in hemlock and ferns (northern exposure) and mountain laurel (southern exposure). The Middle joins the Little Patuxent a half mile above the first convenient take-out in Savage. It is this last half mile that holds the whitewater climax of the cruise, The Falls. See the description of Section 1 on the Little Patuxent for details.

HAZARDS: Trees on upper river. Falls of the Little Patuxent. Scout and, if in doubt, carry.

WATER CONDITIONS: Runnable only with a day of hard rain. Best times are winter and spring.

GAUGE: The staff gauge on the downstream end of the pier of the Homewood Road bridge should read at least minus 0.2 feet. You can count grooves on the pier or left abutment of the Rte. 32 bridge near West Friendship. Zero is about 6 inches below the fifth groove down from the top. Roughly, 240 cfs (4.5 feet) on the USGS gauge (see USGS website) on the Little Patuxent at Rte. 1 is minimum.

Western Branch Patuxent River

INTRODUCTION: Joining the main Patuxent just above Jug Bay, the Western Branch drains about 90 rapidly suburbanizing square miles of northeast Prince George's County. With much of its floodplain protected by county parks, a state wildlife management area, and a University of Maryland farm, it offers within a few miles of the Beltway a handy escape, if you are patient enough to put up with it flashy flows and hearty enough to brave its woody obstacles. If you care not to combine pain with paddling, the final two miles provide a scenic, usually unobstructed, tidal path that is easily accessible from Patuxent River Park's Jackson Landing.

Section 1. Lottsford Road to mouth						
Gradient	Difficulty	Distance	Time	Width	Scenery	Map
7	A	14.2	5.0	25-50	Fair to Good	46

TRIP DESCRIPTION: The put-in is below the confluence of streams that are even smaller than the insignificant rivulet that you are contemplating. Much of the path that follows is enveloped by a rank floodplain forest whose beauty is somewhat compromised by the great amount of trash washed down from surrounding streets and highways. The passage through Upper Marlboro in contrast involves a straightened and leveed channel with views of buildings. Below there, the river retreats into woods, swamp, and then marsh.

The modest gradient is spent over pea-gravel riffles. Of more significant concern are the trees, which besides being obstacles and hazards, can be poison ivy-encrusted annoyances. Also watch for a old mill just below Rte. 214, unusual in that it spans the stream. It is possible to squeeze underneath at low levels after scouting carefully. Tidewater starts about a mile below Rte. 301.

There is no access at the mouth. The nearest exit is almost a mile down the Patuxent at Jackson Landing.

HAZARDS: Anticipate a normal number of strainers for a steam this size. Watch for old mill span below Rte. 214.

WATER CONDITIONS: In late fall, winter, and spring, runnable within four days of hard rain and, in summer, within a day of rain. Last two miles are always passable.

GAUGE: The functioning USGS gauge located on the left bank about 200 yards above Water Street in Upper Marlboro (see USGS website) should run over 300 cfs (4.0 feet) to start at Lottsford Road. There are staff gauges that you can visit about 100 feet above Rte. 202, on the right bank, and on the upstream side of the right abutment of the Water Street bridge in Upper Marlboro. They should be about 3.0 feet and 2.0 feet, respectively, to start at Lottsford.

Calvert Coast
St. Mary's Coast

To Waldorf

Access

SOLOMONS

4

CALIFORNIA

Patuxent River

8.5

Patuxent River
Naval Air Station

LEXINGTON
PARK

ST.

7.1

235

MARY'S

Elms
Beach
Park

BAY FOREST RD

COUNTY

Chesapeake

Bay

7.6

To Leonardtown

St. Jerome Creek

5

RIDGE

AIREDELE RD

Marina

Point No Point

6.9

N

Point Lookout

CHESAPEAKE BEACH

Bayside Park

261

4.2

BREEZY
POINT RD

Park

To Upper Marlboro

263

CALVERT

5.7

PRINCE FREDERICK

Parker Creek

Chesapeake

COUNTY

4.9

2
4

ST LEONARD

CALVERT BEACH RD

Matoaca Beach

2.1

Flag
Ponds
Park

Bay

N

6.1

Cove Point Light

SOLOMONS

Access

3.4

5.4

Patuxent

River

Drum Point

Calvert Coast and Parker Creek

INTRODUCTION: In Calvert County, the shoreline of the Chesapeake Bay is well worth a visit. In contrast with the mushy, marshy eastern side of the bay, Calvert puts a bold face forward — mostly in the form of fossil-laden clay cliffs. In contrast to Anne Arundel County to the north, the shoreline is not totally trashed by waterside development. This might be a paddler's paradise, except that there is pitifully little public access available. So if you do not own land in one of the several little, bayside communities nearby, or have a friend who does, then you must prepare for long excursions to enjoy most of this stretch. And nowhere is this more true than if you wish to enjoy its pristine centerpiece called Parker Creek.

Section 1. Chesapeake Beach (Bayside Park) to Solomons (Md. Rte. 4)						
Gradient	Difficulty	Distance	Time	Width	Scenery	Map
0	A	31.8	17.0	5-10 miles	Good	48

TRIP DESCRIPTION: While this description follows from north to south, let the winds determine the direction of your trip, for this certainly is exposed water. Tides are weak, so do not worry about them, except for probing up sidestreams.

Bayside Park is Chesapeake Beach's sweet, little secret. Look for its barely marked entrance off of Rte. 261 a few blocks south of 13th Street. Using it entails about a 300-yard carry to the beach. If that is too much effort, you can pay for access via the commercial marinas in downtown Chesapeake Beach.

A cruise from Chesapeake Beach to Breezy Point is the best option for short-distance paddlers. It gives a taste of this section's pretty cliffs and narrow beaches. With the U.S. Navy installation at Randall Cliffs and other settlements, however, you will not mistake this reach for wilderness.

A county beach at Breezy Point is convenient for launching, as is an adjacent private marina, and that is your last opportunity for access until Matoaka (pronounced Mat' ta walk' a) Beach Cabins and Flag Ponds Nature Park. For variety, you can start with a short side trip up Plum Point Creek. A high tide will get you almost three quarters of a mile up into its marshes and swamp. From the settlements at Breezy and Plum points to Parker Creek, much of the shore remains undeveloped and is graced by relatively low, fossil-bearing cliffs. Here, as on much of the stretch to Cove Point, the near-shore waters are shallow — often less that two feet deep. So it is difficult for the paddler to closely examine the cliffs without landing.

Parker Creek is one of the jewels of the Chesapeake region. Through the efforts of the American Chestnut Land Trust, The Nature Conservancy, and the Maryland Department of Natural Resources, most of the view from the creek and much of its watershed are now permanently protected. This is an unusual waterway in that it is what geologists call a "captured stream," which means it once flowed westward to join the Patuxent. A sand bar guards its mouth, and at low tide you will probably need to carry over the bar to enter the creek. With high tide, one can ascend about two miles up the winding channel. It passes through wide marshes which then narrow. The marshes change to swamp, and finally the channels ends at the base of beaver dams. High forested ground frames it all in complete, bald eagle-patrolled isolation. If there were only an easier way to get here.

Cliffs almost continuously line the way south of Parker Creek. Unfortunately, the communities at the top crowd the edge and are all too visible. The aesthetic insults end at Flag Ponds Park. There is one intermediate access point on this reach via Matoaka Beach Cabins. For a token fee, the owners of this small private development graciously share access to their beach with boaters, hikers, and fossil hunters.

Flag Ponds Nature Park is a county reservation that features a wild sand beach, shallow ponds, a lush forest, and a trails system to explore it all. With about a half mile separating the parking area from the beach, it is an access for the more energetic, though a boat carriage can greatly ease the pain. The park is open during daylight hours seven day a week from Memorial Day to Labor Day, weekends only in the off season. There is a modest entry fee.

The stretch from Flag Ponds to Cove Point is the best of the Calvert coast. The cliffs are the tallest. The beaches are the loneliest. This is no accident, as the much of the land is within the bounds of a state park, a nuclear power plant, and a liquefied natural gas terminal. Big as the industrial projects are, they are less obtrusive than the shoreline housing to the north. This reach ends at Cove Point, with its lovely old lighthouse.

The remaining miles to Solomons takes you past shoreline development interrupted by more nice cliffs. You can take out at the public ramp at the Rte. 4 bridge, or save yourself a mile of paddling and a ramp fee by exiting at the south end of the Riverwalk.

HAZARDS: None.

WATER CONDITIONS: Tidal.

GAUGE: None.

West River and Rhode River

INTRODUCTION: The West and its tributary, the Rhode, are two stubby inlets of the Chesapeake about six miles south of downtown Annapolis. What they lack in length, however, is more than made up for in shoreline, with over 50 miles of it. While many of these miles are thoroughly developed waterfront, two large tracts of open space, one belonging to the Smithsonian Environmental Research Center, the other to the YMCA's Camp Letts, have made the heart of this estuary system a worthy destination.

Section 1. Carrs Wharf to Rte. 255, Galesville						
Gradient	Difficulty	Distance	Time	Width	Scenery	Map
0	A	Variable	Variable	0 to 1.5 mi.	Good to Fair	49

TRIP DESCRIPTION: The best of this waterway is well suited for a circuit paddle, starting at either Carrs Wharf — a small public landing in Mayo, or Contees Wharf — an even smaller public landing southeast of the crossroads of South River. Other public access points are the fishing pier at the foot of Md. Rte. 255 in Galesville and the dock at the foot of Woods Wharf Road in Shady Side.

Most of the structures in Camp Letts and the Smithsonian Center are concentrated in two small areas. This leaves the rest of their 10 miles of waterfront wild. The ground is high and wooded, decorated with holly and mountain laurel. Marshes frame the heads of most creeks. Perhaps the most rewarding path to explore is Muddy Creek, which reaches back almost two miles into the refuge.

The Smithsonian Center was established to conduct programs of ecological research and public education. The latter includes a self-guided nature trail, organized canoe trips, and seminars. For more information, write the center's Education Department, P.O. Box 28, Edgewater, MD 21037; or call (301) 261-4190 from D.C. area, (410) 269-1412 from Baltimore area, or (410) 798-4424 from Annapolis area.

HAZARDS: Motorboat traffic and personal watercraft.

WATER CONDITIONS: Tidal

GAUGE: None.

Severn River

INTRODUCTION: The Severn is a watery highway through the heart of suburbia. Hence, most of its miles would appeal only to ones who live on it or who are visiting friends that do. Of more general interest is the waterfront of Annapolis. This charming old capitol of Maryland and sailing Mecca puts it best face towards the water, and is well worth a visit.

Severn River

Section 1. Veterans Hwy. to Greenbury Point Shoal Lighthouse						
Gradient	Difficulty	Distance	Time	Width	Scenery	Map
0	A	13.5	7.0	10 ft. to 1 mi.	Fair to Good	50

TRIP DESCRIPTION: The source of the Severn is Severn Run, a swampy, nontidal rivulet that is mostly too small and congested to navigate. This is unfortunate, as much of it flows through the wilds of a state environmental area, and its waters are one of the few in the coastal plain that support trout. By starting at Veterans Highway, you catch the last little bit of the run, which is a 10-foot-wide path rushing over pea gravel riffles or shallow sand-bottomed pools through the last of the swamp. In a good year, you may actually find it free of strainers.

With the beginning of tidewater comes the beginning of the houses, billions and billions of them, lining both the main river and almost every creek and cove. On the positive side, the Severn waterfront is upscale real estate, so the domiciles range from comfortable on up to monuments to conspicuous consumption. So if you enjoy architecture and landscaping, this might just be your cup of tea. On the negative side, there is absolutely no place to land if nature calls, etc. There is also no public access between Veterans Highway and U.S. Rte. 50. One large undeveloped tract along the south side of Round Bay (the bulge below Severna Park) is the sole reminder of how pretty this river once was.

Though just as civilized as the upper river, the Severn below Rte. 50 offers much more variety. Starting at the north shore, just below Rte. 50 are some beautiful red cliffs composed of sharp, scalloped rock almost resembling coral. Below Rte. 2 bridge, the the site of the former Navy's David Taylor Research Center occupies much of the shore. At its lower end, a complex of extraordinarily high communications towers dominate the scenery. Hidden in this metallic forest is a pleasant side trip up lonely and otherwise undeveloped Carr Creek.

The south side of the river is dominated by Annapolis. The U.S. Naval Academy occupies about a half mile of the shore. Then, branching off into the heart of Annapolis is Spa Creek. Spa Creek gives you a good view of the town's historic district and its landmarks. You will share these waters with more sailboats than you ever thought could exist. And if you want to see even more, turn up the next creek down river, Back Creek, which seems like one big marina. A particularly interesting time to visit Spa Creek is between 6 and 8 p.m. on the second Saturday of December, when holiday-lit boats shine for the annual Christmas Lights Parade.

Compared to the upper river, access around Annapolis is good. Within the city, most streets that end at the water are designated as public landings, though parking is tight. Truxton Park, a pleasant island of green on Spa Creek, has a launching ramp. A tiny park (off Edgewood Road) along the east bank of Back Creek is also a good put-in.

HAZARDS: Strainers on Severn Run. On the river, beware of heavy motorboat traffic and personal watercraft.

WATER CONDITIONS: Most of this is tidal. As for Severn Run, catch within a week or two of rain during late fall, winter, or spring.

GAUGE: None.

Patapsco River

Patapsco River

INTRODUCTION: The Patapsco flows through the geographical heart of Maryland and down the State's most important valley to join the Chesapeake Bay near Baltimore — Maryland's largest city, transportation center, and industrial powerhouse. Part of the estuary of the Patapsco is Baltimore's harbor, one of the country's busiest ports.

The nontidal portion of this river remains a paddler's retreat and is surprisingly isolated, considering that it is located just 10 miles from the center of a metropolitan area. The Patapsco Gorge itself was once a major industrial area, made up of factories powered by the river's falling waters. Floods, time, and obsolescence have, however, silenced most of these mills. And the valley, now mostly within the bounds of a state park, is slowly reverting to a more primitive condition.

Section 1. Woodstock to Gun Road						
Gradient	Difficulty	Distance	Time	Width	Scenery	Map
14*	1 to 3-	15.9	5.0	50-100	Fair to	51
*2.7 @ 30fpm					Good	

TRIP DESCRIPTION: Woodstock, located 1.7 miles below the confluence of the North and South branches, is the first available access point on the main stem. If conditions are sufficiently wet, however, a delightful alternative is to start on the North Branch at Marriottsville Road. The North Branch flows through a shallow, wooded gorge decorated by many rock outcrops and marred (only briefly) by a nearby quarry. Although Liberty dam normally lets only a trickle pass down its bed, the course is largely free of trees, both living and fallen. Swift current and easy riffles hurry you to the confluence with the South Branch.

Below the confluence of the branches, the river continues to wind peacefully through an attractive, wooded gorge. At Daniels, there is a 15-foot dam that requires a carry (on the right). A few more riffles and rocks appear, but otherwise all is calm until the river passes beneath the high U.S. Rte. 40 bridge. Immediately below this bridge is the hulk of the old Union Dam, now breached on the far right. The twisting chute through here can be nasty at any water level, so scout first. Most would be wise to carry.

The next few miles are almost continuous whitewater. Look for complex and sometimes tedious rock gardens at low levels and an uncomplicated, bouncy chain of waves at high water. This section climaxes in a steep, bouldery rapid below the old Dickey Mills at Oella. The rapids continue on past Ellicott City until reaching a short backwater formed by a 12-foot dam at Thistle (steep carry on right). Paddlers who are only interested in the best of the whitewater can start at Old Frederick Road (Hollofield) and finish just above the Rte. 144 bridge, Ellicott City, for a run of four miles. After a few riffles comes another pool ending about a half mile downstream at a 25-foot dam, also carried on the right. Below here, there are plenty of easy rapids and riffles until the take-out at the Glen Artney Area of Patapsco State Park, at the foot of Gun Road. This is below some old dam ruins. The scenery along many of these miles below Daniels was severely butchered in 1972 by Hurricane Agnes' floodwaters. It is still healing.

HAZARDS: Dams at Daniels, Thistle, and a half mile below Thistle all require carries. Carrying the crumbling Union Dam is also a good idea considering its nasty hole and the jagged crumbling gabions on the right bank.

WATER CONDITIONS: If Liberty Reservoir is not full, easy parts are canoeable winter and spring within three days of hard rain, but harder parts seldom longer than a day. If Liberty is overflowing (and it takes a wetter than normal winter to reach that state) acceptable levels even on the steep stretch may last three or four days. The North Branch is passable only if Liberty is overflowing.

GAUGE: There is a UGSG gauge (see USGS website) at Old Frederick Road, near Hollofield. Minimum level is roughly 150 cfs (2.0 feet). A check of the rapids below Rte. 144 bridge in Ellicott City provides an adequate indication of water conditions upstream, except for the North Branch, which you must observe at Marriottsville Road.

Section 2. Gun Road to mouth						
Gradient	Difficulty	Distance	Time	Width	Scenery	Map
0*	A to 1-	8.2	3.0	100-200	Fair to	51
*1 @ 8fpm					Poor	

TRIP DESCRIPTION: This run is for local paddlers only—ones who just desire some convenient, secret, watery alcove on which to escape. Wedged between freeways, industry, and city, few others will care to go out of their way to visit this segment.

Most of this run is on tidewater. In fact, Elkridge, just a little more than a mile below the put-in, was once a port for ocean-going sailing ships coming to receive loads of tobacco. But years of man-accelerated erosion have filled the stream bed with sediments, while surrounding wetlands have been intentionally filled for highways, factories, and even an old landfill (long closed). So the trip starts with some fast water and easy, rocky riffles. Between Elkridge and Rte. 295, sandy, beer-can-studded shallows can make progress tedious at low tide. The rest is deep.

The surroundings are fairly woodsy and pleasant until the Harbor Tunnel Thruway crossing. Below here you see a lot more of the surrounding dingy neighborhood. There are patches of tall reed grass and, near the mouth, the high, forsaken grounds of the old landfill are now officially a park. In between, there are some side channels and lagoons into which you can probe. This section is best in summer when the foliage blocks some of the ambient noise and urban ugliness. Finish just west of the mouth at the park east of the South Baltimore General Hospital.

HAZARDS: None.

WATER CONDITIONS: Above Elkridge, you will be dragging if the water is low. So catch within three days of hard rain or almost anytime during normal winter or spring. Below Elkridge, it is always passable, though you will be happiest with a start at high tide.

GAUGE: None. Judge riffles at put-in.

Baltimore Harbor

While not exactly a retreat into the wilderness, a canoe tour of Baltimore Harbor is most interesting and enjoyable. Water pollution control has worked wonders here, allowing the return of fish, crabs, and waterfowl. You still do not want to swim in it, especially after a rain, but it is just fine for boating. The Inner Harbor, with its pavilions, aquarium, ships (sailing frigate USS Constellation, submarine USS Torsk, etc.), and backdrop of glittering, downtown office buildings, is now the pride of Baltimore. What were once dingy, decaying, old surrounding neighborhoods, such as Fells Point or Federal Hill, are now being restored and are regarded as fashionable places to live. Beyond the Inner Harbor are the more traditional trappings of a major port. There are big plants, such as Domino Sugar and Bethlehem Steel, shipyards, coal terminals, docks, and, of course, the big ships. Your car may have rolled off one of the huge freighters docked at Dundalk Marine Terminal. The cranes, trains, ships, and miscellaneous machinery are fascinating, at least if you are just an aging little boy like the author.

One particularly interesting arm of the harbor is what starts as Marley Creek, next becomes Curtis Creek, and then finishes as Curtis Bay. Together they reach back almost seven miles from the Patapsco. Curtis Bay represents industrial Baltimore in all it grimy steel, concrete, and oil-stained majesty. What sets the waterway apart is a long, largely vacant tract of real estate that lines the eastern side of much of Curtis and Marley creeks. I do not know why it remains undeveloped, and maybe I do not want to know. But its wooded expanse, often filled with holly, is pretty, and the tract is wild enough that you might even spot a bald eagle overhead. If you probe up Tanyard Cove, you can easily forget that you are in the heart of a metropolitan area.

Good access is, unfortunately, limited. You can get into the Middle Branch via a launching ramp at the south end of the Hanover Street Bridge, via the park east of the South Baltimore General Hospital, or via Ferry Bar Park (behind Locke Insulators) in Locust Point. For the Inner Harbor, park as close as possible and carry your boat to the steps at the southwest corner, by the Maryland Science Center. For the Northwest Harbor, the ramp at Canton Waterfront Park, on Boston Street just west of Clinton, is excellent. For access to the lower harbor, near Bethlehem Steel, a variety of little parks along the west side of Bear Creek, in Dundalk, will do. For getting to Curtis Bay and environs, there is access at the south side of the Key Bridge via a ramp at Fort Armistead Park. Finally, to slip into the upper end of Marley Creek, try the foot of Chain O Hills Road in Harundale.

South Branch Patapsco River

INTRODUCTION: The South Branch Patapsco River bubbles out of Parrs Spring on the Frederick County line to flow eastward, forming the boundary between Howard and Carroll counties, and finally joining the North Branch Patapsco near Woodstock. For all practical purposes, this is just the upper Patapsco, because Liberty Reservoir usually completely bottles up all flow in the North Branch. As it rolls across the Piedmont Plateau (land of flat rivers), this little creek pulls a pleasant surprise by rushing over miles of moderate but interesting whitewater. If you like your streams tiny and your whitewater rocky and twisting, then head for this stream after the next hard rain.

Section 1. Woodbine to Woodstock						
Gradient	Difficulty	Distance	Time	Width	Scenery	Map
17	A to 3-	14.0	4.5	20-80	Good	52

TRIP DESCRIPTION: The first four miles flow through fields and woods, but the scenery is cluttered by too many houses, too much trash, and an obtrusive railroad. As if to distract you, however, there are easy riffles over gravel bars and through rock gardens, the bouldery ruins of an old milldam at Rte. 97, and a mess of fallen trees between Morgan Station Road and Rte. 97. Below Gaither Road the valley narrows into a wooded gorge that confines the river all the way to Elkridge and tidewater on the main stem. In this gorge the stream begins tumbling over complex, little boulder-patch rapids that continue through Sykesville and on a few more miles below. When the whitewater starts

South Branch Patapsco River (52)

letting up, there is a short stretch of fallen trees and logjams to add interest or aggravation to the trip. Most of the remaining few miles are smooth, with the notable exception of the Falls of the Patapsco, about a half mile below Marriottsville. Here the creek, suddenly, with no warning, plunges over a high, sloping ledge which, while probably runnable, should be carried on the left by most paddlers. There is no convenient access to the mouth of the South Branch, so continue down the Patapsco 1.7 miles to Woodstock.

HAZARDS: Count on battling fallen trees and logjams below Morgan Station Road and below Sykesville. There is a small falls a half mile below Marriottsville, after the stream makes a short bend away from the railroad tracks. Get out well above and scout before approaching.

WATER CONDITIONS: Runnable winter and spring within a day of hard rain.

GAUGE: There is a paddler's gauge painted on the downstream side of the right abutment of the Woodbine Road bridge. Also, if the riffles below that bridge are cleanly runnable, then there is adequate water. Roughly, the USGS gauge at Hollofield (see USGS website) should report at least 400 cfs. Keep in mind, however, that this gauge is about 20 miles downstream of the put-in and its readings may be skewed in wet years by inflow from the North Branch.

Piney Run Lake

Located just northwest of Sykesville, Piney Run Lake provides a fine destination for paddlers seeking quiet water, particularly beginners looking for an unthreatening setting to develop their skills. Formed by the damming of tiny Piney Run, the lake is about a mile and a half long, though one could get about a six- and a half-mile work-out by circling its shoreline closely.

A county park surrounds the waters, forming an attractive, woodsy buffer that screens the view of most of the spreading, suburban cancer beyond. The park provides a launch area, canoe and kayak rentals, and a string of boat-accessible picnic areas. All this comes at a price, so prepare to pay both a park entry fee and a separate launch fee. The lake is open from April 1 through October 31 during daylight hours.

To get there, approach from MD Rte. 97 and turn off on either Streaker or Obrecht roads. If you use Streaker, turn right on White Rock Road and left on Martz Road. For Obrecht Road, it is left on White Rock and right on Martz.

Gwynns Falls

INTRODUCTION: Baltimoreans will be pleased to know that when the big rains hit town, they can break the whitewater gypsy routine and save some gas by looking inward from the Beltway to little and forgotten Gwynns Falls. Although over 200 years of habitation, civilization, and industrialization have exacted a heavy toll from this once clear, wild torrent, all those abuses did not destroy the rapids, which remain in quantity and quality found on few other Fall Line streams.

Gradient	Difficulty	Distance	Time	Width	Scenery	Map
38	A to 3	9.0	3.0	25-200	Poor	53

Section 1. Liberty Heights Ave. to Washington Blvd.

TRIP DESCRIPTION: While not the head of navigation, the put-in at Liberty Heights Avenue marks the transition from mellow headwaters to Fall Line whitewater. The creek soon starts dropping over gentle rock gardens as it passes first through woods and then through Woodlawn Cemetery. Following a short interlude in a pool backed by a three-foot weir (carry), the riffles resume and the gradient increases. The creek rushes through an attractive residential neighborhood climaxing in the charming, restored mill town of Dickeyville. Allow some time to explore its narrow streets lined by white stone and frame houses, and notice the white mill factory across the creek. Also notice the five-foot weir, which you should portage. The rapids, formed by sharp, black rocks, become more challenging now and some are notably steep. While the woodland setting of Gwynns Falls Park is pleasant, the increasingly common odor of raw sewage bubbling forth from Gwynns Falls' infamous leaky sewers begins to offend the nostrils and make one wary about unscheduled immersions. Next the creek eases off into a stretch of long, gentle, gravel-formed rapids until Edmondson Avenue. Be sure that you can identify this bridge, because just downstream, on a blind, swift bend, is a double iron pipe which at minimal levels crosses at a canoeist's chest height. In addition, this pipe often supports a frightening strainer of jammed debris. The short carry is least rotten on the right. Then, shortly below is surprise number two, a five-foot ledge that is runnable by a nasty, tortuous chute on the left or a shear drop on the right. A few more ledges shortly below maintain the excitement. This is a good place for rough rapids as they might distract you from the surrounding grotesque canyon of natural rock outcrops, glaciers of poured waste concrete, and assorted trash. Below Baltimore Street the

Gwynns Falls

scenery gets really revolting while the whitewater mellows to well-spaced riffles and easy rapids. The most exciting activity here is watching the crane at the junkyard feed cars into the compactor machine. Take out at a small park on the right at Wilkens Avenue or at Carroll Park Golf Course at Washington Boulevard.

HAZARDS: Two weirs, the pair of iron pipes, the big ledge (which has serious pinning potential), and the filthy water.

WATER CONDITIONS: Runnable only within 12 hours of a hard and intense rain. I also have a theory that if everybody in western Baltimore flushed their toilets at the same time, we might get a runnable surge in Gwynns Falls.

GAUGE: None.

Jones Falls

INTRODUCTION: This guidebook attempts to be complete—a book to provide a stream for every paddling taste, no matter how demented. So assuming that someone in Maryland, besides myself, would enjoy paddling the ultimate looser stream, here is Jones Falls.

Jones Falls flows down the heart of Baltimore, just like the Seine flows through Paris, the Thames through London, the Potomac through Washington, or the Danube through Budapest. There the similarity ends. For unlike these other nice towns, Baltimore has turned its back on poor, old Jones Falls. Some of it the city has buried, some of it the city has paved, and the remainder the city has used as a freeway right-of-way. Jones Falls' neighbors are factories and railroad yards. Unlike nearby Gwynns Falls or Herring Run, nobody ever enveloped this stream in parks. And unlike the Harbor, its banks are not being renovated and gentrified. But for all this abuse, Jones Falls makes an interesting canoe trip. It is at least a chance to see Baltimore from an unusual angle.

Section 1. Lake Roland Dam to Lafayette Street & Falls Road						
Gradient	Difficulty	Distance	Time	Width	Scenery	Map
23	1 to 2	6.1	2.0	25-50	Unusual	None

TRIP DESCRIPTION: The trip starts off nicely enough, at the foot of Lake Roland Dam in a park. But it quickly carries you out of this leafy setting into the backside of ugly industrial and commercial properties and then to the Jones Falls Expressway (I- 83). This road not only runs by the creek but, for long stretches, right over it. This arrangement treats you to a unique slalom down a forest of concrete supporting pilings. Through much of this section the stream bottom and sides are paved in concrete, or the sides are fortified by massive walls of stacked, stone gabions. You will see some very old factories along the way. These were all mills at one time, some over 150 years old, once powered by the stream's falling water. Some are a beauty to behold, in contrast with the numerous ugly, more contemporary structures. Surprisingly, in this seemingly raped environment, you will see an amazing abundance of bird life. I have observed egrets, flocks of green herons, ducks, and geese on this forlorn waterway. So, it is not all bad.

This is mostly an easy run. It is always swift and, where its bed is natural, it rushes over lots of gravel riffles and rapids. The best evidence of the Fall Line is downstream of 41st Street. There are some rocky rapids and behind an old mill is an eight-foot falls split by a rocky island. The falls is runnable, but a carry across the island is more reasonable for many. At high water a portage may not be an option at this steep-walled spot. Shortly below is a 15-foot dam. A steep carry up to Falls Road (left) and along the road for about a hundred yards is your only choice. The take-out is easy, up a concrete bank, just below the high North Avenue bridge. Make sure you recognize this spot. Just downstream the Falls slips off into a tunnel, running for almost two Stygian miles before emerging in the Inner Harbor.

There is no shuttle map for this stream because of the way the stream and Expressway overlap. The simplest shuttle is via Falls Road and, at the northern end, Lakeside Drive. If you know your way about Baltimore, taking the Expressway may be faster.

HAZARDS: Concrete pilings of the Expressway have potential for a boat-breaking, boater-entrapping broach. Watch for the falls and dam between 41st Street and North Avenue. Both would be extremely dangerous at high water.

WATER CONDITIONS: Up only within 24 hours of a hard rain.

GAUGE: There is a yellow painted gauge on retaining wall across the creek from the red brick sewage pumping station on Ash Street , at the south end of Clipper Mill Road. A level of 2 feet is a fine, minimal, conservative level for a first time down.

Herring Run

INTRODUCTION: Herring Run is a true urban canoe stream. Its watershed is almost completely paved. Its source is literally the gutters of Towson. Its destination is Back River, which is also the destination for half of Baltimore's sewage (treated, fortunately). But buffered by parkland and one college campus, Herring Run is a surprisingly pleasant retreat. Wait for the next downpour, and try it.

Section 1. Echodale Avenue to U.S. Rte. 40						
Gradient	**Difficulty**	**Distance**	**Time**	**Width**	**Scenery**	**Map**
35*	1 to 2+	5.7	1.5	15-25	Fair to	54
*1.5 @ 57					Good	

TRIP DESCRIPTION: The put-in is in an old residential neighborhood. But the creek quickly disappears into a little, densely wooded ravine with steep walls and some attractive rock formations. In the summer, lush foliage blocks out most sight of the surrounding city as far as Rte. 147. Below Rte. 147 the walls diverge, but a wide strip of parkland separates you from the neighborhood. In fact, it starts to feel fairly remote in the last mile and a half. There is an amazing abundance of birdlike seeking refuge here, and you may see ducks, geese, kingfishers, and herons. On the negative side, the water quality is poor. At best, it is street runoff. Then shortly into the trip, a large sanitary sewer tends to spew its contents into the creek when it rains, which is of course when you will be floating by.

Herring Run

The other attraction of Herring Run is its whitewater. It ascends a steep fall line between Echodale Avenue and Rte. 147, providing a menu of rock gardens, cobbles, and ledges, with little slack water in between. The gradient levels off around Rte. 147, but starting just above that point is the first of a long series of gabion dams, with sharp drops of up to three feet. All are runnable. Otherwise, the last half of the run offers mostly gravel-formed rapids and riffles.

Take out just upstream of Rte. 40, at the entrance to the city auto impoundment facility, where a road swings almost down to the edge of the water.

HAZARDS: This is a narrow stream, so beware of fallen trees. The gabion dams can throw up some powerful holes at high water.

WATER CONDITIONS: The drawback of a completely urban stream is that it is incredibly flashy (see last chapter). Generally, to run Herring Run you must wait for an intense rain and go put in before it stops. Runnable levels may last, at best, two hours after the rain.

GAUGE: There is a staff gauge on the right bank under the bridge at the take-out. At minimal levels, it will read about 6.2 feet at the end of your trip. Because of the fast crest, this should roughly read at least seven feet before you start.

Gunpowder Falls

INTRODUCTION: Gunpowder Falls rises in the low hills along the Pennsylvania line, zigzags a southeastward course through beautiful upper Baltimore County, and finally tumbles over the Fall Line to the tidal Gunpowder River east of Baltimore. Partially inundated by two big reservoirs, the

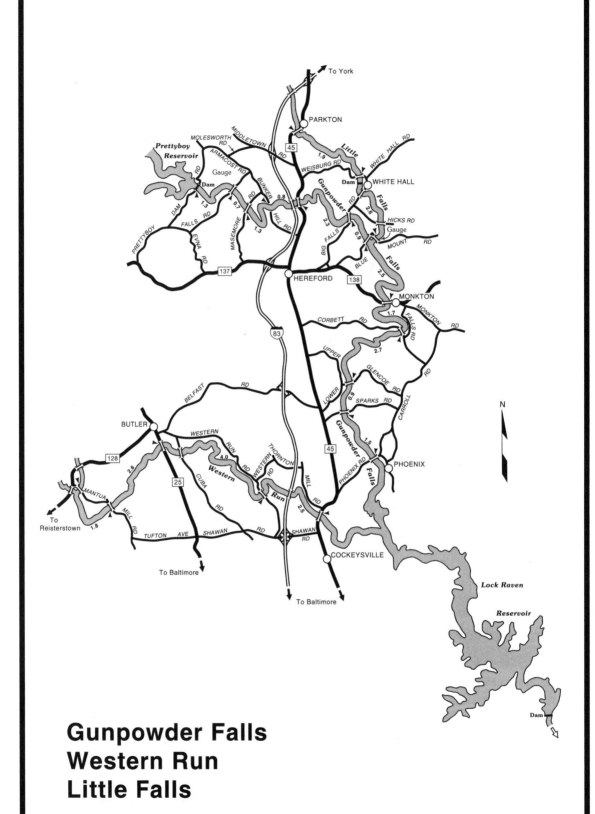

Gunpowder Falls
Western Run
Little Falls

stream provides most of metropolitan Baltimore's water supply. So there is good flatwater paddling, for those so disposed, and still many miles of creek paddling for those who like current underneath them. Its proximity to Baltimore and relatively long-lasting flows in wet years have made this a favorite of Maryland paddlers.

Section 1. Prettyboy Dam to Md. Rte. 45						
Gradient	Difficulty	Distance	Time	Width	Scenery	Map
18*	1 to 3-	4.1	1.5	25-35	Very Good	55
*1 @ 40fpm						

TRIP DESCRIPTION: This short section is a tantalizing appetizer to the exploration of the Gunpowder System. The price of admission is difficult put-in access. You have a choice. You can start at the dam, providing reservoir guards do not catch you, and scramble down a slippery, breakneck path of about a hundred vertical feet to the foot of the south end of Prettyboy Dam. Be sure to have a shuttle driver as no parking is allowed at or near the dam. A better idea is to park at a gated fire road entrance, at the first crest of the hill on Falls Road, a half mile south of its bridge over the Gunpowder. Then carry in a quarter mile, all downhill via the fire road and then foot trail. This tiring, but not killing, approach puts you in at the end of the long straightaway about a half mile below the dam.

The reward for this effort is the pleasure of travelling through a beautiful, wild, steep, wooded gorge. The tiny stream starts by tumbling and dashing down almost continuous boulder gardens and broken ledges, sometimes through the tightest of chutes. After Falls Road it all eases off to easy riffles and fast flat water and stays that way on down to Rte. 45.

HAZARDS: The carry at either put-in, and there is always a possibility of fallen trees on this narrow stream.

WATER CONDITIONS: Canoeable winter and spring within three or four days of a hard rain, providing that Prettyboy Reservoir is full. Normally, if the reservoir is not full (a condition most common in summer and fall or after a prolonged dry spell), the regular discharge from the dam is insufficient for boating this section. However, because the city water-supply people must maintain a certain minimal level in Loch Raven Reservoir where their water intakes are situated, they do so during dry spells by releasing moderate but canoeable volumes of water from Prettyboy. In a really prolonged drought these releases also become increasingly prolonged or frequent. Experience has shown that we can often expect about a two-week release to occur in late August. So far, the city has made no provisions for public notification of these releases.

GAUGE: There is a staff gauge about 50 feet below Falls Road, on the left, on the downstream side of a rock ledge. About 2.0 feet would be zero above Falls Road but still about two inches in the shallowest spots downstream.

Section 2. Md. Rte. 45 to Phoenix Road						
Gradient	Difficulty	Distance	Time	Width	Scenery	Map
7	A to 1	12.5	4.0	30-50	Good	55

TRIP DESCRIPTION: This portion of the Gunpowder is most popular with novices. It is generally a smooth but swift path with enough riffles to keep life interesting. A rocky rapid by the quarry below Big Falls Road will prove the big thrill of the day for the unprepared. During summer release flows, the water is usually clear and cold.

Gunpowder Falls
Little Gunpowder Falls

The river is generally shut off from the rest of the world by the pretty, rock-studded walls of a wooded gorge. But there are also views into the surrounding countryside of horse farms, fields gone to seed, more woodlands, and scattered, attractive homes, both old and new. Except at road crossings, the setting is relatively isolated, though a hiker-biker trail on an old railroad grade often means you will be sharing the gorge with terrestrial types. Unfortunately, the combination of high-priced desirability of the adjacent lands and incidents of abuse stemming from the popularity of this stream has brought some inevitable landowner-visitor conflicts. Many locals resent the influx of park users, which includes hikers, bikers, fishermen, and droves of tubers. There have been access problems at times at such points as Monkton Road and Sparks Road. So please go to extra lengths to be the model visitor. The recommended take-out for this segment is about 2,000 feet downstream of the high Phoenix Road bridge at the hiker-biker access.

HAZARDS: Occasionally a new tree strainer will appear here or there.

WATER CONDITIONS: Runnable winter and spring within a week of hard rain if Prettyboy Reservoir is full or during the summer releases described in Section 1. Normal summer flows are barely sufficient for passage. Also, high water on Little Falls will create runnable levels below Blue Mount Road regardless of the outflow from Prettyboy.

GAUGE: There is a canoeist's gauge painted on the downstream side of the right abutment of Big Falls Road bridge. If most of your flow is coming from Prettyboy, the staff gauge on Section 1 should read at least 1.8 feet.

Section 3. Lower Loch Raven Dam to U.S. Rte. 40						
Gradient	**Difficulty**	**Distance**	**Time**	**Width**	**Scenery**	**Map**
15*	1 to 3+	10.4	4.0	100-150	Good	56
*2@30fpm						

TRIP DESCRIPTION: This section of Gunpowder includes the exciting descent over the Fall Line. If you would like some easy water on which to warm up, put in along Loch Raven Road above Cromwell Bridge Road. This allows you over six pleasant miles where there is nothing more complicated than scattered riffles.

The Fall Line begins just below Rte. 1. If you do not care to warm up, this is where most whitewater boaters start. The river soon begins to earn its name as it tumbles down a bouldery and ledgy bed. At low levels this is a rocky and complex passage. High conditions create a big flush down one long, roaring, heavy, hole-studded rapid. The entire trip runs within the confines of a shallow, wooded gorge, protected by a state park. Take out at Rte. 7 for convenience or at Rte. 40 if you want to catch every last rapid. Rte. 40, unfortunately, bristles with "no parking" signs, but there is a park users' access just upstream on the left off Jones Road. It is about a 200-yard walk up from the river. Make sure you recognize the take-out.

HAZARDS: None.

WATER CONDITIONS: Flow is dependent on the condition of the reservoirs. If the weather has been dry and Prettyboy and Loch Raven are down, then the only water in this section will be that fed by some small side streams. If the reservoirs are full, then a hard rain during winter or spring can sustain runnable levels for a week or more.

GAUGE: There is a canoe gauge painted on the downstream side of the left arch of the U.S. Rte. 1 bridge.

Section 4. U.S. Rte. 40 to Mariner Point Park						
Gradient	Difficulty	Distance	Time	Width	Scenery	Map
1	A to 1-	4.1	2.0	100-150	Good	56

TRIP DESCRIPTION: The remainder of the Gunpowder is a good beginner's trip. After a few gravel riffles and sandy shallows, the path becomes tidal. Most of the passage is through lush woods, but this changes to marsh near the end. Once past the shallows at the mouth, bear left to the take-out at Mariners Point Park. If the water is too low at Rte. 40, just start at Mariners Point and do this trip as a circuit. But be forewarned that identifying the mouth from this direction may be difficult.

HAZARDS: None.

WATER CONDITIONS: Same limitations as Section 3 at start. The remaining tidal reach is fine anytime except for deep winter freeze.

GAUGE: None. Judge shallows at Rte. 40.

Baltimore City Reservoirs

Baltimore has three reservoirs: Liberty on the North Branch Patapsco River and Prettyboy and Loch Raven on Gunpowder Falls. The City strictly regulates and protects these lakes. For that reason (providing that they are full), they are very pretty bodies of water with hilly, wooded shores and no development. On the other hand, this protectiveness makes boating on the lakes a pain in the stern for the would-be paddler. The first obstacle is the requirement that boats used on the reservoirs may not be used elsewhere, in deference to zebra mussel paranoia. Next, only seasonal permits are offered, and they are not cheap ($50 as of this printing). Next, only canoes are allowed on Liberty and Loch Raven, and this would be a great place for sea kayaks. Finally, there are woefully few places where launching is allowed. For Liberty, there two ramps off Oakland Mills Road near Eldersburg, for Loch Raven, there is the Fishing Center at 12101 Dulaney Valley Road, and for Prettyboy, there is an access at the intersection of Spook Hill and Kidds Schoolhouse roads. For more information on current rules, costs, and how to obtain a permit, call the boating information line at 410-795-6150.

Little Falls

INTRODUCTION: Not to be confused with its namesake rapid on the Potomac, this Little Falls is a delightful, little brook that rushes through the rich and rolling countryside of upper Baltimore County to join Gunpowder Falls near Monkton. Endowed with lovely scenery and exciting whitewater, this stream makes an ideal extension to an upper Gunpowder trip or an excellent whitewater duo with the Prettyboy-to-Rte. 45 run on the Gunpowder.

Section 1. Parkton (Md. Rte. 45) to mouth						
Gradient	Difficulty	Distance	Time	Width	Scenery	Map
20*	1 to 3-	4.9	1.5	25-35	Good	55
*1 @ 50fpm						

TRIP DESCRIPTION: This delightful trip begins at Parkton, a lovely, little hamlet of vintage houses clustered about Md. Rte. 45. Immediately below, the creek rushes into a wooded gorge that is decorated by a variety of black rock outcrops and cliffs. The stream bed is filled with boulders, and sometimes the downstream view is totally blocked. But, altogether, this section does not exceed intermediate difficulty. A bicycle trail along the bank provides good rescue or walk-out opportunity. The scenery opens up approaching White Hall, where a five-foot dam with a nasty reversal requires a carry. Below White Hall, the stream flows again into a pretty gorge, this one extending to the confluence with the Gunpowder. One can take out a quarter mile short of the mouth, at Blue Mount Road, or continue on down the Gunpowder to Monkton Road or beyond.

HAZARDS: You will need to carry a dam at the upper end of White Hall and possibly some fallen trees.

WATER CONDITIONS: Canoeable winter and spring within a day of hard rain.

GAUGE: The USGS gauge just upstream of Blue Mount Road (see USGS website or read staff on bicycle trail bridge) should be at least 290 cfs (1.9 feet). Also, the water should be up to at least the bottom of the arch on the Rte. 45 bridge at Parkton.

Western Run

INTRODUCTION: Western Run is a tiny, meandering brook that flows across a peaceful and genteel valley in upper Baltimore County to join Gunpowder Falls east of Cockeysville. It is a fairly unexciting but extremely picturesque run, best recommended for the lover of fine architecture, fine horses, and manicured landscapes.

Section 1. Dover (Mantua Mill Road) to Md. Rte. 45						
Gradient	Difficulty	Distance	Time	Width	Scenery	Map
11	A to 1	10.9	3.5	15-30	Good	55

TRIP DESCRIPTION: Western Run is formed by the union of McGill and Piney runs. Put in on Piney Run at Mantua Mill Road, about a hundred yards east of Butler Road (Md. Rte. 128). There is some very limited parking space on the shoulder of Butler Road.

The creek is tiny to Falls Road, usually only 15 to 20 feet wide. It meanders about an open, gently rolling valley that is dotted by beautiful, old farmhouses, horse farms, and huge mansions. Unfortunately, eroded mud banks tend to bracket the stream. But they are low enough, often enough, to view the surrounding countryside. Although possessing only a modest gradient, the creek rushes over countless riffles formed by fine gravel and over some rubbly rapids formed by the remains of old dams. While this is all very easy, you can count on fallen trees and barbed wire, wooden, and electric fences to complicate navigation throughout the trip. Blackrock Run adds noticeable volume to Western Run just below Falls Road. About this point, the surrounding hills close in, and the remainder of the course is hidden in an attractive, partially wooded gorge.

Much of this cruise passes through an essentially residential neighborhood occupied by people who put out a lot of cash to enjoy some elbow room. Please make an effort to maintain a low profile and travel in small, quiet groups when paddling through. Considering how close this valley is to the big city, it is amazing (as of this writing) how few "posted" signs there are along this stream.

HAZARDS: Beware of strainers, which include barbed wire fences, electric fences, cattle gates, trees, and logjams. Cattle gates, if you are not familiar with the term, are wooden fences suspended in short sections from a cable across the creek. Those on Western Run mostly seem to be loosely suspended, allowing a paddler to squeeze through rather than carry. Watch out for a hard-to-see barbed wire strand underneath the Cuba Road bridge (a steel truss below Falls Road).

WATER CONDITIONS: Canoeable winter and spring not more than two days after a hard rain.

GAUGE: None.

Little Gunpowder Falls

INTRODUCTION: Nestled along the border between Harford and Baltimore counties, this tiny stream dashes down a rocky Fall Line route to tidewater, northeast of Baltimore. Though now just another little creek beneath busy I-95, the Little Gunpowder and its valley were a major center of commerce during colonial times. At that time, the estuary could float ocean-going ships to Joppa, a booming tobacco port, while the upstream Fall Line gradient provided power for mills. But the harbor succumbed to siltation and the town to competition from the new port of Baltimore, so that today Joppa, a bedroom community for Baltimore, remains a town in name only. The value of the stream now is recreational, probably most appreciated by the opportunistic whitewater paddler and the trout fisherman.

Section 1. Md. Rte. 146 to Md. Rte. 147						
Gradient	Difficulty	Distance	Time	Width	Scenery	Map
14	1 to 2	10.7	3.0	15-35	Good to Very Good	56

TRIP DESCRIPTION: This is a delightful passage. After a start in a harmonious, pastoral setting, the Little Gunpowder ambles down a wooded gorge. Its attributes include striking rock outcrops, a rock-studded stream bed, and a well developed surrounding forest of unusually straight, tall trees. You will see little development because much of this land lies within Gunpowder Falls State Park. Most of the gradient is expended as gravel riffles, but occasional ledges or patches of boulders form easy rapids. Being a small stream, expect to find a few fallen trees blocking the way. A sharp, two-foot weir about a quarter mile below the put-in is runnable.

HAZARDS: Fallen trees, a two-foot weir below Rte. 146, and possibly a barbed wire in the first half mile.

WATER CONDITIONS: This stream has a narrow, pastoral, and in some places suburbanizing, watershed. So the runoff is quick. Catch in winter or spring within a day of hard rain.

Section 2. Md. Rte. 147 to U.S. Rte. 40						
Gradient	Difficulty	Distance	Time	Width	Scenery	Map
36	1 to 3–	6.2	2.0	25-35	Fair	56

TRIP DESCRIPTION: The Little Gunpowder now accelerates into almost continuous action, dropping over gravel bars, rock gardens, and, below Jerusalem Road, a variety of interesting ledges. While generally an excellent intermediate trip, high water conditions here create big waves, frightening velocity, and vicious hydraulics that will thrill even the advanced paddler. At any level, approach the sharp drop behind the factory (Belko Co.) at Franklinville with caution.

Although the stream runs through the deepest part of its Fall Line gorge, the scenery is degraded by trash, graffiti on rock formations, and residential development. The gorge ends at U.S. Rte. 40 where civilization really takes over. Your take-out is a shopping center on the right.

HAZARDS: Fallen trees and, at high water, some of the ledges on this creek form powerful holes.

WATER CONDITIONS: Runnable winter or spring within a day of hard rain.

GAUGE: There is a canoe gauge painted on the downstream side of the right abutment of the Rte. 1 bridge. If it is too faded, use the grooves on the left abutment of that bridge. Six grooves down from the bottom of the span roughly indicates about six inches of canoeable water. It takes the same amount of water to do both sections, so you can also use the groove reference on Rte. 165, Section 1.

Winters Run

INTRODUCTION: Winters Run starts in the beautiful Piedmont hills west of Bel Air, Harford County, and rushes down a narrow, wooded valley to the tidal Bush River. It makes a graceful descent over the Fall Line, usually hidden away from the growing suburbia through which it flows.

Section 1. Pleasantville Road to Md. Rte. 7						
Gradient	Difficulty	Distance	Time	Width	Scenery	Map
18	1 to 2–	13.6	4.0	15-25	Good	57

TRIP DESCRIPTION: Enter via steep banks at Pleasantville Road. The stream winds through a shallow, wooded gorge filled with many beautiful beech trees, some of which, unfortunately, have fallen across the creek. There are continuous easy riffles of gravel bars and rock gardens, and, above Carrs Mill Road, a relatively steep, twisting rapid through the ruins of an old milldam. Below here, the topography opens up and the gradient slows somewhat. At U.S. Business Rte. 1 there is a sloping, four-foot-high dam with a strong hole at the bottom. Experienced paddlers can consider running this. Below Business Rte. 1, the stream enters a gorge again, which, except for the presence of a few attractive houses, is essentially wild. The whitewater here is almost nonstop over a rocky and uncomplicated bed. Passing Ring Factory Road, Winters Run enters the backwater of the narrow, attractive, but silt-

Winters Run

(57)

ing-in, Atkisson Reservoir. It is a one- and-a-half-mile paddle across the lake, which is becoming a marsh, to the 60-foot-high dam, portaged on either side. Below the dam, the stream resumes its busy descent, but the scenery degrades to a drab and trashy condition.

HAZARDS: Fallen trees, a dam above Business Rte. 1 (with a powerful hydraulic), and the 60-foot dam that backs up Atkisson Reservoir.

WATER CONDITIONS: Only up within 24 hours of a hard rain, during winter or spring.

GAUGE: USGS gauge near Rte. 1 (see USGS website) should read at least 240 cfs (2.7 feet) Approximately nine inches of water over the dam at Business Rte. 1 should be adequate.

Susquehanna River Tributaries

Chapter 5
The Susquehanna River Basin

The Susquehanna River starts in the heart of New York State at Cooperstown and from there it flows 444 crooked miles to the Chesapeake Bay at Havre de Grace. It has the largest drainage on the east coast, covering almost 28,000 square miles in New York, Pennsylvania, and Maryland. But only 254 square miles lie in Maryland. The Susquehanna, nevertheless, may be Maryland's most important river and basin for its estuary is the Chesapeake Bay, probably the State's foremost natural resource. It is the Susquehanna's tremendous influx of fresh water (or sometimes the lack of it) that virtually determines the character and health of the Bay. It affects, for example, such diverse features as the abundance and quality of the Bay's renown seafood species, silt deposition patterns that can affect navigation, and dispersion of any pollutants that enter these waters. The direct importance of this basin to the canoeist is that it remains a rural, still sparsely populated territory in the heart of a growing eastern seaboard strip city. It is a nice refuge that is still close to home for several million people.

The following streams are described in this chapter:

Susquehanna River
    Conowingo Creek
    Octoraro Creek
    Deer Creek

Susquehanna River

INTRODUCTION: The Susquehanna stands out boldly in this state of small streams, for no other nontidal river in Maryland comes close to matching its nearly mile width. Although most of its long descent over the Fall Line to tidewater at Port Deposit has been reduced to a chain of pools behind hydroelectric dams, there remain a few free-flowing miles below Conowingo Dam that will interest the novice whitewater canoeist.

Paddling this section, one cannot help but speculate on what a majestic and possibly exciting run the Fall Line of the Susquehanna might have been to the turn-of-the-century canoeist. But while the whitewater paddlers might have once enjoyed the lower Susquehanna, commercial boatmen found the rock-strewn, natural Susquehanna most objectionable. During the nineteenth century, navigational interests wrote off the rocky river as a lost cause and bypassed it with canals on both banks from tidewater on upstream as far as Nanticoke, Pennsylvania, 180 miles above its mouth. In addition, these canals tied in with a cross-state system that ran from Philadelphia to Pittsburgh. Ruins of these works on the lower Susquehanna are still evident, where not inundated by the dam pools, at Norman Wood Bridge (Pa. Rte. 372) near Holtwood, Pennsylvania, and along U.S. Rte. 222 above Port Deposit, Maryland.

The Susquehanna can be a powerful and destructive river, for it is capable of gathering up a heckuva lot of water by the time it reaches Maryland. During the great flood of 1936, over 800,000 cfs poured past Conowingo. Then Hurricane Agnes topped that in 1972 with 1,100,000 cfs. Conowingo Dam can pass up to 80,000 cfs just through its turbines, and for those occasions when there is an excess of water, there are 30 huge spillway gates to accommodate it. In spite of all that capacity, there were still some tense moments when Agnes' waters threatened to top the dam.

About the only thing worse than floodwaters is floodwaters with ice. The excessive width of the Susquehanna allows great quantities of ice to form during the winter. And if quick, early snow melt or heavy winter rains bring the river up before the ice can significantly melt, this ice can transform into a frightening, floating glacier that can scrape away almost anything that stands in its path. Understandably, towns close to the Susquehanna face each spring with great apprehension.

The Susquehanna once supported a great fishing industry, based on the harvesting of shad. Shad, like salmon, are anadromous fish, that is, they migrate from the sea to the river to breed. The construction of Conowingo Dam and two more dams upstream totally blocked this migration, and shad ceased to visit the river. Currently the Pennsylvania Fish & Boat Commission is experimenting with portaging the shad around the dams by tank trucks. If the experiment is successful, permanent fish ladders or elevators may be constructed, and perhaps some day the annual shad run will once again become a regular feature of life along the Susquehanna.

Section 1. Broad Creek Access to Susquehanna State Park						
Gradient	Difficulty	Distance	Time	Width	Scenery	Map
3*	A to 1	10.1	3.5	2,500-	Good	58
*between dam and tidewater				4,000		

TRIP DESCRIPTION: About five miles of Conowingo Dam's pool is in Maryland. It is wide, the scenery is bland, winds can whip its surface, motorboats can run you down, and the water just sits there. But if you like canoeing in such a setting, a public ramp at Broad Creek or the power company's ramps at the mouth of Conowingo Creek and at Glen Cove Marina provide easy access.

If you are taking a long trip down the Susquehanna and must portage Conowingo Dam, you have two options. The traditional one is to land at the south (right) end of the dam (steep, weed-choked exit possibly with a debris-jammed approach), walk up Rte. 1 to Shures Landing Road and down that street to the tailrace, an exhausting ordeal. The smart option is to land at Glen Cove Marina and call the power company, which will truck you and your boat to the fishing area below, free of charge. This same public service, incidentally, is offered at Holtwood and Safe Harbor dams, upstream in Pennsylvania.

One can put in at the tailrace of the powerhouse at the fishing access area on Shures Landing Road. For the next four miles, the river drops gently over an incredibly ledgy and jagged bottom. At low water this creates a rocky maze, without parallel, that not only demands good water reading ability, but also requires the boater to have an intuitive sense to decipher where, in a 3,000-foot-wide panorama of pure rock, enough water gathers to float a boat. Higher water simplifies the river to a lot of fast water, spotted with rocks, eddys, little waves, and little holes. Because of the difficulty of rescue, novices should avoid this section in cold weather or if the water level is high. These rocks and riffles, which bear the impressive title of Smith Falls (this is as far as Capt. John Smith got in his exploration of the Chesapeake Bay and Susquehanna River), end at the upstream side of Port Deposit. From there it is about a mile-long paddle down tidewater to the launching ramp in Susquehanna State Park, at the foot of Lapidum Road.

HAZARDS: Be prepared for rapidly fluctuating water levels, varying as much as eight feet at the tailrace launching area. So heed the warning signals. Conversely, the conclusion of power generation can leave the hapless paddler stranded high and dry in a sea of wet rocks. So check the generating schedule before launching. The width of this river makes cold weather paddling risky to the unskilled. And winds can plow up some boat-swamping waves or just plain blow you away.

WATER CONDITIONS: Flow on this section is frustratingly variable, depending on the flow in the river above the hydro dams, power generation at three upstream plants, level of Conowingo Lake, and, of course, power generation at Conowingo. Generally, most or all of your water will be coming from the powerhouse. Historically, if the Susquehanna was low above the reservoirs, the powerhouse would run only during peak demand periods, i.e. Monday through Saturday, in the afternoon. Generation on Sunday during summertime would be undependable. Fortunately, to protect the fishery in the river, the power company now has committed to maintaining a flow of 3,500 cfs at all times between March 1 and November 30. The flow is interruptible during the remaining, three chilly months. While 3,500 cfs spreads pretty thin on such a wide river, it certainly beats the total shut-offs that used to occur.

GAUGE: None. An on-the-spot inspection and check of the generating schedule will tell you everything.

Susquehanna River
Conowingo Creek

To Quarryville

SWIFT RD

GOSHEN MILL RD

PILGRAMS PATHWAY

0.8

1.1

1.3

To Lancaster

272

1.0

ULRICH RD

To Nottingham

SOAPSTONE HILL RD

WAKEFIELD

1.0

GOAT HILL RD

PENNSYLVANIA

PILOT TOWN RD

1.0

Conowingo

222

BLACK BARON RD

1.6

DIXON RD

CORNWALL LA

MASON RD

0.8

OLD MILL RD

Creek

MARYLAND

2.6

PLEASANT GROVE RD

PILOT TOWN RD

BELL MANOR RD

1.9

CONOWINGO RD

222

MT ZOAR RD

To Philadelphia

Access

Access

Broad Creek

Access

3.4

Susquehanna

623

Dam

Octoraro Creek

BERKLEY RD

GLEN COVE RD

1.3

Glen Cove Marina

SHURESVILLE RD

SHURES LNDG RD

River

222

To Baltimore

1

DARLINGTON

161

Deer Creek

STAFFORD RD

5.0

PORT DEPOSIT

To US Rte 40, I-95

Access

WEBSTER LAPIDUM RD

LAPIDUM RD

To Havre de Grace

To Rte 155

N

58

Conowingo Creek

INTRODUCTION: Conowingo Creek is a small stream that flows peacefully out of Lancaster County, Pennsylvania into Cecil County, Maryland, only to end its journey with a violent plunge into the Susquehanna River upstream of Conowingo Dam. It is best classified as a quick, cheap thrills run, ideal as a chaser to any of the other neighborhood streams when the water is up.

Section 1. Swift Road to Pilot Town Road						
Gradient	**Difficulty**	**Distance**	**Time**	**Width**	**Scenery**	**Map**
16	A to 1	9.9	3.5	20-30	Good	58

TRIP DESCRIPTION: Tiny as Conowingo Creek is up there, one can start at Swift Road, just down the hill from the birthplace of Robert Fulton (the father of motorboating). The brook introduces you to a beautiful, pastoral setting. Though the view is sometimes blocked by the creek's eroded banks, you will appreciate seeing so many of the type of well-kept farms that have made Lancaster County famous. Eventually woodlots appear, and by the end of the trip, the passage is hidden entirely back in the woods and in a shallow gorge. One nice cedar grove and a few rock outcrops further complement the scenery.

Though this is a novice run, one must have the experience to handle strainers. There may be only a few fallen trees, but count on lots of fences and one low-water bridge. The water itself is often smooth, broken by short, gravel riffles. Farther down there are a few boulder patches, and almost continuous rock garden mark the final leg to Pilot Town Road.

HAZARDS: Expect trees, fences, and, at Goat Hill Road, a low-water bridge.

WATER CONDITIONS: Catch within 24 hours of a lot of rain.

GAUGE: None on creek. As a very rough indicator, the USGS gauges (see USGS website) on Deer Creek at Rocks and White Clay Creek near Newark should probably be running over 250 cfs.

Section 2. Pilot Town Road to mouth						
Gradient	**Difficulty**	**Distance**	**Time**	**Width**	**Scenery**	**Map**
50*	1 to 5	1.9	1.0	20-30	Very Good	58
* reaches 200 fpm						

TRIP DESCRIPTION: Put in on the road branching due west off U.S. Rte. 222 at Oakwood, Maryland. You have about three quarters of a mile to warm up, as riffles progress to easy rapids, then medium difficulty rapids, and onward and upward. Then comes a four-foot dam, runnable through a breach on the right, after which the creek gets down to serious business. From here to the end, it is one steep, complex, snaggle-toothed rapid that is occasionally filtered through a fallen tree. At best, there are only postage stamp eddies, and they exist only at minimal levels. At higher levels the run is one long uncontrolled flush. Do not attempt this run without first scouting, on foot, every inch between the dam and the mouth, most importantly to identify any tree hazards. Take out at the launching ramp on the backwater of Conowingo Lake.

Octoraro Creek

HAZARDS: The whole run is a hazard, especially if there are any trees in the picture.

WATER CONDITIONS: Winter and spring within 24 hours of a hard rain.

GAUGE: None. Judge while scouting. As a very rough indicator, the USGS gauges (see USGS website) on Deer Creek at Rocks and White Clay Creek near Newark should probably be running over 150 cfs.

Past Prosperity

This sleepy corner of Cecil County was once a busy place. Nearby Conowingo Creek is the site of the Line Pits. This is an abandoned chromium mine that operated between 1828 and 1880. During its first 22 years of operation it was the source of most of the world's chrome supply. This of course is not necessarily saying much since the two major uses for chrome, for electroplating and as an ingredient of stainless steel, had not been developed yet. Nevertheless, a substantial market must still have existed as other chromium deposits were also worked during that period around Rocks State Park, in Harford County, and near Soldiers Delight, in upper Baltimore County. The industry died when its overseas market turned to richer deposits discovered in Asia Minor (Turkey).

Octoraro Creek

INTRODUCTION: Octoraro Creek drains the rolling, rich farm country of southern Lancaster and Chester counties in Pennsylvania. Formed deep beneath the waters of Octoraro Lake by the confluence of the East and West branches, the creek rushes (Octoraro is Indian for "rushing waters") on into Cecil County, Maryland for a rendezvous with the Susquehanna River.

Section 1. Forge Road to Md. Rte. 222						
Gradient	**Difficulty**	**Distance**	**Time**	**Width**	**Scenery**	**Map**
10*	1 to 2−	20.7	7.0	30-50	Good	59
* 3 @ 20fpm						

TRIP DESCRIPTION: The put-in is at the covered bridge just below the little dam, below the big dam that backs the reservoir. The creek follows a mellow course of long, slow pools separated by enjoyable gravel bar riffles, all the time wandering through attractive, rolling fields and woodlands. If you are fortunate enough to catch this stream up in late May, the air will be laced with the fragrance of the flowering Russian olive trees that seem to grow everywhere in this valley.

The creek then enters a shallow, wooded gorge, which is pretty, except for one eyesore, a huge gravel pit. After passing this pit and the beginning of a boy scout camp, Octoraro begins a long and delightful descent through a series of rock gardens that ends in the pool behind a four-foot rubble dam, just above U.S. Rte. 1. The dam is runnable, but is usually scratchy.

The stretch below Rte. 1 comprises the liveliest portion of the Octoraro. Those wishing just to run this section should put in and park along Colora Road. The stream rushes through a fairly isolated gorge filled with numerous easy rapids formed by rock gardens, gravel, and small ledges. A few power line crossings mar the otherwise wild setting. The gorge ends at Rowlandsville, once a busy 19th-century industrial village that manufactured iron and paper. Take out just below here on a side road that branches off Rte. 222 toward Rowlandsville about a thousand feet west of the bridge over Octoraro Creek. It is another third of a mile from Rte. 222 to the Susquehanna, where there is no convenient access.

HAZARDS: Rubble dam just above Rte. 1.

WATER CONDITIONS: Canoeable winter and spring within three days of hard rain, providing that Octoraro Lake is full.

GAUGE: Count the grooves on the downstream end of the pier of U.S. Rte. 1 bridge. Six grooves down from top is zero. Also you can judge by the riffle beneath the covered bridge at Forge Road. Roughly, USGS gauge at Chadds Ford, on Brandywine Creek (see USGS website), should read at least 450 cfs (2.4 feet), providing that the lake is full.

Deer Creek

INTRODUCTION: Deer Creek rises in the pasturelands of York County, Pennsylvania, and from there wanders across a corner of Baltimore County and the width of Harford County to join the Susquehanna River below Conowingo. Composed of a pleasant mixture of woodlands, working farms, and country estates, there is no prettier countryside in Maryland. Unfortunately, this is also very prized, high priced, and jealously defended real estate, which means that there is a lot of posted land, especially at many potential access points. So when running this popular stream, please be on your best behavior and be sure to obtain permission before crossing private land.

Section 1. Gorsuch Mills (Bond Road) to Fawn Grove Road						
Gradient	Difficulty	Distance	Time	Width	Scenery	Map
15	1 to 2	13.1	4.0	15-50	Very Good	60

TRIP DESCRIPTION: This far upper portion of this long stream offers the most pleasant cruising on Deer Creek. Just large enough on which to fit a canoe at Bond Road, the creek starts out by twisting about a flat, agricultural bottomland fringed by pastoral or forested hillsides. The hillsides then converge at Green Road, and for the remaining miles Deer Creek rushes through a chain of wild, wooded ravines. Though interrupted by two summer camps and a few road bridges, these miles offer the paddler plenty of quiet and solitude; a fascinating display of unusually sharp, jagged rock formations; cool, hemlock-shaded bends; and assorted fond memories.

The creek is always in a hurry, rushing over numerous riffles and easy rapids formed by gravel, rock gardens, boulders, and ledges, with swift current in between. One particularly boulder-constricted rapid below Green Road should be scouted by novices. Fences come and go on the civilized parts of this section, and occasional fallen trees, especially on the first few miles, will require carries.

The run concludes at Eden Mill, which in contrast to most long-abandoned and crumbling relics about the State, stands well preserved and was still operating, grinding local corn, as recently as 1965. Eden Mill Dam backs up water for about three quarters of a mile and is easily portaged on the left.

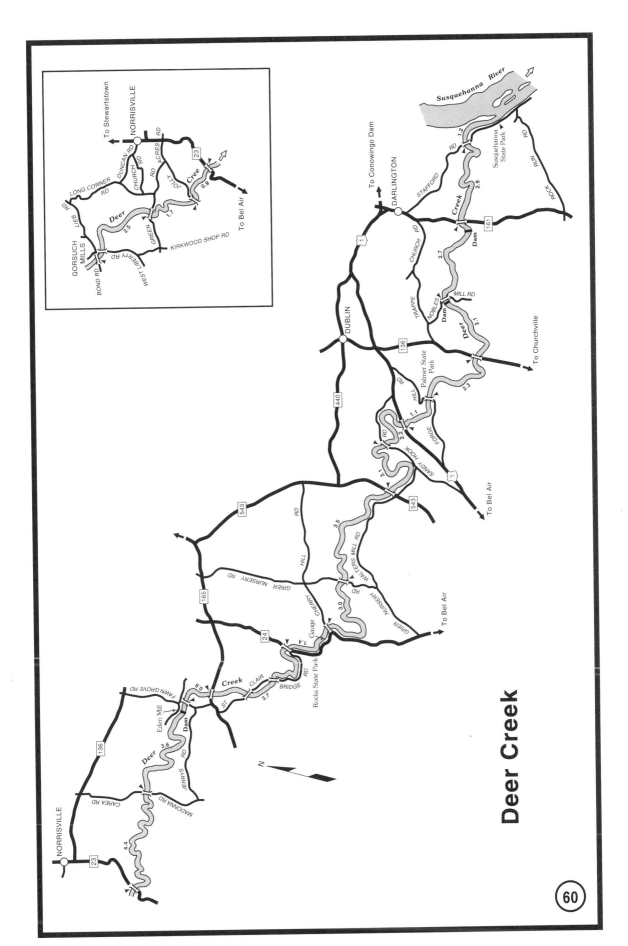

Deer Creek

60

HAZARDS: Strainers include fences on the first two miles and fallen trees throughout. The trees decrease in frequency as the stream grows. There is a low-water bridge below Jolly Acres Road, requiring a carry, and the 12-foot dam at Eden Mill should also be portaged on the left (it has been run by at least one adventuresome sort).

WATER CONDITIONS: Runnable winter and spring after a hard rain. Most reliably passable within a day of rainfall, but if the ground is really wet, then it may last two or three days.

GAUGE: There is a yellow flood staff gauge on the right upstream end of Bond Road bridge. Six inches is zero canoeable level. USGS gauge at Rocks (see USGS website or inspect on site) should report over 500 cfs (3.5 feet).

Section 2. Fawn Grove Road to mouth						
Gradient	Difficulty	Distance	Time	Width	Scenery	Map
11	A to 1,3	30.1	10.0	25-40	Good	60

TRIP DESCRIPTION: One can start at Fawn Grove Road or, better yet, just upstream at the rustic Eden Mill. The initial miles to Rocks State Park take you down swift, flat water spiced with some gravelly riffles and sometimes obstructed by an ill-placed fence or fallen tree. The creek winds about a narrow, rural valley, views of which are, unfortunately, often blocked by eroded mud banks.

At Rocks State Park, Deer Creek breaks through the hard, crystalline mass of Rock Ridge and tumbles down a short, violent series of narrow chutes. Considering the strong potential for broaching and the sharpness of the rocks, novices would be wise to take advantage of the nearby highway and carry. After decelerating through a stretch of gentle rock gardens, the creek then settles down once again to an easy pace as it weaves through hilly countryside. There is still, however, a lively, rock-filled, wooded gorge below U.S. Rte. 1 and a riffly, gorge-like section approaching Stafford Bridge to add variety. The ruins of a three-and-a-half-foot dam above Nobles Mill form a better-than-average rapid (run middle). A sloping, three-foot dam at Wilson Mill is runnable anywhere, though you will clunk over. Possibly the finest quality of Deer Creek though is that through most of these miles, the banks have remained unblemished by the vacation cottages, shacks, and other eyesores that plague so many otherwise beautiful creeks in this area.

You can break this section down into any number of runs of comfortable length, with the best combinations including the passage through Rocks or the gorge below Rte.1. Access points that are presently unposted and offer some degree of parking space include Md. Rte. 165, along Md. Rte. 24, Grier Nursery Road, Md. Rte. 543, Sandy Hook Road, Md. Rte. 136, and Stafford Road. With a muddy take-out at the mouth, the last mile may be worth skipping. But if you visit the stretch near Stafford Bridge, be sure to stop at Susquehanna State Park and check out its old furnace and restored mills.

HAZARDS: The sloping weir at Wilson Mill is runnable anywhere at moderate levels. At high water, a carry would be safer. Fences and trees come and go. So be prepared.

WATER CONDITIONS: Canoeable winter and spring within a week of hard rain.

GAUGE: The USGS gauge (see USGS website or inspect on site) along Md. Rte. 24 at the lower end of Rocks State Park should read at least 140 cfs (2.5 feet) to scrape through the shallowest rock gardens. There is a canoe gauge painted on the right downstream concrete support of the Sandy Hook Road bridge. For rough estimate, the USGS gauge on Codorus Creek near York (call State College or see USGS website) should read over 170 cfs (2.6 feet).

Making Iron

In the late 18th and early 19th centuries, an iron industry operated on a small and localized scale throughout the Middle Atlantic states. Remains of the old blast furnaces stand scattered about the countryside and include among them the well preserved structures at Stafford Bridge on Deer Creek, Lonaconing on Georges Creek, Catoctin Furnace south of Thurmont, and between Metal and Richmond Furnace along the West Branch Conococheague Creek. Local sources supplied the furnaces with raw materials. Various forms of iron ore were found throughout the region, even on the coastal plain of the Eastern Shore where it was called bog iron. Fuel was usually charcoal, made from the wood of the surrounding forests. The final ingredient, limestone, could be mined in much of central and western Maryland and adjacent Pennsylvania. On the coastal plain seashells were used. The furnaces were usually located near running water, which was used to power the bellows that provided the essential blasts of hot air. Pig iron from these mills supplied most local needs, were a major source of cannon and cannon balls during the Revolution and War of 1812, and Rogers Mill on Deer Creek even supplied part of the iron that covered the Civil War iron-clad "Monitor."

Finally, did you ever wonder why the call it pig iron? It seems that to receive the molten iron that was tapped from from the base of the furnace, a narrow channel was dug in the dirt floor in front of the furnace and branching off of this channel were identically shaped molds, also dug in the ground. This configuration reminded somebody of a liter of piglets nursing on a sow. Hence the term pigs for the molded iron forms.

East Chesapeake Bay Tributaries

Chapter 6
Rivers of the Eastern Shore

The "Eastern Shore" is generally the term used to describe Maryland east of the Chesapeake Bay. But this book uses it to describe that portion of the Delmarva Peninsula that drains to the Bay. This includes portions of Maryland, Delaware, and Virginia.

This is a flat, low-lying area dedicated to agriculture and harvesting the Bay's seafood treasures. When you talk about rivers and creeks around here, you are usually talking about tidal estuaries. Tidewater has its drawbacks for canoeing. Many of these waters are wide, windy, and rough, and the current is often going in the wrong direction. You must share these waters with motorboats and sail boats, while the shores, prime waterfront property, may be extensively developed. But there are some intimate and still unspoiled streams left, and they are described here.

There is rarely time for enough branches to gather to form a canoeable-sized stream before tidewater. But those few that do exist, navigable by the swamp-loving river rat, are also covered. There is even some light whitewater, on the Big Elk, which flows along the edge of this arbitrary geographical division. Finally, there are many old millponds that form quiet refuges on streams that would otherwise be too small to paddle.

The following waterways are described in this chapter:

Northeast River Tributaries
Big Elk Creek
Great Bohemia Creek
Chester River
Wye River
Choptank River
    Tuckahoe Creek
    Kings Creek
    Miles Creek
Taylors Island Passages
Honga River
    Worlds End Creek
Farm Creek
Blackwater River
    Little Blackwater River
Transquaking River
    Chicamacomico River
Island Creek
    Pokata Creek

Nanticoke River
    Broad Creek
        James Branch
            Hitch Pond Branch
    Marshyhope Creek
    Barren Creek
        Rewastico Creek
        Quantico Creek
Wicomico Creek
Monie Creek
Manokin River
    Kings Creek
Janes Island and Cedar Island
Pocomoke River
    Nassawango Creek
    Dividing Creek
    Pitts Creek
    Marumsco Creek

Northeast
Creek
Little Northeast
Creek

Principio
Creek

Northeast River Tributaries

INTRODUCTION: The Northeast River is a tidal estuary at the northeast end of the Chesapeake, though the neighboring Elk River reaches farther east and a bit farther north. With largely developed shores, it is not a particularly inviting destination. Far more worthy of mention is a cluster of wet weather, whitewater tributaries nearby. Northeast Creek and Little Northeast Creek feed into the head of the Northeast River estuary. Principio Creek feeds Furnace Bay, which is close enough to be conveniently included in this description. Each cuts a delightful gorge in its decent over the Fall Line. Each offers a touch of wildness in this busy and rapidly developing interurban corridor.

Section 1. Principio Creek. Theodore Road to Md. Rte. 7						
Gradient	Difficulty	Distance	Time	Width	Scenery	Map
46	1 to 2+	4.6	1.5	20-40	Good	61

TRIP DESCRIPTION: This run hides down in a shallow gorge, mostly back in the forest, which at one point is dominated by lovely stand of hemlock. Perhaps the most interesting point is where the creek files through a spooky tunnel beneath the railroad grade. The whitewater, though easy, is a delight as it runs with little interruption, climaxing with a nasty falls at Principio Furnace (Rte. 7). Carry this.

HAZARDS: Expect a moderate number of strainers and a falls at the end.

WATER CONDITIONS: Catch within 24 hours of a lot of rain.

GAUGE: There is an old USGS gauge with an outside staff at Belvidere Road. Look for at least 3.0 feet. To judge from afar, a crude indicator would be the USGS gauges on Deer Creek at Rocks and White Clay Creek near Newark (see USGS website), both of which should be over 1,500 cfs.

Section 2. Northeast Creek. Crothers Road to North East (Walnut Street)						
Gradient	Difficulty	Distance	Time	Width	Scenery	Map
41*	A to 5+	8.4	3.0	20-40	Good	61
*reaches 500 fpm						

TRIP DESCRIPTION: With its extreme range of difficulty and access problems, this is an unusual run. For the first few miles from Crothers Road to Md. Rte. 272 , the creek is mostly flat, crooked, and plagued by logjams and fallen trees. Though framed by the creek's mud banks, the setting is a pleasant mix of fields and woods. A covered bridge graces the end of this section.

Below the bridge, the creek thunders over a dam and then a bouldery fall line. I have not attempted this, but it may within the skill range of the most cutting-edge steep creek paddlers. More of a problem is that the banks are private and outsiders have not been traditionally welcome here. So for most of us, the next point of access (not for the lazy) is from Cecil Community College. Park at the north side of the physical education building and walk down the road on the north side of the baseball diamonds. Behind the first scoreboard is a rip rapped embankment. A good footpath starts at the base of the riprap. The total hike is a bit over a quarter mile.

The reward for this effort is a few miles of almost continuous rocky rapids and riffles (Class 2 maximum) carrying you between equally rocky banks in a shallow, beech-filled gorge. It might be best to finish at Rte. 40, as the scenery is much less satisfying below. Below Rte. 40, the gradient flattens, with the exception of a dam-capped falls beneath the Amtrak bridge. The only carry is up over the railroad grade. Be very careful, as the swift and silent trains can really sneak up on you. Finish on tidewater at the community park at the foot of Walnut Street.

HAZARDS: Strainers, the fall line below Rte. 272, and a falls beneath the Amtrak bridge.

WATER CONDITIONS: Catch within 24 hours of a lot of rain.

GAUGE: None. A crude indicator would be to use the USGS gauges (see USGS website) on Deer Creek at Rocks and White Clay Creek near Newark, both of which should be over 1,500 cfs.

Section 3. Little Northeast Creek. Warburton Road to U.S. Rte. 40						
Gradient	Difficulty	Distance	Time	Width	Scenery	Map
37	A to 3	5.0	3.0	20-40	Good to Fair	61

TRIP DESCRIPTION: This is a lively run with almost continuous rapids and riffles. It is at its best where it dashes through a series of boulder rapids and over one challenging five-foot ledge by the quarry below I-95. Another five-footer below Mechanics Valley Road provides a final splash. The setting, where it is natural, is pleasant, but the quarry and other incursions take their toll. The Little joins Northeast Creek a few hundred yards below Rte. 40.

HAZARDS: Strainers.

WATER CONDITIONS: Catch within 24 hours of a lot of rain.

GAUGE: Use same estimate as on Northeast Creek.

Big Elk Creek

INTRODUCTION: Big Elk Creek flows out of the rolling Piedmont of southern Chester County, Pennsylvania, into Cecil County and the head of the Chesapeake Bay. It drains a small, narrow pastoral valley and, accordingly, it is difficult to catch up more than a day after a good rain. Perhaps the best attraction of this run is that, from the state line to Elk Mills, it passes through what was once the huge DuPont Fair Hill Estate, now owned by the State of Maryland. Described as a "Natural Resources Management Area," this is a place where one can enjoy a remarkably serene, manicured, unlittered, and practically unpopulated landscape in the heart of the great eastern seaboard megalopolis.

Section 1. Oxford Elkdale Road to Elkton, Md. (Md. Rte. 279)						
Gradient	Difficulty	Distance	Time	Width	Scenery	Map
16	1 to 2–	20.2	5.0	15-30	Good	62

TRIP DESCRIPTION: At the suggested put-in you will find just a rivulet, as this is only the East Branch of Big Elk Creek (which in itself is not so big). After a pastoral start, the stream wriggles into a

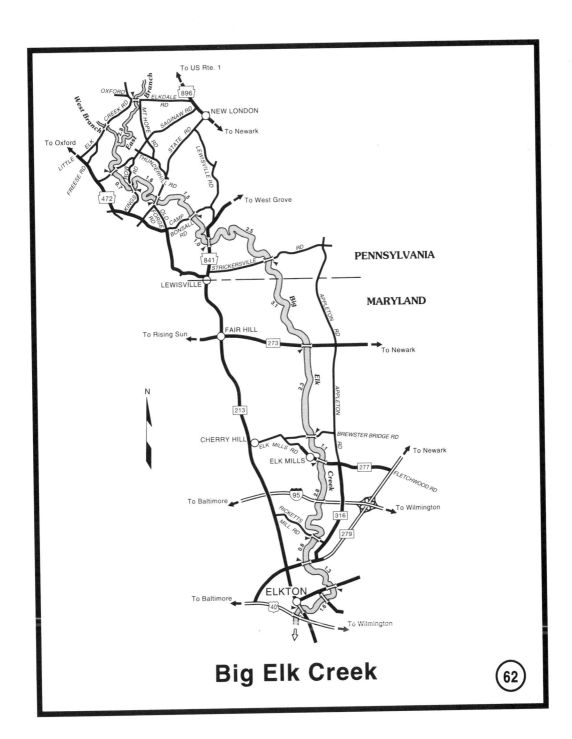

Big Elk Creek

62

lovely, shallow, rock-bound, laurel-filled gorge whose lonesome character is marred but by a few houses and one camp. The West Branch boosts the flow a bit. Two covered bridges add to the ambience.

Around Pa. Rte. 841, the character of the surroundings change. Except where high mud banks block your view, a landscape of rolling pastures and wooded hillsides soon unfolds. As in many other stream valleys in this corner of the state, the hillsides are forested with some beautiful stands of beech trees. A covered bridge and distant farm structures round out the New England-like scene.

The stream is basically easy. There are numerous riffles and small rapids of a rock garden nature that, at low water, are quite tedious, but not dangerous. But there are some difficulties. Expect at least a few fallen trees, a concrete ford, and barbed and woven wire fences. Most of these fences, used to facilitate fox hunting when this was still an estate, are washed out with only the supporting booms or cables remaining. But on the author's last visit there was one troublesome fence still intact, with just a small canoe-size breach that is exposed at low levels. At higher levels, the breach would be impassable and, since the high and difficult-to-scale fence continues on both banks, the paddler should seriously consider carrying along a strong pair of wire cutters (Note: The author in any other situation advocates leaving fences alone.).

The creek leaves Fair Hill above Elk Mills. The topography now flattens out and the scenery seems drab. But the riffles are still numerous and speed you to the finish. Take out on the downstream left at the Rte. 279 bridge.

HAZARDS: Trees, a sharp, two-foot ford (about a mile below Strickersville Road), and fences. The woven wire fence mentioned above warrants special attention, as at high levels it blocks all progress downstream.

WATER CONDITIONS: Paddleable winter or spring within 24 hours of a hard rain.

GAUGE: None. A rough indicator would be over 400 cfs (5.0 feet) at USGS gauge at Strickersville on nearby White Clay Creek (see USGS website).

Great Bohemia Creek

INTRODUCTION: The upper Chesapeake Bay presents a superb mix of land and water that would charm just about anyone. Unfortunately, that charm combined with proximity to Washington, Baltimore, Philadelphia, and Wilmington has lured thousands of individuals into building their homes, estates, and vacation retreats along hundreds of miles of shoreline. There remains very little waterfront bearing the wild beauty that so impressed Captain John Smith almost four centuries ago and which would be of the most interest to the touring paddler today. However, there are fortunately a few pockets of, if not wild, at least fairly undeveloped tidal creek on the upper Eastern Shore. Great and Little Bohemia creeks are two of them.

Section 1. Telegraph Road to Md. Rte. 213						
Gradient	Difficulty	Distance	Time	Width	Scenery	Map
0	A	5.4	2.0	15-2,000	Good	63

Great Bohemia Creek

DELAWARE

To Middletown

ROAD 437

OLD TELEGRAPH RD

BOHEMIA MILLS

OLD TELEGRAPH RD

Creek

OLD TELEGRAPH RD

To Mt. Pleasant

SOUTH ST. AUGUSTINE RD

MARYLAND

342

ST. AUGUSTINE

310

Bohemia

5.4

Creek

CAYOTS

To Elkton

Great

Little

Bohemia

BOHEMIA CHURCH RD

N

213

To Cecilton

63

TRIP DESCRIPTION: If the tide is high, it is possible to put in at Telegraph Road, Bohemia Mills, but once again, only if the tide is high. Even at such times, a little bushwhacking and perhaps a little dragging may be necessary. But this soon gets you out to a shallow, narrow, but floatable, creek that meanders through a freshwater marsh. In about a half mile, Sandy Branch joins from the southeast and that marks the head of navigation for even low tide conditions. The problem with this creek is that it has been choked with silt over the years, leaving only a narrow channel over most of its length, bracketed at low tide by either mud flats or four-inch-deep water. The channel through these unusually murky waters can often be elusive, thus testing your depth-finding intuition. So if you arrive in this neighborhood at low tide, cancel your one-way trip plans, just put in at Md. Rte. 213, and then paddle as far up the creek as you like and return. A short side road at the foot of the south approach to the bridge provides easy access.

Compared to the rest of the Eastern Shore, Cecil County is "mountainous." So the Bohemia cuts through a rolling countryside graced by attractive grain and horse farms. The shores, especially the south shore, tend to be wooded and sometimes break away into low, eroded bluffs. There are narrow, sandy beaches along the lower creek and narrow marshes along the middle and upper reaches. The usually wooded north shore is broken by views across farm fields and is dotted by a few attractive houses, barns, and docks. It is a really nice and peaceful place to spend your time.

You can have a pleasant side trip by poking up Little Bohemia Creek. The Little Bohemia is even prettier and less developed than the Great. On its upper reaches are bluffs clothed in hemlock, a relatively uncommon tree on the Eastern Shore. This creek, unfortunately, is even more silted in than the Great Bohemia and, at low tide, you will only be able to ascend it about a mile and a half above its mouth.

HAZARDS: Being stuck in the middle of a black, gooey, bottomless mud flat on an ebbing tide.

WATER CONDITIONS: Tidal and thus canoeable all year, except when frozen.

GAUGE: None.

Chester River

INTRODUCTION: The Chester is one of the longer and larger rivers of the Eastern Shore. Starting just upstream of Millington with the confluence of a few, tiny branches, this river is an estuary for its entire length. Only several yards wide at its start, it expands to over three miles wide by the time it reaches the Bay at the northern tip of Kent Island. As you might guess, the Chester is a fine river for power boats, sailboats, and sea kayaks. Canoes would probably do best on the more sheltered upper reaches.

Section 1. Millington (Md. Rte. 313) to Chestertown (High Street)						
Gradient	Difficulty	Distance	Time	Width	Scenery	Map
0	A	15.4	7.0	50-2,400	Fair to Good	64

Chester River

To Wilmington

MILLINGTON

291

313

1.6

301

To Bay Bridge

4.5

River

290

544

2.2

CRUMPTON

Access

BUCKINGHAM RD

Access

MORGNEC

DEEP LANDING RD

3.6

Chester

DOUBLE CREEK RD

Morgan

Creek

544

To Elkton

Access

291

213

3.5

HIGH ST

213

CHESTERTOWN

Access

To Sudlersville, Rte. 301

300

4.2

Southeast Creek

CHURCH HILL

RD

SOUTHEAST CREEK RD

289

Access

Creek

1.2

4.5

2.9

ISLAND CREEK RD

Granny Finley Branch

NECK

QUAKER NECK LNDG. RD

OLD TOWN RD

Access

LANDS END RD

Island

MILL RD

2.0

SPARKS

QUAKER

3.2

213

CLIFFS CITY RD

Access

Chester

River

River

7.0

Access

Corsica

304

1.3

CENTREVILLE

Old Mill Stream

To Rte. 301

N

64

TRIP DESCRIPTION: The Chester gets off to an only mediocre start. It banks are lined with houses, and much of its channel can get shallow at low tide, even by a canoeist's standards. But at least it is small and cozy, and you will find some pretty and still undeveloped bends.

From Crumpton to Morgan Creek, the Chester is at its best. Houses are far apart and generally set back from the river. The paddler beholds mostly patches and strips of marshes backed by high ground that is covered by both farms and forest. This is the way one would expect prime Bay country to appear.

Below Morgan Creek, the shores are again lined with houses. While most of this remaining stretch is of no redeeming scenic value, the riverfront of Chestertown, in contrast, is a pleasure to behold. The houses here are stately, 18th-century structures. Be sure to allow some time to explore on foot the old sections of this charming college town and county seat. A public access at the foot of High Street provides an easy exit from the water.

Those wishing to do only the prime, middle section can find good access via Rte. 291, over Morgan Creek (0.8 miles down to the Chester); at Buckingham Road; at Deep Landing; and at Crumpton, via an access at the foot of Market Street. Note that Queen Anne's County Recreation and Parks Department charges a fee for use of its public landings. For Maryland residents, it is $5 daily or $25 annually, and for nonresidents, it is $10 daily and $50 annually. The department's address is 1945 4-H Park Road, P.O. Box 37, Centreville, MD 21617. You can also purchase permits at several shops and marinas about the county, or for those approaching from the Western Shore via the Bay Bridge, at Anglers Sport Center near Sandy Point. The names and locations are listed on signs at the landings and in a brochure published by the county. For more information, call 410-758-0835. Kent County public landings require fees only from boaters pulling trailers.

HAZARDS: None.

WATER CONDITIONS: Tidal and, hence, always runnable.

GAUGE: None.

Section 2. Chestertown (High Street) to Corsica River

Gradient	Difficulty	Distance	Time	Width	Scenery	Map
0	A	12.5	7.0	1,600-6,500	Good to Very Good	64

TRIP DESCRIPTION: This is a lovely reach of the Chester with some tributaries that are even nicer. Development follows both shores for about a mile below Chestertown. After that, the right side is typically wooded and undeveloped. It is often edged by high, eroded banks, sometimes of dirt, sometimes of soft orange rock that is studded with shells and fossils. In between are little patches of marsh. The left side of the river is typically marsh-fringed, beyond which dry land slopes gently to farms and scattered farm structures. The country ambience is punctuated by a marina at Rolph's Landing and a few houses here and there.

About four miles below Rte. 213, Southeast Creek enters from the southeast. It and its tributaries can easily occupy you for a day. There is access to the creek via a public landing at the foot of Southeast Creek Road. The north side of the creek presents a largely unspoiled mix of farms and woods, while the other side supports several houses. There are also marshy spots and, near the mouth, high cut banks. Near the head of the wide part of the creek, the waters can get uniformly shallow at low tide. But be persistent, because where it narrows, the channel deepens and leads you up to the head of a lovely cattail marsh.

Island Creek joins Southeast Creek about a mile above the mouth. This is a pretty passage that you can ascend all the way to the culvert at Sparks Mill Road. Development is light and uneven, leaving you all alone back in the marsh and woods. But the best feature of Island Creek is its tributary,

Granny Findley Branch. Joining just above Island Creek Road, this gem is completely wild and passable for about a mile and a half. If only creeks like this were the rule, not the exception.

Returning to the Chester, the route continues to be nice. Narrow bands of marsh and cedar-studded shores frame a rural landscape. Shoreline development remains light, particularly on the south side. There is no access at the mouth of the Corsica River, so take out at Cliff City Public Landing, across the river, just upstream. Or you can continue on by turning up the Corsica.

The Corsica looks much like the Chester, just slightly smaller. As you ascend, however, development increases, particularly along the south shore. If the tide is in, you can make it all the way up to Rte. 213 in Centreville, where there is a small town park. The last mile, which is actually on Old Mill Stream, is a contrasting, narrow channel through a pretty marsh on the edge of town. If the tide is out, finish at the Centreville Wharf, where Old Mill Stream and Three Bridges Branch join northwest of town (reached by Rte. 304 and Burrisville Road).

HAZARDS: None.

WATER CONDITIONS: Tidal.

GAUGE: None.

Wye River

INTRODUCTION: The Wye River stands out as one of the few relatively unspoiled Eastern Shore estuaries close to the Washington-Baltimore-Annapolis area. With the suburbs enveloping even Kent Island, this is amazing. Depending on where you look at it, this body of water is called the Wye River, Wye East River, or Wye Narrows. It forms part of the border of Talbot and Queen Anne's counties—an area where waterfront property is at a premium and where precious few miles of shoreline remain undeveloped. The Wye is less than 12 miles from the Bay Bridge. So go enjoy it while it is still nice.

Section 1. Wye Mills (Md. Rte. 404) to Wye Landing						
Gradient	Difficulty	Distance	Time	Width	Scenery	Map
0	A	5.5	3.0	10-1,000	Good to Fair	65

TRIP DESCRIPTION: This being tidal, you can start at either end. If you start at Wye Mills, you must pick your way down just a ribbon of shallow water that for the first few hundred yards will be complicated by deadfalls. Bring along a saw. A few hours of labor by you and a few others can create clear floating for all who follow. At least half of this route stays narrow and crooked. There are few houses visible up there, so you are mainly treated to a vista of wooded hillsides and little marshes. There is a tributary on the right, elegantly named Madam Alices Branch, about a mile and a half below Wye Mills. Ignore the discouraging shallows at its mouth and go explore it. It is completely wild up there, and you can follow its path for over a mile. The good times end approaching Wye Landing as the river broadens and development takes over the left shore. A public launching ramp makes an easy take-out.

HAZARDS: None.

Wye River

(65)

WATER CONDITIONS: Tidal, so always canoeable. Timing your trip to hit high tides at the upper end will make things much easier.

GAUGE: None.

Section 2. Wye Island Circuit						
Gradient	Difficulty	Distance	Time	Width	Scenery	Map
0	A	15.0	7.0	500-4,000	Good to Fair	65

TRIP DESCRIPTION: The lower Wye is unusual in that it is split by a huge island. The island, Wye Island, is unusual in that 2,450 of its 2,800 acres are state-owned and remain undeveloped. This is no accident. Just a few years back, Wye Island was destined to become one big, planned, residential and resort development. The state intervened in the mid-70's and purchased the island. Wye Island, like Big Elk Creek's Fair Hill Estate, is now administered as a natural resources management area. You can get out to it by bridge and then walk, cycle, or drive its network of country lanes past cultivated fields, old farm structures, and woodlots. One of these woodlots, on the western half of the island, is a long, narrow stand of virgin oak forest, also worth a walk.

212

Of course, since you are reading this book, you might enjoy paddling around the island, starting at Wye Landing. In doing so you are likely to see lots of waterfowl and maybe even an eagle. Except for one stretch between Wye Landing and the bridge to the island, the opposite shores, unfortunately, are lined with houses, docks, etc. Just stick to the island side and the width of the river will soften the impact of the other shore.

HAZARDS: Wind can be a problem on this wide river.

WATER CONDITIONS: Anytime.

GAUGE: None.

Choptank River

INTRODUCTION: The Choptank River starts in Kent County, Delaware, west of Dover. It winds its way through swamp forests to tidewater at Greensboro, Maryland, and sloshes still onward to the Chesapeake Bay, just west of Cambridge. This is a typical swamp river above Greensboro with typical swamp hardships, and one must be truly dedicated to the outdoors, not to mention slightly crazy, to subject oneself to this sort of masochism, even if it is a lovely place to visit. Less athletic seekers of solitude will most prefer the segment between Greensboro and Denton, while only those paddlers not discouraged by wide waters, pesky winds, and sometimes built-up shores will venture below.

Section 1. Mud Mill Road to Greensboro, Md.						
Gradient	Difficulty	Distance	Time	Width	Scenery	Map
4	A to 1–	10.7	8.0	10-100	Good	66

TRIP DESCRIPTION: Mud Mill Road is the technical head of navigation only. Put in here and you subject yourself to a cellulose hell: logs, trees, bushes, vines, thorns, poison ivy, etc., seemingly without end. It is almost nonstop wrestling with this mess. Do yourself a favor and put in a mile downstream at Bee Tree Road. There are still a lot of deadfalls, but at least you get a chance to paddle in between. As you progress downstream, obstacles become fewer and by the end it is pretty easy going. Also, with each mile downstream, the scenery improves, the surrounding swamps widen, and the trees get bigger. One interesting feature is the unusual number of holly trees along this river. Also, some of the adjacent land has some elevation, allowing you to enjoy some pretty, beech-covered hillsides and interesting, gray cliffs. Finally, last but not least, there is some elementary whitewater here in the form of gravel bar riffles below Red Bridges Road (this spot, incidentally, is a popular springtime destination for perch-seeking fishermen). The finish though is smooth, on tidewater, at a public boat ramp downstream and around the bend from the Sunset Avenue bridge in Greensboro.

HAZARDS: Trees and exhaustion.

WATER CONDITIONS: Passable late fall, winter, and spring except after a drought.

GAUGE: There is a USGS gauge (see USGS website or inspect on site) at Red Bridges Road. A level of 45 cfs (2.75 feet) is about zero for canoeing.

HENDERSON

MUD MILL

BEE TREE RD

RD

1.5

311

GOLDSBORO

JACKSON LA

2.6

287

JARRELL RD

RD

10
To Dover

311

3.6

RED BRIDGES RD

River

MILL

DRAPERS

Gauge

3.0

SUNSET AVE

GREENSBORO

Access

BOYCE MILL RD

DELAWARE

480

314

MARYLAND

HOLLY

RD

7.7

Choptank

313

RIVER RD

To Hillsboro

404

317

328

Access

DENTON

313
404

To Federalsburg

N

Choptank River

Section 2. Greensboro to Denton						
Gradient	Difficulty	Distance	Time	Width	Scenery	Map
0	A	7.7	3.5	100-1,000	Good	66

TRIP DESCRIPTION: While this section lacks the intimacy of the upper Choptank, it also lacks the hardships. Once beyond Greensboro, it offers relative isolation amidst both high and swampy, wooded banks. Access is certainly easy—a public boat ramp about a third of a mile downstream of the Sunset Avenue bridge in Greensboro and a public ramp in Denton, just above the old bridge to West Denton.

HAZARDS: None.

WATER CONDITIONS: Tidal and hence canoeable all year.

GAUGE: None.

Section 3. Denton to Windyhill Landing						
Gradient	Difficulty	Distance	Time	Width	Scenery	Map
0	A	22.8	11.0	200-3,000	Good	67,68

TRIP DESCRIPTION: The Choptank begins to grow big now, but not huge. The river for the first few miles below Denton has too much development. But as the miles pass, the houses appear farther apart. Wooded banks and, farther down, big expanses of marshland dominate the scenery. Some of the shoreline and marshes have been preserved by The Nature Conservancy and the state. Access through here is ample, and this section combines well with trips on Tuckahoe, Kings, or Miles creeks.

HAZARDS: None.

WATER CONDITIONS: Always canoeable.

GAUGE: None.

Section 4. Windyhill Landing to Cambridge (U.S. Rte. 50)						
Gradient	Difficulty	Distance	Time	Width	Scenery	Map
0	A	12.0	6.0	1,000-8,000	Good	68

TRIP DESCRIPTION: Now the Choptank starts getting seriously big. The above distance is the most direct, following the centerline of the river. But if you favor a shoreline, and then start exploring its many beautiful tributaries, it will take you days to cover this reach.

For about the first half of this section, as far as Raccoon Creek on the right, and as far as Warwick River on the left, the shores of the Choptank remain in a largely natural state. That means more marsh backed by wooded high ground. All of the major tributaries are worth investigating.

The first tributary, on the left, is Marsh Creek. This is a gem. After ascending its marshy first half mile, low-slung Poplar Neck Road bridge requires an awkward lift-over. At least with a high tide, this creek allows you to probe way back into a most wild of swamps. The clear but tannin-stained water and exotic vegetation will delight you.

Tuckahoe Creek
Choptank River
Kings Creek

After the village of Choptank's developed shores comes Hunting Creek. You can follow this for at least four and a half miles at low tide and maybe, with possibly some bushwhacking, make it up to the Rte. 16/331 bridge at high tide. There are a few houses along the lower creek, but otherwise the view is of an attractive wooded facade backed by farm fields.

After some development at Wrights Wharf, the marshy shores of the Choptank lead to Blinkhorn Creek. You can follow that creek for about a mile through minimally spoiled marsh and then swamp.

More marshy shores (on both sides of the river) lead to Cabin Creek next. You can follow this back about two and a half miles. Cabin's shores are heavily developed up to Suicide Bridge, with its popular restaurant and garish riverboat replica. Above there, it leads past high, wooded shores and just a bit of marsh with navigation ending (just barely, at low tide) at a little, old mill and milldam.

The next tributary is on the right. Raccoon Creek is not very big, but it compensates for that in quality. You can ascend up its narrow, twisting channel about a mile through a narrow marsh backed by deep woods.

The Warwick River enters about two miles farther, on the left. It is fairly attractive, in spite of its developed shores. You can follow it about a mile and a quarter to its forks in the town of Secretary, where there is a public ramp. With a high tide, each of the forks will wriggle into marshy and still largely natural surroundings, with the southern fork being the nicest.

For the remainder of the way to Rte. 50, usually well-spaced housing and some riprap detract from the quality of the close-up view. The left shore continues mostly marshy while extensive development crowds the shores of all of the remaining tributaries. You can take out at either end of the old Rte. 50 bridge, which is now a public fishing pier, or at the visitor center in Cambridge, just a few yards downstream.

HAZARDS: None.

WATER CONDITIONS: Tidal. Always paddleable.

GAUGE: None.

Tuckahoe Creek

INTRODUCTION: Tuckahoe Creek forms the twisting border between Caroline and Queen Anne's counties. Tiny, tangled, and swampy above Rte. 404 and wide, placid, and tidal below, it offers a satisfying escape from the congested, nearby megalopolis.

Section 1. Crouse Mill Road to Hillsboro Access

Gradient	Difficulty	Distance	Time	Width	Scenery	Map
2*	A	5.3	2.4	15-100	Good	67

*down to tidewater

TRIP DESCRIPTION: Much of this run is within the bounds of Tuckahoe State Park. It is possible, but not recommended, to put in seven miles upstream of Crouse Mill Road at Md. Rte. 304, Bridgetown, on the Mason Branch. The first two miles of Mason Branch are now, thanks to the magic of the Natural Resources Conservation Service, an ugly and straight channelized ditch. This is followed by about three miles of tangled, woody jungle, followed by two miles of pond, most of which is flooded swamp forest. The paddler would find it much more worthwhile to put in on the pond at Crouse Mill Road, paddle upstream to observe the tremendous flocks of waterfowl that winter there, and then proceed downstream. This also gives one the opportunity to run the three- and-a-half-foot dam at the end of the pond.

The section below Crouse Mill Road is reasonable. Part is nontidal with a good current. Thanks to the spare-time efforts of some park employees, many of the deadfalls that used to plague the paddler now have passages sawed through them. You will still have to carry some trees, but not so many as to make you wish you were elsewhere. And if you too take along a saw, you can help to keep this creek open.

This is a pretty section. The surrounding forest is deep, dense, and contains a lot of really big, beautiful trees. The water is fairly clear and slightly tannen-stained. The silence of the swamp is wonderful. The creek slinks into tidewater subtly and does not widen much until approaching Hillsboro. Take out in Hillsboro at a public ramp downstream of the Main Street bridge.

HAZARDS: Sharp dam at Crouse Mill Road can be dangerous when the water is up. Fallen trees are usually not much of a hazard as strainers, but be careful not to slip when climbing over them.

WATER CONDITIONS: Above Crouse Mill Road, usually floatable through any normal winter or spring. Below Crouse Mill Road, this is probably passable through all but the driest years, though a bit of dragging may be necessary at the start.

GAUGE: None.

Section 2. Hillsboro Access to mouth						
Gradient	Difficulty	Distance	Time	Width	Scenery	Map
0	A	13.0	4.5	100-1,500	Good	67

TRIP DESCRIPTION: The preferred put-in is the public ramp off Main Street in Hillsboro. More suited for the casual paddler, this section meanders placidly past large tracts of marsh and mostly high, wooded banks touched by little development. The woods include even a hemlock or two and the more common sight of holly patches. The width of this stream regularly swings from very wide to narrow, adding even more variety to the cruise. Rte. 328 concludes the best of the Tuckahoe, as the last two miles are more developed. There is no public access at the mouth. So those going the whole way should continue a mile down the Choptank and take out on the other side at Ganeys Wharf.

HAZARDS: None.

WATER CONDITIONS: Runnable all year.

GAUGE: None.

Choptank River
Miles Creek

68

Kings Creek and Miles Creek

INTRODUCTION: They seem to usually hide the best rivers from us. In the mountains, they hide them down in deep canyons and, on the Piedmont Fall Line, down in narrow gorges. And out on the flat Eastern Shore, they hide them out in the middle of soybean fields and off broad estuaries where you could cruise right by five times without noticing their mouths. They hid the two tiny Choptank tributaries called Kings Creek and Miles Creek out on the eastern edge of Talbot County, but now we are letting the creek out of the bag.

Section 1. Kings Creek. Kingston Landing to head of creek						
Gradient	Difficulty	Distance	Time	Width	Scenery	Map
0	A	5.0	2.5	15-200	Very Good	67

TRIP DESCRIPTION: This is a most beautiful, watery byway. The paddler will see few structures from the water, and only a few farm fields hint of the intensely cultivated land beyond its high, wooded banks. Expansive marshes surrounding the mouth of this creek shrink as you progress upstream. It is possible to enjoy some of these marshes on foot also. The Nature Conservancy has bought some of the marsh and constructed a boardwalk through it. Approached by a small landing about a quarter mile up from the mouth of the creek, this will certainly round out your perspective.

After passing Kingston Road, swampy shores just about replace the marsh. But there is still always a thin fringe of cattails and reeds. If you have time, a short side trip up Beaverdam Branch (on your right facing upstream) treats you to more undisturbed marsh and forest. Heading farther upstream, Kings Creek gradually narrows until the end is suddenly reached in a tangle of fallen trees.

You can start on Kings Creek near its mouth by putting in at Kingston Landing, a third of a mile up the Choptank, or halfway up the creek where Kingston Road crosses. Watch your approach as the turnoffs to Kingston Road and Kingston Landing Road are poorly marked.

HAZARDS: None.

WATER CONDITIONS: Always canoeable, except when frozen. Upper creek is best with high tide.

GAUGE: None.

Section 2. Miles Creek. Windyhill to head of creek						
Gradient	Difficulty	Distance	Time	Width	Scenery	Map
0	A	5.5	3.0	50-250	Good	68

TRIP DESCRIPTION: Miles Creek is not as pretty as Kings Creek because it is more developed in spots. Like Kings Creek, you can approach it from near its mouth, via the public boat ramp at Windyhill on the Choptank, or enter midway, via Bruceville Road. The lower creek winds through broad wetlands, while the portion above Bruceville Road begins bumping a lot against high, wooded banks. This upper section of creek shallows to only inches at low tide, so just how far you ascend varies considerably with how much tide you have.

HAZARDS: None.

WATER CONDITIONS: Always canoeable. Above Bruceville Road, it is best with high tide.

GAUGE: None.

Tidal Navigation Hints

While your typical tidal estuary usually gives the impression of substance and depth when viewed from shore, the paddler soon finds that in reality these waterways are often only inches deep with only a narrow, elusive channel suitable for even canoe navigation. If you are cognizant, however, of a few basic rules, you can pick your way down these passages with all the confidence of a veteran waterman.

First, channels on estuaries, as on nontidal streams, tend to hang to the outside of bends, especially on the lower reaches of the stream where bottom-scouring tidal currents are strongest. Be aware, however, that on tight s-turns the channel often tends to diagonal across to the other side much sooner than on a nontidal river.

Next, look where the duck blinds are. Blinds are usually serviced by motorboaters, who want deep water even more than you do. So the conservative navigator in shallow waters might choose to simply zigzag from blind to blind.

Look for markers. On the upper reaches of estuaries, where channels really start withering, look for strange sticks or clusters of sticks that seem to unnaturally protrude from the murky shallows. These are often some waterman's crude buoy system.

Nature sets out markers too. On the really upper reaches, watch for vegetative patterns. Lily pads, arrowhead plants, etc. usually only grow in shallows. So watch for the gaps and go for them.

Finally, if you still insist on messing up, do it at low tide. Then you just have to wait six hours and you get lifted off for a second chance.

Taylors Island Passages

INTRODUCTION: Taylors Island is a big parcel of land out on the west side of Dorchester County, down at the end of Rte. 16. Barely above sea level, the island has an ambiguous boundary of wild marshland. The open water that officially separates Taylors Island from the mainland is a complex series of passages bearing at least a half dozen different names. Somehow, waterside development has bypassed these beautiful waters. As a result, here lies one of the most extensive tracts of unspoiled tidewater canoeing in Maryland.

Section 1. Md. Rte. 335 to Taylors Island Public Access						
Gradient	Difficulty	Distance	Time	Width	Scenery	Map
0	A	10.2	5.0	50-2,500	Excellent	69

To Cambridge

16

Access
TAYLORS
ISLAND

ROBINSON NECK RD

Slaughter Creek

Slaughter Creek Broads

SMITHVILLE

5.1

Slaughter Creek Narrows

RD

Slaughter Creek

PUNCH ISLAND RD

Jacks Creek

1.8

1.6

Access

0.8

Beaverdam Creek

Upper Keene Broad

Chesapeake Bay

Punch 1.0 Island Creek

0.8

Dunnock Slough

1.9

0.5

Dunnock Island Creek

N

Lower Keene Broad

2.8

HIP ROOF RD

Great Marsh Creek

To Church Creek

335

Honga River

To Honga

Taylors Island Passages

69

TRIP DESCRIPTION: There is no upstream or downstream here. Start where you want or can, with a tide that looks like it will help you along. But realize that the routes here can be complex enough that sooner or later you will have to fight the tide. The distance described above is just that of the most direct route between the two points. But varying the route up side channels or alternate forks, such as Dunnock Island Slough, will make your trip much more interesting. In fact, if the day is calm and you are energetic and adventuresome, you could combine these passages with the bay side of Taylors Island for a circumnavigation of the island. This watery maze is certainly one place where you would profit by bringing along $7^{1}/_{2}$-minute USGS topographic maps (Taylors Island and Golden Hill sheets) and a compass. There are many opportunities back here for making wrong turns—time consuming errors that could transform your afternoon outing into a moonlight canoeing excursion. There are only three access points to this waterway, and they are far apart. So allow lots of time, even if you are a good navigator. Besides, this is too nice a place through which to hurry.

Almost any passage that you follow will be beautiful. Other than at the mouth of Punch Island Creek and at the village of Taylors Island, you see few houses or docks. Some channels, like Jacks Creek, are pristine. Really the biggest civilized intrusion on this tract, and an annoying one, are low-flying jets out of Patuxent Naval Air Station. This is a world of wide marshes and piney hummocks. Canoe camping possibilities are tempting, though many shores are posted. Waterfowl is usually plentiful. In fact, a corner of this area, Beaverdam Creek, is within the Blackwater National Wildlife Refuge. So if you can just combine all this with some favorable weather, you will have a perfect trip.

HAZARDS: Getting lost, so bring a map.

WATER CONDITIONS: These are all tidal waters and always canoeable.

GAUGE: None.

Honga River

INTRODUCTION: Forget its name. The Honga is not really a river, not even an estuary. It is a bay, separated from the main Chesapeake by the string of Hoopers Islands. Be it a river or bay, this is a destination for those who like their water open, but not infinitely so.

Section 1. Md. Rte. 335 to Hoopersville						
Gradient	Difficulty	Distance	Time	Width	Scenery	Map
0	A	12.0	6.0	0.3 to 2 miles	Good	70

TRIP DESCRIPTION: You will want to tailor your own tour of this rambling body of water and wetland. The above distance describes only the most direct route from Md. 335, the uppermost access point, to Hoopersville, the lowermost. But you have many more choices. To better acquaint you with the possibilities, the following description of the the Honga is from the perspective of a circuit trip that follows the shoreline. This route covers more miles than most could do in a day, especially if one chooses to probe every little bay and gut. Wind will be the most important factor in deciding where and what direction to go. Tidal currents are not a concern on the Honga itself, but they can be stiff on the sidestreams and the narrow passages between islands.

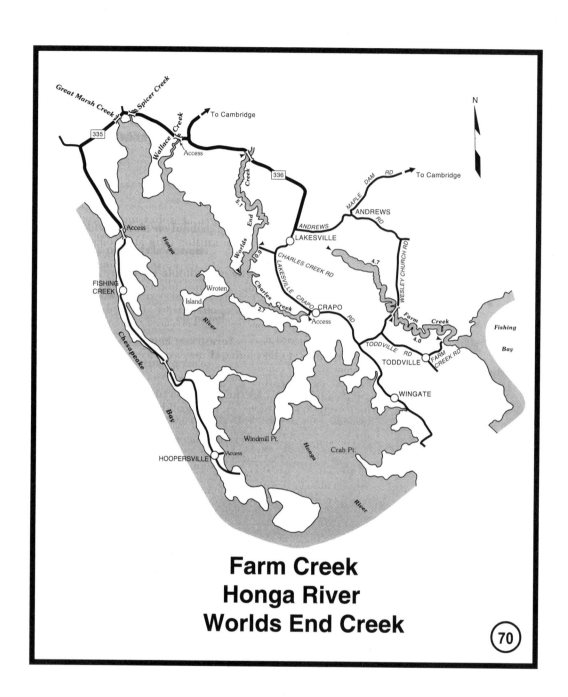

Farm Creek
Honga River
Worlds End Creek

(70)

The put-in is on Great Marsh Creek, a fitting name. Heading east from its mouth, the first few miles of shoreline are mostly undisturbed marsh, except for a patch of higher ground with structures, and unsightly bank erosion protection of riprap and old tires. A side trip up Spicer Creek offers a short tortuous passage up to some pretty ponds. A bit farther, Wallace Creek offers a bigger and longer diversion in a mostly unspoiled setting. You can follow it up to Rte. 355 and beyond. To explore that final reach, however, you may have to portage, as there is only a foot of clearance beneath the bridge span at high tide.

A few more miles past marsh and forest bring you to Charles Creek. This is a lovely path that slowly narrows between also narrowing marsh backed by piney, high ground. It has an even prettier tributary, Worlds End Creek, that is described separately. You can ascend Charles Creek up to an access at Crapo. Return to the Honga through a slot between the mainland and Wroten Island called The Canal. A loop around the mostly deserted and marshy Wroten Island is well worth the nearly five-mile detour. About five more miles of mostly deserted shore brings you to Windmill Point. Here you have the choice of making the relatively narrow crossing to Hoopersville or exploring the final lobe of the Honga. The serrated remainder of the eastern side of the Honga provides a lot of shoreline in a small area, much of it equally scenic, though a bit more settled than the stretch to the north. The logical final crossing to the west is near Crab Point.

The west side of the Honga is less wild than the east, as the Hooper Island chain is relatively settled. Marshy Lower Hooper is the exception. High ground (which down there seems to mean anything over an inch above high tide) on Middle and Upper Hooper is occupied by sort of a linear settlement. The population congeals at the villages of Hoopersville and Fishing Creek, both of which have lovely, little harbors that would probably delight an artist as much as the paddler. Once you get a little bit north of the strait called Fishing Creek, the shore again seems remote and hardly disturbed.

HAZARDS: None.

WATER CONDITIONS: Tidal.

GAUGE: None.

Worlds End Creek and Farm Creek

INTRODUCTION: There is probably no wetter place in Maryland than the southern half of Dorchester County. The roads down there wind almost as much as the ones in the mountains do. But here they carefully thread a trail from one precious high ground to the next, linking little places like Honga, Crapo, Bishops Head, and Crocheron to the higher and drier world beyond. It stands to reason that this would be the right place to which to take a small boat. And if you follow these long, winding roads down to Farm Creek or Worlds End Creek, surely you will agree.

Section 1. Worlds End Creek: Md. Rte. 336 to mouth						
Gradient	Difficulty	Distance	Time	Width	Scenery	Map
0	A	6.0	3.0	20-1,500	Excellent	70

To Cambridge

16

CHURCH CREEK

To Taylors Island

335

Little Blackwater River

MAPLE DAM RD

Hughs Dam Creek

EGYPT RD

3.2

GREENBRIER RD

KEY WALLACE DR

Blackwater River

footbridge

4.5 Access

Visitor Center

Lookout Tower

2.8

To Honga

Blackwater

National

Wildlife

Refuge

3.9

6.4

N

SHORTERS WHARF

MAPLE DAM RD

Blackwater

7.3

5.0

ANDREWS

Raccoon Creek

Fishing

Bay

To Lakesville

ANDREWS RD

WESLEY RD

River

Blackwater River
Little Blackwater River

TRIP DESCRIPTION: Worlds End Creek provides a perfect way to survey that unspoiled expanse of intimidatingly titled wetland called Hell Hook Marsh. This is one of those rare creeks where you can stand up in your canoe and look out across a vast area and see nobody nor any sign of them. The major portion of Worlds End Creek remains a terribly twisting thread down the middle of ever-widening salt meadows bounded by an unbroken wall of forest. While this may be a lonely canoe trail today, old, rotting, black pilings and timbers protruding from the bank muck at low tide remind one that this was once an important artery of local commerce in the pre-automobile era. The creek widens suddenly at about the five-mile point to an estuary fringed by tall pines whose skyline, as viewed from a boat, eventually vanishes in the distance and then returns as a mirage.

Public access to this beauty is limited to the narrow right-of-way of Rte. 336. The marsh is private property, as is the landing at the foot of Charles Creek Road. Please respect this and, unless you can secure permission to cross private land, either consider this a circuit tour or continue another three and a half miles to the end of this creek and then up Charles Creek to the public landing at Crapo.

HAZARDS: None.

WATER CONDITIONS: Always canoeable.

GAUGE: None.

Section 2. Farm Creek: Toddville to head of creek						
Gradient	Difficulty	Distance	Time	Width	Scenery	Map
0	A	8.7	4.0	30-400	Very Good	70

TRIP DESCRIPTION: Beginning as a pond in the heart of wild Beech Ground Swamp, tiny Farm Creek follows the crookedest path possible to its meeting with Fishing Bay. Start your journey just above the mouth at the public boat ramp on Farm Creek Road near Toddville, and head upstream. As far as Wesley Church Road, the narrow channel is usually hemmed in by tall reeds and, hence, that is most of what you see. Above there, however, the reeds disappear, affording a wonderful panorama of wide, green marsh meadows and dense pine forests. The trip climaxes in a shallow wilderness pond, and then it is time to turn back.

HAZARDS: None.

WATER CONDITIONS: Always boatable. But upper sections are best with high tide.

GAUGE: None.

Blackwater River and Little Blackwater River

INTRODUCTION: The area surrounding Fishing Bay in southern Dorchester County is Maryland's convincing imitation of the Everglades. If you care to survey it by foot, bike, or automobile, follow the road to Elliott Island. If you want to see it from a boat, the Blackwater system will introduce you to a king-size chunk of it.

The Blackwater and Little Blackwater drain much of Dorchester County south of Cambridge. This is a markedly low area where the difference between wetland and terra firma is often only two or three feet. Much of the Blackwater passes through lands and wetlands protected by either a national wildlife refuge or a state wildlife management area, and those remaining areas that are privately owned are so remote that nobody has ever even bothered to post them, much less develop them. In fact, there are only two points of access to the whole 28 miles of the Blackwater and only two on the relatively civilized Little Blackwater.

Section 1. Blackwater River: Md. Rte. 335 to head of river						
Gradient	Difficulty	Distance	Time	Width	Scenery	Map
0	A	6.0	3.0	15-500	Excellent	71

TRIP DESCRIPTION: This is the best of the Blackwater, and you must handle it as a circuit tour. Heading upstream from the boaters' access at the Rte. 335 bridge, the still relatively wide river zigzags into the wilderness of Moneystump Swamp. Development back here consists of a few duck blinds, some wildlife refuge markers, and one improbable footbridge. In general, the river passes through forests of almost pure pine fronted by freshwater marsh. The Blackwater, which now begins to live up to its name, eventually narrows on past the footbridge and finally dissolves into a vast, cattail-filled marsh. These upper reaches of the river support a beautiful floating garden of water lilies. In summer their blossoms will delight you, but their thick, interwoven growths will also frustrate and probably block your upstream progress short of the true head of navigation.

HAZARDS: None.

WATER CONDITIONS: Tidal, so there is always water. Daily tidal fluctuations are slight up here, but longer term effects caused by sustained northwesterly or southeasterly respectively driving extra water out or in can influence your success in shallow stretches.

GAUGE: None.

Section 2. Blackwater River: Rte. 335 to Shorters Wharf (Maple Dam Road)						
Gradient	Difficulty	Distance	Time	Width	Scenery	Map
0	A	10.0	6.0	150-6,000	Good	71

TRIP DESCRIPTION: There are two significant hurdles to clear to do this section. First of all, most of this section flows within the Blackwater National Wildlife Refuge, which is closed to river traffic from October 1 to April 1. This means that, except for April and maybe early May, you must endure bug season to tour this place. Remember that in bad years even the locals are driven to distress by the little vampires. And besides being potentially tormenting, it is against the rules to feed the wildlife. As hard a pill as all this is to swallow, at least rest assured that this rule was not made with malice to canoeists. The Refuge is an important avian rest stop on the Atlantic Flyway, which is a goose's version of the New Jersey Turnpike. While some birds winter here, the major crush hits in late fall and early spring on their way through. The Refuge's goal is to keep as many birds as possible within its boundaries during that busy period. This is so that during hunting season the birds do not get shot and at other times to assure that these feathered locust do not descend on neighboring farmers' fields and devour the newly-sprouted winter wheat, etc., thereby incurring great wrath. So the

Refuge prohibits boating and other backcountry travel to avoid spooking the nervous honkers and quackers, causing them to prematurely flee to the troubled world beyond the refuge.

The other problem with this stretch is that to navigate it is an exercise in aquatic orienteering. Do not even consider venturing below Rte. 335 unless you have a good sense of direction and good eyesight. The entire reach from Rte. 335 to the confluence with the Little Blackwater is, contrary to what the topographic maps show, a huge lake. The lake is plenty deep where the old river flowed, but where the islands and marshes once lay is now only a few inches deep. Of course, to the uninitiated it all looks the same, just a big lake. Much of the channel on the eastern half of the lake is marked by sticks or poles protruding from the water. These often require sharp vision to see, and sometimes more than one channel is marked. You should bring along the Golden Hill and Blackwater River USGS 7$\frac{1}{2}$-minute quadrangle sheets and a compass to try to follow the old channel by map, using the stick markers to then verify your estimates. There are few markers in the first two miles. Generally that part of the channel describes a gentle arc from the Rte. 335 bridge, off of the southern tip of Spriggs Island by 1,000 feet, and across Raymond Pond. You will find sticks beginning to appear again approximately 2,000 feet north of Bull Point. The mouth of the Little Blackwater is marked by a yellow refuge sign instructing you to "Maintain Speed for Next Mile." This is because this is a bald eagle nesting area. So please obey the signs and do not land or linger.

The rest of the channel to Shorters Wharf is easy to follow. Reed grass on this section is usually low, especially in the spring after winter fires have leveled much of it. So wide open views are plentiful.

HAZARDS: Getting lost in plain view of where you are headed.

WATER CONDITIONS: Tidal. Ideally, an extraordinarily low tide might be an asset, as the shallows would be exposed, thus revealing the elusive channel.

GAUGE: None.

Section 3. Blackwater River: Shorters Wharf to mouth						
Gradient	Difficulty	Distance	Time	Width	Scenery	Map
0	A	12.5	6.0	150-500	Good	71

TRIP DESCRIPTION: This section passes through a beautiful marsh that is dotted with waterfowl-filled ponds and sloughs, but, alas, the tall riverside reeds block your view of it. So unless you go ashore now and then, you will not see very much, though admittedly it is nevertheless a fine form of solitude.

There is no access to the mouth, so your options are to simply turn around, forge across Fishing Bay to Elliott Island (risky in canoe), ascend the nearby Transquaking River to Bestpitch, or paddle about five and a half miles down the west shore of Fishing Bay to the boat ramp at Toddville. You will get good exercise from any of these options. Wesley Road, a mass of mud and ruts, might allow you to take out on Raccoon Creek, but it is not recommended.

HAZARDS: None.

WATER CONDITIONS: Always runnable.

GAUGE: None.

Section 4. Little Blackwater River: Key Wallace Drive to head of river						
Gradient	Difficulty	Distance	Time	Width	Scenery	Map
0	A	7.0	3.5	20-800	Good	71

TRIP DESCRIPTION: Unlike the wild Blackwater, for most of its length the Little Blackwater is a wide, winding river coursing through attractive farm country. There are patches of woods between farms and there is still plenty of marshland, but you will seldom be out of sight of someone's house, except on the more remote upper reaches. Most paddlers will prefer this portion of the Little Blackwater above Key Wallace Drive. Also, you can shorten this run by using a midpoint access via Maple Dam Road where it crosses Hughs Dam Creek.

The two-and-a-half-mile section below Key Wallace Drive partly flows through the refuge. Thus it is also subject to the seasonal use restrictions and, in addition, the same navigational challenges as found on Section 2 of the Blackwater. A better way of seeing this lower section is from the observation tower on the scenic drive.

HAZARDS: Watch out for spikes in an old railroad trestle pier near the head of the creek.

WATER CONDITIONS: Always runnable.

GAUGE: None.

Transquaking River

INTRODUCTION: The Transquaking River provides a serene tidal trail through the heart of flat, oh so flat, Dorchester County. Although beginning only a few miles south of busy U.S. Rte. 50, thoroughfare of thousands of shore-bound vacationers, the Transquaking meanders into one of Maryland's true geographical backwaters. This is some of the most thinly populated territory in the state, with most people situated along a few narrow roads that thread through vast expanses of impenetrable swamp and marsh and, on higher ground, endless corn and soybean fields. In mild weather, the river is most suitable for beginners. However, if you possess the skills and knowledge to handle cold weather paddling, winter and early spring are the recommended seasons as minimal motorboat traffic and absence of blood-sucking insects allow one to most enjoy this quiet setting of land and water.

Section 1. Drawbridge Road to Bestpitch Ferry Road						
Gradient	Difficulty	Distance	Time	Width	Scenery	Map
0	A	11.7	4.0	100-300	Good	72

TRIP DESCRIPTION: As on most tidal waterways, the put-in is arbitrary, all depending on which way the tide is flowing. Starting at Drawbridge Road, where there is the luxury of a public launching ramp, parking, and pit privies, puts you just below the head of navigation, which is the dam of Higgins Millpond. It is possible to paddle upstream to the dam, lift over, and then explore the two-mile length of this pretty pond.

Heading downstream from Drawbridge Road, initially the river courses past swampy shores broken by occasional solid ground and a few lonely farms. The black-stained water provides a deep channel. About four miles downstream, marshlands replace the swamps, and these marshes gradually widen to one to two miles. In winter these broad meadows turn golden brown, contrasting boldly with the distant skyline of gray forests crowned by stately green pines. The claustrophobic paddler will revel in this Maryland version of the big sky country. Bestpitch Ferry Road pops up suddenly and offers an easy exit via another public launch area.

Transquaking River
Chicamacomico River

There are an additional five to eight and a half miles of river below Bestpitch (depending on your choice of routes) through even grander and vaster wetlands. There is, however, no access to the mouth. So the paddler then has the choice of either doubling back; if one is a good navigator, finding the mouth of the Blackwater River and ascending that stream to Maple Dam Road; or, finally, crossing Fishing Bay to Elliott Island. Only consider this last option if you are a strong and competent paddler with a good assessment of the impending weather. Make a mistake out there, and you will be crab food.

HAZARDS: Mosquitos the size of B-52s and wind.

WATER CONDITIONS: Navigable all year, except when frozen.

GAUGE: None.

Chicamacomico River

INTRODUCTION: The Chicamacomico River (pronounced Chi' ca ma com' i co; say it fast five times) is a slightly longer and slightly prettier version of the Transquaking River to which it is a tributary. It rises as a handful of insignificant trickles and drainage ditches located about five miles east of the Transquaking's similar humble beginnings and matures to a navigable stream only upon reaching tidewater, a short distance south of Rte. 50.

Section 1. U.S. Rte. 50 to Bestpitch Ferry Road						
Gradient	Difficulty	Distance	Time	Width	Scenery	Map
0	A	15.4	6.5	15-500	Good	72

TRIP DESCRIPTION: It is possible to put in at U.S. Rte. 50 just below Big Millpond IF you are a truly dedicated, hardcore swamp rat. That little, ten-foot-wide, two-inch-deep trickle, jammed with fallen trees and debris, can get you to where you want to go. Honest. Just walk west from the Rte. 50 bridge, along the guardrail, and about a hundred feet past the end of the guardrail you will observe a little, five-foot-wide side channel that runs along the foot of the embankment and then bends off into the woods. You can put in there. The channel immediately rejoins the main flow, and for about the next 200 yards this shallow rivulet rushes over a sandy bottom, twisting and turning through a gauntlet of low limbs, bushes, and toppled trees. With a low-profile boat such as a kayak, or with a lot of skill in an open canoe, one can wriggle through this mess with only a few carries. Others will probably fare worse, but because the surrounding jungle is so dense and tangled, the creek route still beats trying to carry or drag through the woods to easier waters. You soon (in distance, if not in time) reach tidewater, and you can now settle down to a peaceful journey down a quickly widening and still twisting route through a swamp forest. In summer, the dark waters will be bountifully decorated by water lilies. The river, unfortunately, remains shallow for these first few miles, so one must be constantly alert for the best channel.

Less adventuresome paddlers will choose to start at the public boat ramp at New Bridge Road. They can probe upstream as far as they dare and then head downstream. The swampy shores continue on for a few more miles, interrupted now and then by a farm or cabin. Below Drawbridge Road, the marshes take over the surroundings and widen dramatically, putting you out in the wide open spaces. Since the river generally trends in a west to southwestward direction, this is a good section for the downstream-bound paddler to avoid late on a sunny afternoon, as the glare will be brutal. The take-out is on the Transquaking at Bestpitch, a mile below the mouth of the Chicamacomico.

HAZARDS: None.

WATER CONDITIONS: Most of this river is tidal and thus suitable to cruise all year. But the short nontidal stretch just below Rte. 50 needs extra water, which is likely only after wet weather.

GAUGE: None.

Island Creek and Pokata Creek

INTRODUCTION: As mentioned earlier, the lands between Fishing Bay and the Nanticoke River are Maryland's answer to the Everglades. The grassy and watery vastness of this remote area is truly awe inspiring. A drive down the road to Elliott Island is a good introduction. But to really experience its charms, get in your boat and follow Island and Pokata creeks.

Section 1. Island Creek: Mouth to Island Creek Pond						
Gradient	Difficulty	Distance	Time	Width	Scenery	Map
0	A	11.2	5.5	15-1,000	Excellent	73

TRIP DESCRIPTION: You cannot put in at the mouth, nor can you start at Island Creek Pond. The road approaches Island Creek only near its midpoint where, for easy access, you will find a ramp about a mile north of Pokata Creek. The trip downstream is on the widest part of Island Creek. High grass here confines your view to the creek corridor, creating a pleasant monotony. If the weather and water are calm, it would be fun to follow the marshy shores of Fishing Bay from the mouth to Elliott Island or even to the Transquaking River and on up to Bestpitch. Otherwise, just double back from the mouth.

Heading upstream yields Island Creek's best rewards. About a mile and a half above the ramp you will arrive at a fork, with both arms the same size, and with the right arm marked by some wooden pilings. The right arm takes you to a maze of small, shallow, marsh-bound ponds with good views of the marsh beyond. The left arm slowly shrinks and shrinks, in an unpromising manner, but continues on and on. The high, creekside spartina grass begins to disappear, offering wonderful views across endless marsh. The passage ultimately delivers you to a long, twisting chain of ponds called Island Pond. The shores are all wooded, some swamp and some hummock. It is a picture of wilderness tranquility. The ponds are crawling with muskrat. Birds come and go. You quickly find that the ponds are all shal-

N

6.8

Island

Creek

Island

1.7

ELLIOTT

Island

Pond

To Vienna

Savanna

Lake

Little
Savanna
Lake

Access

1.3

Creek

1.4

0.7

Fishing
Bay

3.8

Creek

Pokata

To Elliott Island

Island Creek
Pokata Creek

low, but you can pick your way all the way to the head of the ponds. Keep in mind that this is a confusing route where a map and compass can save you from a lot of dead ends.

HAZARDS: Winds. As on most tidal creeks, this is an exposed area. Definitely stay off of Fishing Bay on a windy day.

WATER CONDITIONS: Tidal, always passable.

GAUGE: None.

Section 2. Pokata Creek: Mouth to Little Savanna Lake						
Gradient	Difficulty	Distance	Time	Width	Scenery	Map
0	A	4.5	2.0	10-100	Very Good	73

TRIP DESCRIPTION: As on Island Creek, the put-in is in between. So start at the bridge of Elliott Island Road (recognized by house on south bank). Since there is only about a mile of creek below the bridge, this lower stretch is best as an alternate start for a lower Island Creek tour. Heading upstream on this narrow creek takes you initially up a twisting corridor of high marsh grass. But the high bank grass soon thins, allowing wonderful views across the short grass meadows beyond. If you have never seen a salt marsh, these meadows resemble a suburban home owner's dream lawn, until you attempt to walk across it and find things very wet. The trip ends as Pokata's waters spread out as Little Savanna Lake. Only inches deep, it does not allow poking around, as on Island Pond. So gaze, enjoy, and head back to the bridge, hopefully on a favorable tide.

HAZARDS: None.

WATER CONDITIONS: Always passable.

GAUGE: None.

Nanticoke River

INTRODUCTION: The Nanticoke gathers its waters from the swamps and extensively cultivated flatlands of Sussex County, Delaware, and then cuts an imposing swath across Maryland's lower Eastern Shore. Most of it is a wide, windy tidal estuary which, while very pretty, should only be attempted by paddlers armed with tide tables, lots of energy, and, during summer, ample bug protection. Meanwhile, back in the headwaters, the U.S. Soil Conservation Service has done its best over the years to channelize all of the freshwater creeks in the neighborhood into drab, quick-draining, scum-filled, straight ditches. But somehow, they missed a few of the best ones, and have left for us canoeists the upper Nanticoke and its tributaries, the upper Marshyhope, James Branch, and Hitch Pond Branch.

Section 1. County Road 545 to Seaford, Del. (U.S. Rte. 13)						
Gradient	Difficulty	Distance	Time	Width	Scenery	Map
3	A	9.6	3.5	20-100	Good	74

To Bridgeville

To Dover

RIFLE RANGE RD
(RD 545)

Gauge

404

1.8

18

18

To Georgetown

To Federalsburg

13

River

4.3

OLD FURNACE RD
(RD 46)

Nanticoke

MIDDLEFORD

(RD 535)

3.5

20

N

SEAFORD

FRONT ST

HIGH ST

MIDDLEFORD RD

Access

1.2

20

ROAD 20

BLADES

ROAD 13

To Salisbury

Nanticoke River

TRIP DESCRIPTION: There is no reason to start above County Road 545 (Rifle Range Road) as the stream has all been channelized. The Nanticoke reverts to its natural channel at this point and commences winding through a pretty swamp, only occasionally marred by views into the surrounding farmland or by logging scars. The most pleasant facet of this run is that it is relatively easy to negotiate. Unlike many other swamps, downed trees block the way with only moderate frequency, and often there is a way around them. The stream turns tidal a few miles below the confluence with the Gravelly Branch (left), but with the right tide, you can enjoy a strong current well past Middleford, after which the river widens out into a slow estuary with residentially developed shores.

The choice of take-outs is a poor one. You can carry up the steep embankment to busy Rte.13, you can continue one mile downstream to the confluence of Williams Pond at the community hospital, or you can continue a half mile farther to a public launching ramp above the DuPont plant at the foot of Porter Street.

HAZARDS: Fallen trees and snags.

WATER CONDITIONS: Runnable late fall, winter, spring, and during a wet summer. Higher levels are desirable to increase options for bypassing trees.

GAUGE: A USGS gauge (inspect on site or see USGS website) is located at Road 545. Given that zero is a function of your tolerance for liftovers, consider 110 cfs (4.4 feet) to 200 cfs (5.5 feet) as a desirable range.

Section 2. Seaford, Del. (Porter St.) to Sharptown, Md. (Md. Rte. 313)						
Gradient	Difficulty	Distance	Time	Width	Scenery	Map
0	A	9.3	4.0	200-1,500	Fair to Good	75

TRIP DESCRIPTION: On this reach, the Nanticoke evolves from the intimate swamp stream of Section 1 to the expansive corridor of water and marsh that leads to the Chesapeake. By entering via the public ramp in Seaford, you bypass the uninteresting passage through town and, at low tide, avoid slogging through muck to launch. Actually the town lingers for many miles in the form of riverside development. But as high ground diminishes, so do the buildings. Once past Woodland, with its active little car ferry, the scenery is primarily natural, and once past Broad Creek, it is practically unspoiled. Most of this route is lined by swamp. Take out at the public ramp and park by the Md. Rte. 313 Bypass at Sharptown.

HAZARDS: None.

WATER CONDITIONS: Tidal.

GAUGE: None.

Section 3. Sharptown (Md. Rte. 313) to Vienna						
Gradient	Difficulty	Distance	Time	Width	Scenery	Map
0	A	7.6	3.5	500-1,000	Good	77

TRIP DESCRIPTION: This is a beautiful section available in an easily handled portion. The riverscape transforms from swamp-lined corridor to a tour of marshes. Except for at Riverton, there is no high ground nearby and thus no development. A ramp at the foot of Race Street in Vienna provides easy egress.

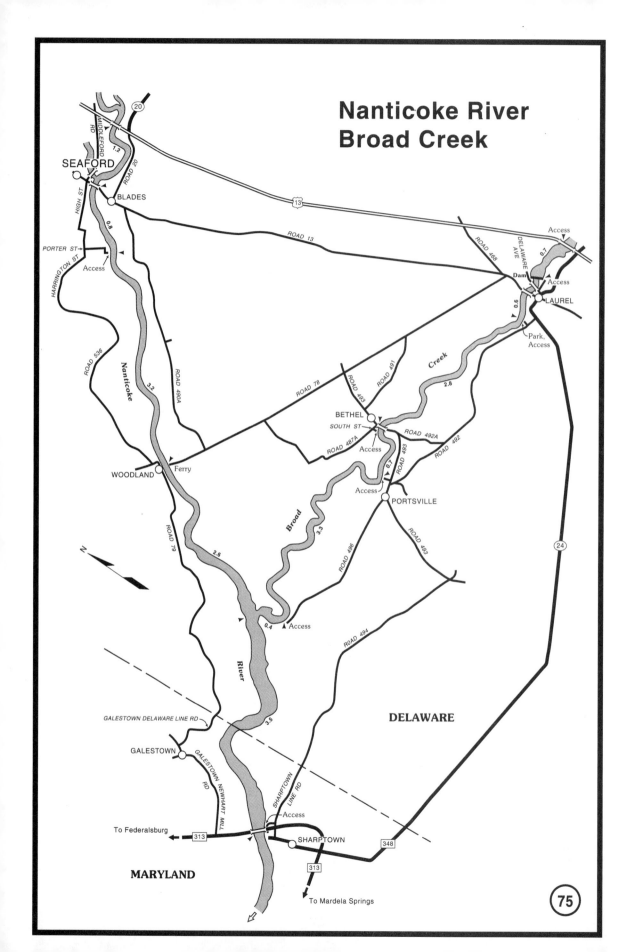

Nanticoke River
Broad Creek

ROAD 20

ROAD 13

U.S. 13

MIDDLEFORD RD

1.2

SEAFORD

BLADES

HIGH ST

PORTER ST

HARRINGTON ST

Access

0.8

ROAD 536

Nanticoke

3.2

ROAD 490A

ROAD 78

ROAD 493

ROAD 491

ROAD 468

DELAWARE AVE

Access

0.7

Dam

Access

0.6

LAUREL

Park, Access

Creek

2.8

BETHEL

SOUTH ST

ROAD 487A

Access

0.7

ROAD 493

ROAD 492A

ROAD 492

Access

WOODLAND

Ferry

PORTSVILLE

Broad

3.3

ROAD 496

ROAD 493

ROAD 79

2.6

0.4

Access

ROAD 494

24

River

N

DELAWARE

GALESTOWN DELAWARE LINE RD

3.5

GALESTOWN

GALESTOWN NEWHART MILL RD

SHARPTOWN LINE RD

Access

To Federalsburg

313

SHARPTOWN

348

313

MARYLAND

To Mardela Springs

Nice side trips are a feature of this section. First, about two miles below the Marshyhope, on the right, is a channel branching perpendicularly from the Nanticoke. It is named The Canal. It ends at a T-intersection with Panguash Creek, whose swampy, twisting channel you can follow in either direction until you are good and lost or maybe until it leads you back to the main river or the Marshyhope via a secret route that you will never be able to retrace. The other good side trip is Chicone Creek. Located also on the right, less than a mile above the take-out, it provides a single, easily-followed passage through more beautiful swamp. With high tide, you can ascend to about a quarter mile above Chicone Road, which crosses on a culvert that you must carry.

HAZARDS: None

WATER CONDITIONS: All tidal.

GAUGE: None.

Broad Creek

INTRODUCTION: Broad Creek is formed at the confluence of James Branch and Elliott Pond Branch, just east of Laurel, Delaware. Starting as a pond and finishing as a relatively narrow estuary, this is a pleasant and accessible route for beginners.

Section 1. U.S. Rte. 13 to mouth						
Gradient	Difficulty	Distance	Time	Width	Scenery	Map
0	A	8.5	4.0	15-800	Fair to Good	75

TRIP DESCRIPTION: If you want to paddle only on Records Pond, you can use the ramp on the north side just upstream of Rte. 13 or the park at the south end of the dam that forms the pond. The park is a block east of Delaware Avenue on Front Street. If you are interested only in the tidal section, a better place to start is Laurel River Park on the west side of town, just below the railroad bridge.

Records Pond between Rte. 13 and the dam is completely lined by houses. In contrast, the remainder of the path through town is mostly screened from the surroundings by dense vegetation, including flourishing brier patches and some lingering cypress trees. Below town, developed high ground alternates with magnolia-studded swampy reaches. Protected as a state wildlife area, the last few miles offer the most natural setting.

Access to Broad Creek is good. You can reach the middle river in Bethel via a tiny park at the foot of South Street (tough at low tide) and another tiny park at the upstream end of Portsville. You can reach the lower end via the boat ramp at Phillips Landing, about a half mile above the Nanticoke.

HAZARDS: None

WATER CONDITIONS: Consisting of tidewater and an impoundment, water is always there.

GAUGE: None.

Hitch Pond Branch
James Branch

To Dover

Records

To Laurel

Access

To Salisbury

ROAD 461

Pond

1.0

James

Branch

2.7

ROAD 462

24

Hitch

ROAD 463

Pond

1.5

Branch

ROAD 449

ROAD 449

Trussum Pond

ROAD 72

Dam

Trap Pond
State Park

Campground

Trap

1.6

Pond

ROAD 72

ROAD 62

To Millsboro

Dam

Davis
Pond

N

Hitch Pond Branch and James Branch

INTRODUCTION: Whoever coined the adage "good things come in small packages" might have been inspired by this remote, little swamp run. Canoeable streams just do not come any smaller, Delaware streams do not come any wilder, and on top of all that, you may be able to get down this beauty without a chain saw.

Section 1. Road 72 to U.S. Rte. 13						
Gradient	Difficulty	Distance	Time	Width	Scenery	Map
4	A	6.8	4.0	5-25	Very Good	76

TRIP DESCRIPTION: This trip begins at the spillway at Davis Pond Dam on the edge of Trap Pond State Park. This park offers fine camping facilities and makes an excellent base of operations for exploring lower Eastern Shore rivers.

You are actually launching on yet another waterway, Raccoon Prong, making this a four-stream tour in less than seven miles. If you have the time, head the short distance upstream on Davis Pond. This gives a taste of open water followed by a beautiful swamp. It also gives an opportunity to shoot the sloping, six-foot, wooden spillway. You can also put in below. The microscopic channel that follows is indeed navigable and usually free of strainers. It is a short passage through cypress swamp that all too soon delivers you into cypress-fringed Trap Pond. You are now on Hitch Pond Branch. At the end of the pond you must make the short carry to the foot of its impassable spillway.

Hitch Pond Branch immediately rushes off into deep, dark, dank, and dense swamp forest that usually completely blots out the endless farms and fields that lie just beyond. Initially the creek is only five to eight feet wide, but additional tributaries swell it to sufficient width that you cannot broach your boat between the banks. Hitch Pond Branch then flows into James Branch below the first road bridge, from which point on there is plenty of elbow room. Amazingly, there are only a few trees blocking the course, partly because in years past the Delaware Department of Parks cleared the stream for canoeists. Bring along a saw and keep this beauty open for the next visitor. But the most outstanding feature of this swamp is its rich growth of cypress trees. Some surprisingly big trees remain, and the weird, grotesque shapes of their unique trunks will never cease to fascinate. The trip ends too soon on the civilized Records Pond where a state launching ramp offers easy exit.

HAZARDS: Trees and overhanging limbs.

WATER CONDITIONS: Runnable all winter and spring and often in wet summers.

GAUGE: There is a USGS gauge at the Trap Pond spillway. A level of 1.3 feet is just fine.

Marshyhope Creek
Nanticoke River

Trussum Pond

One should not visit this neighborhood without at least a short visit to Trussum Pond. Formed by an old dam across James Branch, just above its confluence with Hitch Pond Branch, this is the closest thing to a bayou in Delaware. Access is via Road 72 at a small state park parking area. Trussum is more of a swamp than a pond. Graceful cypress protrude everywhere from its black, lily pad dappled waters, creating a bit of a challenge to navigation. While a main channel is often difficult to identify, a variety of routes and some persistence in pursuing them can lead you almost a mile and a half above the dam. This place is really special in late autumn when the cypress stand like great rusty mops against the now bare hardwood forests.

Marshyhope Creek

INTRODUCTION: Marshyhope Creek oozes out of Kent and Sussex counties, Delaware and flows through Caroline and Dorchester counties, Maryland to join the Nanticoke River below Sharptown. Channelization has devastated the upper river, but nine miles of prime swamp cruising remain between Woodenhawk, Delaware and tidewater at Federalsburg, Maryland, and there are then over 16 miles of easy tidal cruising below.

Section 1. Woodenhawk, Del. (Del. Rte. 404) to Federalsburg, Md.						
Gradient	Difficulty	Distance	Time	Width	Scenery	Map
2	A	9.5	4.0	20-30	Good	77

TRIP DESCRIPTION: Do not be distressed by the dredged channel that you find at the put-in. A few hundred yards downstream it abruptly ends and, after a brief introductory tangle with some trees, the creek begins its narrow, winding, and sometimes subtle route through a very wet swamp forest. This is a pretty swamp without too many civilized inroads, except for a a noisy sawmill above Noble Road. Like the Nanticoke, the going is relatively easy as fallen trees do not occur too often, at least compared to other small coastal plain streams. The flooded nature of the surrounding woods, fortunately, often allows a bypass route around deadfalls that would otherwise mean a liftover. On the other hand, there are a few braided channels that can easily lead you into a dead end. Take out at the town park behind the Union United Methodist Church (entrance easy to miss) a few hundred yards above the Rte. 318 bridge.

HAZARDS: Fallen trees and snags.

WATER CONDITIONS: Catch in late fall, winter, spring, and wet summers. Higher water increases options for avoiding fallen trees.

GAUGE: None on creek. Roughly, USGS gauges on Choptank at Greensboro and on Nanticoke at Bridgeville should read over 110 cfs (4.4 feet) and 85 cfs (3.0 feet) respectively for a comfortable level on Marshyhope. Remember that low levels (i.e. uncomfortable levels) mean lots of liftovers.

Section 2. Federalsburg (Md. Rte. 318) to mouth						
Gradient	Difficulty	Distance	Time	Width	Scenery	Map
0	A	16.6	8.0	100-700	Good	77

TRIP DESCRIPTION: The tidal Marshyhope should have been named the "Swampyhope," as it flows for much of its length past wild and wet, wooded fringes. Scattered patches of high ground are usually private and built upon. Together, these characteristics make this mostly attractive river only marginally desirable to cruise as there are few places where you can stop along the way. Put in at the public marina above Rte. 318 and take out one mile down the Nanticoke at Riverton, or at any bridge in between.

HAZARDS: None.

WATER CONDITIONS: Tidal and always navigable.

GAUGE: None.

Barren Creek

INTRODUCTION: Looking for a short, convenient canoe trip to combine with an Ocean City weekend? Here is the creek for you. Located about halfway between Cambridge and Salisbury, just off of Rte. 50, but not so close as to be ruined by that busy highway, Barren Creek will please you. It is a small, tidal tributary of the mighty Nanticoke that has somehow, so far, escaped civilization's destructive hand.

Section 1. Mardela Springs (Bridge St.) to mouth						
Gradient	Difficulty	Distance	Time	Width	Scenery	Map
0	A	6.8	3.0	60-200	Good	78

TRIP DESCRIPTION: The put-in is easy—a small town park with a boat ramp, set by the bridge on Bridge Street. Barren Creek is different from most Dorchester County tidal streams in that more than half of its length passes between entirely wooded banks. Swampy here, high and dry there, this is a delightful, closed-in setting. There are a few houses and farms along here, but mostly the surroundings are wild. Background noise from Rte. 50 is surprisingly negligible. Eventually, the expected marshes do appear, and they soon stretch out forever as part of the wetlands you view from the Rte. 50 bridge over the Nanticoke. When you reach the mouth, you are in the middle of nowhere. You can either double back or ascend the Nanticoke for a little over a mile to a public access in Vienna.

HAZARDS: Steer clear of commercial barge traffic on the Nanticoke.

WATER CONDITIONS: Tidal, always canoeable.

GAUGE: None.

Rewastico Creek and Quantico Creek

INTRODUCTION: Rewastico and Quantico creeks are tributaries of the broad, windswept, lower Nanticoke River, diverging from almost a common mouth to wind their way back past marsh, forest, and farm to headwaters that are only a dozen miles east of downtown Salisbury. These can be difficult waterways to completely explore as there is access only at their upper ends, meaning that it takes a fairly long trip to explore their entire lengths, and this may include battling the wind and tide in addition. With a more modest itinerary, these creeks will please anybody.

Section 1. Rewastico Creek: Athol Road to mouth						
Gradient	Difficulty	Distance	Time	Width	Scenery	Map
0	A	6.3	3.0	30-400	Good	79

Quantico Creek

Rewastico Creek

To Hebron

QUANTICO

To Salisbury

347

349

To Mardela Springs

ATHEL RD

HOLLAWAY RD

HURLEYS NECK RD

RD

CHERRY WALK RD

CHERRY WALK RD

ROYAL OAK

To Nanticoke

ROYAL OAK RD

ROYAL OAK RD

4.8

Creek

Creek

Quantico Creek

Manumsco Creek

Renasitico

1.5

Quantico Creek

11.0

0.9

Nanticoke River

N

79

TRIP DESCRIPTION: The put-in is at the head of tidewater at the old, crumbling, gray mill and earthen dam forming Rewastico Mill Pond. Access here requires crossing private property, so be sure to ask permission first. The creek quickly widens from the little, dark pool at the mill but never really grows very big. The route is generally pretty with marsh-fringed shores backed by often wooded high ground. But too many houses and farms occupy the surrounding high ground to generate a very remote atmosphere. Gradually though the marshes widen, farms disappear, and by the time you reach the mouth, you will feel far from anywhere. And in a way you are, because the take-out is way back where you started or, if you are really energetic, it is a short hop down the Nanticoke and then a long haul up Quantico Creek to Rte. 347.

HAZARDS: None.

WATER CONDITIONS: Tidal, always runnable.

GAUGE: None.

Section 2. Quantico Creek: Quantico (Md. Rte. 347) to mouth						
Gradient	Difficulty	Distance	Time	Width	Scenery	Map
0	A	11.0	5.5	15-500	Good	79

TRIP DESCRIPTION: Public access is available only off of the Rte. 347 right-of-way through a mess of mud, briers, and brambles to a shallow and narrow creek. Since the first 100 yards are complicated some by snags and deadfalls, you might consider seeking permission to put in across private property down an unnamed side street on the river right. The creek continues to be narrow and shallow for less than a mile, but now at least free of obstructions, running through woods until, like Rewastico Creek, it widens to modest dimensions. Quantico Creek proves to be pretty as, unlike Rewastico, there are few buildings crowding it, leaving mainly a tour of broad, lonely wetlands and deep, pine woods. These woods possess an understory of cedar and holly whose wonderful greenness will be most appreciated in winter when they so contrast with the golden marshes.

HAZARDS: None.

WATER CONDITIONS: Runnable all year, but the upper reaches are marginal at low tide.

GAUGE: None.

Wicomico Creek

INTRODUCTION: Wicomico Creek is a nice, but hardly outstanding, tidal stream that is conveniently close to Salisbury. You may ask then, why not do the Wicomico, which flows right out of the heart of Salisbury. The Wicomico River is just too big, too straight, and, hence, too monotonous. It has some attractive, swampy fringes, but most of the high ground is occupied by houses. They are mostly attractive houses, but attractive houses are not as desirable as wide, open spaces. The River is

Wicomico Creek

80

also popular with motorboaters, is windswept, and is the route of commercial barge traffic. So assuming that you would enjoy something more quiet and sheltered, try Wicomico Creek.

		Section 1. Loretto Allen Road to Redden Ferry Road				
Gradient	Difficulty	Distance	Time	Width	Scenery	Map
0	A	6.2	3.0	20-600	Good	80

TRIP DESCRIPTION: The put-in is a nice little county park on the right bank below an old milldam. The creek here is just barely ready to receive you, and at low tide you may have a little dragging in the first 100 yards. The creek remains narrow as far as Somerset Creek (large tributary on left, one and a half miles down). The banks are unusually high for the lower Eastern Shore and mostly wooded. The gently winding course is usually fringed by relatively narrow marshes with the high ground beyond occupied by both woods and farms. You are seldom out of sight of a house on this creek, but they are still far apart and mostly attractive structures.

It is best to finish your trip at Redden Ferry at either the south approach or at a publicly-leased boat ramp and parking spot on the north approach. The latter is a good take-out, but has had some security problems from time to time. The mouth is one mile beyond, but with an oversized marina marring the view and an absence of access, there is little reason to go that far.

248

Monie Creek

HAZARDS: None.

WATER CONDITIONS: Always canoeable, but it is best to catch the upper end at high tide.

GAUGE: None.

Monie Creek

INTRODUCTION: Most of Somerset County's estuarine waters are wide open expanses, more suitable for sea kayaking and sailing than for canoeing. So Monie Creek is special in that it offers a relatively sheltered path through this pretty tidewater setting. It starts just a few miles northeast of Princess Anne. But when you get just a few miles into rural Somerset County, you feel far from anywhere.

Section 1. Md. Rte. 362 to mouth						
Gradient	Difficulty	Distance	Time	Width	Scenery	Map
0	A	8.3	4.0	20-800	Good to Very Good	81

Manokin River
Kings Creek

To Salisbury

PRINCESS ANNE

0.4

SOMERSET RD

363

STP

0.5

675

OLD PRINCESS ANNE WESTOVER RD

To Deal Island

Manokin

1.4

Taylor Branch

1.2

13

0.3

PERRY RD

Prison

River

1.8

STEWART

Creek

3.5

Kings

1.0

NECK RD

To Pocomoke City

NECK RD

5.5

River

REVELLS RD

Monokin

Raccoon
Point
Park

Access

82

TRIP DESCRIPTION: Access to this crooked creek is limited, with Rte. 362 getting right to the head of navigation and Drawbridge Road touching the creek at mile five. At Rte. 362, with its beautiful, old, colonial mansion, respect the no trespassing signs and stick to the highway right-of-way, south side of bridge. The easiest way to use Drawbridge Road is from the south, where it deadends right at the water's edge. The north approach ends at a wildlife management area parking place, about a hundred yards short of the river. A subtle but dry path through the marsh will get you to the water.

The narrow, looping upper portion of this route passes many farms and houses. But it is all set in the middle of a pretty marsh that will draw most of your attention. The section below Drawbridge Road is by far the prettiest. The marshes are wide, wild, and backed mostly by the face of a forest. Mostly within the bounds of the Deal Island Wildlife Management Area, this is an unspoiled setting. When you reach Nail Point, the mouth, you stare down Monie Bay into seemingly endless water. This can be a particularly pretty place to be at sunset.

HAZARDS: None.

WATER CONDITIONS: Tidal and passable even at low tide.

GAUGE: None.

Manokin River and Kings Creek

INTRODUCTION: The Manokin and its tributary, Kings Creek, are two convenient streams, flowing westward from busy U.S. Rte. 13 in Somerset County. And since they are so easy to reach and do, maybe they will be worth your time to paddle them.

Section 1. Manokin River: Princess Anne (N. Somerset St.) to mouth						
Gradient	Difficulty	Distance	Time	Width	Scenery	Map
0	A	9.6	4.5	20-3,000	Fair to Good	82

TRIP DESCRIPTION: North Somerset Street is the head of navigation, at high tide only. At low tide, a deep channel does not form until about a half mile below Md. Rte. 363. So either you can pole your way down from Rte. 363 or try to find some way in behind the town sewage treatment plant.

To Kings Creek, the Manokin offers mixed aesthetics. On the good side, the river is usually accompanied by a narrow band of marshes backed by a ragged skyline of pine and hardwood forest. But this is offset by high ground that is usually taken up by houses, farms, and, worst of all, chicken houses. Yes, part of the experience of paddling the Manokin is sucking up deep breaths of essence de poulet, or in plain English, the stench of chicken manure. The price we pay for a taste of fried chicken.

Below Kings Creek the Manokin steadily widens, and by the end the banks are over a half mile apart. But the houses and farms thin out down here, making for more attractive shores. Take out at the public ramp at Raccoon Point County Park.

HAZARDS: None.

Big Annemessex River

N

To Princess Anne

Janes

Island

Daugherty Creek Canal

Access
ALFRED LAWSON RD
PLANTATION DR
413
358

State

Park

Sound

CRISFIELD

SOMERSET AVE

River

CALVERY RD

Access

Little Annemessex

Jenkins Creek

Tangier

Cedar
Island

Wildlife

Management Area

Broad Creek

Sound

Cedar Straits

Pocomoke

Janes Island
Cedar Island

WATER CONDITIONS: All tidal, but attempt uppermost mile only at high tide.

GAUGE: None.

Section 2. Kings Creek: U.S. Rte. 13 to mouth						
Gradient	Difficulty	Distance	Time	Width	Scenery	Map
0	A	4.5	2.0	15-100	Good	82

TRIP DESCRIPTION: Kings Creek is a small and pleasant tributary to the Manokin. All of its detractions, a prison, a feedmill, and a trailer park are clustered near Rte. 13. But even up there, one beautiful old house and some banks clad in bayberry thickets partially compensate for these blemishes. As for the rest of the creek, it is a mostly undeveloped mix of marsh and woods.

At high tide it is reasonable to start a third of a mile higher (and in less traffic) at the Old Princess Anne Westover Road. There is no access at the mouth, so either double back to Stewart Neck Road or continue up or down the Manokin.

HAZARDS: None.

WATER CONDITIONS: Tidal, though high tide is probably needed in the upper end.

GAUGE: None.

Janes Island and Cedar Island

INTRODUCTION: Perhaps Somerset County's best-known landmark is Crisfield. Its fame has long been as a seafood capital. Now more and more visitors are finding that it is also a good base for paddling. One might wish to start by exploring the two islands that flank the town — Janes and Cedar.

Janes Island makes up the bulk of a state park of the same name. It is an island because the Daugherty Creek Canal separates it from the mainland. The park encourages canoeing and kayaking here to the extent that it charges no fee for launching, allows year-round and 24-hour access, provides for back-country camping, and best of all, has established a system of marked canoe trails. This latter feature makes this an exceptionally good venue for paddlers who are just beginning to venture into the world of tides and confusing marshy mazes.

Cedar Island is protected as a state wildlife management area. It is smaller than Janes, but every bit as wild. There are no marked trails here, but plenty of routes to follow. Try it when you graduate from Janes' protective setting.

Section 1. Janes Island						
Gradient	Difficulty	Distance	Time	Width	Scenery	Map
0	A	Variable	Variable	30+	Good	83

WILLARDS

To Salisbury

346

50

354

BENT PINE RD

MASSEY CROSSING RD

LOGTOWN RD

To Ocean City

2.4

MT. PLEASANT RD

River

Pocomoke

2.3

TIMMONSTOWN RD

To Berlin

POWELLVILLE

PURNELL RD

CROSSING RD

LEE 2.2 RD

374

1.7

NINEPIN BRANCH RD

QUEPONCA RD

WHITON CROSSING RD

FIVE MILE BRANCH RD

N

5.0

To Salisbury

Gauge

PORTERS CROSSING RD

To Berlin

2.3

OLD FURNACE RD

354

River

12

RED HOUSE RD

1.6

5.1

Nassawango

Access

113

NASSAWANGO RD

2.3

Creek

394

Pocomoke

SNOW HILL
City Park

2.1

1.0

To Pocomoke City

Pocomoke River
Nassawango Creek

84

TRIP DESCRIPTION: The primary put-in is the state park ramp at the end of Alfred Lawson Drive. From here you can strike out on any or all of five color-coded trails, not to mention invent your own routes. All of the trails are passable at low tide, though the blue trail gets a bit shallow. Tidal currents on the interior trails are moderately strong. Much of the exposed brown trail, which follows the perimeter, would challenge many paddlers on windy days.

Much of Janes Island would more appropriately called "Janes Marsh." Its south and west rim, however, form a delightful, low, narrow beach. If the beach is all that you want, a mere mile-long paddle on the yellow trail gets you to a dock and a short trail to the beach. There are also some scattered hummocks. These provide a foundation for the back-country campsites. Call the park at 410-968-1565 to obtain permits and to learn the stringent back-country rules of etiquette.

HAZARDS: Wind and bugs.

WATER CONDITIONS: All tidal.

GAUGE: None.

Section 2. Cedar Island						
Gradient	Difficulty	Distance	Time	Width	Scenery	Map
0	A	Variable	Variable	200+	Good	83

TRIP DESCRIPTION: The best approach to Cedar Island is from the county launching ramp by the Calvary Road bridge over Jenkins Creek. Circumnavigating Cedar is the easiest approach for the directionally impaired. The east side, Broad Creek, even has navigation markers. Contrary to what is shown on the USGS quadrangle, the southwest side, Cedar Straits, is deep enough to paddle at a normal low tide. A variety of guts and ponds penetrate the interior. Though their pattern is maze-like, the small size of the territory assures that most will find their way out.

Like Janes, Cedar is mostly just a big, beautiful marsh. The Tangier Sound side has a low, narrow beach. There are some jungle-covered hummocks along Broad Creek, one of which yields a bountiful crop of wild persimmons come November, i.e. if you can get past the tangled shield of poison ivy.

HAZARDS: Wind and bugs.

WATER CONDITIONS: All tidal.

GAUGE: None.

Pocomoke River

INTRODUCTION: The Pocomoke drains out of a big swamp in Sussex County, Delaware to eventually reach the Chesapeake Bay at the Maryland-Virginia line. What you see now is what remains of a once huge cypress swamp forest that has long since succumbed to logging, draining, and massive fires. The swamp was for a long time logged to supply a thriving cypress shingle industry. But that industry withered when cypress was replaced by the use of redwood. Then in 1930, a fire ravaged the swamp (supposedly started by an exploding moonshine still), burning out not only trees, but more importantly, several feet of very slowly deposited peat. Even the river has been changed under past channelization efforts. But time has softened the scars, the forests are growing back, and wildlife and waterfowl abound. This is now probably the best opportunity in the State for the beginner paddler to escape the civilized world.

Section 1. Md. Rte. 346 to Whiton Crossing Road						
Gradient	Difficulty	Distance	Time	Width	Scenery	Map
1	A	8.6	2.5	15-35	Good	84

TRIP DESCRIPTION: This part of the Pocomoke has long been channelized and it gives one the feeling of paddling down a canal, not a river. The banks, however, are now densely wooded, as is the surrounding, swampy territory. So one enjoys a feeling of remoteness. There is initially a strong current, but this slows down considerably as the river widens.

HAZARDS: None.

WATER CONDITIONS: All of the time, except for dry summers.

GAUGE: What you see at the put-in represents the most marginal conditions on this section. This corresponds to about 45 cfs (4.45 feet) as measured by the USGS gauge at the put-in (see USGS website).

Section 2. Whiton Crossing Road to Snow Hill City Park						
Gradient	Difficulty	Distance	Time	Width	Scenery	Map
2*	A	10.5	4.0	15-200	Excellent	84
*above tidewater						

TRIP DESCRIPTION: The channelization ends below Whiton Crossing Road, and the river commences twisting through a deep, swamp forest. It is a forest of holly trees, maple, sweet gum, and, best of all, cypress. Even with all the past devastation, some of the trees have survived to a giant size. The canoeist is carried through this wilderness by a remarkably fast and powerful current of dark, tea-colored water (Pocomoke is Indian for "black water"). If you run this stretch when the water is low, be prepared, unfortunately, for many deadfalls blocking the section between Whiton and Porters.

Below Porters Crossing, the river becomes tidal, but remains relatively narrow and easy to paddle. Cypress continue to line the dark waters, but reeds and other still water plants now decorate the scenery. Take out at Snow Hill City Park, which is on the left about a half mile below the Md. Rte. 12 bridge, or with permission, you can exit at the Pocomoke River Canoe Company, by the bridge.

HAZARDS: Numerous deadfalls.

WATER CONDITIONS: All year except during prolonged dry periods.

GAUGE: The USGS gauge near Willards (see USGS website) should read at least 45 cfs (4.45 feet) for a comfortable run. You can float the stream with much less water, but the liftovers will increase exponentially. Tidal below Porters Crossing.

Section 3. Snow Hill City Park to Pocomoke City (U.S. Rte. 13)						
Gradient	Difficulty	Distance	Time	Width	Scenery	Map
0	A	13.8	6.0	250-900	Good	85

TRIP DESCRIPTION: This is a very convenient and attractive piece of the Pocomoke to paddle. Still relatively narrow, the river rolls past wild, tangled, cypress-studded swamp, interrupted here and there only by a few farms and houses and facilities of two state parks. You are more likely to see motorboats on this section than above, and you may even have to dodge an oil or gravel barge. There is a variety of access points at Pocomoke City: the park under the south end of the Rte. 13 bridge, a mile upstream at Winters Quarters Landing, or a mile downstream of Rte. 13 at the Williams Street Boat Ramp.

HAZARDS: Stay out of path of commercial shipping.

WATER CONDITIONS: Tidal and exceptionally deep.

GAUGE: None.

Section 4. Pocomoke City (U.S. Rte. 13) to Shelltown						
Gradient	Difficulty	Distance	Time	Width	Scenery	Map
0	A	15.3	7.0	250-1,000	Good	85

TRIP DESCRIPTION: This section of the Pocomoke would be the least interesting to the paddler. The river as far as Rehobeth remains narrow as it continues past wild cypress swamp. There is, however, much more high ground along this portion, and most of it is built upon. Past Rehobeth, the cypress disappear and marshes begin to bracket the river with scattered farms occupying the solid ground just beyond. You can take out at Cedar Hall Wharf, which is upstream of a lovely, old, colonial-style house, or at the ramp in Shelltown. The mouth lies two miles beyond Shelltown where the Pocomoke rounds the sandy tip of Williams Point on aptly named Fair Island into big, blue Pocomoke Sound. This little island is probably the nicest feature of the lower river.

HAZARDS: Give commercial shipping a wide berth.

WATER CONDITIONS: Tidal, always canoeable.

GAUGE: None.

Nassawango Creek

INTRODUCTION: Nassawango Creek is the Pocomoke's largest canoeable tributary, entering the Pocomoke about a mile and a half below Snow Hill. In its nontidal portion, it is tiny, but it usually carries enough water to float a canoe through its lovely cypress swamp. Most people explore the equally beautiful, but much easier, tidal portion. And its popularity continues to grow. Thanks to a

Pocomoke River
Dividing Creek
Pitts Creek

Nassawango Creek

NASSAWANGO RD

12

0.4

SNOW HILL

City Park

1.7

394

1.0

1.9

Pocomoke River

4.0

Shad Landing State Park

113

Milburn Landing

State Park

DIVIDING CREEK RD

3.7

Dividing Creek

1.9

364

1.1

1.4

To Princess Anne

13

WINTERS QUARTERS DR

756

PEACH ORCHARD RD

1.0

Pocomoke City

667

11.1

371

13

MARYLAND

TULLS CORNER RD

REHOBETH

BACK SHELLTOWN RD

Pocomoke

CEDAR HALL WHARF RD

Little Mill Creek

COLONA RD

To Norfolk

707

1.1

705

SHELLTOWN RD

River

Pitts Creek

3.6

709

2.3

5.4

VIRGINIA

SHELLTOWN

0.5

0.4

709

2.0

Pocomoke Sound

N

85

long effort by The Nature Conservancy to preserve the surrounding and upstream swamp, this is one stream that we can look forward to paddling for many years to come.

Section 1. Md. Rte. 12 to mouth

Gradient	Difficulty	Distance	Time	Width	Scenery	Map
2*	A	7.2	5.0	10-500	Excellent	84

*above tidewater

TRIP DESCRIPTION: What you see at Rte. 12 seems awfully small, but you will notice that there is a good bit of water flowing over the gauging station weir under the bridge, and that is enough to float you. Like the Pocomoke, the water flows swiftly and clearly, but stained dark brown by tannic acid leached from decaying vegetation. Like the Pocomoke, it flows through a deep, lovely, cypress swamp forest. Unlike the Pocomoke, nobody ever came in and cut away the fallen trees. So it is rough going, but well worth it.

Below Red House Road, where the Conservancy has built a canoe launch, the stream is tidal, easy to paddle, and continues to be pretty. It is initially tiny, but eventually it opens up and is not nearly so wild. Most people will choose to paddle here, if only to bypass the upstream hardships. There is no access at the mouth, so either end your trip one mile upstream at Nassawango Road or head 1.7 miles up the Pocomoke to the city park at Snow Hill.

HAZARDS: Fallen trees.

WATER CONDITIONS: Above tidewater, you can float it in late fall, winter, and spring, except after a prolonged dry spell. The tidal section is always boatable.

GAUGE: USGS staff gauge (see USGS website or inspect on site) at Rte. 12 should read at least 20 cfs (2.1 feet) for the nontidal section.

Dividing Creek

INTRODUCTION: Dividing Creek is an aquatic gem known to but a few while so suitable for all. It provides an intimate, hidden path into the twilight recesses of the vast Pocomoke Swamp. While it possesses a remote atmosphere as fine as is found anywhere in Maryland, it is easily accessible from nearby Pocomoke City. Being tidal, Dividing Creek is always runnable, except maybe in the deepest, iciest months of winter. It needs no shuttle. In fact, it has none. The creek is remarkably deep and narrow and consistently so for an unusually great distance. Study a map of the Delmarva Peninsula and you will find few, if any, estuaries with these combined characteristics. The upper reaches of this creek and swamp have been targeted for years by some politicians and the eager engineers of the Natural Resources Conservation Service for channelization to reclaim its "worthless" swamplands. Fortunately the State of Maryland seems to have come to recognize the importance of its wetlands, and we hopefully should no longer have to worry about the day when this becomes the Dividing Creek Canal.

Section 1. Pocomoke River to who knows where						
Gradient	Difficulty	Distance	Time	Width	Gradient	Map
0	A	5.0	2.5	15-25	Excellent	85

TRIP DESCRIPTION: Unlike most streams, start Dividing Creek at the bottom. The nearest convenient put-in is a public launching ramp on the Pocomoke River, located in a park at the foot of Winters Quarters Drive in Pocomoke City. Paddle upstream on the Pocomoke past some houses on your right, cross to your left side of the river (northwest bank), and then, when the last house begins to fade from view about a mile above your put-in, watch for an unimpressive-looking break in the cypress on your left. Enter, for that is your creek.

The stream winds in an unspoiled manner until it approaches and passes beneath Md. Rte. 364, Dividing Creek Road. There are a few house here, but the dark waters quickly lead you back into the deep swamp. The swamp forest is a combination of cypress and hardwoods. There is little solid ground touching on the creek, so plan lunch and rest stops accordingly. Most of the going is easy and unimpeded by fallen trees, a rare luxury when it comes to exploring swamps. Do not worry too much about tides, as the current is relatively moderate. As you reach the final stretches of navigability, the creek begins to shallow somewhat, and you will encounter forks to test your sense of direction. If you choose correctly, you will stretch a few hundred extra yards out of the trip. Finally and suddenly the channel dissolves into the sodden no-man's-land, and it is time to turn back.

HAZARDS: None.

WATER CONDITIONS: Canoeable all year.

GAUGE: None.

Pitts Creek

INTRODUCTION: Pitts Creek is a twisty, tidal path that straddles the Maryland-Virginia border. Depending on what map you look at, its upper reaches are also called Wagram Creek. Whatever its correct name, you will call it beautiful. Together with its little tributary, Little Mill Creek, this waterway offers over 10 miles of backwoods and back-marsh cruising.

Section 1. Va. Sec. Rte. 707 to mouth						
Gradient	Difficulty	Distance	Time	Width	Scenery	Map
0	A	9.0	4.0	15-150	Good to Very Good	85

TRIP DESCRIPTION: The put-in is at a remote wooden bridge over a deep channel of black water. You can start by exploring about a half mile of lonely, freshwater marsh upstream of the bridge, via just a tiny channel. Heading downstream, the path is past dense swamp. Only a few cypress trees hint that this is a Pocomoke tributary. A sand pit and a power line are the only blemishes on this wild stretch. After about two miles, the swamp changes to marsh, which grows wider throughout the trip.

Marumsco Creek

Occasionally the creek bumps up against high ground, which is usually occupied by farms. About three and a half miles into the trip, Little Mill Creek enters on the right. If the tide is in, take a side trip up to Colona Road. It gets tight and tangled towards the end, but it is all passable. The chances of stirring up lots of ducks are excellent on this intimate channel of black water.

More twists and turns through marsh eventually deliver you to the Pocomoke. There is no access at the mouth, but a short way downstream is Va. Rte. 709 on the left, or you can take out a bit farther down the Pocomoke on the right, at Shelltown (long shuttle though). If the tide is coming in, you might want to finish the trip up the Pocomoke at Cedar Hall Wharf.

HAZARDS: None.

WATER CONDITIONS: Tidal.

GAUGE: None.

Marumsco Creek

INTRODUCTION: Marumsco Creek is a tidal tributary to beautiful Pocomoke Sound, draining the south side of Somerset County, near Crisfield. If marsh touring is your pleasure, this is probably the nicest place to paddle this side of Dorchester County.

Section 1. Md. Rte. 667 to Rumbly Point						
Gradient	Difficulty	Distance	Time	Width	Scenery	Map
0	A	12.2	6.0	15-3,000	Fair to Very Good	86

TRIP DESCRIPTION: At high tide, it is possible to start as high as Rte. 667, Hudson Corner. Unlike most of its length, Marumsco Creek here is tiny, flows by wooded and dry banks, and twists past farm fields and various buildings. But marsh soon follows.

A better idea is to start at Bryan Hall Road. Below here the creek meanders through broad marsh meadows backed by forest. You see few houses on this reach. Occasionally the creek bumps up against a hummock, allowing you to get out and stretch, a luxury on these wetland streams. Most of the creek is narrow, but the final mile and a half balloons into almost a bay. When you get to the lonely road head at Rumbly Point and gaze out into Pocomoke Sound, you will really feel exposed. As long as you have a calm day, this will all be just fine.

HAZARDS: None.

WATER CONDITIONS: Tidal. Upper stretch, above Bryan Hall Road, can get tedious at low tide.

GAUGE: None.

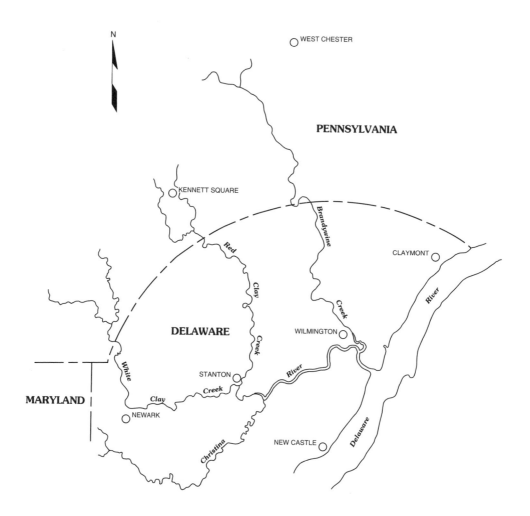

N

WEST CHESTER

PENNSYLVANIA

KENNETT SQUARE

CLAYMONT

DELAWARE

WILMINGTON

MARYLAND

STANTON

NEWARK

NEW CASTLE

Red

Clay

Creek

Brandywine

Creek

River

White

Clay

Creek

River

Christina

Delaware

Christina River Tributaries

Chapter 7
Christina River Basin

The Christina River Basin covers about 500 square miles of northern Delaware and southeastern Pennsylvania, emptying its waters into the Delaware River. It is drained by a few small streams that rise in the Pennsylvania Piedmont and rush to tidewater at or near Wilmington. The basin includes headwater areas that are mostly, peacefully rural; midlands that mix farmland with prosperous and tasteful outlying residential areas; and lowlands that are covered by the busy, crowded urban and industrial complex of the Wilmington-Newark corridor. One who paddles these streams will see it all, along with a fascinating exposure to 300 years of history that are so intertwined with these waters.

The following streams are described in this chapter:

Christina River
    White Clay Creek
      Red Clay Creek
    Brandywine Creek

Christina River

Christina River

INTRODUCTION: The Christina is a pathetic, little dribble extending over three states, starting in some pastures west of Strickersville, Pennsylvania; cutting across a small corner of Maryland; and then spanning New Castle County, Delaware to join the Delaware River at Wilmington. This is not the type of stream for which one travels great distances. Hemmed in by mud banks, plagued by deadfalls, and surrounded by only average woodlands, the Christina possesses little to be called outstanding. Time and place, however, make the little Christina shine. For as a parcel of open space and an intimate, woodland canoe trail that carries fairly reliable water levels by the doorstep of 400,000 people, it must be regarded as no less than a precious natural resource. Novices will find this run, at reasonable levels, quite safe and suitable to attempt.

Maryland and Delaware managed to mostly avoid the brunt of the action during the Revolutionary War. But the Christina Valley became one exception in September of 1777, when British troops, lead by General William Howe, sailed up the Chesapeake Bay, landed at the head of the Elk River (now Elkton), and marched eastward across the Christina Valley to Philadelphia. They skirmished with a small Continental detachment at Cooch's Bridge (next bridge above your put-in) on the Christina and then proceeded to the Brandywine at Chadds Ford, where they met the main American forces under General Washington. The 12,000 American troops, however, were no match for 18,000 British and Hessian troops plus a thick fog that Howe used to his advantage. Washington's forces were badly beaten, thus opening the way for the subsequent British occupation of Wilmington and then Philadelphia. Just think, if the British had possessed this guidebook, they could have canoed to Philadelphia and avoided a lot of bloodshed.

Section 1. Sunset Lake Road to New Churchman Road						
Gradient	Difficulty	Distance	Time	Width	Scenery	Map
3	A to 1–	11.4	5.5	20-40	Fair	87

TRIP DESCRIPTION: Put in at the crossing of Sunset Lake Road (Del. Rte. 72). That teeny, murky brook, all of 15 to 20 feet wide, is your "river," and it quickly wriggles off into the forest. That forest, unfortunately, seems to be initially a forest of high voltage power lines, power lines, and more power lines. Eventually the more traditional woodland decor of wall to wall trees takes over, broken only occasionally by some encroaching homes or a road crossing. Except for the inescapable drone of distant roadways, the atmosphere is almost wild. The creek is generally entrenched in four- to six-foot mud banks which, oddly, by restricting one's field of vision to the adjacent jungle, tend to enhance the illusion of remoteness.

The Christina is basically a novice or beginner stream. It has no rapids, just frequent, gentle riffles where its waters rush over bars of pea gravel or sand. But that does not necessarily mean that it is an easy trip. In the tradition of all small Coastal Plain streams, the Christina bristles with snags, fallen trees, logjams, and overhanging vegetation. Quite remarkably though, the agile and perceptive paddler can usually bypass, bump over, or squeeze under most obstacles. Partial thanks for this condition can be given to some unknown heroes who have sawed passages through some of these troublesome logs and limbs. If some local paddlers could continue this practice (how about you?), this will continue to be a reasonable canoe trail.

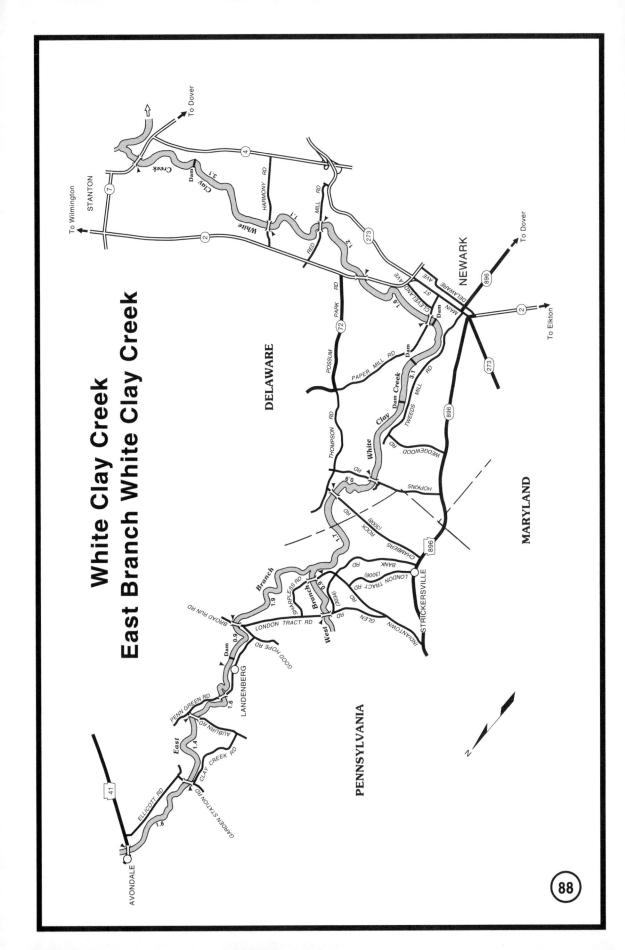

White Clay Creek
East Branch White Clay Creek

As the stream progresses onward, little tributaries subtly trickle in, and the creek soon swells from teeny to tiny. Below Walther Road (sand and gravel operation on right), the Christina really broadens as it enters Smalleys Pond, which is formed by a six-foot dam that is easily carried on the right.

Tidewater begins shortly below Smalleys Dam. The banks now become increasingly developed. But stretches of primitive swampy and marshy shores prevail and, thus, these last few miles will still appeal to some. Those venturing past New Churchman Road will gaze upon vast stands of phragmites reeds; behold vistas of freeways, junk heaps, scattered industry, and the distant skyline of Wilmington; and, if they go all the way, will look up at the big ships docked at the Port of Wilmington.

HAZARDS: Carry the six-foot dam at Smalleys Pond and do not get entangled in the woody strainers on this creek. Respect commercial shipping near the Port of Wilmington (those big ships move quickly).

WATER CONDITIONS: Usually up in late fall, winter, and spring, except after prolonged dry spell. Tidal stretch always up.

GAUGE: USGS gauge (see USGS website) at Sunset Lake Road near Coochs Bridge should read at least 20 cfs (3.7 feet).

White Clay Creek

INTRODUCTION: The lands along the great arc of the Delaware-Pennsylvania line are remarkable in that they transform in just a few miles from one of the nation's foremost industrial areas—a vast sea of refineries, chemical complexes, power plants, and shipyards—to a serene, sparsely populated landscape of old farms and country estates. White Clay Creek is born and matures in this rolling countryside, but then finishes its short career in the fringes of the great sprawl of the northeast urban corridor. Somehow even through those crowded lower reaches it does an admirable job of gerrymandering a fairly pleasant path amongst the scattered remaining patches of fields and woods all the way to its finish, near Stanton. While hardly special enough for which to warrant driving great distances, this creek fits the bill perfectly for the local paddler desiring a quiet day floating through the countryside.

White Clay received its name from the extensive, local deposits of white kaolin clay, possibly the richest deposits in the nation. The clay traditionally was the raw material for fine china, but today the bulk of it finds its way into a variety of industrial applications. The largest customer is probably the paper-making industry which uses it as a filler in the manufacture of fine, white paper. This all goes to prove that there is money in even mud.

Section 1. East Branch: Avondale (Rte. 41) to West Branch						
Gradient	Difficulty	Distance	Time	Width	Scenery	Map
19	A to 2-	7.6	2.5	15-30	Good	88

TRIP DESCRIPTION: Come here when the weather has been very wet. You may perhaps question why you chose this destination, as the narrow, mostly smooth path initially leads you through the kind of suburbia you probably sought to escape. But things change for the better. After Auburn Road, the creek burrows into a shallow gorge, just filled with little boulder-patch rapids, decorated by pretty rock formations, and unfortunately also occupied by too many houses. The gorge continues just beyond Landenberg, not far below which is a sharp three-foot weir to carry. While the rapids end back in the gorge, long riffles continue for the remainder of the way. The remainder of the way, while passing through more open country, is a delight as it meanders through the fields and woods of the White Clay Creek Preserve. There is no convenient take-out at the mouth, so use that as an excuse to continue down through more of the park.

HAZARDS: Weir below Landenberg Road, and strainers. Also, as of the publication date, boating is prohibited on the Pennsylvania section of the White Clay Preserve for no logical reason. Any activists out there?

WATER CONDITIONS: Catch within a day of hard rain during late fall, winter, or spring.

GAUGE: None on the East Branch, so use the USGS gauge on White Clay just below the confluence with the West Branch near Strickersville (see USGS website). To get down the rockiest rapids of the gorge, look for at least about 400 cfs (5.0 feet).

Section 2. Sharpless Road to Stanton, Del.(Del. Rte. 7 & 4)						
Gradient	Difficulty	Distance	Time	Width	Scenery	Map
10	A to 1	12.9	4.5	20-40	Good to Fair	88

TRIP DESCRIPTION: The cruise can start on the tiny West Branch at Sharpless Road, less that a quarter of a mile above the East Branch. The stream zigzags down a mostly forested, narrow valley and through short ravines. As along most other streams in this area, the surrounding woods are graced with some beautiful beech trees. The preserve protects about the first three miles of this section. The creek moves along nicely, dropping over plenty of gentle rock gardens and gravel riffles, and it may be blocked once or twice by some fallen trees. Adding some spice to the run are a two-foot rubble dam early in the trip and a rough rubble dam at the water intake above Newark. Farther down, a sloping, six-foot dam, located about a mile above Paper Mill Road bridge, is often too scrapey to run, but has a great playing hydraulic at its foot, at least at moderate levels. White Clay almost sneaks by Newark, now a college town, but once very much dependent on the falling creek to power its grist and paper mills. One subtle reminder of that past, a sloping four-foot dam at Paper Mill Road (called Chapel Street in Newark), can be run anywhere. Paper Mill Road is at mile 5.9, and most people will choose to finish their trip here.

Below Paper Mill Road, White Clay works its way onto the coastal plain and past considerably more civilization, including apartment houses, roads, and the busy tracks of Conrail. Still, the majority of the passage is through open space or woods. To keep things interesting there are many riffles; two runnable weirs, each about two feet high; and one, sharp, three-foot weir (carry) about a mile above Del. Rte. 7 and 4. A short, steep, muddy scramble on the right at that bridge marks the end of the trip.

HAZARDS: Be prepared for little dams and weirs, some of which form powerful hydraulics at high water, and for fallen trees.

WATER CONDITIONS: You must catch this usually within a day of hard rain, during winter or spring.

GAUGE: There are USGS gauges just below the confluence of the branches near Strickersville, at Paper Mill Road in Newark, and near Newark at Delaware Park Boulevard, all reporting on the USGS website. Look for at least 80 cfs at Strickersville (3.6 feet), 95 cfs (6.35 feet) at Newark, and 120 cfs (5.9 feet) near Newark. If there is enough water to smoothly slide over the dam at Paper Mill Road, then the level is adequate.

Red Clay Creek

INTRODUCTION: Red Clay Creek gathers its waters from the hilly countryside surrounding Kennett Square, Pennsylvania and then winds down through northern New Castle County, Delaware to join White Clay Creek midway between Wilmington and Newark. The course is set mostly on the Piedmont and on the Fall Line, passing through a semirural, semisuburban landscape in an old and affluent neighborhood. Needless to say, the human influence is strong, but really quite pleasant, manifesting itself in the form of covered bridges, ancient stone and stucco buildings, old mills, and a touch of Victorian gingerbread. The stream is punctuated by numerous old dams which testify to the former water-powered industrial might of this now peaceful valley.

Today industry still thrives, but the most important and famous industry of this region is very subtle and easy to overlook. It takes place in dozens of big, drab, mysterious sheds that dot the surrounding countryside, it is carried on in the dark, and it runs on horse manure. It is the growing of mushrooms, tons and tons of them, to smother the nation's steaks, to complement its sauces, and to top its pizzas. Which all goes to prove, there is money in manure.

Section 1. Marshall Bridge Road to Del. Rte. 41						
Gradient	Difficulty	Distance	Time	Width	Scenery	Map
14	A to 2–	10.5	3.0	25-45	Good	89

TRIP DESCRIPTION: Red Clay Creek is born at the confluence of its East and West branches just above Marshall Bridge Road. It is possible for the dedicated paddler to put in farther up on the West Branch, though it is pretty small. If you decide to do so, there is a four-foot dam just above Marshall Bridge Road that can be run down the middle. It is hardly more than a half mile to the next dam, a sloping four-footer that can be run anywhere with enough water. Shortly downstream, the creek winds through the village of Yorklyn, identified by its sprawling fibers plant and some dank and pungent odors wafting through the air from the mushroom sheds across the stream. There is a very gently sloping dam in Yorklyn, runnable anywhere.

From Yorklyn on down, for most of the way, a railroad track and various roads follow near the creek. Traffic, however, is generally light on both, thus maintaining the quiet nature of the run. The creek flows through alternating stretches of wooded gorge and narrow, grassy valley and, since the banks range from medium to low, the paddler sees most of whatever is going on in the neighborhood.

The dams do not stop at Yorklyn. Just below Yorklyn, above a railroad trestle, is the fourth dam, a sharp five-footer that should be carried. Less than a half mile and you will encounter a fifth dam, a sharp four-footer that also should be carried. It is over a mile and a half to the next dam, five feet high and unrunnable, located on a pretty, wooded loop above Mount Cuba. About a mile farther is a sharp, four-foot dam that should be carried.

Except for the short pools behind the dams, most of Red Clay down to Lancaster Pike (Del. Rte. 48) is characterized by plenty of gravel-formed riffles and swift current. But then below Rte. 48, Red Clay begins to display a little spunk as it dashes over some short, exhilarating rapids formed by boulder patches and rock gardens. There is an old, broken-out dam on this section that can be run on the left, but scout first as the breach tends to be complicated by debris. Unfortunately, just as things start really becoming enjoyable, the take-out at Rte. 41 appears (the bridge 200 yards upstream affords a much easier exit). Easy rapids and riffles do continue well past Rte. 41. But industry, shopping centers, houses, noise, trash-cluttered mud banks, and a poor selection of take-outs offset the rewards of some extra fast water. Also, there are two more dams to portage, a six-footer beneath the Rte. 2 bridge

271

Red Clay Creek

89

and an eight-footer under the high railroad bridge. But for those who still want to run the final two and a half miles below Rte. 41, a small park at the end of Netherfield Street, located above the mouth, is the best take-out. Do not continue below here unless the tide is going out, as the tidal currents in lower White Clay Creek and the Christina are horrendous.

HAZARDS: Nine dams described above, the lower seven of which require portages. Also, the creek is spanned by several railroad trestles whose multiple piers could easily function as deadly strainers at high levels.

WATER CONDITIONS: Canoeable winter and spring within a day of hard rain.

GAUGE: A UGSG gauging station at Rte. 48 bridge has no outside staff, but you can use the concrete weir as a reference. You want enough water to cleanly clear the middle of the weir to make it over the rockier riffles far upstream. For checking in advance, USGS gauges near Kennett Square (located along Rte. 82 above the West Branch) and near Stanton (located on the downstream side of the westbound lane of Rte.4) are available on the USGS website. You want at least 50 cfs (3.8 feet) and 100 cfs (8.9 feet) respectively.

Brandywine Creek

INTRODUCTION: Brandywine Creek drains the heart of Chester County, Pennsylvania, and New Castle County, Delaware, emptying into the tidal Christina River in downtown Wilmington. This is a valley with a long and rich history. Settled over three and a quarter centuries ago, first by the Swedes, then the Dutch, and finally the English, it did not take long for its residents to recognize the enormous energy potential of the Brandywine's steep Fall Line gradient. By the Revolutionary War, the lower valley had developed into the most important milling center in the English colonies. Appropriately enough, this area was fought over during the Revolution, and George Washington even slept here. But the valley's real claim to fame arrived in 1802, when a French immigrant with the improbable name of Eleuthere Irenee du Pont de Nemours, also eyeing that beautiful falling water, established a powder mill outside of Wilmington. Needless to say, the business was a success and over the years, as one of the world's corporate superpowers, DuPont has brought prosperity to the valley and, for that matter—as a manufacturer of plastic resins, nylon, and Kevlar—may perhaps even be credited with having brought you your boat and equipment.

It is also worth visiting the Brandywine Valley not only as a paddler, but also as a tourist. Among its attractions are the Hagley Museum, which includes the restored DuPont powder works; Winterthur, a DuPont estate renown for its gardens and interior design; the Brandywine Museum, featuring works of the Brandywine Valley's most famous artist, Andrew Wyeth; and just over the hill in the Red Clay Creek Valley, the Longwood Gardens. If you are an admirer of fine architecture and carefully landscaped grounds or just plain would like to see how the other half lives, then you will love shuttling on the Brandywine. The drive out Del. Rte. 100, Rte. 52, and various interconnecting lanes offers an incredible display of rolling, manicured estates, beautiful and diversely styled mansions, and on a less pretentious level, dozens of old stucco, brick, or stone farm and mill houses that date back into the 18th century.

Brandywine Creek

Section 1. Confluence East and West branches to Rockland						
Gradient	Difficulty	Distance	Time	Width	Scenery	Map
4	A to 1	12.7	4.0	60-150	Fair	90

TRIP DESCRIPTION: You can put in at the Pa. Rte. 842 bridge over either the West or East Branch, the latter being preferable at low water levels. This is mostly a smooth water run—the backwaters of four old milldams, with easy riffles in between. The first two dams—one just above the amusement park at Lenape, the next about a mile above U.S. Rte. 1—are three to four feet high, built of rubble, and are canoeable at fairly high levels, though beginners should carry each on the left. The little two-foot weir, just above Rte. 1, has an easily-shot breach on the right. The last dam is at Rockland, just below the take-out.

Above Chadds Ford, the valley is open, attractive, and fairly visible from the creek. Unfortunately, a persistent high voltage power line sullies the view. Below Chadds Ford, attractive wooded hills hem the creek. Both sections are nicest after summer foliage softens the scenery.

Take out on the left at the Brandywine Creek State Park access (Doe Skin Access) located about 200 yards above Rockland Road, or if you would like to avoid a mile and a half of sluggish water, at the park access at Thompson Bridge. The park is quite strict about closing (and towing away vehicles) at sundown. So make sure that you allow enough time for your trip.

HAZARDS: Three small dams.

WATER CONDITIONS: Canoeable winter, spring, and usually into mid-summer. In wet years it stays up all summer.

GAUGE: The USGS gauge at Chadds Ford (see USGS website) should read at least 1.4 feet for the discriminating boater, though livery canoes keep grinding down all summer, regardless of level. There is also a staff gauge on the right abutment of the U.S. Rte. 1 bridge. Zero on this gauge is approximately zero canoeing level.

Section 2. Rockland to Market Street						
Gradient	Difficulty	Distance	Time	Width	Scenery	Map
20	A to 3–	6.5	3.0	100-150	Good	90

TRIP DESCRIPTION: This is an excellent intermediate run, but if you despise dams, then skip this section as there are 11 of them. The put-in is the state park access on the left about 200 yards above Rockland Road. The first dam is a jagged, sloping, and probably runnable barrier located just upstream of the Rockland Bridge. It is easily carried on the right, but the portage involves trespass on land very explicitly posted against boaters, so proceed only at your own risk. Strong current and a few riffles carry you into the grounds of the Hagley Museum (also posted), and about three quarters of a mile below Rockland appears the next dam. This one is only about three and a half feet high, but because of an ugly roller, carry on the left. Not far downstream is a gently sloping, five-foot dam best run to the right of center. This is followed by a long, complex, boulder-studded rapid that carries you past the old powder works.

The right bank of the creek here is lined by three-sided, stone-walled buildings of heavy construction. They originally had a relatively flimsy fourth wall on the side facing the stream. The logic was that if there was an explosion, the streamside wall would go, thus directing the force of the blast harmlessly (except for those workers in the building or any canoeist happening by) across the creek and thus saving neighboring buildings from destruction.

Shortly below, and still on the Hagley property, is a vertical five-foot dam that should be carried on the left. An easy rapid and some strong current carries you past some beautiful, old industrial structures and to the next dam (a coarse, sloping five-footer) which is run toward the right. Shortly below this is a classic sloping, eight-foot, concrete dam that is runnable right of center. When apartment houses appear on the right bank, watch out for a dangerous, vertical seven-foot dam with a tight carry on the left that would be dangerous to approach at high water. This is followed by an interesting, long, steep boulder-studded rapid that ends in a short pool by a huge, old mill. The pool ends with a dangerous, six-foot vertical dam with a carry on the concrete fish ladder on the left. This also would be dangerous to approach at high water. A short distance below this is a runnable, sloping four-foot dam. Next comes a vertical four-foot dam with a nasty roller that is easily carried on the left. The final dam, below the high Baynard Street Bridge, is a vertical three-footer that can be clunked over on the far right, with caution. The dam is followed by a short, rocky rapid, once the site of an old and popular springtime whitewater slalom race, which brings you to tidewater above Market Street. Take out on the left at the foot of the rapid.

HAZARDS: Eleven dams described above. Even those described as runnable could be hazardous at high water. Finally, watch out for playful tykes, especially around Baynard Street, who love to toss rocks at passing canoeists.

WATER CONDITIONS: Runnable winter and spring within two days of rain or right after heavy local summer showers.

GAUGE: USGS gauge at Chadds Ford (see USGS website) should read at least 2.0 feet. Rapids above Market Street should have at least a foot of runnable water for a good trip.

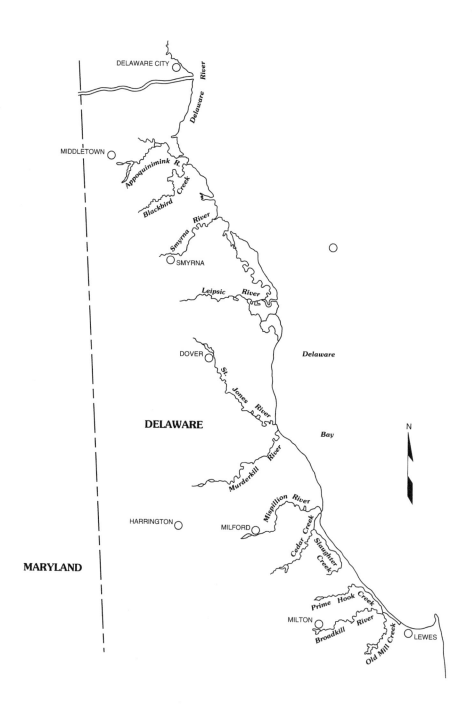

DELAWARE CITY

MIDDLETOWN

Appoquinimink R.

Blackbird Creek

Smyrna River

SMYRNA

Leipsic River

Delaware

DOVER

St. Jones River

DELAWARE

Bay

N

Murderkill River

Mispillion River

HARRINGTON

MILFORD

Cedar Creek

Slaughter Creek

MARYLAND

Prime Hook Creek

MILTON

Broadkill River

Old Mill Creek

LEWES

Delaware Bay Tributaries

Chapter 8
Delaware Bay Drainage

The edge of Delaware Bay is a beautiful, ragged swath of vast marshes, tangled swamps, and thin, sandy beaches, periodically interrupted by narrow, twisting, tidal rivers that penetrate back almost to the centerline of Delaware. Long ago these rivers were centers of activity for this region. They were major commercial passages that made busy ports and shipbuilding centers out of now sleepy little towns such as Smyrna, Odessa, and Frederica. But today the value of these waters is mainly recreational.

If you have never visited this region, drive down Del. Rte. 9 from Delaware City to Leipsic and you will quickly appreciate the beauty and canoeing potential of this slice of the State. To paddle here requires a minimum of canoeing skill, but one must learn to use the tides as they can be fierce. Once you have figured out the tides, you can ascend or descend a stream; descend one stream and then ascend a tributary or neighboring river; or simply put in and paddle one way until the tide changes and then ride the tide back, thus eliminating the need for a shuttle. The difference between a high or low tide can make the difference in whether you can peer across miles and miles of open marsh meadow or just stare up at a cellulose wall of cattails or spartina grass. Overall, the paddling here is best during the cooler months when biting, stabbing, and gnawing bugs are gone and motorboats are few. All seasons, however, are beautiful here, and with year-round assured water, decide for yourself.

The following waterways are described in this chapter.

Appoquinimink River
Blackbird Creek
Smyrna River
Leipsic River
St. Jones River
Murderkill River
Mispillion River
Cedar Creek
    Slaughter Creek
Broadkill River
    Old Mill Creek
    Prime Hook Creek

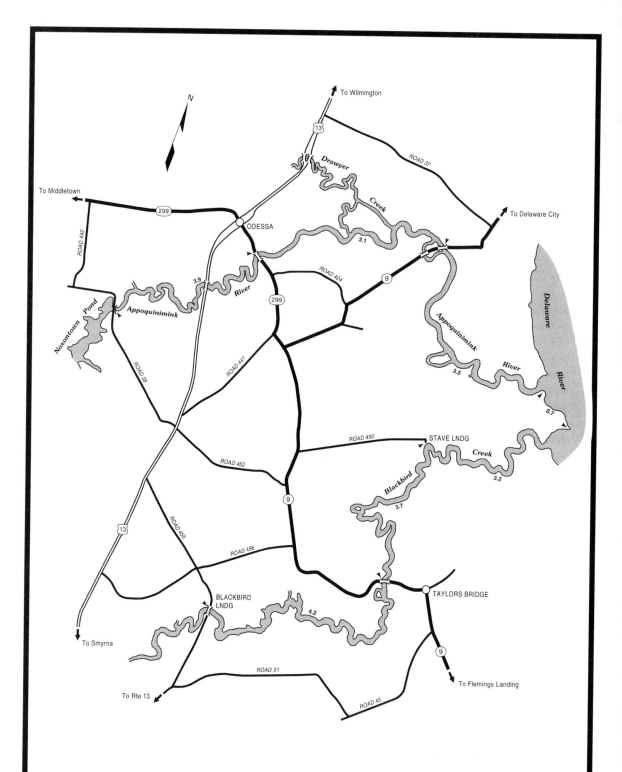

Appoquinimink River
Blackbird Creek

Appoquinimink River and Blackbird Creek

INTRODUCTION: The Appoquinimink River and Blackbird Creek, located in middle New Castle County, where Delaware is skinniest, are the northernmost creeks of any length in this state's great band of tidal wetlands. Sharing almost a common mouth, they enter the Delaware River just upstream of where it officially becomes Delaware Bay. Together, these winding tidal waterways offer over 23 miles of exploring (not to mention the extra miles from getting lost on side channels) all within 25 miles of downtown Wilmington.

Both creeks, unfortunately, lack any good access to their mouths. So what this means is that if you desire to paddle the entire length of either creek, you must also plan to tack on three to six extra miles, possibly against the tides, to reach a roadhead. Use the accompanying maps and plan accordingly.

Section 1. Appoquinimink River: Road 38 to mouth						
Gradient	Difficulty	Distance	Time	Width	Scenery	Map
0	A	10.5	5.0	100-300	Good	91

TRIP DESCRIPTION: Put in right by the spillway of the dike that separates freshwater Noxontown Pond from tidewater. The first quarter mile can be terribly shallow at low tide, so at such times consider starting at Odessa. The river above Odessa winds through narrow, marshy bottoms that are fringed by wooded higher ground, while downstream it flows through mainly open marsh. The open marsh, however, tends to be closed, screened off by a cellulose curtain of riverside phragmites reeds. Thus, except for some occasional peeks out to the adjacent farmlands, you will be subject to hemmed in solitude.

HAZARDS: Exceptionally strong tidal current rips through the piers of the Rte. 299 bridge in Odessa.

WATER CONDITIONS: Tidal and always runnable, except for the uppermost quarter mile, which is only passable at high tide.

GAUGE: None.

Section 2. Blackbird Creek: Blackbird Landing (Road 55) to mouth						
Gradient	Difficulty	Distance	Time	Width	Scenery	Map
0	A	11.1	5.0	100-500	Good	91

TRIP DESCRIPTION: Put in at Blackbird Landing because there is no direct access to the head of the creek. But before going down, go up. The riverscape above Blackbird Landing is exceptionally pretty as the creek flows through swamps and past beech-covered hillsides. The swamps vanish below Blackbird Landing and the rest of the creek's twisting path passes through the heart of lovely, unspoiled marshlands. But as on Appoquinimink, the paddler has limited opportunity to appreciate this beauty as he or she stares up at the endless, towering wall of reedgrass (phragmites). The graceful monotony of these reeds, however, are regularly broken by clear and pleasing views out at the farmland perched on the adjacent high ground. Just go with the tides and you will have a good trip.

HAZARDS: None.

WATER CONDITIONS: Can be paddled all year, except when frozen.

GAUGE: None.

Smyrna River and Leipsic River

INTRODUCTION: The Smyrna and Leipsic rivers are two similar tidal streams that flow through northern Kent County, Delaware. Until the late 17th century, the Leipsic was a tributary of the Smyrna, which then meandered for a long way parallel to Delaware Bay to find its outlet near Port Mahon. It would still be possible for an energetic paddler to retrace much of this old route by following what is now Duck Creek.

Section 1. Smyrna River: Smyrna Landing (Road 76) to mouth						
Gradient	**Difficulty**	**Distance**	**Time**	**Width**	**Scenery**	**Map**
0	A	8.5	4.0	50-400	Good	92

TRIP DESCRIPTION: It is possible to put in at U.S. Rte. 13, but highway noise, sumptuous views of fast food joints, and a possible carry around the low Road 76 bridge at high tide do not make it worth the trouble. The first mile and a half below Smyrna Landing runs past high, wooded banks that appear to be man-made, probably dredge spoil from years past. But once beyond Mill Creek (first major tributary on right), this becomes a marsh tour. The limited perspective of a canoe hurts here as the height of the riverside reeds often denies the paddler of an appreciation of the beauty and vastness of the wetlands that lie beyond. There is no access at the mouth, so you can either double back to Rte. 9 or, if the wind and tide are with you, head three and a half miles down the bay to the town park at Woodland Beach.

HAZARDS: Jetty pilings at the south side of the river entrance can form a barrier at low tide.

WATER CONDITIONS: Paddleable all year except when frozen.

GAUGE: None.

To Odessa

River

FLEMINGS LANDING

3.4

ROAD 30

9

WOODLAND BEACH

Delaware

ROAD 485

Smyrna

5.1

ROAD 317

To Odessa

ROAD 8

Bay

6

SMYRNA LANDING

1

ROAD 76

SMYRNA

Duck

ROAD 325

ROAD 12

Creek

13

ROAD 448

ROAD 84

ROAD 85

Bombay Hook National Wildlife Refuge

Leipsic

5.0

River

8.4

42

LEIPSIC

To Dover

9

PORT MAHON

DOVER

ROAD 89

To Dover

8

LITTLE CREEK

To Rte. 113, Rte.1

N

Smyrna River
Leipsic River

Section 2. Leipsic River: U.S. Rte. 13 to Delaware Bay						
Gradient	Difficulty	Distance	Time	Width	Scenery	Map
0	A	13.4	6.0	50-500	Good	92

TRIP DESCRIPTION: Put in at the Garrison Lake Fishing Access Area, north side. The first part of this run, down to Rte. 9, is very pretty, leading you first through swamps and then through a narrow marsh. Below Rte. 9, the river is similar to the Smyrna in that it winds through the heart of a vast, beautiful marshland of which little is visible because of the tall reeds. It is still pretty though, and because it flows through Bombay Hook National Wildlife Refuge, the lower part of this river is one of the few stretches in southern Delaware where you do not encounter duck blinds on every corner. Access to the mouth is also nonexistent on this river, so you can either double all the way back to Rte. 9 or paddle nearly five miles down the bay to the boat ramp at Port Mahon.

HAZARDS: None.

WATER CONDITIONS: Tidal, so there is always enough water.

GAUGE: None.

St. Jones River and Murderkill River

INTRODUCTION: Please be assured that in spite of such bloodstained names as Murderkill, Broadkill, and Slaughter Creek, Delaware is a very peaceful and friendly place to paddle.

The Murderkill and St. Jones rivers are almost tributaries of each other, entering Delaware Bay but a half mile apart at Bowers Beach. The former begins in the quiet farmlands between Harrington and Felton while the latter starts within the shadow of the State Capitol in busy Dover. This is another pair of streams where, with favorable tides, you can conveniently embark on an extended two-river journey.

Section 1. St. Jones River: Dover (Silver Lake Dam) to mouth						
Gradient	Difficulty	Distance	Time	Width	Scenery	Map
0	A	12.3	4.5	20-400	Good	93

TRIP DESCRIPTION: If you care to explore upstream and paddle around Silver Lake, you need to secure a permit from the Dover Police Department to do so. The permit runs for a year, starting in February, and costs $5.00 for Dover residents and $10.00 for outsiders. There is excellent and free access to the creek at the foot of the Silver Lake spillway at the city recreation area, reached by

To Smyrna

Silver Lake

PARK DR

DOVER

E. LOOCKERMAN ST

STP

2.0

Dover Air Force Base

CAMDEN

footbridge

ROAD 26

ROAD 351

St.

4.8

Jones

ALT 113

ROAD 107

River

3.8

Delaware

Bay

MAGNOLIA

N. FLACK AVE

BOWERS BEACH

ROAD 18

River

Murderkill

7.4

FREDERICA

ROAD 389

5.0

ROAD 10

Killen Pond State Park

ROAD 386

ROAD 388

ROAD 384

1.2

1.2

ROAD 426

ROAD 390

ROAD 119

To Milford

ROAD 384

ROAD 35

To Milford

To Harrington

N

St. Jones River
Murderkill River

driving north off of East Loockerman Street on Park Drive. Three scrapey drops in the first half mile, however, may encourage some, especially those who are ascending the river, to skip this passage through a parcel of attractive, manicured city parkland and put in or exit next to the town sewage treatment plant behind the corner of East Avenue and East Water Street.

The stream forges a narrow, swampy path through Dover and its suburbs and remains surprisingly attractive, considering its urban location. Buildings and trash, nevertheless, do take their aesthetic toll here. But then again, it is only on this section that one can best admire the St. Jones' most unique feature—it is on the approach path to Dover Air Force Base. The base specializes as the home for a huge squadron of gigantic jet transport planes. It is unlikely that you will ever see a larger flying object, except perhaps a Delaware salt marsh horse fly.

Below the town, the planes, and Rte. 113, the river returns to a natural state, a winding channel through a soggy sea of reeds. Sadly, the mouth of this pretty river is marked by a small garbage dump. You can take out here, reached by North Flack Avenue, or a half mile beyond in Bowers Beach, on the Murderkill, at the public boat ramp.

HAZARDS: None.

WATER CONDITIONS: Tidal and always runnable except for the upper half mile between Silver Lake and the sewage treatment plant. The upper section is best in late fall, winter, and spring within a week of rain.

GAUGE: None.

Section 2. Murderkill River: Road 384 to mouth						
Gradient	Difficulty	Distance	Time	Width	Scenery	Map
0	A	15.2	6.0	15-400	Good	93

TRIP DESCRIPTION: Road 384 crosses the Murderkill on the dam that backs up Killen Pond. Protected by a state park, this is one of the prettiest and least developed ponds in Delaware and is well worth exploring. The tiny outflow from the pond is actually nontidal and offers a short, shallow run through the woods to the backwaters of Coursey Pond. This is also a very attractive pond with high, wooded, undeveloped shores. There is public access at the dam for both above and below, the foot of the dam marking the beginning of tidewater.

The Murderkill next offers a forest-bound passage almost to Frederica, first bordered by high banks on one side and swamp on the other, then total swamp. Incidentally, this swamp bears the wholesome name of Big Cripple Swamp. A few houses occupy some of the high ground along here. Approaching Frederica, the marsh completely inherits the river for good. So reed grass is most of what you will see from here on down to Delaware Bay. This section is fairly undisturbed, except for a power line, the no trespassing signs, and the ubiquitous duck blinds. If you decide to stop at Frederica, the best access is found a few yards up Spring Creek at the Rte. 12 bridge. Access to the mouth is via a public boat ramp at Bowers Beach.

HAZARDS: Stay away from the spillways of Killen Pond and Coursey Pond dams.

WATER CONDITIONS: Tidal, except for the ponds and the short section in between them. That section may be too low in summer and fall.

GAUGE: None.

Tides And Tide Tables

There are four changes of tides, evenly spaced, in any 24 hours. The tide coming in from the sea is called the flood tide, going out is called the ebb tide, and the pauses in between are called slack water. You can know in advance when these phases are to occur by consulting a tide table. You can purchase tables directly from the U.S. Coast and Geodetic Survey in Washington, D.C., from the Maryland Department of Natural Resources (for a Chesapeake Bay Table only) in Annapolis or from your local marine supply store. While formats may vary, they all include the same basic information.

To understand the use of a tide table, let us take an example; say you want to paddle up the Smyrna River from its mouth on May 1, this year. First you consult this year's table (these are annual publications) which gives the tide schedule at the nearest major point, in this case the entrance to Delaware Bay, on each day of the year. The chart has columns for time of slack water, time of maximum current velocity, and maximum current velocity. The velocity column also indicates the tide's direction, ebb(E) or flood(F). So after checking out May 1, you determine that maximum flood tide will be at 1110 (they use military time) and 2331 and that slack waters preceding these tides are 0812 and 2021 respectively. Now if you want to paddle by daylight, you would choose to time your trip to the first tide and start on the slack at 8:12 A.M., figuring to have a maximum favorable current at 11:10 A.M. and dead slack about six hours after you put in (remember, four tides per day). But wait! This is the schedule of the tides at the Delaware Bay entrance. What about at the mouth of the Smyrna, 45 miles up the Bay? For it takes longer for the tide change to reach up here. So you now consult another table which lists various points up and down the Bay and then lists the time difference between that point and the entrance. The lag times vary slightly between ebbs and floods since there is always a net flow down the Bay because of the Delaware River's inflow. So looking up the Smyrna River entrance in the table you see the time difference at just before flood is +1 hour, 48 minutes and for maximum flood is +1 hour, 42 minutes. Therefore, you add these to the schedule at the Bay entrance, and now you know that on May 1 you should start at 10:00 A.M. (8:12 + 1:48) and be moving along fastest around 12:52 P.M. and should be hitting slack again around 4:00 P.M. This is just the minimum that you can learn from a tide table, but it is enough to canoe by.

Mispillion River, Cedar Creek and Slaughter Creek

INTRODUCTION: The waters of the Mispillion, Cedar, and Slaughter all spill into Delaware Bay at a place called Mispillion Light. They share a common quality, along with Broadkill, Old Mill, and Prime Hook, of remoteness, minimal development, and a variety of distracting scenery. Their marshes are exceptionally pleasant to explore as the grass is relatively short, allowing good views from the boat of the wet landscape.

This is a good place to view all sorts of creatures, beautiful and strange. Walk the beaches at the mouth and you will find the sands littered with those living fossils, the horseshoe crab. Float through the marsh at low tide and see comical fiddler crabs scurrying for little holes in the muck as you approach. Of course there will be flocks of waterfowl, perhaps some muskrat, and, if you are dumb enough to paddle here in the summer, watch your bow partner be carried off by greenheads and mosquitos with six-foot wingspans.

Mispillion River
Cedar Creek
Slaughter Creek

Section 1. Mispillion River: Milford to mouth

Gradient	Difficulty	Distance	Time	Width	Scenery	Map
0	A	10.5	3.5	100-300	Good	94

TRIP DESCRIPTION: The banks of the Mispillion in Milford are heavily developed and often bulkheaded. As a result, the best and one of the only points of entry is a public launching ramp located behind the town police station on the north bank about three tenths of a mile above Del. Rte. 14 bridge. The first few miles pass by relatively high, wooded banks. Some lingering development persists, such as power lines, a marina, and the Rte. 1 Bypass, before the stream loses itself in the wide, unspoiled marshes fanning out from the bay. In summer this solitude is likely to be disturbed by the heavy motorboat traffic that frequents this waterway.

For the indecisive, this river has two mouths—a man-made, jettied exit at the lighthouse and a relatively new, eroded break in the barrier beach about a hundred yards to the north. One can take out at the public boat ramp, about three quarters of a mile up Cedar Creek. Also, if you are energetic and the tides are right, it is possible to ride the strong ebb tide down the Mispillion, hit slack at Mispillion Light, and then ride the swift flood tide up the Cedar to Rte. 1.

HAZARDS: None.

WATER CONDITIONS: Tidal and always passable.

GAUGE: None.

Section 2. Cedar Creek: Del. Rte. 30 to mouth

Gradient	Difficulty	Distance	Time	Width	Scenery	Map
0	A	9.6	3.5	100-200	Excellent to Good	94

TRIP DESCRIPTION: A steep, sandy descent along the edge of the Swiggetts Pond spillway brings you to a pool of clear, tea-colored water seeping off into the woods. The creek will demand, for a short distance, some tight maneuvering around sharp turns and under low-hanging limbs and deadfalls to reach open water. If you prefer to avoid these trials, put in at the old highway approach just above Rte. 1. But by all means paddle upstream as far as you can go before heading down to the sea. This segment between Rte. 30 and Rte. 1 is the prettiest on the Cedar, for this is where it earns its name. Dense stands of fragrant white cedar envelop the dark, still waters. This is swamp scenery at its best. You can enjoy it at a distance from the creek's deep main channel, or enjoy it close up by poking up any of several side channels past the shaggy, gray trunks.

Passing Rte. 1, the swampy fringe and cedars continue for a while. But then this all opens up to a wide marsh lined by distant pine forest. There are a few summer homes scattered through here, but generally the atmosphere is primitive. While the surrounding scenery is spread way out, the creek is usually narrow. The wild part of the journey ends near Rte. 36 as Cedar transforms into a long harbor for pleasure boats and commercial fishing vessels. The best take-out is a public boat ramp about a quarter mile below Rte. 36 on the left.

HAZARDS: None.

WATER CONDITIONS: Tidal, and always runnable.
GAUGE: None.

Section 3. Slaughter Creek: Road 38 to mouth						
Gradient	Difficulty	Distance	Time	Width	Scenery	Map
0	A	6.5	2.5	50-70	Good	94

TRIP DESCRIPTION: Much of this run is within Prime Hook National Wildlife Refuge, so that during fall, winter, and spring, you should be rewarded with, if not the sight of waterfowl, at least a cacophony of nearby and far away quacks, honks, and whistles. It can definitely be the wrong place to be if you have a headache.

This trip starts as a narrow ribbon of dark water weaving through a freshwater marsh bordered by dark, tangled forests of pine and cedar. The creek is initially shallow, but still deep enough to float a canoe, including on about a half mile of creek above the put-in. About a mile and a half downstream of Road 38, just short of Delaware Bay, the creek swings hard left and parallels the bay, following what reveals itself, in a very subtle way, to be a man-made channel. Studying the map, you can see that Slaughter Creek formerly turned hard right and emptied directly into the bay.

The lower creek flows fairly straight through vast, unspoiled salt marshes, the view of which is partly obstructed by the dense vegetation that grows on the often slightly raised banks, further evidence that this is a dug channel. The vegetation is not all bad though, as many of the little trees that you see are persimmons. If you paddle this creek after the first frost, give this much maligned and misunderstood, ping pong ball sized fruit a try, that is if the possums do not beat you to the punch. A road bridge to Fowler Beach crosses the creek and not far beyond an abandoned bridge crosses, both of which may lack clearance at high tide. For a little variety, you can land at that first bridge and walk the quarter mile of road to a bayside lunch stop or hike on lonely Fowler Beach. After passing the village of Slaughter Beach, the creek passes more wild marsh and joins Cedar Creek. Take out a mile and a quarter down Cedar Creek at the public boat ramp.

HAZARDS: None. You may have to portage two low bridges. Also, a low weir (a tide gate), located just upstream of Road 199, will require a carry.

WATER CONDITIONS: Tidal and thus always runnable.
GAUGE: None.

Broadkill River and Old Mill Creek

INTRODUCTION: Broadkill River is the southernmost tributary of Delaware Bay, entering at the old port of Lewes. Like most Delaware Bay tributaries, it is formed by a handful of unnavigable branches and ditches, many dammed to power long gone or crumbling grist mills. It is also fed by Old

Prime Hook Creek
Broadkill River
Old Mill Creek

Mill Creek, one of the loveliest tidal creeks in Delaware and a highly recommended side trip. Either run combines nicely with a day of beachcombing at nearby Cape Henlopen or Beach Plum Island.

Section 1. Milton (Del. Rte. 5) to Oyster Rocks						
Gradient	Difficulty	Distance	Time	Width	Scenery	Map
0	A	9.9	5.0	100-300	Good	95

TRIP DESCRIPTION: There is a public launching ramp in Milton, off Chandler Street, located on the north bank. The dark waters meander for the first mile past pretty, wooded, mostly swampy shores. Here and there is the only high ground that you will see by the riverside on this cruise, so enjoy its beech-dotted slopes while you can. All too soon, the woods recede a bit and are replaced by a narrow margin of freshwater marsh. The marshes gradually widen and then turn to lush salt meadows which, after Rte. 1, dominate the scenery. Except around Rte. 1, most of this passage is through undeveloped territory, if you do not count the numerous duck blinds. Oyster Rocks is a nice place to take out, although a short downstream excursion to Beach Plum Island is recommended. Beach Plum, which is owned by the State, is a relatively wild stretch of beach that is part of a narrow spit diverting the Broadkill to its man-made mouth at Roosevelt Inlet. Those desiring to paddle to the bitter end soon encounter built-up shores, but if that does not bother you, then proceed up the Lewes and Rehobeth Canal to the public landing at Rte. 9.

HAZARDS: None.

WATER CONDITIONS: Tidal, always runnable.

GAUGE: None.

Section 2. Old Mill Creek: Del. Rte. 1 to Oyster Rocks						
Gradient	Difficulty	Distance	Time	Width	Scenery	Map
0	A	5.7	3.0	20-100	Very Good	95

TRIP DESCRIPTION: Old Mill Creek has a lot going for it, including its quaint name. It is narrow, intimate with its wet surroundings, and, most importantly, it is wild. This is one stream where six miles may seem entirely too short a run. The creek amounts to almost nothing at its put-in behind the old, red mill at Rte. 1, so be prepared for some slogging if you do not depart on a high tide. Like the Broadkill, this trip starts in the woods, here a wild and lonely swamp. Marsh soon takes over, but this marsh's lawnlike uniformity is broken by pine and cedar-covered hummocks—islands of solid ground in this sea of muck. The mouth dumps you about a half mile downstream of Oyster Rocks, which unfortunately means a short fight against Broadkill's stiff tidal currents (still easier than going down to Lewes).

HAZARDS: None.

WATER CONDITIONS: Canoeable all year, but you need a high tide to float as far upstream as Rte. 1.

GAUGE: None.

Prime Hook Creek

INTRODUCTION: Do you seek smooth water to paddle on, but not if it means dealing with wide, exposed, wind-swept river? And does getting those tides straight, and enduring the exhausting, long haul that ensues if you do not, make staying home and mowing the lawn even look good? Then maybe you should come on down to Prime Hook Creek. Hidden away in the soggy heart of a national wildlife refuge, this is one of the nicest canoe streams in Delaware. This is one tidal stream that remains mostly narrow and is usually sheltered, as it is snugly guarded by either forest or tall reeds. And although it is tidal, the range is small and the current relatively weak. You will never find a more forgiving stream near the shores of Delaware Bay.

Section 1. Del. Rte. 1 to Refuge Headquarters						
Gradient	Difficulty	Distance	Time	Width	Scenery	Map
0	A	7.0	3.0	10-800	Good	95

TRIP DESCRIPTION: The start of this route is one of the most unpromising that you will see anywhere, for that eight-foot-wide dribble behind the tavern is for what you just drove all this way. But be patient. Duck those low-hanging limbs and in a few yards you will be gliding quietly across the head of a string of swamp-fringed ponds. The ponds invite poking and probing around their back-waters—a good way to see wildlife. But if you are in a hurry, generally bear left as you cross the ponds, except at the first island, and when far ahead you spot a white sign, then paddle for it. If the sign says "To Blinds 27,28," then you are doing just fine. Continue straight and in a short distance the last of the ponds will funnel into a tiny, tea-colored creek. From here the route meanders initially through a swamp forest which then slowly evolves to just a wooded facade that screens out the vast freshwater marsh that lies beyond. While the place generally remains in a primitive state, the woods are peppered with little white signs, most of which point the way to public, waterfowl hunting blinds. The blinds, incidentally, are located on little side channels which once again are the best place to spot wildlife. While the signs can be a bit of an eyesore, the ones saying "To Refuge HQ" can save the day for you (and maybe part of the night also) when you confront the confusing intersections with major ditches. Amazingly, there are few deadfalls complicating this creek, and those that exist have been sawed out.

About a mile or so past Foord Landing, which is closed to public use, you can kiss the last tree goodbye as the creek burrows into a reed-lined corridor. To navigate here, just continue to follow the signs, which means that you will turn right at each of the two major intersections. Just for the record, the last two miles of this tour are not really on Prime Hook Creek, but first on Petersfield Ditch and then on Headquarters Ditch.

When paddling Prime Hook, keep in mind that this flows through the Prime Hook National Wildlife Refuge. Be sure you are familiar with their rules, such as daytime use only and no camping. We are fortunate that there are no seasonal paddling prohibitions here as there are at Blackwater National Wildlife Refuge.

HAZARDS: None.

WATER CONDITIONS: Always canoeable, except when frozen. By nature, this is all tidal, i.e., at sea level. But when the weirs on Section 2 are in place, there is no tidal influence as this is then really a freshwater impoundment.

GAUGE: None.

Section 2. Lower Prime Hook Circuit Tour						
Gradient	Difficulty	Distance	Time	Width	Scenery	Map
0	A	10.4	4.0	25-400	Good	95

TRIP DESCRIPTION: All in all this is a nice paddle. But after the upper creek, you may find it a letdown. Prime Hook Creek once dumped directly into Delaware Bay. But storms and shifting sand blocked its path, and now the creek has two outlets to the Broadkill River, an arrangement well suited to a circuit paddle.

Arbitrarily starting at the Refuge Headquarters and arbitrarily going clockwise (in practice you should plan your direction and put-in according to direction of wind and tides), head out Headquarters Ditch to Petersfield Ditch, turn left and head northwest for about a half mile to a fairly important looking ditch (with the "To HQ" sign pointed toward the channel that you are on) and turn right. You are now back on Prime Hook Creek, headed downstream. This stretch is quite shallow at low tide, except when the weir is in, and its narrow channel is squeezed within a corridor of towering, 12-foot phragmites. When you spot the houses of Broadkill Beach, follow the deeper fork to the right and you will now be on Broadkill Sound, which is just another ditch. Here you may encounter a temporary weir, which if it is in place, will require a short carry. To your right are nice views across salt meadows of the Refuge while on your left is the sprawling clutter of Broadkill Beach, a bayside resort community. Upon entering Broadkill River, turn right. As you ascend the river you will notice a white, cone-crowned structure, probably a beacon. Petersfield Ditch, which is much larger than any others that have branched off of the north side of the Broadkill so far, lies on the right about a mile past this landmark. The ditch offers good views of the attractive marsh and has no complications, except at Rte. 16 Bridge. At high tide there is inadequate clearance to float beneath its span, and another temporary weir sometimes blocks the ditch about a hundred feet upstream. At the second major ditch intersection north of Rte. 16, which is Headquarters Ditch, turn left. This ditch is marked by a sign.

HAZARDS: More an annoyance than a hazard, there are two weirs, one on Broadkill Sound opposite California Avenue in Broadkill Beach and one on Petersfield Ditch about 100 feet north of Rte. 16. These are temporary structures in that the Refuge managers can add or subtract logs from the weirs' center sections according to the amount of flooding desired. Their purpose is to improve waterfowl habitat by, among other things, flooding out weedlike phragmites reeds with freshwater. When they are functioning, which is usually from late October through early March, and at times during summer, these weirs will add two short carries. But on the other hand, they eliminate fighting adverse tidal currents which do indeed exist on this circuit tour.

WATER CONDITIONS: Tidal and, hence, always navigable. But avoid low tide on Primehook Creek and upper Broadkill Sound.

GAUGE: None.

Beware Of Fowl Play

One of the greatest natural resources of the Eastern Shore is its waterfowl. Located in the middle of the great Atlantic flyway, the Delmarva Peninsula is the wintering ground or stopover point for tens of thousands of geese, swans, ducks, and other migratory birds. Laced with waterways and wetlands, spotted with enticing fields of corn, and normally subject to a fairly temperate winter climate, what more could a goose or duck want? There are four national wildlife refuges situated here to provide safe accommodations for the wandering waterfowl. They are Bombay Hook, east of Dover, Prime Hook, southeast of Milford, Eastern Neck, southeast of Rock Hall, and Blackwater, south of Cambridge. Blackwater is probably the most famous and certainly the most accessible for the casual tourist. They have a scenic drive, a watch tower, and a staffed visitor's center. The center has interpretive exhibits inside, and outside you can count on a few docile birds to strut around the yard for close observation.

Chapter 9
Atlantic Ocean Drainage

Technically, every stream in this book belongs in this chapter, because every stream drains ultimately to the Atlantic Ocean. But this chapter addresses only that narrow strip of land in Sussex County, Delaware and Worcester County, Maryland that drains neither to the Delaware nor Chesapeake bays, but straight to the Atlantic. This is flat, featureless, agricultural land, interrupted only by a few small towns and some chicken plants. On its east side is the sandy edge of the ocean, part of which is buried beneath seaside resorts and part of which is an unspoiled national seashore.

There are no canoeable freshwater streams here. There are, however, broad and shallow bays and a few estuaries. From Ocean City north, these waters are blighted by the backside of the resorts on one side and second home communities on the other. But between Assateague Island and the mainland is beautiful Chincoteague Bay, whose marshy shores are still mostly wild and invite exploration by the paddler.

There is but one canoe route described in this humble chapter:

Assateague Island Canoe Trail

To Ocean City, Berlin

SOUTH POINT RD

611

Access

Sinepuxent Bay

Access

State Park

Ferry Lndg

N

Seashore

2.0

Tingles Island

3.0

National

Chincoteague Bay

Pine Tree

Atlantic

2.0

Island

Jims Gut

Ocean

6.0

Assateague

Pope Bay

MD

VA

Assateague Island Bays

Assateague Island Canoe Trail

INTRODUCTION: Most waters described in this book are not really trails in the usual sense. Nobody blazed them. And, at least on the nontidal streams, you cannot take many wrong turns or paddle them in two directions. Here now is something different.

Assateague Island is what is known as a barrier island—a relatively high and dry bar of sand, kicked up by the ocean and storms, which in turn serves as an energy absorbing shield for the mainland when the sea turns its fury landward. It could have been developed as "Ocean City South," but thanks to the hard work of conservationists, it has instead been preserved in a wild state as a national seashore. Most people come here to enjoy the seashore only. But there is another side to Assateague—the back side, i.e. the bay side. Here is a ragged shoreline where vast marshes merge with shallow waters. It is a world where a canoe or kayak is the best means for exploring.

The National Park Service has assisted the paddler by blazing a canoe trail, that is they erected numbered markers to keep you on a reasonable course down the shore. This is good, for it is possible to lose your bearings out there, and it is very easy to stray into an undesirable direction. In addition, the Park Service has established four primitive back country campsites. Most people will agree that an overnight excursion, using these campsites, is the best way to enjoy this trip.

Section 1. Old Ferry Landing to Pope Bay Campsite						
Gradient	Difficulty	Distance	Time	Width	Scenery	Map
0	A	13.0	6.0	5 miles	Very Good	96

TRIP DESCRIPTION: Most paddlers start their trip at Old Ferry Landing, near the North Beach Campground in the national seashore. But if the weather is right and you are comfortable crossing a mile of open water, you can also start at public accesses at South Point or the northwest end of the Md. Rte. 611 bridge. Finally, you can also start in Virginia, in the town of Chincoteague or in the Chincoteague National Wildlife Refuge at Toms Cove.

At first glance, if you have seen one mile of this trip, you have seen it all. To one side is the broad Chincoteague Bay or Sinepuxent Bay, on the other is endless marsh bordered by sandy woods. But the vastness of it all will charm you. And it is so wild. Closer up, there are more distractions. You do not have to be an ornithologist to appreciate the birding. There are all kinds of ducks, geese, gulls, wading birds like herons and egrets, and even pelicans. Imagine that, pelicans in Maryland! Down in the shallow water you may see blue crabs scurrying out of your shadow. And on shore there are deer and wild horses.

Just because there are no rocks and rapids, the canoeing here is by no means idiot proof. For one thing, the water is often extremely shallow for great distances out from shore. It is often only three inches deep at low tide. Paddling through minimal depths is not fun and soon tiring. Luckily the bottom is sandy and firm and thus conducive to poling and, if necessary, wading. Such wide, shallow, and exposed water is very sensitive to wind and can get very rough. So avoid this place on windy days. Also, watch the tides, as they can leave you stranded, especially if you are exploring some of the shallow back passages. Finally, this low-lying shoreline challenges your navigation skills, especially in the mass of islands near the Virginia border. Take along a good map and compass and keep careful track of your progress. Even the park's numbered trail marker signs can be confusing at times.

Camping really rounds out this trip. Unfortunately, the Park Service only allows use of its campsites from March 1 through October 31, most of which is bug season. If you have no tolerance for mosquitoes, stay away after early May. The campsites are primitive, with only fire rings, chemical toilets, and a picnic table. Bring along your own drinking water. The sites are set in attractive, woodsy locations (pretty but prone to being buggy) along back passages of the bay. They can be somewhat difficult to find. To stay here you need a permit, obtainable from the Seashore Visitor Center (at the Rte. 611 bridge), Toms Cove Visitor Center (at the national wildlife refuge), and at the national seashore campground registration office. No camping, or even landing, is allowed in the national wildlife refuge.

HAZARDS: Wind is the most serious navigation hazard. Keep in mind that this area can also be an unusually harsh environment for the inexperienced paddler or camper. The hazards include blazing midsummer sun, early and late season cold water, ravenous blood-sucking insects, and tidal currents.

WATER CONDITIONS: Tidal and hence always boatable. But low tide can make approaching shore most difficult.

GAUGE: None.

Chapter 10

Storm Drains and Flash Floods

Paddlers living amid the vast sprawl of the Washington-Baltimore Metropolitan Area will be pleased to know that there are dozens of runnable whitewater streams right at their doorsteps. Disguised as mild-mannered trickles that meander about parklands, shopping centers, factories, and houses, they can be almost instantly transformed by a summer shower into roaring, raging, whitewater wonders. These phenomena, often dubbed with the unflattering title of storm drain, are the products of extensive urbanization that results in almost complete and immediate runoff of any rain that should fall in that watershed. Riding such floods can be both thrilling and even aesthetically rewarding. But it is essential that the paddler be aware that urban canoeing is also fraught with perils and peculiarities and should thus be prepared for some of the following problems before ever putting in.

First of all, there are the obstacles. Of course, as on their country cousins, the ill-placed fallen tree, undercut banks, and snags are an ever present problem. But this situation is noticeably aggravated by the highly errosive nature of these flash flooding monsters. Then many of these streams flow through developed parklands where numerous, low footbridges hovering over high velocity current threaten to brain the unwary boater. Many streams have seen past development such as dams, sewers, bridge piers, and retaining walls, which have long since washed, crumbled, or dissolved away, but often with ugly, iron reinforcement rods still remaining. Camouflaged by the extremely muddy waters, these can often account for those mysterious, gaping holes that suddenly appear in your "indestructo" boat. Not all of the obstacles stand still. By the time that you put in, the stream may have already flooded and receded back within its banks, but in the process may have accumulated such wealth as picnic tables, shopping carts, logs, and, in winter, ice flows. Remember, on a really small stream there is seldom much room to outmaneuver such tumbling, thrashing battering rams. Unidentified flying objects can also on odd occasions menace you, as storm drains have been known to flow through golf courses, rifle ranges, archery ranges, and past bored juveniles who love to toss rocks and bottles. Finally, there are the hazards involved in the ultimate in urban storm drains, the concrete-paved channels. Scout every inch of these before attempting, as the danger of all hazards described above are magnified by the inability to stop in these flumes. In addition, such channels are sometimes strained through concrete energy dissipators, narrow culverts, pipe crossings, and some really exotic predicaments such as the "bottomless pit" on Little Falls Branch below Massachusetts Avenue in Montgomery County or the two-mile-long tunnel on Jones Falls beneath downtown Baltimore.

Next, the paddler must be fully aware of the abysmal quality of the water that he or she is about to boat on and possibly bathe in. For you see, that brown water roaring past you is not all just mud. Street runoff also includes such appetizers as motor oil, lawn and garden fertilizer, pesticides, doggy dung, garbage, and anything else that can wash off of the ground. Furthermore, it is common practice to run sanitary sewers down stream valleys and even stream beds, and these sewers often overflow, especially during storms. There is not much that you can do about this except stay upright and keep your mouth shut in heavy whitewater.

Boating in highly populated areas can attract considerable attention, which can create problems. Local police sometimes react unfavorably to the sight of some fool flushing down a swollen creek, interpret this as a self-destructive act, and thus may move to save you from yourself by ejecting you from the subject stream. A more substantial problem is that of "attractive nuisance." Attractive nuisance means that just the sight of you causes trouble in the eyes of the law. Many storm drains are parallelled by parkways and highways where drivers can be easily distracted by your interesting activity, thus setting the stage for some really juicy accidents. You can argue that that is not YOUR fault, but local administrators subsequently drafting regulations prohibiting boating on local streams may not see it that way. And it is their opinion that counts. So keep a low profile, and stay off such creeks during rush hour.

You have to be quick and sharp just to catch these streams up. A creek draining a totally urbanized basin is purely dependent on rainfall intensity, i.e. it has to rain very hard. In fact, you often must arrive at some of your smaller selections while it is still raining, and a mere half hour afterwards could be too late. Locating an area of intense rainfall is difficult, as storms, even the widespread winter type, tend not to be uniform. With summer showers, conditions are so extreme that it can be pouring on your house, but the sun may be shining a mile away. A telephone call to friends or relatives in the targeted basin can be your best scouting, keeping in mind that nonpaddlers seldom have the same concept of what "a lot of rain" is as paddlers. Otherwise, finding your water is a game of chance.

Finally, good luck and be careful.

Index

(*denotes stream with Class 3+ whitewater, or greater)

Accotink Bay, 58
Anacostia River, 136
Antietam Creek, 107
Appoquinimink River, 281
Aquia Creek, 61
Assateague Island Canoe Trail, 299

Back Creek, 104
Barren Creek, 244
Bear Creek,* 22
Bennett Creek, 127
Big Cove Creek, 99
Big Elk Creek, 204
Big Pipe Creek, 123
Blackbird Creek, 281
Blackwater River, 227
Brandywine Creek, 273
Breton Bay, 56
Broad Creek (DE), 239
Broadkill River, 290
Brush Creek,* 82
Burgess Creek, 140

C&O Canal, 133
Calvert Coast, 163
Casselman River, 23
Catoctin Creek, 113
Cattail Creek, 151
Cedar Creek, 287
Cedar Island, 253
Chester River, 208
Chicamacomico River, 232
Chicamuxen Creek, 55
Chopawamsic Creek, 59
Choptank River, 213
Christina River, 267
Coan River, 64
Conococheague Creek, 101
Conowingo Creek,* 193
Corsica River, 211

Deer Creek, 196

Dividing Creek, 259

East Branch Antietam Creek,* 110
East Branch White Clay Creek, 269
Evitts Creek, 84

Farm Creek, 225
Fifteenmile Creek, 89
Flintstone Creek, 88

Georges Creek,* 77
Great Bohemia Creek, 206
Gunpowder Falls,* 177
Gwynns Falls, 173

Herring Run, 176
Hill Top Fork, 140
Hitch Pond Branch, 241
Honga River, 223

Island Creek, 233

James Branch, 241
Janes Island, 253
Jennings Run,* 83
Jones Falls, 175

Kanes Creek, 58
Kings Creek (Somerset), 251
Kings Creek (Talbot), 220

Leipsic River, 282
Licking Creek, 97
Linganore Creek, 127
Little Blackwater River, 227
Little Falls, 182
Little Gunpowder Falls, 184
Little Northeast Creek, 203
Little Patuxent River, 158
Little Pipe Creek, 125
Little Seneca Creek, 130
Little Tonoloway Creek, 95

Little Wills Creek, 83
Lower Machodoc Creek, 64

Manokin River, 251
Marsh Creek, 119
Marshyhope Creek, 243
Marumsco Creek, 260
Mattawoman Creek, 139
Mattox Creek, 63
Middle Creek, 121
Middle Patuxent River, 160
Miles Creek, 220
Mispillion River, 287
Monie Creek, 249
Monocacy River, 114
Murderkill River, 284

Nanjemoy Creek, 140
Nanticoke River, 235
Nassawango Creek, 257
Neabsco Creek, 59
Nomini Creek, 63
North Branch Casselman River, 25
North Branch Potomac River,* 65
Northeast Creek,* 203
Northwest Branch, 137

Occoquan Bay, 58
Octoraro Creek, 195
Old Mill Creek, 290

Parkers Creek, 163
Patapsco River, 169
Patuxent River, 149
Piney Run Lake, 173
Piscataway Creek, 52
Pitts Creek, 260
Pocomoke River, 255
Pohick Bay, 58
Pokata Creek, 233
Pomonkey Creek, 52
Popes Creek, 63
Port Tobacco River, 55
Potomac Creek, 61
Potomac River,* 31
Powells Creek, 59
Prime Hook Creek, 293
Principio Creek, 203

Quantico Creek, 245

Quantico Creek (VA), 59

Red Clay Creek, 271
Rewastico Creek, 245
Rhode River, 165
Rock Creek (PA), 120
Rock Creek (Montgomery),* 133
Rosier Creek, 63

St. Clements Bay, 56
St. Jones River, 284
St. Mary's Coast, 149
St. Mary's River, 56
Savage River,* 73
Seneca Creek, 129
Severn River, 165
Sideling Hill Creek, 91
Slaughter Creek, 287
Smyrna River, 282
South Branch Patapsco River, 171
Southeast Creek, 210
Susquehanna River, 190

Taylors Island Passages, 221
Toms Creek, 121
Tonoloway Creek, 93
Town Creek, 85
Transquaking River, 230
Tuckahoe Creek, 217

Upper Machodoc Creek, 63

West Branch Antietam Creek, 110
West Branch Conococheague Creek, 104
West River, 165
Western Branch Patuxent River, 161
Western Run, 183
White Clay Creek, 269
Wicomico Creek, 247
Wicomico River (Charles), 141
Wills Creek,* 79
Winters Run, 185
Worlds End Creek, 225
Wye River, 211

Yeocomico River, 64
Youghiogheny River,* 17

Zekiah Swamp Run, 141